MICROPROCESSORS:

Fundamental Concepts and Applications

MICROPROCESSORS:

Fundamental Concepts and Applications

Victor E. Gibson

Delmar Publishers Inc.

I⟨T⟩P™

NOTICE TO THE READER

Cover photo courtesy of Tom Way / IBM

Figures 1-1, 1-2, 1-3, 1-4, 1-5, 1-6, 1-7 Courtesy of IBM Archives
Figures 1-8, 1-9, 8-30, 15-1, 15-5, 15-6, 15-7, 16-4, 16-8, 16-9, 16-10, 16-11, 16-14, 16-15, 16-16, 16-18, 16-19, and
    Tables 15-1, 15-2. Reprinted by permission of Intel Corporation.
Figures 3-7, 3-11, 3-13, 3-17, 5-5, 5-14, 14-4, 14-9 and Tables 14-1, 14-2, 14-3, 14-4, 16-2, 16-3, 16-20. Reprinted by
    permission of Motorola Corporation.
Figure 13-16. Reproduced by permission of Hayes Microcomputer Products, Inc.

Delmar staff
    Administrative Editor: Wendy Welch
    Project Editor: Theresa M. Bobear / Barbara Riedell
    Production Coordinator: James Zayicek / Larry Main
    Art Coordinator: Brian G. Yacur
    Design Coordinator: Lisa L. Bower

For information, address Delmar Publishers Inc.
3 Columbia Circle, Box 15-015
Albany, New York 12212-5015

Printed in the United States of America
Published simultaneously in Canada by Nelson Canada, a division of The Thomson Corporation

1 2 3 4 5 6 7 8 9 10 XXX 99 98 97 96 95 94 93

Library of Congress Cataloging-in Publication Data

Gibson, Victor E.
        Microprocessors: fundamental concepts and applications / Victor E. Gibson.
        p. cm.
        Includes index.
        ISBN 0-8273-4761-8
        1. Microprocessors.   I. Title.
QA76.5..G497   1993   92-21490
004.16—dc20   CIP

CONTENTS

CHAPTER 8 Elements of a Microprocessor 149

CHAPTER 9 Microprocessor Status 178

CHAPTER 10 Microprocessor Instructions and Programming 192

CHAPTER 11 Addressing Techniques 211

CHAPTER 12 Interrupts and Stacks 238

PREFACE

Microprocessors: Fundamental Concepts and Applications is designed to be a first course in microprocessors. It is intended for engineering or electronic technology students in two- or four-year colleges, tech schools, or technical high schools.

It is assumed that the student has completed a course in digital electronics, a usual prerequisite for a microprocessor course. While this background is not absolutely essential, it is highly recommended.

This book has a specific philosophy in mind. All microprocessors have certain elemental building blocks in common. Microprocessors become much easier to understand when they are broken down into fundamental block functions.

Mastery of the elemental blocks will allow the student to grasp more complicated devices later, as the more sophisticated and powerful processors use these same fundamental elements. The major difference between simple and sophisticated microprocessors is that better manufacturing techniques and enhanced architectures are employed with the latter. To a very large extent, this book is meant to be "generic." In this way, the student is prepared to continue study of more advanced devices and to keep up with the latest introductions from the manufacturers.

This book is not limited to microprocessors. The processor is not a "stand alone" device. It is surrounded by other electronic devices with which it has fundamental contact and working relations. Therefore, to fully understand the microprocessor, it is necessary to understand the devices immediately surrounding it and to study microprocessor applications.

Chapter 1 starts things off by presenting a brief history of the computer, concentrating primarily on those events which led to the microprocessor. This is not a history lesson; rather it is a fun look at some of the people who played a part in the events that culminated with the invention of the microprocessor.

Chapter 2 is an introduction to the binary number system. As this system is the basis of microprocessor language, microprocessors will remain a mystery without a fundamental knowledge of binary numbers.

Chapter 3 covers registers, comparators and adders, digital blocks which are elementary parts of the microprocessor. An understanding of these elements is assumed in later chapters.

Probably the most vital part of any microprocessor system is its memory. Memory has been divided into two major categories: nonvolatile and volatile.

Chapter 4 explores the basic concept of memory and covers nonvolatile memory from the diode matrix to bubble memory. Chapter 5 focuses on volatile memory, including static and dynamic RAM as well as CCD's.

As many of the crucial concepts in microprocessor systems, for example DMA, depend on a basic understanding of mass storage, and some of the fundamental abilities of the microprocessor are dependent on the existence of mass storage, the student of microprocessors needs to have a background in mass storage devices. Chapter 6 provides this background.

In addition to an understanding of binary numbers, familiarity with other number systems is also vital in the study of microprocessors. Chapter 7 concentrates on the other number systems, such as hexadecimal, which are used extensively with microprocessors.

Chapter 8 looks at the basic building blocks of microprocessors. Understanding each of these elements is the key to understanding all microprocessors.

Chapter 9, The Microprocessor Status, focuses largely on the status register and the meaning of the various status flags. Here the concept of carry and overflow is introduced and the states which a microprocessor can enter is covered.

Chapter 10 approaches programming in a general way, with the intention of showing that the programming required for basic microprocessors is neither mysterious nor difficult.

Chapter 11 is devoted to the basics of addressing. With a thorough study of this chapter, the student should have no difficulty grasping some of the more advanced forms of addressing used in modern microprocessors.

The ability of the microprocessor to handle interrupts is not only a measure of its sophistication but also contributes to its complexity. Chapter 12 studies interrupts in conjunction with the concept of the stack. This chapter provides a basis for understanding the various interrupt routines established in microprocessors, regardless of manufacturer.

Chapter 13 provides an introduction to microprocessor communication (a field of study in its own right). Because microprocessors must communicate with various devices, a fundamental study of microprocessors cannot ignore communications.

Chapter 14 focuses on the MC6800, one of the most popular and widely used microprocessors. As the MC6800 employs all fundamentals covered earlier in the text, this chapter clearly illustrates the necessity of studying the basic elements of the microprocessor.

The 8080A/8085A, like the MC6800, are also extremely popular. Many pieces of equipment used today were designed around these processors and will be with us for some time to come. Chapter 15 studies the 8080A/8085A microprocessor.

Chapter 16 is devoted to interfacing the microprocessor. This chapter looks at the microprocessor in its normal environment—namely, in the midst of other IC chips. The first portion of the chapter describes several of the IC chips used to interface the microprocessor, while the second portion explains some of the common bus structures.

Microprocessor Fundamentals, is intended to prepare the student to work with microprocessors by providing an understanding of how electronic devices using microprocessors operate. In addition, this text is designed to prepare the student to study more advanced microprocessors and assembler language.

Finally, the author would like to thank the people who have helped make this book possible. The support and encouragement from Nan Carol as well as the technical advice and help from L. Robin Akers have been invaluable. The reviewers, whose comments and suggestions have been most useful, provided welcomed assistance in the preparation of this text: Steven D. Banta, James E. Boyer, Ronald Brehmer, Rick Burgess, William A. Campbell, Joseph R. Delfino, Tim Goulden, Audrie E. Hall, Verne Hansen, Michael P. Jacobs, Raymond C. LaPrade, Vaughn K. Lester, Thomas Lombardo, Gorden W. Martin, Michael E. Pelletier, Ronald F. Ravenelle, J. William Ray, Jr., Cheryl M. Reed, and James M. Rhodes. And last, to all the staff members at Delmar Publishers, my everlasting gratitude for their patience and graciousness.

OUTLINE

NEW TERMS TO WATCH FOR

Abacus

Brattain

Babbage

UNIVAC

Hollerith

Silicon Valley

Mauchly

Von Neumann

Shockley

Leibnitz

ENIAC

Analytical Engine

Kilby

Atanasoff

Intel

4004

Pascal

Bardeen

Difference Engine

Noyce

Punch Cards

Fairchild

Eckert

Hoff

After completing this chapter, you should be able to:

1. Describe the first computer used by man.
2. Explain how early computers differed from modern versions.
3. Name the inventor of the first American computing machine.
4. Identify the three individuals who claim to have invented the first electronic computer.
5. Describe the first truly modern computer.
6. State the significance of the invention of the transistor as it relates to the development of computers.
7. Name the company that invented the microprocessor.
8. Explain how and why the development of the microprocessor came about.

1-1   WHY LOOK AT COMPUTER HISTORY?

No one would question the relevance of computers in contemporary society. There are few, if any, people on the face of the earth today whose lives have not been touched in some way by these marvelous devices.

Today, everything is "in the computer." From birth to death, our lives are carefully tracked, recorded, and filed using computers, and everything from satellites to CDs is computer dependent.

It is, therefore, appropriate to ask, how did things get this way? Who were the key players responsible for the developments that have so affected our lives? Nearly all sports fans know who Ty Cobb was and what Hank Aaron did. And we all, at some point in our education, have learned who the founding fathers of our country were. As a career in electronics will almost certainly include use of the computer and more than likely an understanding of microprocessor chips at some level, it only makes sense to provide some brief but pertinent information on the history of computers. Simply put, the microprocessor *is* a computer. We will follow the development of the computer up to the introduction of semiconductors. At this point, we'll branch into the evolution of solid state devices, which led to the development of the microprocessor. This chain of events and related history leads right to you, the student, now on the threshold of this fascinating world.

1-2   HOW OLD IS THE COMPUTER?

The Abacus

No one is absolutely certain just when the first mechanical computing device was invented. However, there is some indication that the abacus was invented around 2600 B.C. (Fig. 1-1). Devised by the Chinese for use in calculation (and familiar to the ancient Egyptians as well), this rectangular wooden frame with beads strung in columns on taut strings is considered by many to be the first computer. It is divided into two parts, with two beads at the top of the column representing heaven and five beads on the lower division representing earth. The mystical connections aside, all four of the basic math operations can be performed on an abacus, and a skilled operator can calculate with surprising speed. These devices are still used and can be found in markets in the Eastern world.

FIGURE 1-1 Abacus

1-3   THE FIRST MECHANICAL CALCULATORS

Pascal

Leonardo da Vinci made sketches of a mechanical computer sometime around the year 1500, but nothing was ever built. More than a century later, in 1642, a Frenchman named Blaise **Pascal** invented a working mechanical calculating machine. He called it the Pascaline and it worked very much like an odometer (Fig. 1-2). One full revolution of a wheel caused the next one to rotate 1/10 of a revolution. The Pascaline, a box full of cogs and wheels, wasn't commercially successful for a couple of reasons: in the first place, Pascal was the only one who could repair it; secondly, human labor was so inexpensive at the time that people could be hired to perform calculations more economically than his machine.

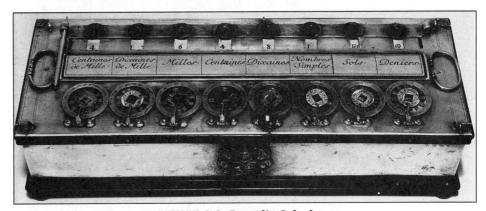

FIGURE 1-2 Pascal's Calculator

Leibnitz

Later in the seventeenth century, Gottfried **Leibnitz**, of calculus fame, used the idea of cogs and wheels to build a mechanical calculator that was a financial success. Not only could the Leibnitz machine add and subtract, but it could multiply, divide, and actually extract square roots. The year was 1694.

1-4   MODERN COMPUTER HISTORY

Babbage

By most accounts, modern computer history started with an Englishman named Charles **Babbage**. Early in the nineteenth century, he wrote a series of scientific papers expounding the principles of a calculating science that are not far removed from the ideas used today in computing.

In 1821, he devised a **Difference Engine** that solved complicated polynomials (Fig. 1-3). He then applied to the Chancellor of the Exchequer for funding to build a bigger and better machine. The approval of his application may be the first recorded instance of a government research grant provided to an individual.

FIGURE 1-3 Difference Engine

Ten years later, however, the Difference Engine wasn't finished. But by then, Babbage was convinced that a general purpose computing machine might be even more useful. He called this the **Analytical Engine**. There was even a ready made market for such a computer. The textile industry of the day was using a new loom invented by Jacquard (Fig. 1-4). Threads were routed through holes punched in cards. The route through the holes constituted a program for the loom pattern. (Strangely, these cards were also 80 columns wide, just like the **punch cards** used by IBM machines today.)

The Analytical Engine was to be a steam-driven, complex construction of mechanical wheels, gears, ratchets, and levers. While it might have worked, the technology of the day failed Babbage; the parts could not be ground and molded to the precision required and by the time he died an embittered man in 1871, the Analytical Engine was still not built. It was left to his son to complete the first Babbage machine in 1910.

FIGURE 1-4 Jacquard Loom

1-5   THE FIRST AMERICAN COUNTING MACHINE

Hollerith

The next chapter in computer history opened with Herman **Hollerith**. In 1879, at the age of nineteen, he accepted a position with the United States Census Bureau to work on the 1880 census. As the census was not complete until 1888, he enjoyed some job security. During this time he was encouraged to work on innovations to improve the efficiency of census tabulation. Because the bureau feared that the next census would take a full ten years to complete, a competition was held to produce machines which might reduce the possibility of error and delay anticipated for the 1890 census. Hollerith won. His machine did the tabulation for the 1890 census in just six weeks (Fig. 1-5).

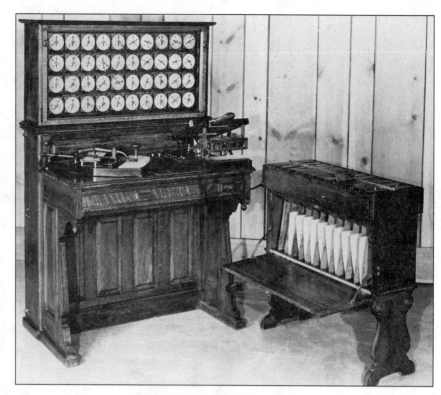

FIGURE 1-5 Hollerith Tabulator

The Hollerith Tabulator Machine utilized the same type of punch cards as the Jacquard loom. The cards were passed over small cups filled with mercury. Pens resting on the cards dropped through the holes into the mercury cups, completing an electrical circuit. The circuit activated mechanical devices that tabulated information recorded on the cards such as age, sex, and race.

Following this successful undertaking, Hollerith struck off on his own in 1896, and founded the Tabulating Machine Company, which he later sold to IBM. Hollerith machines were improved and sold by IBM right up to the advent of the electronic digital computer.

1-6   THE FIRST COMPUTER

Atanasoff

The electronic digital computer owes its existence to three inventors. The first was John **Atanasoff**, a Ph.D. who taught at Iowa State in Ames, Iowa. A volatile, hyperactive man given to all-night work binges, he was obsessed with finding a way to speed the calculation of complex equations with up to twenty-nine variables. At the time, the calculations had to be done by hand and the job was laborious and time consuming.

The temperature was well below zero one December night in 1937 when Atanasoff was working late in the physics building. Tormented by the lack of a solution to the automated calculating problem, he leaped in his car and drove non-stop over more than 180 miles, crossing the Mississippi river into Illinois. Late that night, attracted by the lights of an all-night roadhouse, he stopped for refreshment. While at the roadhouse he contemplated the work of Babbage. Atanasoff, like Babbage, wanted to use a punch card system with binary numbers, but he was afraid that users could not master it.

Then he made three important decisions. First, he concluded that the advantages of a binary number system would far outweigh the disadvantages of mastering it. Second, he decided that a serial calculating method akin to the way the human mind works should replace the *ratcheting* method used in the Babbage machines. And finally, he decided that a regenerative memory should be employed.

Armed with these three decisions, he was able to coax a $650 grant from Iowa State University, and with the assistance of Clifford Berry, he built the first electronic digital computer in the fall of 1939. Atanasoff and Berry called their computer the ABC machine. For years, Atanasoff urged Iowa State to patent the device, but the university never did.

We might not have known so much about the work of Atanasoff except for a patent suit brought by Sperry Rand against Honeywell. The suit centered on who actually first had the idea for the electronic computer. On October 19, 1973, after 6 years of litigation that included 78 witnesses, 135 days of testimony, and 25,686 exhibits, the judge for the U.S. court ruled that the ideas of John Atanasoff were *borrowed* by the other claimants. But who were these other claimants, and why were *they* working to develop computers?

1-7   THE ENIAC

Mauchly and Eckert

At a scientific conference in 1940, John Atanasoff met John **Mauchly**, one of the other claimants to the invention of the electronic computer. At that time, Mauchly was head of a project at Ursinus College that studied atmospheric electricity. The research required tabulating huge amounts of weather data. He was hiring students at $.50 per hour to do the work but had concluded that it would take a lifetime to complete the project with human calculators. Naturally, Mauchly was interested when Atanasoff told him about the ABC machine.

That summer, Mauchly hitched a ride to Ames, Iowa, where he spent five days in Atanasoff's home as a guest. He saw the ABC. He read and requested copies of Atanasoff's papers. Atanasoff turned down the request. Later in court, Mauchly claimed to have gained nothing from this experience. He was not able, however, to produce any papers, notes, materials, witnesses, or other proof that he had conceived of the electronic computer prior to meeting Atanasoff.

In the summer of 1941, Mauchly met J. Presper **Eckert**. The two became staffers at the Moore School of Engineering at the University of Pennsylvania. The Moore School was participating in a joint project with the United States Army Ordinance Department's Aberdeen proving ground. There, ballistic research was being performed to compute all of the Army and Air Corps artillery firing tables. Although they were using a special analog device invented for this purpose, it still took thirty days to compute a table for the most advanced artillery.

In 1943, Mauchly and Eckert were given the go ahead to develop an electronic computer that would be capable of rapidly computing missile trajectories. They proposed that their machine be called Electronic Numerical Integrator And Computer or **ENIAC** (Fig. 1-6). The estimated cost of development was $150,000. By the time it was finished, however, the price tag had climbed to more than $485,000, thereby establishing the first cost over-run—and the subsequent tradition of underestimating anything to do with computer costing.

FIGURE 1-6 ENIAC

Eckert was the hardware man. He applied the concept of using the presence or absence, rather than the magnitude, of a voltage to represent information. He believed this method to be more reliable. And it was ideal for a binary system. For his part, Mauchly, who was responsible for the calculating methods, chose an analog decimal system because he, like Atanasoff, thought binary code would prove too difficult for users.

ENIAC was a monster of a machine. It had over 17,000 vacuum tubes and occupied the entire basement of the engineering building. It was one hundred feet long, ten feet high, and, when operating, sometimes heated the room to 120 degrees. Even worse, it was programmed with plug board wires; there were over 6,000 switch connections spread over three walls (Fig. 1-7).

FIGURE 1-7 ENIAC Plug Boards

Not only was ENIAC able to perform the desired trajectory calculations, but it did so in about thirty seconds, as opposed to the previously required thirty days. ENIAC, finished too late for the war, was first used in December of 1945 for a calculation needed by Los Alamos.

Despite tales of vacuum tube replacements by the cartful, ENIAC functioned well and was used until 1955. And until the 1973 court decision, nearly everyone considered it to be the first electronic computer. The court decision aside, Mauchly and Eckert earned their place in the history of computer development and deserve the credit for building ENIAC. ENIAC can now be found in the Smithsonian museum in Washington, DC.

von Neumann

ENIAC obviously needed something better than plug boards to program it. A more efficient method was devised by John **von Neumann** who became a consultant with the ENIAC group in 1944. In 1945, he wrote a paper on binary coding, serial calculation, and the stored program. His boss at the time, an army Lieutenant, thought the paper so good, he had it printed and distributed to scientists in both the United States and Britain. The theories presented in this paper serve as the basis for computers built today; virtually all modern computers use the idea of a stored program and today's microprocessors still employ the von Neumann architecture.

1-8 UNIVAC

In 1946, Eckert and Mauchly contracted with the United States Census Bureau, an old computer customer, to develop a Universal Automatic Computer or **UNIVAC**. But due to financial troubles, Eckert and Mauchly eventually sold out to Remington Rand. UNIVAC-I was delivered in 1951.

1-9 SOMETHING HAPPENED IN NEW JERSEY

While IBM was busily engaged in selling desk calculators full of mechanical parts and Rand was out peddling electronic computers made with tubes, something truly startling was about to happen at Bell Laboratories in Murray Hill, New Jersey. On December 23rd, 1947, the transistor was invented by three physicists. John **Bardeen**, Walter **Brattain**, and William **Shockley** eventually earned a Nobel Prize for their work.

The beginnings were humble, with the first transistors being made from a relatively rare substance called germanium. Then, in 1954, future player Texas Instruments announced the development of the silicon transistor. Making these transistors, however, was a difficult proposition. Controlling the production environment and eliminating impurities proved particularly exasperating. Satisfactory yields were typically 20% to 30%, with the rest having to be thrown away. At one point, a mythical and undiscovered element humorously called deathnium was theorized to be destroying purity and, hence, reducing transistor yields. But ultimately, and rather anticlimactically, *deathnium* turned out to be copper.

Transistorized Computer

In 1955, IBM marketed its first transistorized computer. The 2200 transistors it contained replaced some 1250 vacuum tubes. Power consumption and the necessary cooling were reduced 95%.

By this time, computers were beginning to make their presence felt. Even so, the Department of Commerce survey of 1955 showed that probably only one hundred such machines would be needed to satisfy our country's needs. After all, the survey concluded, only elite organizations like the Census Bureau would need to compute with such magnitude.

1-10   THE BEGINNING

Shockley

Also in 1955, Mountain View, California welcomed back a long-lost son, William Shockley. The following year he would be one of the Nobel Prize winners for that 1947 invention, the transistor. But this year, wanting a piece of the high-tech pie, Shockley opened his newly-formed Shockley Semiconductor Laboratories in a shed. There among eight or ten other young Ph.Ds in Shockley's Lab, was one Robert **Noyce**, the MIT graduate who would one day run the company that invented the microprocessor.

Bill Shockley was a showman and an eccentric, not uncommon traits among future gurus and entrepreneurs in the microelectronics industry. His eccentricity was often evident when he lectured. On one occasion in particular, he began a lecture by saying that he was speaking on a hot subject that night. He then opened what looked like a book to the accompaniment of a loud bang and smoke rising from the lectern.

Underneath the showmanship, however, Shockley was a skilled communicator. This is evidenced by the explanation he provided one of his students who was having difficulty grasping the concept of an amplifier: "If you take a bale of hay and tie it to the tail of a mule and then strike a match and set the bale on fire and if you compare the energy shortly expended by the mule to the energy expended by yourself in striking the match, you will understand the concept of amplification."

But one area in which William Shockley's skills were sorely lacking was people management. He swore that one person in ten was psychotic and, therefore, was convinced that at least one of the people working for him was crazy. Because of this conviction, he required each of his employees to complete a psychological profile. His idea of preventing salary disputes was to post each employee's salary on the company bulletin board. When he once suspected someone of sabotaging experiments, he strapped the embarrassed employee into a lie detector harness. (No saboteur was ever found.) And whenever one of his employees developed an innovative scientific idea, Shockley would call his cronies at Bell Labs in an attempt to verify the validity of the idea. Robert Noyce was subjected to this treatment more than once.

1-11   THE TRAITOROUS EIGHT

Not surprisingly the atmosphere Shockley created at his company prompted eight of his employees to resign en masse. Shockley referred to those who defected in 1957 as the Traitorous Eight. Among them was Robert Noyce, the elected leader. A venture capitalist then introduced the group of eight defectors to personnel at **Fairchild** Camera and Instrument Corporation, who were willing to lay out three million dollars to found Fairchild Semiconductor. It is interesting to note that this defection began a trend of mass defections that plagued the industry for years to come.

1-12   THE FIRST INTEGRATED CIRCUIT

The IC

The next major event in the history of the computer took place in February of 1959. Jack **Kilby** of Texas Instruments was awarded the first patent of an integrated circuit. Although he preferred to work with silicon, his integrated circuit was constructed from germanium. Texas Instruments touted the invention as a semiconductor solid circuit no larger than a match head.

In July of that same year Robert Noyce, head of the team at Fairchild, also filed a patent for an integrated circuit, having never heard of Jack Kilby's developments at Texas Instruments. Noyce's IC was made from silicon and his new planar production technique was eminently more practical than Kilby's.

These first integrated circuits were the result of constant pressure from the electronics industry to produce smaller equipment with yet more features. Naturally more transistors in a smaller area was more economical. The invention of the integrated circuit marked the beginning of a numbers game still played today. For instance, in 1950, one thousand tubes occupied one cubic foot. By 1956, it was ten thousand transistors to one cubic foot. In 1959, it was one million components. And recently, Intel announced a microprocessor chip that integrates more than a million transistors on a chip measuring 1 by 1.5 centimeters.

By 1962, large computers had over 200,000 separate components, and this more and smaller trend marked the semiconductor industry throughout the 60's.

Supercomputer

Even when computers were being built with discrete transistors, the results were impressive. In 1966, *Fortune* magazine reported that the latest supercomputer could multiply every number in the New York telephone book by the number following it, add the sums of all these products, divide the total by any other number, and print the answer—all in two seconds.

The Valley

In the 1960s, small semiconductor companies began to gravitate towards the Santa Clara Valley just south of San Francisco. So many semiconductor and electronic firms gathered there that it became known as **Silicon Valley**, and each new company seemed to inspire entrepreneurs to defect and begin yet another company. Fairchild itself inspired and spawned so many defections and new startups that Adam Smith named the leaders of these groups Fairchildren.

1-13   THE INTEL DEFECTION

By 1968 the man who had originated defection was getting restless again. Bob Noyce didn't like running the very large company Fairchild Semiconductor had become. He hankered for his old white lab coat, as he was, after all, a hands-on man. So in June of that year, he left to found a new company. Investors stood in line to hand Bob Noyce money. He called the new company **Intel**. At the time, Noyce hadn't envisioned making microprocessors at Intel; in fact, no one had yet heard of such a thing as the microprocessor.

First Product

Intel's first product was a 64-bit, bipolar memory chip that was destined to replace the then state-of-the-art ceramic core memory. This was shortly followed by a 256-bit MOS memory chip. These products represented a spectacular start, introducing Intel as a company with both bipolar and MOS technology—an achievement unmatched by most other companies for another ten years. Participating in all this was a young genius fresh from performing research at Stanford University—employee number twelve of Intel (Fig. 1-8), Marcian "Ted" Hoff.

1-14   THE JAPANESE CONNECTION

Hoff

Hoff had been assigned to work with a Japanese company called Busicom. Busicom made desktop calculators (pocket calculators weren't even a possibility yet). The Japanese were interested in having Intel design and build custom circuitry for the calculator. Their engineers wanted the product to have six or eight large complex IC chips, and each chip was to have specific calculator functions.

Hoff believed there was a better way. He had worked with Digital Equipment Corporation and was impressed with the way its computer could perform extremely complex tasks by way of relatively simple software instructions. Why not place all the calculator building blocks on a single chip and program it with memory?

This idea was proposed to the group of Japanese engineers in July of 1969. They didn't like it. Nevertheless, Noyce told Hoff to keep on working to develop the idea. When the Japanese returned in October, they had a change of heart. They were buying.

FIGURE 1-8 When development of the microprocessor was underway at Intel in 1969, the company had only 106 employees. Since then it has grown into a worldwide corporation with more than 20,000 employees. The three Intel founders are (front row - left to right) Robert Noyce, vice chairman, and Gorden E. Moore, chairman and CEO. Andrew S. Grove, president, is in the second row, far right. Standing next to Grove (with glasses) is Marcian E. "Ted" Hoff, the inventor of the microprocessor.

1-15 THE VERY FIRST MICROPROCESSOR

Early in 1971, the first microprocessor chip, called the **4004**, because of its 4-bit architecture, was delivered to Busicom. The Japanese balked again; the price was too high and they wanted to renegotiate.

In an odd reversal of traditional roles, Hoff the inventor, urged a reluctant marketing group to secure the rights from the Japanese so that Intel could sell the device to others. One member of the marketing group reportedly told Hoff that the computer industry might sell twenty thousand units a year, and that Intel, if lucky, could get a ten percent market share amounting to two thousand chip sales a year. To the marketing group, it was hardly worth the effort—an amazing attitude when we consider the millions upon millions of chips sold today.

Intel was granted the right to sell the 4004 in May of 1971 (by which time most of the marketing department had been eased out). The world's first computer chip was now for sale (Fig. 1-9).

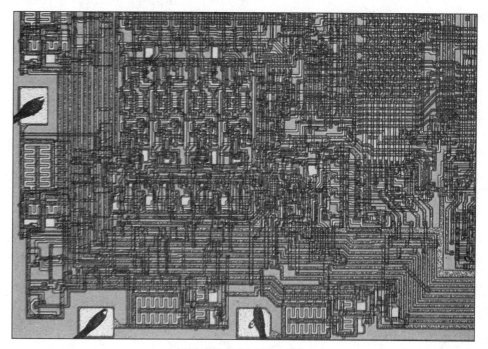

FIGURE 1-9 4004 Chip

TI

There are a couple of footnotes to the history of the first microprocessor. Also during 1971, Intel and Texas Instruments were each working on a request from Display Terminal Company (now called Datapoint) for a modular processor that could control a terminal. Texas Instruments announced its solution early in 1972. Intel followed in April of the same year with its answer: the 8008, an 8-bit processor. The 8008 is hardly worth mentioning except that it fathered a new offering from Intel; the now famous Model 1 8080 chip contained many of the features the market thought important at the time of its introduction in 1974. In fact, this chip may well turn out to be the most important product of the century, and it came from what some have called the "most important company in America."

This chapter has presented the history of computers from the abacus to the development of the microprocessor. And computers continue to make history. The development of new and better chips continues unabated, helping to spur other advancements in the world of computers, including the introduction of Apple I in 1975 and IBM's entrance into the PC market in 1983. And glory days are surely not over. New uses are still being found for microchips. Computers hundreds of times more powerful than ENIAC sit on desk tops everywhere—and every one of them uses a microprocessor.

SUMMARY OF IDEAS

- The abacus could rightly be called the first mechanical computing device. It was used as far back as 2,600 B.C. and is still used today.
- The first mechanical calculating machines were built in the seventeenth century by Pascal and Leibnitz.
- Modern computer history began with Charles Babbage and his Difference Engine.
- The American chapter of computer history began when Herman Hollerith successfully completed his tabulating machine for the Census Bureau in 1890.
- John Atanasoff is generally credited with building the first electronic computer at Iowa State University.
- Mauchly and Eckert are credited as having invented ENIAC, the computer designed to calculate missile trajectories.
- John von Neumann is credited with being the first to conceive of the stored program.
- The transistor was invented by John Bardeen, Walter Brattain, and William Shockley, who shared a Nobel Prize for their efforts.
- Robert Noyce and seven others defected from Shockley Labs to form Fairchild Semiconductor.
- Jack Kilby and Robert Noyce patented the first integrated circuits.
- Robert Noyce left Fairchild to found Intel, the company that introduced the first microprocessor in 1971.
- Marcian "Ted" Hoff was in charge of the project that produced the first microprocessor. It was his idea to put all the calculator building blocks on one chip.

CHAPTER QUESTIONS & PROBLEMS

True or False
1. Charles Babbage invented the first mechanical calculator.
2. John Atanasoff patented the first electronic computer while at the University of Iowa.
3. ENIAC was developed for the United States Census Bureau.
4. Robert Noyce was one of the co-inventors of the transistor.
5. Ted Hoff of Intel is credited with inventing the microprocessor.

Fill in the Blanks
6. Charles Babbage called his first calculating machine the _____ _____.

7. The three Nobel Prize-winning inventors of the transistor were: _____, _____, _____.

8. The huge computer developed at the University of Pennsylvania was called ____________________.
9. The first integrated circuit may well have been invented by two people, each working separately without the knowledge of the other's efforts. The names of these individuals were ____________________ and ____________________.
10. The first microprocessor was introduced in the year _____.

Multiple Choice

11. Which of the following individuals was able to secure government funding?
    a. Gottfried Pascal
    b. Robert Noyce
    c. Charles Babbage
    d. Jack Kilby
12. Which of the following inventors was an advocate of digital electronics?
    a. John Mauchly
    b. Blaise Pascal
    c. John Atanasoff
    d. Charles Babbage
13. When was the first electromechanical computer available commercially in the United States?
    a. 1871
    b. 1896
    c. 1910
    d. 1947
14. ENIAC was designed to:
    a. tabulate the United States Census.
    b. make computers commercially available to American business.
    c. compute missile trajectories.
    d. facilitate the calculation of weather statistics.
15. The first microprocessor chip was designed to:
    a. enhance the sale of Intel memories.
    b. control a computer terminal.
    c. build a desk calculator.
    d. introduce Personal Computers.

THE BINARY NUMBER SYSTEM

OUTLINE

NEW TERMS TO WATCH FOR

Decimal
Carry
Binary
Borrow
Positional Notation
9's Complement

Radix
10's Complement
Base
1's Complement
Exponential Notation
2's Complement

Decimal Point
End Around Carry
Binary Point
Signed Binary

After completing this chapter, you should be able to:

1. Describe how the **decimal** number system works.
2. Define and understand **positional notation**.
3. Explain what the radix or base is when referring to a number system.
4. Understand how both integers and fractions are represented in the binary number system.
5. Convert decimal numbers to binary numbers.
6. Convert binary numbers to decimal numbers.
7. Add binary numbers.
8. Form the complement of both decimal and binary numbers.
9. Subtract binary numbers.
10. Represent signed numbers in binary form.
11. Demonstrate how multiplication and division are performed with binary numbers.

2-1   INTRODUCTION

Virtually all computers today work with the **binary** number system rather than the decimal system. There is, of course, a very good reason for this. Binary numbers are microprocessor friendly. Fortunately, the use of the binary number system is not nearly as complicated and difficult as some of the early computer inventors believed. But before introducing the binary system, a brief look at our decimal system is in order.

2-2   THE FIRST NUMBERS

Counting

Most historians and anthropologists believe that our number system, which is based on the value 10, is the result of efforts by early man to keep track of his possessions. The first counting system symbolically represented objects. The most convenient symbols were fingers. In fact, anthropologists have found that the majority of systems were based on either 5, 10, or 20, which of course, corresponds with fingers and toes. But most systems were based on the number 10.

Nevertheless, the possession of ten fingers may not have given us the most effective number system. Twelve would certainly be more convenient for time, inches, feet, and the degrees of angles, and for the true mathematician, a prime number base like 5 or 11 might have been more agreeable.

2-3   POSITIONAL NOTATION

Symbols

The symbols we use are of Hindu-Arabic origin and are thousands of years old. But the most notable characteristic of our number system is **positional notation**. This idea is ascribed to the Babylonians from whom we also get the idea of *zero* or the absence of a value. They were using it about 400 B.C. Historians note, however, that it wasn't until about A.D. 700 that the Hindus recognized zero not only as an absence but also as a number for computational purposes.

The value of positional notation is enormous. The Roman numeral system did not survive, possibly because it does not use positional value with any consistency. Positional notation means that while we use only ten different symbols, it is possible to represent any value we desire. The ten symbols are:

0	5
1	6
2	7
3	8
4	9

The Base

The number of symbols used in a number system is called the **radix** or **base**. The base denotes the number of unique symbols possible.

It is a simple matter when counting, if the number of objects exceeds the number of symbols, to use the same symbols again. The number 99 for example, uses the same two symbols, but these two symbols can represent a large number of objects due to the *position* of the symbols.

Fixed Value of Position

Each position has a fixed value in relation to each other position in a string of numbers. The value of each succeeding position is found by multiplying the next lower position by the base.

In our decimal system, the positional values are:

100,000	10,000	1,000	100	10	1
5th	4th	3rd	2nd	1st	Single
Place	Place	Place	Place	Place	Units

Each place or position has a value ten times greater than the preceding one. A symbol found in the second place has a value 10 times greater than the same symbol found in the first place.

Interpreting

As an example, the number 4,937 uses only four of the possible ten symbols. How, then, do we interpret this notation?

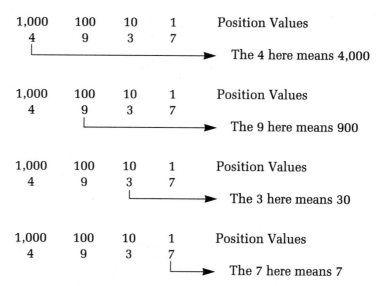

Here is how the number is interpreted:

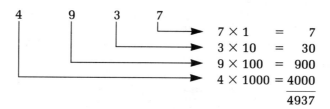

Significant Digits

The left most digit is the most significant as it denotes the largest value. The number systems we use, are all read from left to right, just like our word and sentence structure. The left most digit is called the Most Significant Digit or MSD and the Least Significant Digit or LSD is the right most one.

While this may sound self evident, pointing this fact out is necessary in order to understand a number system other than the base ten system we habitually use. So understanding the rationale behind our system must be very clear.

2-4 EXPONENTIAL NOTATION

Scientific Notation

The exponential or scientific notation system also makes implicit use of positional value. The position values can be represented as powers of 10. Recall that any number raised to the "0" power is always "1" and that any number raised to the 1st power is always the number itself. Thus:

$$
\begin{aligned}
10^0 &= 1 & &= & 1 \\
10^1 &= 10 & &= & 10 \\
10^2 &= 10 \times 10 & &= & 100 \\
10^3 &= 10 \times 10 \times 10 & &= & 1,000 \\
10^4 &= 10 \times 10 \times 10 \times 10 & &= & 10,000 \\
10^5 &= 10 \times 10 \times 10 \times 10 \times 10 & &= & 100,000
\end{aligned}
$$

We can represent the values of the positions by using powers of 10. The powers or exponents correspond to the position number.

10^5	10^4	10^3	10^2	10^1	10^0
100,000	10,000	1,000	100	10	1
5th Place	4th Place	3rd Place	2nd Place	1st Place	Single Units

Fractions

It is possible to represent fractional parts of numbers by establishing a radix point. The radix point in the base 10 system is called the **decimal point**. All numbers positioned to the right of this point are fractional numbers, that is, less than 1.

The positional values to the right of the decimal point are 1/10 of the value of each preceding one. We have,

$$
\begin{aligned}
.1 &= 1/10 &= 10^{-1} \\
.01 &= 1/100 &= 10^{-2} \\
.001 &= 1/1,000 &= 10^{-3} \\
.0001 &= 1/10,000 &= 10^{-4}
\end{aligned}
$$

With these additional positions, we can now represent all possible integers and fractions.

Interpreting Fractions

Here is how we interpret the number 3,297.023

$$
\begin{aligned}
&3{,}297.023 \\
3 &= 3 \times 10^3 = 3000.0 \\
2 &= 2 \times 10^2 = 200.0 \\
9 &= 9 \times 10^1 = 90.0 \\
7 &= 7 \times 10^0 = 7.0
\end{aligned}
$$

Decimal Point .

$$
\begin{aligned}
0 &= 0 \times 10^{-1} = .0 \\
2 &= 2 \times 10^{-2} = .02 \\
3 &= 3 \times 10^{-3} = \underline{.003} \\
& \qquad\qquad\qquad 3297.023
\end{aligned}
$$

It is not our objective to belabor the obvious but to fix clearly in your mind, just how the decimal positional system actually works. The reason for the foregoing will become obvious in the next section.

 SELF-CHECK FOR SECTIONS 2-1, 2-2, 2-3, 2-4

1. Explain the value of positional notation.
2. Explain a number base.
3. What is the decimal value of the 9 in the number 944?
4. Is the MSD the right most or left most digit?
5. Does exponential notation use positional values?

2-5   INTRODUCTION TO BINARY

The Base 2

Now that we have a thorough grounding in how the decimal number system works, we are ready to examine the binary number system. Binary is nothing more than a number system that has a base of 2 instead of 10. While Leibnitz, one of the early calculator inventors, didn't invent binary numbers he certainly was one of their first advocates. He saw binary numbers as a sort of esoteric truth. The first binary number symbol, "0," represented for him, non-being, nothing, or the void. While the other symbol, "1," represented the creator and all of creation. No mean feat for a number system.

Symbols

The good news for us is that instead of dealing with 10 unique symbols, we now have only 2 to contend with.

They are:

0

1

There are no more symbols available in binary.

To represent larger numbers, we have only to use the same two symbols over but in different *positions*. As in the decimal system, the value of a position is based on the one preceding it.

In the base 10 system, each place has a value of 10 times the one preceding it. In the binary system, each place has a value of 2 times the position preceding it.

Binary Positional Values

So the binary positional values are:

32	16	8	4	2	1
5th	4th	3rd	2nd	1st	Single
Place	Place	Place	Place	Place	Units

But we have already discovered that **exponential notation** is an efficient system for noting positional values, so,
The powers of 2 are:

$$2^0 = 1 \qquad\qquad = 1$$
$$2^1 = 2 \qquad\qquad = 2$$
$$2^2 = 2 \times 2 \qquad\qquad = 4$$
$$2^3 = 2 \times 2 \times 2 \qquad = 8$$
$$2^4 = 2 \times 2 \times 2 \times 2 \quad = 16$$
$$2^5 = 2 \times 2 \times 2 \times 2 \times 2 = 32$$

The value of each position then looks like this:

2^5	2^4	2^3	2^2	2^1	2^0
32	16	8	4	2	1
5th	4th	3rd	2nd	1st	Single
Place	Place	Place	Place	Place	Units

Binary Counting

To count in binary, we begin,

BINARY	DECIMAL
0	0
1	1

But in binary, we are now out of symbols so we must start again in another position,

10	2
11	3

And again we must start a new position,

100	4
101	5
110	6

Quite obviously, many more positions are necessary to represent numbers in binary. The fewer the symbols, the more positions needed, and, as you can see, binary numbers quickly grow larger than their corresponding decimal or base-ten numbers.

Table 2-1 is a table of all binary numbers and their decimal equivalents through the number 15.

TABLE 2-1

Binary	Decimal
0000	0
0001	1
0010	2
0011	3
0100	4
0101	5
0110	6
0111	7
1000	8
1001	9
1010	10
1011	11
1100	12
1101	13
1110	14
1111	15

Interpreting Binary

How would we interpret a binary number such as 1011?

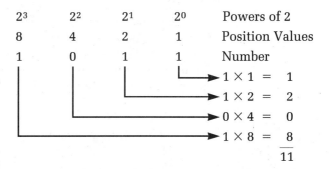

2^3	2^2	2^1	2^0	Powers of 2
8	4	2	1	Position Values
1	0	1	1	Number

$$1 \times 1 = 1$$
$$1 \times 2 = 2$$
$$0 \times 4 = 0$$
$$1 \times 8 = \underline{8}$$
$$11$$

With binary, the method of finding the value of a symbol in a given position is actually easier than in decimal. If a "1" is found in any position, then the value of that "1" is the same as the value of the position. If a "0" is in a given position, then the value of the position is "0." Incidentally, each position in a binary number is called a *bit*, rather than a digit.

2-6 BINARY FRACTIONS

Binary Fractions

Fractional parts of binary numbers are represented in the same way as decimal fractions, with negative exponents. The radix point for the binary system is called the **binary point**. All numbers to the right of the point are less than one. The place values are:

. 1/2 1/4 1/8 1/16 1/32 etc.
. Binary point

The exponential values are:

$$2^{-1} = 1/2$$
$$2^{-2} = 1/4$$
$$2^{-3} = 1/8$$
$$2^{-4} = 1/16$$
$$2^{-5} = 1/32$$
$$2^{-6} = 1/64$$

Interpreting Binary Fractions

As an example, here is how we interpret 1001.011

$$1 = 1 \times 2^3 = 8.0$$
$$0 = 0 \times 2^2 = 0.0$$
$$0 = 0 \times 2^1 = 0.0$$
$$1 = 1 \times 2^0 = 1.0$$

Binary Point   .

$$0 = 0 \times 2^{-1} = 0.0$$
$$1 = 1 \times 2^{-2} = 0.25$$
$$1 = 1 \times 2^{-3} = 0.125$$
$$\overline{9.375}$$

1001.011 base two or binary system is equal to 9.375 in the base ten or decimal system.

Relating to Binary

Now we can represent all possible integers and fractions in binary notation. For human beings at least, binary numbers are more cumbersome and certainly base two numbers are not as easily recognizable as decimal numbers. In addition, binary does require more places than decimal numbers. For example, it is easier to relate to 42,500 than it is to 10101110101101010.

Still, there are some clues that can be used to get a "feel" for binary numbers. For example, which number is larger?

10110101011011
or
10110111011011

At first glance, it may be difficult to determine the greater value. But remember, significance is always read from left to right. The bits to the left are always more significant than the ones preceding them.

10110101011011 = 11,611
or
10110111011011 ≐ 11,739

When we compare 11,611 to 11,739, we immediately see that 11,739 is larger. The reason is that reading from left to right, we find a larger significant digit in 11,739 in the same position as compared to that position in the smaller number.

11,⑥11
11,⑦39

In the binary numbers shown, the key is the 7th bit from the left. In the larger number, the "1" in the position shown, is larger than the "0" found in the same position in the smaller number.

$$101101\textcircled{0}1011011$$

$$101101\textcircled{1}1011011 \; = \; \text{Larger Number}$$

2-7   USEFULNESS OF BINARY

Two Conditions

The real usefulness of the binary number system becomes apparent when we apply it to electronics. The two number symbols available, namely, 0 and 1, are analogous to a yes/no situation. Any situation which is typified by only two conditions lends itself to binary representation.

Electronics

Almost nothing is more common and more easily understood than an on/off switch. It has two states—either on or off. This reflects the presence or absence of an electrical condition. The presence of a voltage, regardless of magnitude, can be represented as "1" and the absence of voltage can be represented as "0." For this reason, electronic computers are well suited to the use of the binary, base-2 counting system. Indeed microprocessors work exclusively by manipulating binary numbers, which are represented in its circuits by either an on or an off electrical state.

Outside the microprocessor, however, we will continue to use the decimal system for their foreseeable future, for human convenience. This make it necessary to learn how to convert from one system to the other.

Note: For a few dollars, a hand held calculator can be had that will convert to and from binary. But in order to quickly grasp the action of microprocessor circuits, it is necessary to understand how to work with simple binary numbers. Because a calculator can easily be operated incorrectly, we highly recommend acquiring a basic understanding of the binary system. If you can handle binary numbers manually, you can monitor the correct use of the calculator, because you can judge the reasonableness *of an answer.*

2-8   BINARY TO DECIMAL CONVERSION

Subscripts

Binary numbers, such as 11011_2, are sometimes written with the subscript $_2$, to indicate the base 2 system is being used. The subscript 10 is used for decimal numbers, like this, 14_{10}. We will, from time to time, be using this system when the possibility of confusing two number systems exists.

We have already seen how binary numbers can be converted to decimal numbers. Here again is how it is done.

Binary to Decimal Conversion

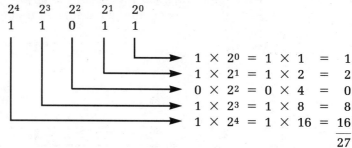

$$1 \times 2^0 = 1 \times 1 = 1$$
$$1 \times 2^1 = 1 \times 2 = 2$$
$$0 \times 2^2 = 0 \times 4 = 0$$
$$1 \times 2^3 = 1 \times 8 = 8$$
$$1 \times 2^4 = 1 \times 16 = 16$$
$$\overline{27}$$

Or a more straightforward way:

2^4	2^3	2^2	2^1	2^0
↓	↓	↓	↓	↓
1	1	0	1	1
↓	↓	↓	↓	↓

$$16 + 8 + 0 + 2 + 1 = 27$$

Recall that in the binary system, if a "1" bit is present in a position, the value to be added is the same as the value of the position.

2-9 DECIMAL TO BINARY CONVERSION

Methods

Converting a decimal number to a binary number is not quite as straightforward. We will present two methods to accomplish this. Whichever method feels the most reasonable and comfortable is the one for you to adopt.

First Method

The first method is based on the fact that a conversion from one base to another can be accomplished by successively dividing by the base to which we wish to convert. It is sometimes called the remainder method.

For instance, the conversion of the decimal number 27 to binary is done by dividing by 2.

Division	Answer	Remainder	
$27 \div 2$	13	1	LSB
$13 \div 2$	6	1	
$6 \div 2$	3	0	
$3 \div 2$	1	1	
$1 \div 2$	0	1	MSB

$$11011 = 27$$

MSB   LSB

TECHNICAL FACT

*Note that in binary, we refer to the most significant **bit** as opposed to **digit**.*

The trick is to place the remainders in a column as shown. Also, when 1 is divided by 2, the quotient is 0 with a remainder of 1.

Second Method

The second method of conversion is less elegant and certainly less scientific. However, it does work and it is a valid way to achieve a conversion. It has proved effective for many students and if it works for you, use it.

Blackjack

This method is reminiscent of the card game *Blackjack* or *21*. A player attempts to draw enough cards to total 21 points, but exceeding this number is not allowed. If you exceed 21, you are said to *bust*.

To begin a conversion, the position values of the binary system are written horizontally as shown below. It is only necessary to write enough values to exceed the number to be converted.

For example, to convert 78 to a binary number:
Write,

$$128 \quad 64 \quad 32 \quad 16 \quad 8 \quad 4 \quad 2 \quad 1$$

The number 128 exceeds 78 so that this will be enough positions. As in blackjack, we may not exceed a given number. The first number we cannot exceed is 78, the number to be converted.

78 − 64 _____	Certainly 128 exceeds 78 so that this position is not usable. However, 64 does not exceed 78 so, write a "1" in that position and subtract 64.

$$14 \qquad \begin{array}{cccccccc} 128 & 64 & 32 & 16 & 8 & 4 & 2 & 1 \\ 0 & 1 \end{array}$$

14   The number we may not exceed is now 14. The next position, 32, exceeds 14. Taking that position would cause us to *bust*, as in blackjack. Write a "0" in that position.

$$\begin{array}{cccccccc} 128 & 64 & 32 & 16 & 8 & 4 & 2 & 1 \\ 0 & 1 & 0 \end{array}$$

14   The next number (card) available is 16. But 16 is also larger that 14 and would caused us to *bust*. Put a "0" in that position.

$$\begin{array}{cccccccc} 128 & 64 & 32 & 16 & 8 & 4 & 2 & 1 \\ 0 & 1 & 0 & 0 \end{array}$$

14 − 8 _____	We can use the next position without exceeding 14 or *busting*, so write an "1" under the 8 position and subtract 8.

$$6 \qquad \begin{array}{cccccccc} 128 & 64 & 32 & 16 & 8 & 4 & 2 & 1 \\ 0 & 1 & 0 & 0 & 1 \end{array}$$

6 − 4 _____	The new number not to be exceeded is 6. The next position is 4, and is acceptable, so write a "1" under the 4 and subtract.

$$2 \qquad \begin{array}{cccccccc} 128 & 64 & 32 & 16 & 8 & 4 & 2 & 1 \\ 0 & 1 & 0 & 0 & 1 & 1 \end{array}$$

2	Two is the number not to exceed. The next position
− 2	is 2, and is acceptable, so write a "1" in that position
_____	and subtract 2.
0	

128	64	32	16	8	4	2	1
0	1	0	0	1	1	1	

0   Zero cannot be exceeded. Simply add a "0" under the
     1 position to indicate we are not using it.

128	64	32	16	8	4	2	1
0	1	0	0	1	1	1	0

The binary equivalent of 78 is 1001110.

✓ SELF-CHECK FOR SECTIONS 2-5, 2-6, 2-7, 2-8, 2-9

6. How many symbols does the binary system use?
7. In the binary system, reading from right to left, each position has a value of _____ that of the preceding position.
8. If a "1" is found in any position, then the value of that "1" is that same as the value of the _____ .
9. If a "0" is in a given position, then the value of the position is _____ .
10. Explain why binary is easily adapted to electronics.
11. Convert the binary number 100101 to a decimal number.
12. Write the binary equivalent of the decimal number 134.

2-10   BINARY ADDITION

Rules for Addition

Binary addition is quite easy. We learned to add in decimal by learning or memorizing the sums of single digit numbers. For binary, there are very simple addition rules to learn. They are:

$$0 + 0 = 0$$
$$0 + 1 = 1$$
$$1 + 0 = 1$$
$$1 + 1 = 0 \quad \text{(with a carry of 1)}$$

Here is an example:

Binary Addition		Decimal Addition
1010	=	10
0101	=	5
1111	=	15

Note that in each of the 4 column additions necessary to complete the problem, we followed the applicable rule.

The last rule indicates that a **carry** of "1" is necessary. If a carry is generated, as it is whenever 1 + 1 is added, the carry is simply added to the next higher position.

For example:

$$\begin{array}{r} 0111 = 7 \\ 0001 = 1 \\ \hline 0 \end{array}$$

The carry is added or *carried* to the next higher position.

Step 1

$$\begin{array}{r} \overset{1}{0}111 = 7 \\ 0001 = 1 \\ \hline 0 \end{array}$$

In the 2nd step, 1 + 1 = 0 and another carry is generated.

Step 2

$$\begin{array}{r} \overset{11}{0}111 = 7 \\ 0001 = 1 \\ \hline 00 \end{array}$$

In the third step, yet another carry is generated.

Step 3

$$\begin{array}{r} \overset{111}{0}111 = 7 \\ 0001 = 1 \\ \hline 000 \end{array}$$

In the last step, the carry plus "0" (1 + 0 = 1) is added.

Step 4

$$\begin{array}{r} \overset{111}{0}111 = 7 \\ 0001 = 1 \\ \hline 1000 = 8 \end{array}$$

Sample Additions

Here are some sample additions. Be sure to understand how they are done.

$$\begin{array}{r} 0101 = 5 \\ 1100 = 12 \\ \hline 10001 = 17 \end{array} \qquad \begin{array}{r} 0011 = 3 \\ 1111 = 15 \\ \hline 10010 = 18 \end{array}$$

$$\begin{array}{r} 0111 = 7 \\ 1001 = 9 \\ \hline 10000 = 16 \end{array} \qquad \begin{array}{r} 1100 = 12 \\ 1110 = 14 \\ \hline 11010 = 26 \end{array}$$

2-11   BINARY SUBTRACTION

Subtraction Rules

Subtraction of binary numbers also requires a set of rules. They are as follows:

$$\begin{array}{l} 0 - 0 = 0 \\ 1 - 0 = 1 \\ 1 - 1 = 0 \\ 0 - 1 = 1 \quad \text{(with a borrow of 1)} \end{array}$$

There are two difficulties that we encounter in subtraction. The first problem occurs when a larger number is subtracted from a smaller one. A **borrow** is generated and must be tracked. The second difficulty appears when we must express an answer that is less than zero, i.e., a negative number.

Tracking a *borrow* is certainly possible but troublesome. Representing a negative number is less obvious. Negative numbers are usually represented with a form of number called a *complement*.

2-12   COMPLEMENTS

Definition

Complements are used to complete the form of something. For example, a 120 degree angle has a 60 degree complement. The 60 degree angle complements the 120 degree angle to complete it, that is, make it a straight line of 180 degrees.

The 9's Complement

Two kinds of complements are common in number systems. The first kind of complement is the value required to complete a number to the highest possible digit in the system. In the base 10 system, the highest digit possible is 9. The **9's complement** is the number necessary to complete a digit to 9. The 9's complement of 3 is 6. The 9's complement of 54 is 99 − 54 or 45.

The 10's Complement

The other type of complement is the difference between a given number and the next higher power of the number base. In the decimal or base 10 system, we speak of the **10's complement**. The 10's complement of 3 is 7. This is because the next highest power of the number base above 3 is 10. 10 − 3 = 7. The 10's complement of 54 is 46. The next higher power above 54 is 10^2 or 100. 100 − 54 is 46.

The 10's complement can be formed by first forming the 9's complement and simply adding one.

For example, the 10's complement of 450 is:

$$
\begin{array}{rcll}
999 - 450 & = & 549 & = \text{ 9's complement} \\
& & \underline{+\,1} & \\
& & 550 & = \text{ 10's complement}
\end{array}
$$

Why Complements?

The reason for discussing complements is that they can not only be used to represent negative numbers, they can also be used to perform subtraction by adding. It is much simpler and less expensive to build microprocessors that need only perform the add function yet can subtract too.

Subtraction by Addition

Lest you think that all of this is double talk, here is how to subtract by adding:

Subtraction Problem

$$
\begin{array}{r}
782 \\
-450 \\
\hline
332
\end{array}
$$

The same problem can be solved with complements. Recall the 10's complement of 450 was 550.

To subtract by adding, we add the 10's complement,

$$
\begin{array}{r}
782 \\
+550 \quad \text{add 10's complement} \\
\hline
332
\end{array}
$$

disregard $+ 1$

The only condition is that we disregard any carry that causes the number to exceed the size of the largest number in the problem. So we strike the 1.

2-13   BINARY COMPLEMENTS

Base 2 Complements

Fortunately, dealing with complements is even easier in the binary number system. In binary, we speak of the **1's complement** and the **2's complement**. They are defined in the same way we defined the two types of complements previously. Both types of complements can be used for subtraction by adding. The first method is called the **End Around Carry** (EAC) or 1's complement subtraction.

2-14   1's COMPLEMENT SUBTRACTION

Complementing a Binary Number

Recall that the first form of complement is the number required to complete a given number to the highest digit possible in the system. The highest digit possible in binary is "1." If the given digit is "0," a "1" will complete it or *complement* it. If the given digit is "1," it is already complete and "0" is the complement. This makes the formation of the 1's complement simplicity itself.

Forming the 1's Complement

To form the 1's complement of any binary number, simply change every bit position to its opposite. In other words, all 0's become 1's and all 1's become 0's.

For example:

$$
\begin{array}{l}
10110011 \\
01001100 \ = \ \text{1's complement}
\end{array}
$$

The EAC Method

To use this method to perform subtraction, we first form the 1's complement of the number to be subtracted (subtrahend), and then we add.

ADD:

$$4 \longrightarrow 0100 \longrightarrow 0100 \longrightarrow 0100$$
$$-2 \longrightarrow 0010 \longrightarrow 1101 = \text{1's complement} \longrightarrow 1101$$
$$(1)\ 0001$$

This is called End Around Carry

$$
\begin{array}{l}
0100 \\
\underline{1101} \\
(1)\ 0001 \qquad \text{When an EAC occurs, it is} \\
\underline{+\ 1} \qquad\quad \text{added to the number.} \\
0010 \qquad = 2
\end{array}
$$

Here is another example:

ADD:

$$
\begin{array}{llll}
27 & 11011 & 11011 & 11011 \\
\underline{-\ 10} & \underline{01010} & \underline{10101}\ \text{1's complement} & \underline{10101} \\
& & & \text{EAC}\ (1)\quad 10000 \\
& & & \qquad\qquad \underline{+\ 1} \\
& & & \qquad\qquad 10001 = 17
\end{array}
$$

Negative Number

It is possible that a subtraction can result in a negative number.

$$
\begin{array}{llll}
2 & 0010 & 0010 & 0010 \\
\underline{-\ 4} & \underline{0100} & \underline{1011}\ \text{1's complement} & \underline{1011} \\
& & & 1101
\end{array}
$$

No EAC

In this case, an EAC is NOT generated. In addition, the answer does not *appear* to be 2. The answer is in fact −2 and 1101 is the way in which −2 is represented in 1's complement form.

To prove this, form the 1's complement of 1101:

$$
\begin{array}{l}
1101 \\
0010 \quad \text{1's complement} = 2_{10}
\end{array}
$$

We have discovered one way of representing negative numbers. In other words, the 1's complement form of a number does represent negative values.

Rules for 1's Complement Subtraction

From these examples, some rules for 1's complement subtraction can be made.

To subtract using 1's complement arithmetic:

1. Form the 1's complement of the number to be subtracted.
2. Add the two numbers using rules for binary addition.
3. When the result generates an EAC, the answer is a positive value. Add the EAC to the LSB.
4. If the result does not generate an EAC, the answer is a negative value.

2-15   THE 2'S COMPLEMENT

Usage

Although 1's complement arithmetic finds some use in the microprocessor world, a more common method for representing negative numbers is the 2's complement form.

The Second Type of Complement

The other form of complement we discussed was defined as the number necessary to complete a given number to the next highest power of the base. The next highest power in the binary number system is always two times the value of the given number. This doesn't necessarily help make formation of the 2's complement easier, however. But remember that it is possible to form the 10's complement by adding +1 to the 9's complement. This same idea can be used to form the 2's complement. All we have to do is add +1 to the 1's complement.

In the complement method of subtraction, we will add the 2's complement of the number to be subtracted (subtrahend), to the other number (minuend), just as we did in the 1's method.

Forming the 2's Complement

To form the 2's complement:
1. Form 1's complement
2. Add + 1

This is analogous to the way in which the 10's complement can be formed from the 9's.   Here is an example:

Form the 2's complement of 00110111.
Step 1: Form the 1's complement

$$00110111$$
$$11001000 \ = \ 1\text{'s complement}$$

Step 2: Add +1

$$11001000 \ = \ 1\text{'s complement}$$
$$\underline{\qquad +1}$$
$$11001001 \ = \ 2\text{'s complement}$$

Negative Numbers

The 2's complement is a very convenient and easy way to form negative binary numbers. And also conveniently, the 2's complement of a decimal number is simply that number with a minus sign. In other words, the 2's complement of 8 is −8. The 2's complement of 114 is −114. This fact is extremely helpful in checking the accuracy of a 2's complement representation, as we will soon see.

✔ **SELF-CHECK FOR SECTIONS 2-10, 2-11, 2-12, 2-13, 2-14, 2-15**

13. Write the four rules for binary addition.
14. The addition of 1 + 1 in binary generates a _____.
15. Explain what complement is.
16. Form the 1's complement of 1010.
17. Form the 2's complement of 1010.
18. Explain the use of the 2's complement.

2-16   2'S COMPLEMENT SUBTRACTION

Subtracting Using 2's Complement

Here is the way 2's complement subtraction is performed.

$$
\begin{array}{rl}
4 & \quad 00000100 \\
-2 & \quad \underline{00000010}
\end{array}
$$

Form the 2's complement of the number to be subtracted by:

Step 1:   Form the 1's complement

$$
\begin{array}{l}
00000010 \\
11111101 = 1's
\end{array}
$$

Step 2:   Add +1

$$
\begin{array}{l}
11111101 = 1's \\
\underline{+1} \\
11111110 = 2's
\end{array}
$$

Now add,

$$
\begin{array}{rl}
00000100 = & 4 \\
11111110 = & -2 \\
\hline
\text{Discard} \quad 1 \qquad 00000010 = & 2
\end{array}
$$

As we did in the 10's complement, discard any carry that exceeds the original number.

The Negative Result

We also need to consider the case where a subtraction results in a negative answer.

$$
\begin{array}{rl}
2 & \quad 00000010 \\
-4 & \quad \underline{00000100}
\end{array}
$$

Form the 2's complement of the number to be subtracted by:

Step 1:   Form the 1's complement

$$
\begin{array}{l}
00000010 \\
11111011 = 1's
\end{array}
$$

Step 2:   Add +1

$$11111011$$
$$+1$$
$$\overline{11111100} \ = \ 2\text{'s}$$

Now add,

$$00000010$$
$$11111100$$
$$\overline{11111110} \ = \ -2$$

The binary number 11111110 is the 2's complement answer and represents −2.

We know that +2 + (− 4) = −2 and this is in effect what has taken place. We also know that the 2's complement of −2 is +2.

The Check

To check the answer, we can form the 2's complement of −2. If the result is +2, then we know that our representation of −2 in binary was correct.

We found that −2 = 11111110

Step 1:   Form the 1's complement

$$11111110$$
$$00000001 \ = \ 1\text{'s}$$

Step 2:   Add +1

$$00000001$$
$$+1$$
$$\overline{00000010} \ = \ 2\text{'s}$$

The result is +2.

2-17   THE SIGN

Sign Bit

We have purposely been using 8-bit numbers. You may have noticed that the MSB is 0 when the number is positive and 1 when the number is negative.

This is, in fact, the convention used in 8-bit **signed binary** arithmetic.

MSB = 1 = Negative number

MSB = 0 = Positive number

Magnitude

By reserving the MSB for the sign of the number, we do limit the magnitude of the numbers possible with 8 bits. In other words, we limit the size of a number to a maximum positive value of +127 and a maximum negative value of −128.

$$0 \quad 0101111$$

Sign   Magnitude

Computers and microprocessors typically work in 8-bit *bytes* or multiples thereof.

Convention for Larger Numbers

Microprocessors usually work in 8, 16, or 32 bit *words*. The convention of using a "1" in the Most Significant Bit position to indicate the sign, still holds. In a 32-bit number, using the MSB position as the sign bit, still allows representation of numbers +2,147,483,647 to −2,147,483,648.

How a Microprocessor Treats Signs

Although the use of the MSB as the sign bit is common, it is necessary to know whether or not you are working with signed binary numbers. In other words, microprocessors work with binary representation but cannot *know* if we have decided to use the MSB as the sign or have decided to use it to represent magnitude.

In either case, the microprocessor will treat the bit in the same way. Later in the book, we will deal with some of the ramifications of this. For now, be aware that:

Signed Number		Unsigned Number
	not equal	
11001100	≠	11001100

Reading Signed Numbers

To determine the value of 11001100, if it is signed, can be done like this:

We know that the "1" in the MSB position means it is a negative value. Negative values are represented in 2's complement. Forming the 2's complement of a negative number will result in the same number with a positive value.

Step 1:   Form the 1's

$$11001100$$
$$00110011 = 1's$$

Step 2:   Add +1

$$00110011$$
$$\underline{+1}$$
$$00110100 = 2's$$

2^7	2^6	2^5	2^4	2^3	2^2	2^1	2^0
↓	↓	↓	↓	↓	↓	↓	↓
128	64	32	16	8	4	2	1
↓	↓	↓	↓	↓	↓	↓	↓
0	0	1	1	0	1	0	0
		↓	↓	↓	↓	↓	↓
		32 +	16 +	0 +	4 +	0 +	0 = 52

If the 2's complement of a negative number, 1100100, turns out to be +52, the number must have been −52.

Signed Number		Unsigned Number
11001100	≠	11001100
−52		?

What is the value of this pattern of bits then, if it is considered to be unsigned?

2^7	2^6	2^5	2^4	2^3	2^2	2^1	2^0
↓	↓	↓	↓	↓	↓	↓	↓
128	64	32	16	8	4	2	1
↓	↓	↓	↓	↓	↓	↓	↓
1	1	0	0	1	1	0	0
↓	↓	↓	↓	↓	↓	↓	↓

$$128 + 64 + 0 + 0 + 8 + 4 + 0 + 0 = 204$$

Signed Number		Unsigned Number
11001100	≠	11001100
−52	≠	204

Now it is more obvious that the two are not equal. Simply be aware that the signed number convention is left to us. The microprocessor cannot be aware of such things.

2-18 BINARY MULTIPLICATION

Binary multiplication is not nearly as difficult as decimal multiplication.

Rules

The rules for binary multiplication are:

$$0 \times 0 = 0$$
$$0 \times 1 = 0$$
$$1 \times 0 = 0$$
$$1 \times 1 = 1$$

When binary numbers are multiplied, the same pattern of partial products used with decimal numbers is followed.

```
       101
   ×   101
   ───────
       101
       000      Partial Products
     101
   ───────
     11011
```

Binary multiplication in microprocessors is sometimes done with a special instruction. If such facilities are not available, it is also possible to perform multiplication by adding. This is in fact what multiplication is. 4×4 is really a shorthand way of expressing $4 + 4 + 4 + 4$. Because of the speed with which microprocessors function, adding 4 several times does not present a problem.

2-19   BINARY DIVISION

Division is also carried out just as decimal division is performed.

$$
\begin{array}{r}
5 \\
5\overline{)25}
\end{array}
\qquad\qquad
\begin{array}{r}
101.0 \\
101\overline{)11001.0} \\
\underline{101} \\
00101 \\
\underline{101} \\
\hline
0 \quad \text{remainder}
\end{array}
$$

Trial subtractions are made as the divisor is subtracted from each successive group in the dividend. From left to right, as soon as the dividend group becomes large enough to subtract the divisor, a "1" is placed in the quotient and the divisor subtracted.

Many microprocessors have division instructions that will perform binary division on two binary numbers and produce both a quotient and a remainder.

 SELF-CHECK FOR SECTIONS 2-16, 2-17, 2-18, 2-19

19. Using the 2's complement method, subtract: $\begin{array}{r} 1011 \\ -\,0010 \end{array}$

20. Which bit position is used as the sign bit for an 8-bit number? For a 16-bit number?
21. If the sign bit is 1, will the number be positive or negative?
22. Explain one way a microprocessor might do multiplication.

SUMMARY OF IDEAS

- Most early number systems used the base of 10. They had ten unique symbols.
- Positional notation is a system that allows the position of a symbol, in reference to other symbols, to denote value.
- In our base 10 system, the value of a position is always 10 times the value of the preceding position.
- The number of unique symbols that a number system contains is referred to as the base or radix.
- The binary system has a radix of 2. Only two unique symbols are possible.
- Each position in the binary number system has a value of twice the preceding one.
- In the binary system, if a "1" bit is present in a position, the value to be added is the same as the value of the position.
- Conversion of a decimal number to a binary number can be accomplished by successively dividing by 2.
- Binary addition is accomplished by the following set of rules. They are:

$$
\begin{array}{rcl}
0 + 0 &=& 0 \\
0 + 1 &=& 1 \\
1 + 0 &=& 1 \\
1 + 1 &=& 0 \quad \text{(with a carry of 1)}
\end{array}
$$

- Complements are used to complete a value. There are two kinds of complements common in number systems.

- The first kind of complement calls for the number necessary to complement a number to the highest possible digit in the system.
- The second kind of complement is the difference between a given number and the next highest power of the number base.
- In binary, an example of the first kind of complement is called the 1's complement.
- The 1's complement is formed by changing every bit position in the binary number to its opposite.
- When the 1's complement is used for subtraction, an EAC or End Around Carry bit is added to the result, if such a bit is present.
- The 2's complement in binary is an example of the second kind of complement.
- The 2's complement is formed by:
  1) Forming the 1's complement
  2) Adding +1
- The 2's complement is the most common way of representing negative binary numbers.
- A "1" in the MSB position of a binary number means a negative number and a "0" in this position means a positive number.

CHAPTER QUESTIONS & PROBLEMS

True or False

1. The decimal number system uses the 10 decimal symbols of 0 through 10.
2. Positional notation, while quite useful in decimal, has little value or use in the binary system.
3. Working from left to right, in the binary system, each position has the value of 1/2 the preceding one.
4. Number complements make it possible to perform subtraction by using addition methods.
5. The 1's complement of a binary number is used to form the 2's complement.

Fill in the Blanks

6. The system of using a limited set of unique symbols by situating the same symbols in different locations is called _____ _____.
7. In the decimal system, reading from left to right, each position has a value of _____ times the preceding one.
8. The 2's complement of +1,345 is _____ (your answer in decimal).
9. In a binary number, a "1" in the fifth position from the left of the binary point is _____ the value of a "1" in the fourth position.
10. In signed binary, a "1" in the MSB position means that the number is _____.

Multiple Choice

11. Which of the following is the larger number? (unsigned numbers)
    a. 11000111101010101
    b. 11000110101010101
    c. 11000111101010111
    d. 11000111101010000

12. The largest decimal number that can be represented with only 4 binary bits is
    a. 10.
    b. 20.
    c. 15.
    d. 16.

13. Forming the 1's complement of 0001_2 will yield
    a. 1111.
    b. 10000.
    c. 1110.
    d. 11110.

14. Forming the 2's complement of 0001_2 will yield
    a. 1111.
    b. 10000.
    c. 1110.
    d. 11110.

15. The decimal value of 11111111 in unsigned binary is
    a. 128.
    b. 256.
    c. 255.
    d. −1.

Problems

16. Add the following binary numbers:

    10110001   10101111
    10001011   00001010

    01010101   11000001
    00010001   11111100

17. Form the 1's complement of each of the following:
    10101000
    10100101
    11111000
    00100100

18. Form the 2's complement of each of the following:
    10101001
    00001111
    11010100
    10100011

19. Write +64 in binary form.
20. Write −64 in signed (2's complement) form.
21. Find the decimal value of 11000110. Assume the number is written in signed 2's complement form.
22. What is the decimal value of 11000110 if it is considered to be an unsigned number?
23. Write +127 in 2's complement form.
24. Write −128 in 2's complement form.
25. Form the 2's complement of 1000.

CHAPTER 3 REGISTERS, COMPARATORS, & ADDERS

OUTLINE

NEW TERMS TO WATCH FOR

D-Type Flip-Flop   Recirculating   JK-Type Flip-Flop
UART   Shift Left   Shift Right
Shift Register   Comparator   SISO
Equality Circuit   SIPO   Adder
Half Adder   PISO   Full Adder
PIPO   Subtracter   Clock Pulse
Adder-Subtracter   Truth Table   XOR

After completing this chapter, you should be able to:

1. Define the term *shift register*.
2. Identify the four major classes of shift registers.
3. Determine the effect of shifting a binary number to the left or to the right.
4. Describe how to connect a serial shift register in a manner that will keep it from losing its data.
5. Calculate the amount of time necessary to load and unload serial shift registers.
6. State one of the major purposes for SIPO and PISO registers.
7. Explain how an XOR gate can be used for determining equalities.
8. Clarify the way in which a microprocessor compares the magnitude of binary numbers.
9. Draw the symbols for adder circuits.
10. Use adder circuits to sum binary numbers and to predict the outputs of such circuits.
11. Describe the operation of an adder-subtracter.

3-1   INTRODUCTION

A microprocessor works exclusively with binary numbers. All math, character representations, data transfers, and instructions must be in the binary form in order for the microprocessor to be able to control, manage, and use them. The microprocessor must manipulate massive quantities of binary numbers. In addition, the numbers must be moved around, stored, and shifted at tremendous speeds. To accomplish this work, the microprocessor needs certain specialized circuits. Since the processor is designed to be as self-sufficient as possible, these circuits are integrated into the microprocessor chip.

Three of these special circuits are the subject of this chapter. They are the **shift register**, the **comparator**, and the **adder** circuits. These circuits are essential to the microprocessor. Later, we will see them interact within the microprocessor as it carries out program instructions. By examining the circuits on the level of their discrete components, a much clearer understanding of the microprocessor will be gained.

3-2   SHIFT REGISTERS

The temporary storage and work space areas for binary number manipulation are provided for by registers or, more properly, **shift registers**. Shift registers are found in several forms in the microprocessor and make up a large part of the internal circuitry.

Flip-Flops

Shift registers are constructed from flip-flops. In digital electronics, a flip-flop is defined as a temporary storage device for a binary bit. A flip-flop can store a logic "1" or a logic "0" condition. One of the simplest forms of a flip-flop, the **D-type**, is shown in Figure 3-1(A). Figure 3-1(B) is the symbol for a D flip-flop, and Figure 3-1(C) is the **truth table** for a D-type flip-flop. We are able to state this truth table in the following words: in a D flip-flop, the logic level on Q follows the logic level on D whenever the flip-flop is clocked.

FIGURE 3-1 (A) Diagram of D Flip-flop (B) Symbol for D Flip-flop (C) Truth Table for D Flip-flop

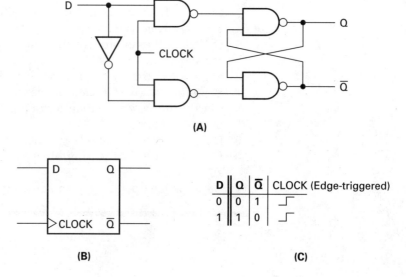

(A)

(B)

D	Q	$\bar{Q}$	CLOCK (Edge-triggered)
0	0	1	⌐
1	1	0	⌐_

(C)

Classification

A group of flip-flops arranged to temporarily store binary numbers is called a shift register. Binary numbers are placed into and removed from a group of flip-flops or shift register in a variety of ways. The way in which binary information is loaded and removed from the register determines the classification. There are four main classifications of shift registers.

SISO	Serial In; Serial Out
SIPO	Serial In; Parallel Out
PISO	Parallel In; Serial Out
PIPO	Parallel In; Parallel Out

Width

Another way of classifying shift registers is according to their *width*. The width of a register is determined by the number of flip-flops it contains. This indicates the width or length of the binary number that can be processed or stored. Common widths are 4-, 8-, or 16-bits, but in certain applications, registers of several thousand bits are used.

Serial In; Serial Out

The simplest type of shift register is the *Serial-In–Serial-Out* type or **SISO**. It simply means that the input to the register is accomplished in serial form, that is, one bit at a time. The output will also be available one bit at a time.

Serial Connections

The D flip-flops in Figure 3-2(A) are connected serially. Note that the Q-output of each stage is connected to the D-output of each following stage. The clock inputs are connected together. The **clock pulse** will cause all flip-flops to clock their D inputs to their Q outputs simultaneously. The **not-Q** outputs are not used.

Timing

The timing diagram for loading the Serial-In–Serial-Out shift register in Figure 3-2(A) is shown in Figure 3-2(B). The Data or D input of the flip-flop is being loaded with the 4-bit binary number, 0001_2. The number, 0001_2 appears on the serial input of the first flip-flop, FF3, one bit at a time. The input remains high or "1" for time period t_a. During time t_a, the first clock pulse arrives. On the positive edge of the clock pulse, the D input is clocked to the Q output of the first stage, FF3. The Q output of this stage remains high for time t_1. At this time, the shift register is storing the binary number 1000_2.

SISO

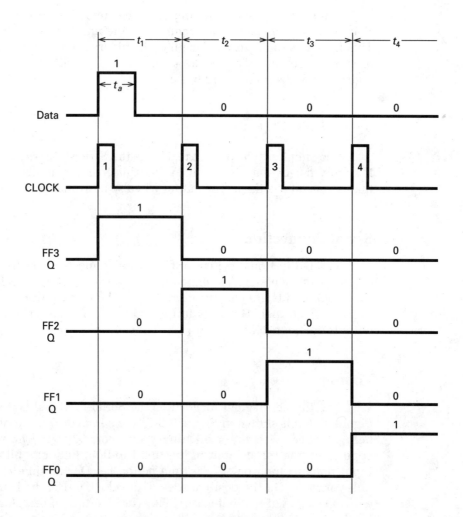

FIGURE 3-2 (A) 4-Bit D Flip-flop Shift Register

FIGURE 3-2 (B) SISO Timing Diagram

When the positive edge of the next clock pulse arrives, at the beginning of time t_2, the "1" on the output of the first stage, FF3, is clocked to the output of the second stage, FF2. (Fig. 3-3 (A and B)) The output to the first stage, FF3, is now "0" again. This is because the data input has returned to "0." The second clock pulse caused this "0" to be transferred to the Q output of FF3. During time t_2, the register contains 0100_2.

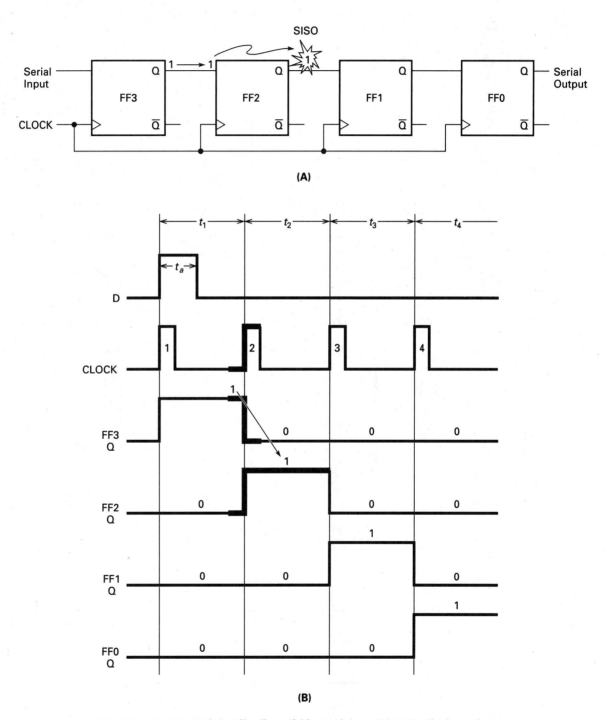

FIGURE 3-3 (A) 4-Bit D Flip-flop Shift Register (B) SISO Timing Diagram

The third clock pulse again triggers all four stages at once. But the only "1" present at this time is on the input to the third stage, FF1. In Figure 3-4 (A and B), the "1" is clocked over to the output of the flip-flop FF1. For the time period t_3, the register contains 0010_2.

Upon the arrival of the fourth clock pulse, the input to flip-flop FF0 is "1." This "1" is now clocked to the output of the last stage, FF0. All other stages are clocking a "0" from **D** to **Q**. During time t_4, the register contains the binary number 0001_2, which is the entire and correct value.

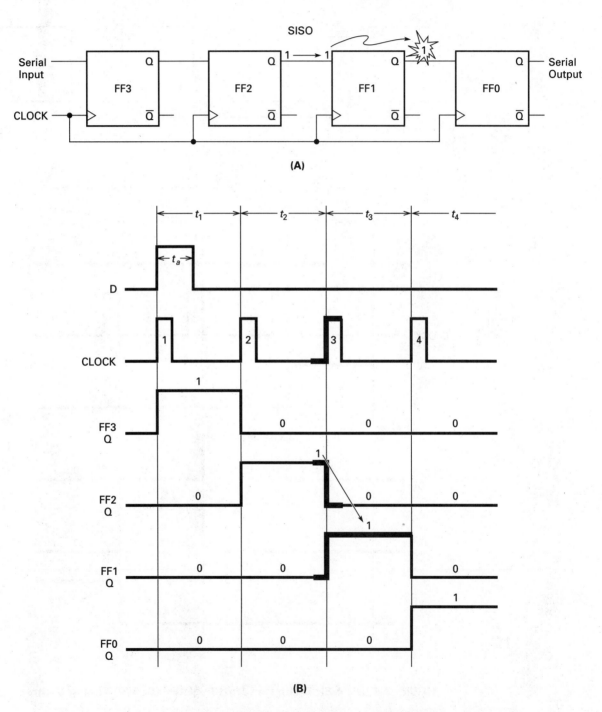

FIGURE 3-4 (A) 4-Bit D Flip-flop Shift Register (B) SISO Timing Diagram

In Figure 3-5, the data input to the shift register is 1001_2. It is shifted in, or loaded one bit at a time. At time t_4, the register is completely loaded and contains a binary 1001_2.

Two Points

There are two important points to be made in reference to Serial-In–Serial-Out shift registers. First, we note that it took four clock pulses to load the register. A serial input register always requires as many clock pulses as it has stages to load it. The second point is that it will also require four clock pulses to unload or *read* out the number it contains. For the 4-bit register discussed, we can say that it only contains accurate data after four clock pulses and until then, it cannot be read.

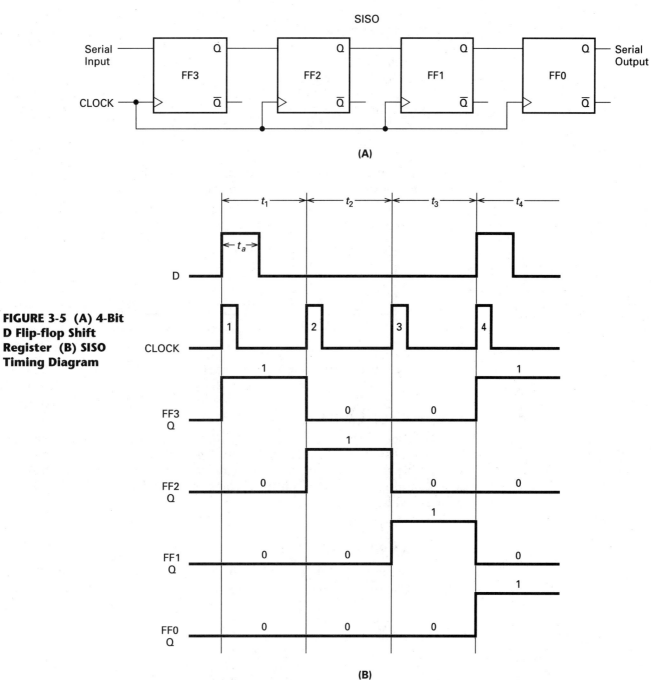

FIGURE 3-5 (A) 4-Bit D Flip-flop Shift Register (B) SISO Timing Diagram

Practical Considerations

In practice, a flip-flop register does require that the data logic on the input be present a few nano-seconds before the clock pulse arrives. This factor is accounted for during design, but not actually reflected in the timing diagrams. For the purposes of our timing diagrams, as the clock pulse goes positive, the data is already assumed to be present on the **D** input.

Recirculating Shift Registers

The timing is critical for shift registers. For the Serial-In–Serial-Out register, data can only be read after the fourth clock pulse. If it is not read or used at that time, the data can be lost when another clock pulse arrives. It would be shifted, so to speak, off the end of the last stage and into "nowhere." It may not be practical in the scheme of things, to read the data at the moment the register is fully loaded. For this reason, provisions must be made to keep the information from being lost. This is accomplished by **recirculating** the data.

Figure 3-6 shows a recirculating circuit. The data input for new data is D1. The recirculating data is input on D2. To recirculate, the output of the last stage is connected back to the recirculate input, D2. The Control input, a signal from the microprocessor's control unit or coordinator, determines whether data is recirculated or new data is accepted. When the Control input is low, the D2 input is active and data is recirculated. If the Control is high, then D1 is active and new data can be input. With this circuit, the information can be constantly renewed until it is *read out,* that is, used.

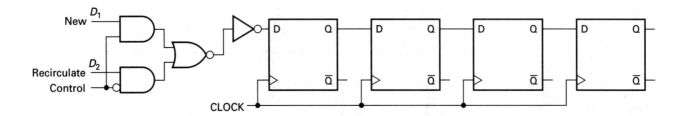

FIGURE 3-6 Recirculating Shift Register

Shift Left; Shift Right

To accomplish certain operations within a microprocessor it is necessary to be able to shift binary numbers both to the right and to the left. For example, shifting all bit positions in a binary number one position to the left is the same as multiplying by 2. Shifting all bit positions one bit to the right is the same as dividing by 2.

Shift Left Connection

The Serial-In–Serial-Out register just discussed, could only shift to the right. It is simply a matter of connecting the outputs of the following stages to the inputs of the preceding stages to change the shift direction to the left. The diagram in Figure 3-7(A) shows how this is done. Note the input is now on the **D** lead of the right most register.

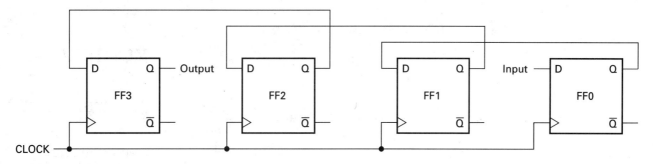

FIGURE 3-7 (A) Shift Left Connection

Combination

In practice, most shift registers are a combination, that is, they can be used in both left and right modes. Figure 3-7(B) demonstrates a way of using control circuitry to operate the shift register in either a **shift right** or a **shift left** mode. When the Mode (control) is low, the register will shift to the right, but if the Mode (control) is high, the register will shift to the left.

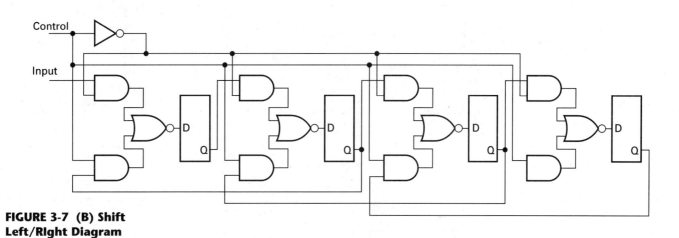

FIGURE 3-7 (B) Shift Left/Right Diagram

The 74F194 by Motorola is shown in Figure 3-7(C). This universal 4-bit register, made with D-type flip-flops, will shift either left or right.

Speed

The rate at which a serial shift register shifts data in and out will depend on the rate at which it is clocked. For a serial shift register this becomes a major factor. A 1,024-bit serial shift register will require 1,024 clock pulses to fully shift and load all bits. If a shift register is clocked at frequency f, then the time T required to load (or unload) it will be,

$$T = 1/f \times \text{number of stages}$$

Even if we clock at a 10 KHz rate, the time to load the 1,024-bit register will be:

$$T = 1/f \times \text{number of stages}$$
$$T = 1/10 \times 10^3 \times 1,024$$
$$T = 102.4 \text{ milliseconds}$$

In the microprocessor world, 100 milliseconds is a relatively long time.

 **MOTOROLA**

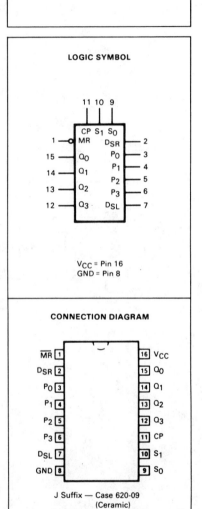

Advance Information

4-BIT BIDIRECTIONAL UNIVERSAL SHIFT REGISTER

DESCRIPTION — The MC54F/74F194 is a high-speed 4-bit bidirectional universal shift register. As a high-speed multifunctional, sequential building block, it is useful in a wide variety of applications. It may be used in serial-serial, shift left, shift right, serial-parallel, parallel-serial, and parallel-parallel data register transfers. The F194 is similar in operation to the S195 universal shift register, with added features of shift left without external connections and hold (do nothing) modes of operation.

- **TYPICAL SHIFT FREQUENCY OF 150 MHz**
- **ASYNCHRONOUS MASTER RESET**
- **HOLD (DO NOTHING) MODE**
- **FULLY SYNCHRONOUS SERIAL OR PARALLEL DATA TRANSFERS**

FUNCTIONAL DESCRIPTION — The F194 contains four edge-triggered D flip-flops and the necessary interstage logic to synchronously perform shift right, shift left, parallel load and hold operations. Signals applied to the Select (S_0, S_1) inputs determine the type of operation, as shown in the Mode Select Table. Signals on the Select, Parallel data (P_0–P_3) inputs and Serial data (D_{SR}, D_{SL}) inputs can change when the clock is in either state, provided only that the recommended setup and hold times, with respect to the clock rising edge, are observed. A LOW signal on Master Reset ($\overline{MR}$) overrides all other inputs and forces the outputs LOW.

MODE SELECT TABLE

OPERATING MODE	INPUTS						OUTPUTS			
	$\overline{MR}$	S_1	S_0	D_{SR}	D_{SL}	P_n	Q_0	Q_1	Q_2	Q_3
Reset	L	X	X	X	X	X	L	L	L	L
Hold	H	l	l	X	X	X	q_0	q_1	q_2	q_3
Shift Left	H	h	l	X	l	X	q_1	q_2	q_3	L
	H	h	l	X	h	X	q_1	q_2	q_3	H
Shift Right	H	l	h	l	X	X	L	q_0	q_1	q_2
	H	l	h	h	X	X	H	q_0	q_1	q_2
Parallel Load	H	h	h	X	X	p_n	p_0	p_1	p_2	p_3

l = LOW voltage level one setup time prior to the LOW-to-HIGH clock transition.
h = HIGH voltage level one setup time prior to the LOW-to-HIGH clock transition.
p_n (q_n) = Lower case letters indicate the state of the referenced input (or output) one setup time prior to the LOW-to-HIGH clock transition.
H = HIGH Voltage Level
L = LOW Voltage Level
X = Immaterial

FIGURE 3-7 (C) MC54/74F194 Data Sheet

MC54F/74F194

LOGIC DIAGRAM

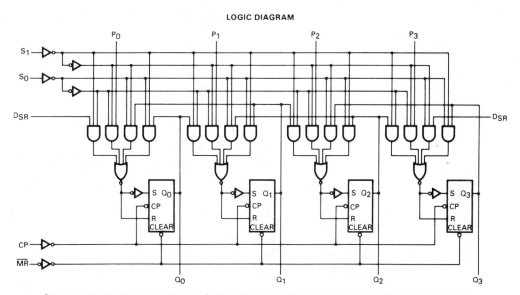

Please note that this diagram is provided only for the understanding of logic operations and should not be used to estimate propagation delays.

GUARANTEED OPERATING RANGES

SYMBOL	PARAMETER		MIN	TYP	MAX	UNIT
V_{CC}	Supply Voltage	54, 74	4.50	5.0	5.50	V
T_A	Operating Ambient Temperature Range	54	–55	25	125	°C
		74	0	25	70	
I_{OH}	Output Current — High	54, 74			-1.0	mA
I_{OL}	Output Current — Low	54, 74			20	mA

DC CHARACTERISTICS OVER OPERATING TEMPERATURE RANGE (unless otherwise specified)

SYMBOL	PARAMETER		LIMITS			UNITS	TEST CONDITIONS	
			MIN	TYP	MAX			
V_{IH}	Input HIGH Voltage		2.0			V	Guaranteed Input HIGH Voltage	
V_{IL}	Input LOW Voltage				0.8	V	Guaranteed Input LOW Voltage	
V_{IK}	Input Clamp Diode Voltage				–1.2	V	I_{IN} = –18 mA	V_{CC} = MIN
V_{OH}	Output HIGH Voltage	54, 74	2.5	3.4		V	I_{OH} = –1.0 mA	V_{CC} = 4.50 V
		74	2.7	3.4		V	I_{OH} = –1.0 mA	V_{CC} = 4.75 V
V_{OL}	Output LOW Voltage			0.35	0.5	V	I_{OL} = 20 mA	V_{CC} = MIN
I_{IH}	Input HIGH Current				20	µA	V_{IN} = 2.7 V	V_{CC} = MAX
					100	µA	V_{IN} = 7.0 V	
I_{IL}	Input LOW Current				–0.6	mA	V_{IN} = 0.5 V	V_{CC} = MAX
I_{OS}	Output Short Circuit Current (Note 2)		–60		–150	mA	V_{OUT} = 0 V	V_{CC} = MAX
I_{CC}	Power Supply Current			33	46	mA	S_n, $\overline{MR}$, D_{SR}, D_{SL} = 4.5 V P_n = Gnd, CP = ⌐	V_{CC} = MAX

NOTES:
1. For conditions such as MIN or MAX, use the appropriate value specified under guaranteed operating ranges.
2. Not more than one output should be shorted at a time, nor for more than 1 second.

FIGURE 3-7 (D) MC54/74F194 Data Sheet (cont.)

Serial In; Parallel Out

The next major classification of shift registers is called **Serial-In–Parallel-Out** or **SIPO**. The name explicitly states the operation of the shift register. The input to this type is in a serial manner, one bit at a time. But the output is taken in a parallel fashion, all the bits at the same time.

Clocking

Figure 3-8(A) shows a Serial-In–Parallel-Out, 4-bit shift register. It still requires four clock pulses to load the register. However, on the fourth clock pulse, the register contains a valid 4-bit number. To read this number, the *read enable* line is pulsed high. This enables the read AND gates, making the binary number contained in the shift register available on the four parallel outputs A, B, C, and D. The number is read at once, all 4-bit positions are present at the same time. The four additional clock pulses, used to read the serial out type, are no longer necessary. Of course, recirculation may still be needed.

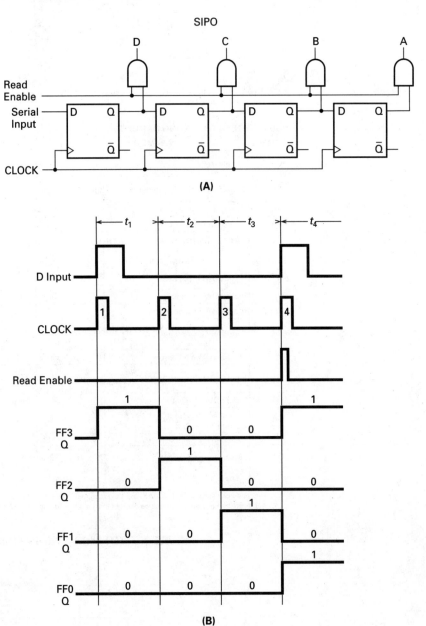

FIGURE 3-8 (A) 4-Bit Serial-In–Parallel-Out Shift Register (B) SIPO Timing Diagram

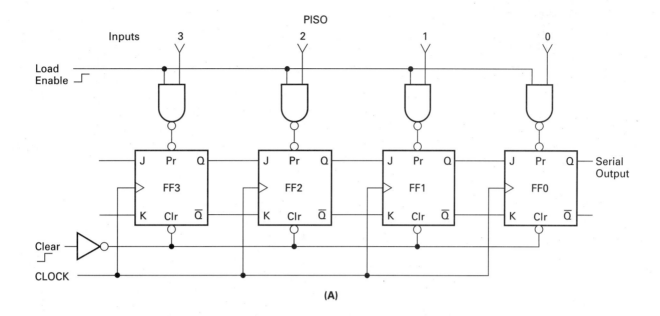

(A)

Preset	Clear	J	K	Q	Q̄	CLOCK
0	1	×	×	1	0	×
1	0	×	×	0	1	×
1	1	1	0	1	0	⌐_
1	1	0	1	0	1	⌐_
1	1	1	1	Toggle		

× = Don't Care

(B)

FIGURE 3-9 (A) 4-Bit Parallel-In–Serial-Out Shift Register (B) JK Flip-flop Truth Table

Parallel In; Serial Out

The third type of shift register is the **Parallel-In–Serial-Out** type, **PISO**. Again, as the name implies, all inputs are simultaneous or parallel. The output, however, must be taken in a serial manner. Figure 3-9(A) is a diagram of a Parallel-In–Serial-Out shift register. This circuit makes use of the **JK-type** flip-flop. By pulsing the *clear* input, the shift register is cleared, that is, all Q outputs are made zero, as can be seen by examining the truth table in Figure 3-9(B).

Loading

In order to load the PISO shift register, the load enable line is brought high. At this time, the binary number present on the parallel inputs is transferred to the Q output of each flip-flop. The truth table for the PISO in Figure 3-9(B) confirms this.

The effect is that the shift register is loaded with a binary number the instant the load enable is brought high. To read or unload it will require four clock pulses.

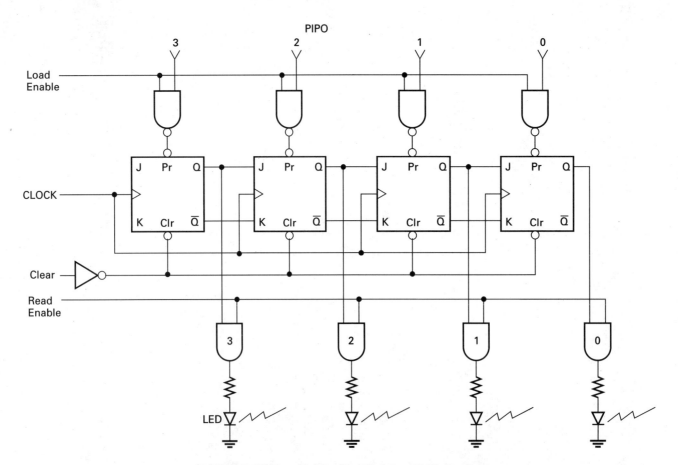

FIGURE 3-10 Parallel-In–Parallel-Out Shift Register

Parallel In; Parallel Out

Figure 3-10 shows a register that is designed to use a parallel input as well as a parallel output. This type is called **Parallel-In–Parallel-Out** or **PIPO**. It is simply a matter of adding a parallel circuit to read what is in the register once it is loaded. For the PIPO register we have added the AND gates connected to the output of each flip-flop. The AND gates are driving LED devices. If a "1" is present, the LED will be on. If a "0" is present, the LED will be off. In this way, the information in the shift register is always available.

Combination Register

Shift registers are available as combination registers. The exact way in which a register can be used must be determined from its data sheet. The *mode control* determines the way in which the register functions. Look at the data sheet for the 74LS299 (Fig. 3-11). There it can be seen how such a device is used in practice. Note for example, the S_0 and the S_1 inputs are the mode select inputs.

Applications

The parallel format for binary numbers is obviously faster and more efficient than the serial format. When data is transferred from place to place within a microprocessor system, the physical distances are not far. Providing parallel electrical pathways on an eight, sixteen, or thirty-two bit bus does not present a problem. In the outside world, however, distances become a consideration. The transfer of data on eight parallel wires becomes a major difficulty when the transmitting device is several hundred feet away or across town.

 **MOTOROLA**

SN54/74LS299

8-BIT SHIFT/STORAGE REGISTER WITH 3-STATE OUTPUTS

LOW POWER SCHOTTKY

DESCRIPTION — The SN54LS/74LS299 is an 8-Bit Universal Shift/Storage Register with 3-state outputs. Four modes of operation are possible: hold (store), shift left, shift right and load data.

The parallel load inputs and flip-flop outputs are multiplexed to reduce the total number of package pins. Separate outputs are provided for flip-flops Q_0 and Q_7 to allow easy cascading. A separate active LOW Master Reset is used to reset the register.

- **COMMON I/O FOR REDUCED PIN COUNT**
- **FOUR OPERATION MODES: SHIFT LEFT, SHIFT RIGHT, LOAD AND STORE**
- **SEPARATE SHIFT RIGHT SERIAL INPUT AND SHIFT LEFT SERIAL INPUT FOR EASY CASCADING**
- **3-STATE OUTPUTS FOR BUS ORIENTED APPLICATIONS**
- **INPUT CLAMP DIODES LIMIT HIGH-SPEED TERMINATION EFFECTS**

**FIGURE 3-11
SN54/74LS299
Data Sheet**

PIN NAMES

PIN NAMES		LOADING (Note a)	
		HIGH	LOW
CP	Clock Pulse (active positive-going edge) Input	0.5 U.L.	0.25 U.L.
DS_0	Serial Data Input for Right Shift	0.5 U.L.	0.25 U.L.
DS_7	Serial Data Input for Left Shift	0.5 U.L.	0.25 U.L.
I/O_n	Parallel Data Input or	0.5 U.L.	0.25 U.L.
	Parallel Output (3-State) (Note c)	65(25) U.L.	15(7.5) U.L.
$\overline{OE}_1, \overline{OE}_2$	3-State Output Enable (active LOW) Inputs	0.5 U.L.	0.25 U.L.
Q_0, Q_7	Serial Outputs (Note b)	10 U.L.	5(2.5) U.L.
$\overline{MR}$	Asynchronous Master Reset (active LOW) Input	0.5 U.L.	0.25 U.L.
S_0, S_1	Mode Select Inputs	1 U.L.	0.5 U.L.

NOTES:
a. 1 TTL Unit Load (U.L.) = 40 μA HIGH/1.6 mA LOW.
b. The Output LOW drive factor is 2.5 U.L. for Military (54) and 5 U.L. for Commercial (74) Temperature Ranges.
c. The Output LOW drive factor is 7.5 U.L. for Military (54) and 15 U.L. for Commercial (74), The Output HIGH drive factor is 25 U.L. for Military (54) and 65 U.L. for Commercial (74) Temperature Ranges.

**CONNECTION DIAGRAM
DIP (TOP VIEW)**

1	S_0	V_{CC}	20
2	$\overline{OE}_1$	S_1	19
3	$\overline{OE}_2$	D_{s7}	18
4	I/O_6	Q_7	17
5	I/O_4	I/O_7	16
6	I/O_2	I/O_5	15
7	I/O_0	I/O_3	14
8	Q_0	I/O_1	13
9	$\overline{MR}$	CP	12
10	GND	DS_0	11

J Suffix — Case 732-03 (Ceramic)
N Suffix — Case 738-03 (Plastic)

NOTE:
The Flatpak version has the same pinouts (Connection Diagram) as the Dual In-Line Package.

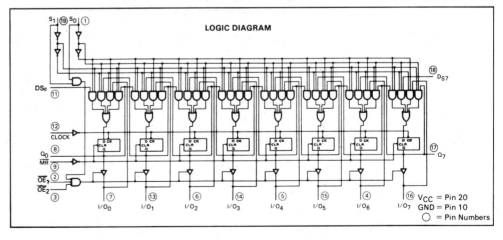

For this reason, data is transmitted on a single pair of wires or telephone lines in serial format. For example, as in Figure 3-12, a host computer may need to be in communication with a remote terminal. Yet inside each electronic device, the data is manipulated in the eight-bit parallel manner that is more efficient. The conversion from one format to another is accomplished by a PISO and a SIPO.

SN54/74LS299

GUARANTEED OPERATING RANGES

SYMBOL	PARAMETER			MIN	TYP	MAX	UNIT
V_{CC}	Supply Voltage		54	4.5	5.0	5.5	V
			74	4.75	5.0	5.25	
T_A	Operating Ambient Temperature Range		54	−55	25	125	°C
			74	0	25	70	
I_{OH}	Output Current — High	Q_0, Q_7	54,74			−0.4	mA
I_{OL}	Output Current — Low	Q_0, Q_7	54			4.0	mA
		Q_0, Q_7	74			8.0	
I_{OH}	Output Current — High	I/O_0—I/O_7	54			−1.0	mA
		I/O_0—I/O_7	74			−2.6	
I_{OL}	Output Current — Low	I/O_0—I/O_7	54			12	mA
		I/O_0—I/O_7	74			24	

DC CHARACTERISTICS OVER OPERATING TEMPERATURE RANGE (unless otherwise specified)

SYMBOL	PARAMETER		LIMITS			UNITS	TEST CONDITIONS
			MIN	TYP	MAX		
V_{IH}	Input HIGH Voltage		2.0			V	Guaranteed Input HIGH Voltage for All Inputs
V_{IL}	Input LOW Voltage	54			0.7	V	Guaranteed Input LOW Voltage for All Inputs
		74			0.8		
V_{IK}	Input Clamp Diode Voltage			−0.65	−1.5	V	V_{CC} = MIN, I_{IN} = −18 mA
V_{OH}	Output HIGH Voltage I/O_0—I/O_7	54	2.4	3.2		V	V_{CC} = MIN, I_{OH} = MAX
		74	2.4	3.1		V	
V_{OH}	Output HIGH Voltage Q_0, Q_7	54	2.5	3.4		V	V_{CC} = MIN, I_{OH} = MAX
		74	2.7	3.4		V	
V_{OL}	Output LOW Voltage I/O_0—I/O_7	54,74		0.25	0.4	V	I_{OL} = 12 mA, V_{CC} = V_{CC} MIN, V_{IN} = V_{IL} or V_{IH} per Truth Table
		74		0.35	0.5	V	I_{OL} = 24 mA
V_{OL}	Output LOW Voltage Q_0—Q_7	54,74			0.4	V	I_{OL} = 4.0 mA, V_{CC} = V_{CC} MIN, V_{IN} = V_{IL} or V_{IH} per Truth Table
		74			0.5	V	I_{OL} = 8.0 mA
I_{OZH}	Output Off Current HIGH I/O_0—I/O_7				40	μA	V_{CC}= MAX, V_{OUT} = 2.7 V
I_{OZL}	Output Off Current LOW I/O_0—I/O_7				−400	μA	V_{CC}= MAX, V_{OUT} = 0.4 V
I_{IH}	Input HIGH Current	Others			20	μA	V_{CC} = MAX, V_{IN} = 2.7 V
		$S_0, S_1, I/O_0$—I/O_7			40	μA	
		Others			0.1	mA	V_{CC} = MAX, V_{IN} = 7.0 V
		S_0, S_1			0.2	mA	
		I/O_0—I/O_7			0.1	mA	V_{CC} = MAX, V_{IN} = 5.5 V
I_{IL}	Input LOW Current	Others			−0.4	mA	V_{CC} = MAX, V_{IN} = 0.4 V
		S_0, S_1			−0.8	mA	
I_{OS}	Short Circuit Current	Q_0, Q_7	−20		−100	mA	V_{CC} = MAX
		I/O_0—I/O_7	−30		−130	mA	V_{CC} = MAX
I_{CC}	Power Supply Current				53	mA	V_{CC} = MAX

FIGURE 3-11 SN54/74LS299 Data Sheet (cont.)

UART

The need for PISO and SIPO shift registers for converting format has become so common that a chip is available containing this combination. These IC chips are called **UART's**, *Universal Asynchronous Receiver Transmitters*. We will learn more about *Asynchronous* data later in the book. For now, it is sufficient to think of asynchronous as a serial data stream.

SN54/74LS299

FUNCTION TABLE

\overline{MR}	S_1	S_0	$\overline{OE}_1$	$\overline{OE}_2$	CP	DS_0	DS_7	RESPONSE
L	X	X	H	X	X	X	X	Asynchronous Reset; $Q_0 = Q_7$ = LOW
L	X	X	X	H	X	X	X	I/O Voltage Undetermined
L	H	H	X	X	X	X	X	
L	L	X	L	L	X	X	X	Asynchronous Reset; $Q_0 = Q_7$ = LOW
L	X	L	L	L	X	X	X	I/O Voltage LOW
H	L	H	X	X	⌐	D	X	Shift Right; $D \to Q_0$; $Q_0 \to Q_1$; etc.
H	L	H	L	L	⌐	D	X	Shift Right; $D \to Q_0$ & I/O_0; $Q_0 \to Q_1$ & I/O_1; etc.
H	H	L	X	X	⌐	X	D	Shift Left; $D \to Q_7$; $Q_7 \to Q_6$; etc.
H	H	L	L	L	⌐	X	D	Shift Left; $D \to Q_7$ & I/O_7; $Q_7 \to Q_6$ & I/O_6; etc.
H	H	H	X	X	⌐	X	X	Parallel Load; $I/O_n \to Q_n$
H	L	L	H	X	X	X	X	Hold: I/O Voltage undetermined
H	L	L	X	H	X	X	X	
H	L	L	L	L	X	X	X	Hold: $I/O_n = Q_n$

H = HIGH Voltage Level
L = LOW Voltage Level
X = Immaterial

AC CHARACTERISTICS: $T_A = 25°C$, $V_{CC} = 5.0$ V

SYMBOL	PARAMETER	MIN	TYP	MAX	UNITS	TEST CONDITIONS
f_{MAX}	Maximum Clock Frequency	25	35		MHz	
t_{PHL} t_{PLH}	Propagation Delay, Clock to Q_0 or Q_7		26 22	39 33	ns	$C_L = 15$ pF
t_{PHL}	Propagation Delay, Clear to Q_0 or Q_7		27	40	ns	
t_{PHL} t_{PLH}	Propagation Delay, Clock to $I/O_0 - I/O_7$		26 17	39 25	ns	$C_L = 45$ pF,
t_{PHL}	Propagation Delay, Clear to $I/O_0 - I/O_7$		26	40	ns	$R_L = 667$ Ω
t_{PZH} t_{PZL}	Output Enable Time		13 19	21 30	ns	
t_{PHZ} t_{PLZ}	Output Disable Time		10 10	15 15	ns	$C_L = 5.0$ pF

AC SETUP REQUIREMENTS: $T_A = 25°C$, $V_{CC} = 5.0$ V

SYMBOL	PARAMETER	MIN	TYP	MAX	UNITS	TEST CONDITIONS
t_W	Clock Pulse Width HIGH	25			ns	
t_W	Clock Pulse Width LOW	15			ns	
t_W	Clear Pulse Width LOW	20			ns	
t_s	Data Setup Time	20			ns	
t_s	Select Setup Time	35			ns	$V_{CC} = 5.0$ V
t_h	Data Hold Time	0			ns	
t_h	Select Hold Time	10			ns	
t_{rec}	Recovery Time	20			ns	

FIGURE 3-11 SN54/74LS299 Data Sheet

**FIGURE 3-12 Data
Transmission Using
Shift Registers**

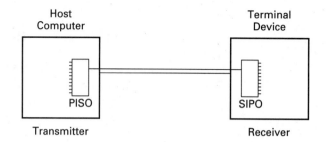

Host Computer — Terminal Device — PISO — SIPO — Transmitter — Receiver

**MOTOROLA
■ SEMICONDUCTOR**
TECHNICAL DATA

MC6850

ASYNCHRONOUS COMMUNICATIONS INTERFACE ADAPTER (ACIA)

The MC6850 Asynchronous Communications Interface Adapter provides the data formatting and control to interface serial asynchronous data communications information to bus organized systems such as the MC6800 Microprocessing Unit.

The bus interface of the MC6850 includes select, enable, read/write, interrupt and bus interface logic to allow data transfer over an 8-bit bidirectional data bus. The parallel data of the bus system is serially transmitted and received by the asynchronous data interface, with proper formatting and error checking. The functional configuration of the ACIA is programmed via the data bus during system initialization. A programmable Control Register provides variable word lengths, clock division ratios, transmit control, receive control, and interrupt control. For peripheral or modem operation, three control lines are provided. These lines allow the ACIA to interface directly with the MC6860L 0-600 bps digital modem.

- 8- and 9-Bit Transmission
- Optional Even and Odd Parity
- Parity, Overrun and Framing Error Checking
- Programmable Control Register
- Optional ÷1, ÷16, and ÷64 Clock Modes
- Up to 1.0 Mbps Transmission
- False Start Bit Deletion
- Peripheral Modem Control Functions
- Double Buffered
- One- or Two-Stop Bit Operation

**MC6850 ASYNCHRONOUS COMMUNICATIONS INTERFACE ADAPTER
BLOCK DIAGRAM**

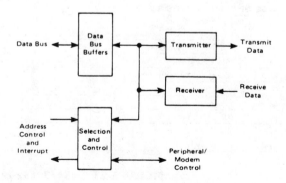

FIGURE 3-13 MC6850 Data Sheet

The UART chip is designed to receive data in a serial form and transfer it into a parallel format and to accept parallel formatted data and transfer it to a serial form. A common application for such a device is to connect an 8-bit, parallel microprocessor bus to the serial data world. An ACIA or Asynchronous Communications Interface Adapter made by Motorola, does just that. Figure 3-13 is the data sheet for an MC6850 ACIA.

MAXIMUM RATINGS

Characteristics	Symbol	Value	Unit
Supply Voltage	V_{CC}	-0.3 to $+7.0$	V
Input Voltage	V_{in}	-0.3 to $+7.0$	V
Operating Temperature Range MC6850, MC68A50, MC68B50 MC6850C, MC68A50C	T_A	T_L to T_H 0 to 70 -40 to $+85$	°C
Storage Temperature Range	T_{stg}	-55 to $+150$	°C

This device contains circuitry to protect the inputs against damage due to high static voltages or electric fields; however, it is advised that normal precautions be taken to avoid application of any voltage higher than maximum rated voltages to this high-impedance circuit. Reliability of operation is enhanced if unused inputs are tied to an appropriate logic voltage level (e.g., either V_{SS} or V_{CC}).

THERMAL CHARACTERISTICS

Characteristic	Symbol	Value	Unit
Thermal Resistance Plastic Cerdip	θ_{JA}	 120 65	°C/W

POWER CONSIDERATIONS

The average chip-junction temperature, T_J, in °C can be obtained from:

$$T_J = T_A + (P_D \bullet \theta_{JA}) \quad (1)$$

Where:

T_A = Ambient Temperature, °C

θ_{JA} = Package Thermal Resistance, Junction-to-Ambient, °C/W

P_D = $P_{INT} + P_{PORT}$

P_{INT} = $I_{CC} \times V_{CC}$, Watts — Chip Internal Power

P_{PORT} = Port Power Dissipation, Watts — User Determined

For most applications $P_{PORT} \blacktriangleleft P_{INT}$ and can be neglected. P_{PORT} may become significant if the device is configured to drive Darlington bases or sink LED loads.

An approximate relationship between P_D and T_J (if P_{PORT} is neglected) is:

$$P_D = K + (T_J + 273°C) \quad (2)$$

Solving equations (1) and (2) for K gives:

$$K = P_D \bullet (T_A + 273°C) + \theta_{JA} \bullet P_D 2 \quad (3)$$

Where K is a constant pertaining to the particular part. K can be determined from equation (3) by measuring P_D (at equilibrium) for a known T_A. Using this value of K, the values of P_D and T_J can be obtained by solving equations (1) and (2) iteratively for any value of T_A.

DC ELECTRICAL CHARACTERISTICS ($V_{CC} = 5.0$ Vdc $\pm 5\%$, $V_{SS} = 0$, $T_A = T_L$ to T_H unless otherwise noted.)

Characteristic		Symbol	Min	Typ	Max	Unit
Input High Voltage		V_{IH}	$V_{SS} + 2.0$	—	V_{CC}	V
Input Low Voltage		V_{IL}	$V_{SS} - 0.3$	—	$V_{SS} + 0.8$	V
Input Leakage Current ($V_{in} = 0$ to 5.25 V)	R/$\overline{W}$, CS0, CS1, $\overline{CS2}$, Enable RS, Rx D, Rx C, $\overline{CTS}$, $\overline{DCD}$	I_{in}	—	1.0	2.5	µA
Hi-Z (Off State) Input Current ($V_{in} = 0.4$ to 2.4 V)	D0-D7	I_{TSI}	—	2.0	10	µA
Output High Voltage ($I_{Load} = -205$ µA, Enable Pulse Width < 25 µs) ($I_{Load} = -100$ µA, Enable Pulse Width < 25 µs)	D0-D7 Tx Data, $\overline{RTS}$	V_{OH}	$V_{SS} + 2.4$ $V_{SS} + 2.4$	— —	— —	V
Output Low Voltage ($I_{Load} = 1.6$ mA, Enable Pulse Width < 25 µs)		V_{OL}	—	—	$V_{SS} + 0.4$	V
Output Leakage Current (Off State) ($V_{OH} = 2.4$ V)	$\overline{IRQ}$	I_{LOH}	—	1.0	10	µA
Internal Power Dissipation (Measured at $T_A = 0°C$)		P_{INT}	—	300	525*	mW
Internal Input Capacitance ($V_{in} = 0$, $T_A = 25°C$, f = 1.0 MHz)	D0-D7 E, Tx CLK, Rx CLK, R/$\overline{W}$, RS, Rx Data, CS0, CS1, $\overline{CS2}$, $\overline{CTS}$, $\overline{DCD}$	C_{in}	— —	10 7.0	12.5 7.5	pF
Output Capacitance ($V_{in} = 0$, $T_A = 25°C$, f = 1.0 MHz)	RTS, Tx Data $\overline{IRQ}$	C_{out}	— —	— —	10 5.0	pF

*For temperatures less than $T_A = 0°C$, P_{INT} maximum will increase.

FIGURE 3-13 MC6850 Data Sheet (cont.)

✔ **SELF-CHECK FOR SECTIONS 3-1, 3-2**

1. A large part of microprocessor circuitry is made up of _____ circuits.
2. A flip-flop stores a _____ or a _____ .
3. What does SISO mean?
4. Explain the concept of a recirculating register.
5. Explain the major difference between shift-left and shift-right registers.
6. What does SIPO mean?
7. A PISO has a _____ input and a _____ output.
8. Explain the mode control on a combination register.

3-3 COMPARATORS

Introduction to Comparators

One of the most important tools used by the microprocessor to make decisions is the comparator circuit. These circuits help determine the arithmetic relationship between two binary numbers. The microprocessor can then make decisions, that is, carry out actions based upon the result of a comparison. In order to understand how a microprocessor can make such comparisons, it is important to know how a comparator circuit works.

Equality Circuits

The Exclusive-OR gate, shown in Figure 3-14 is an example of a simple equality circuit. In other words, it is a logic block for determining if two binary bits are equal. Referring to Figure 3-14, if A and B inputs are equal, that is, either both "0" or both "1," then the output of the gate is "0." If the bits are not equal, the output will be "1," indicating an inequality.

4-Bit Numbers

If four **XOR** gates are arranged in parallel, as in Figure 3-15, they can be used to determine if two 4-bit binary numbers are equal.

As long as the 4-bit number applied to the A inputs is equal to the 4-bit number applied to the B inputs, all the outputs O_0 to O_3 will remain at "0." If any corresponding bit position of the two numbers is different, an output of "1" will result, indicating an inequality. Examples 1 and 2 of Figure 3-15 depict the actions of XOR gates.

Inequality

A simple circuit like this could handle all cases where A ≠ B or A = B.

But what about the nature of the inequality? There will be a case for A > B and A < B. The determination of relative magnitude is the real function of a comparator.

(A)

A	B	A ⊕ B
0	0	0
0	1	1
1	0	1
1	1	0

(B)

FIGURE 3-14 (A) Exclusive-OR Gate (B) Truth Table for XOR

FIGURE 3-15 (A) Equality Circuit

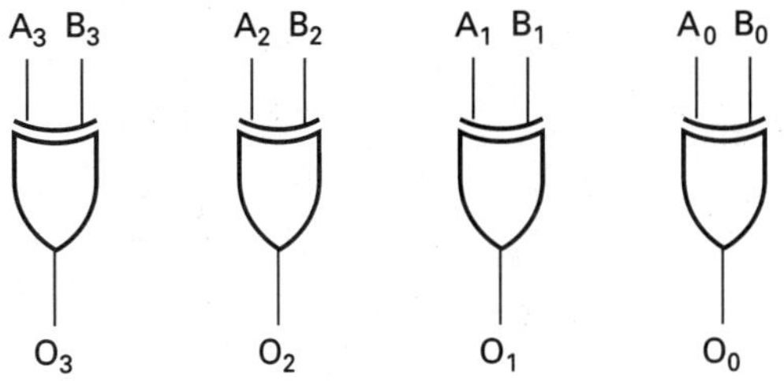

(A)

Example 1 –All outputs are Zero, Indicating an Equality.

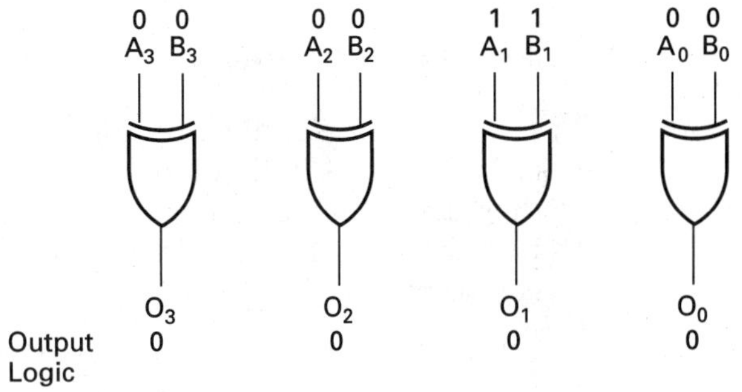

Output Logic

A input	A_3 0	A_2 0	A_1 1	A_0 0
B input	B_3 0	B_2 0	B_1 1	B_0 0
Output	O_3 0	O_2 0	O_1 0	O_0 0

Example 1

Example 2 –One Output is not Zero, Indicating an Inequality.

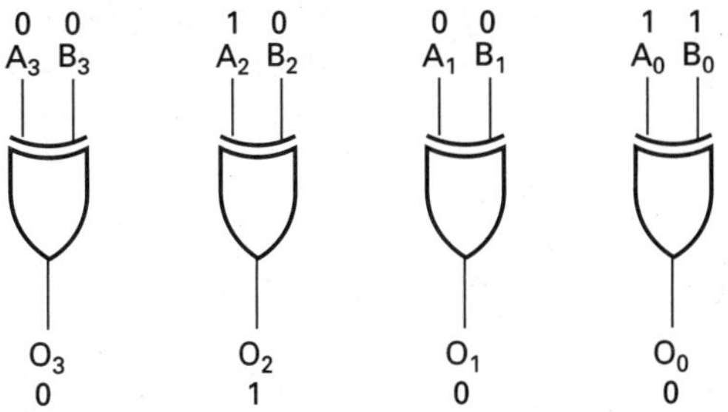

A input	A_3 0	A_2 1	A_1 0	A_0 1
B input	B_3 0	B_2 0	B_1 0	B_0 1
Output	O_3 0	O_2 1	O_1 0	O_0 0

Example 2

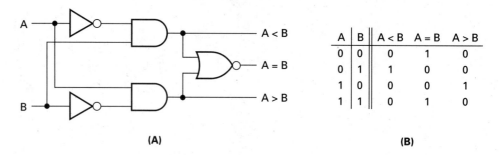

A	B	A < B	A = B	A > B
0	0	0	1	0
0	1	1	0	0
1	0	0	0	1
1	1	0	1	0

(A)   (B)

FIGURE 3-16 (A) A Comparator (B) Comparator Truth Table

The 3 Conditions

The circuit shown in Figure 3-16(A) will compare A and B and furnish an output that will comply with the 3 necessary conditions. When A = B, then the output A = B is a logic 1. If A > B or A < B, the corresponding outputs are logic 1. This is, of course, a simple circuit and is only capable of comparing two bits.

A Comparator Chip

Circuits that compare larger binary numbers are more complex. The reason is that the number of combinations double every time another bit position is added. The data sheet in Figure 3-17 is for an 8-bit comparator circuit chip.

3-4   ADDERS

In the last chapter, binary addition was examined. The importance of binary adder circuits becomes evident when we remember what we learned in Chapter 2, that it is also possible to subtract by adding complements.

Basic Addition Logic Block

The truth table for the Exclusive-OR gate is almost an exact replica of the rules used for binary addition:

Rules for Addition   XOR Truth Table

A	B	A + B
0	0	0
0	1	1
1	0	1
1	1	0

0 + 0 = 0
0 + 1 = 1
1 + 0 = 1
1 + 1 = 0   (with carry of 1)

 **MOTOROLA**

SN54/74LS682
SN54/74LS684
SN54/74LS688

**8-BIT MAGNITUDE
COMPARATORS**

LOW POWER SCHOTTKY

DESCRIPTION — The SN54LS/74LS682, 684, 688 are 8-bit magnitude comparators. These device types are designed to perform comparisons between two eight-bit binary or BCD words. All device types provide $\overline{P=Q}$ outputs and the LS682 and LS684 have $\overline{P>Q}$ outputs also.

The LS682, LS684 and LS688 are totem pole devices. The LS682 has a 20 kΩ pullup resistor on the Q inputs for analog or switch data.

FUNCTION TABLE

	INPUTS			OUTPUTS	
DATA	ENABLES				
P, Q	$\overline{G}, \overline{GT}$	$\overline{G2}$	$\overline{P=Q}$	$\overline{P>Q}$
P = Q	L	L	L	H
P > Q	L	L	H	L
P < Q	L	L	H	H
X	H	H	H	H

H = high level, L = low level, X = irrelevant

TYPE	$\overline{P=Q}$	$\overline{P>Q}$	OUTPUT ENABLE	OUTPUT CONFIGURATION	PULLUP
LS682	yes	yes	no	totem-pole	yes
LS683	yes	yes	no	open-collector	yes
LS684	yes	yes	no	totem-pole	no
LS685	yes	yes	no	open-collector	no
LS686	yes	yes	yes	totem-pole	no
LS687	yes	yes	yes	open-collector	no
LS688	yes	no	yes	totem-pole	no
LS689	yes	no	yes	open-collector	no

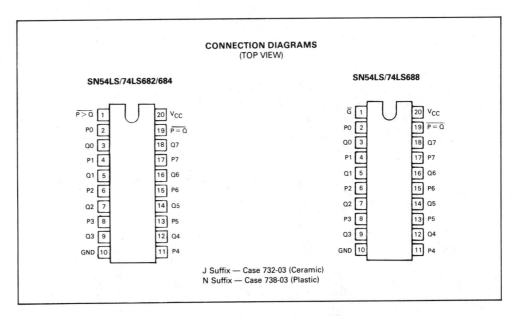

FIGURE 3-17 SN54/74LS682 Data Sheet

SN54/74LS682 • SN54/74LS684 • SN54/74LS688

GUARANTEED OPERATING RANGES

SYMBOL	PARAMETER		MIN	TYP	MAX	UNIT
V_{CC}	Supply Voltage	54	4.5	5.0	5.5	V
		74	4.75	5.0	5.25	
T_A	Operating Ambient Temperature Range	54	−55	25	125	°C
		74	0	25	70	
I_{OH}	Output Current — High	54,74			−0.4	mA
I_{OL}	Output Current — Low	54			12	mA
		74			24	

DC CHARACTERISTICS OVER OPERATING TEMPERATURE RANGE (unless otherwise specified)

SYMBOL	PARAMETER		LIMITS			UNITS	TEST CONDITIONS
			MIN	TYP	MAX		
V_{IH}	Input HIGH Voltage		2.0			V	Guaranteed Input HIGH Voltage for All Inputs
V_{IL}	Input LOW Voltage	54			0.7	V	Guaranteed Input LOW Voltage for All Inputs
		74			0.8		
V_{IK}	Input Clamp Diode Voltage			−0.65	−1.5	V	V_{CC} = MIN, I_{IN} = −18 mA
V_{OH}	Output HIGH Voltage	54	2.5	3.5		V	V_{CC} = MIN, I_{OH} = MAX, V_{IN} = V_{IH} or V_{IL} per Truth Table
		74	2.7	3.5		V	
V_{OL}	Output LOW Voltage	54,74		0.25	0.4	V	I_{OL} = 12 mA V_{CC} = V_{CC} MIN, V_{IN} = V_{IL} or V_{IH} per Truth Table
		74		0.35	0.5	V	I_{OL} = 24 mA
I_{IH}	Input HIGH Current				20	μA	V_{CC} = MAX, V_{IN} = 2.7 V
		LS682-Q Inputs			0.1	mA	V_{CC} = MAX, V_{IN} = 5.5 V
		Others			0.1	mA	V_{CC} = MAX, V_{IN} = 7.0 V
I_{IL}	Input LOW Current	LS682-Q Inputs			−0.4	mA	V_{CC} = MAX, V_{IN} = 0.4 V
		Others			−0.2	mA	
I_{OS}	Short Circuit Current		−30		−130	mA	V_{CC} = MAX
I_{CC}	Power Supply Current	LS682			70	mA	V_{CC} = MAX
		LS684			65	mA	
		LS688			65	mA	

FIGURE 3-17 SN54/74LS682 Data Sheet (cont.)

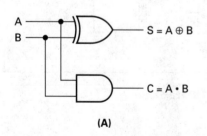

A Addend	B Augend	S Sum	C Carry
0	0	0	0
0	1	1	0
1	0	1	0
1	1	0	1

(A)   (B)

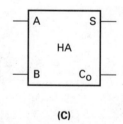

(C)

FIGURE 3-18 (A) Half Adder (B) Truth Table for Half Adder (C) Symbol for Half Adder

Half Adder

In order to build a **half adder**, all that is needed is to include a circuit that will provide the "1" necessary for the carry. Such a circuit is shown in Figure 3-18 along with the truth table.

When both A and B are logic "1," the AND-gate will generate a carry. This is called a *half-adder* circuit. The half adder will take care of a carry should one occur as the result of adding A and B. But there is no provision made in the half adder for a carry input from a preceding stage.

Full Adder

A **full-adder** circuit is shown in Figure 3-19. It is constructed from two half adders and an OR-gate. As can be seen from the truth table in Figure 3-19(B), the carry-in (**C**), from a preceding stage is now accounted for.

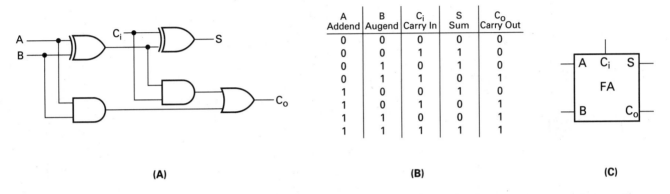

A Addend	B Augend	C_i Carry In	S Sum	C_o Carry Out
0	0	0	0	0
0	0	1	1	0
0	1	0	1	0
0	1	1	0	1
1	0	0	1	0
1	0	1	0	1
1	1	0	0	1
1	1	1	1	1

(A) (B) (C)

FIGURE 3-19 (A) Full Adder (B) Truth Table for Full Adder (C) Symbol for Full Adder

The full-adder circuit can be used for parallel addition. The block diagram for a 4-bit adder appears in Figure 3-20. The 4-bit numbers are applied to the A and B inputs. A slight propagation delay will occur as the outputs will not settle until all the carry inputs *ripple* through. The output is then available on the S-leads.

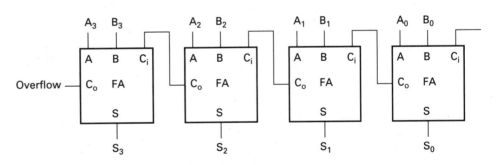

FIGURE 3-20 4-Bit Parallel Adder

If the sum should exceed 4-bit positions, there will be an overflow output on the carry lead of the fourth stage (C_i).

Subtraction

Recall that in Chapter 2 we established the rules for binary subtraction as follows:

$$0 - 0 = 0$$
$$1 - 0 = 1$$
$$1 - 1 = 0$$
$$0 - 1 = 1 \quad \text{(with a borrow of 1)}$$

By adding the invertor to the half-adder circuit, as shown in Figure 3-21(A), we can create a half **subtracter**. Note that the truth table shown in Figure 3-21(B) reflects the rules for binary subtraction.

The subtraction circuit does generate the proper signals and follow the truth table. On the other hand, we have already discovered a more efficient way of doing subtraction, the 2's-complement method.

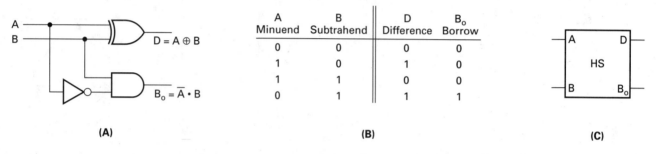

FIGURE 3-21 (A) Half Subtracter (B) Truth Table for Half Subtracter (C) Symbol for Half Subtracter

Adder-Subtracter

Figure 3-22 is a block diagram of an **Adder-Subtracter**. The logic level supplied by the microprocessor's control unit to the Control lead of the Adder-Subtracter determines whether the circuit will add two numbers or subtract them.

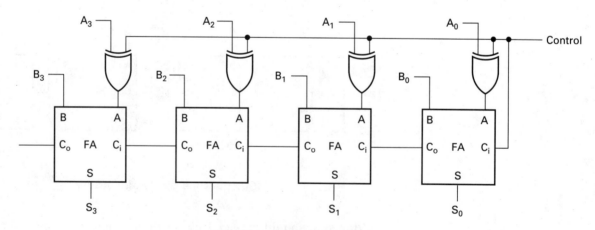

FIGURE 3-22 Adder-Subtracter

Addition Function

When the Control input is at logic "0," the circuit will add two 4-bit binary numbers placed on the A and B inputs. The "0" on the Control lead causes each of the XOR gates to have a "0" on one input. This means the XOR gates will then function as buffers, that is, they will output the same logic as is input on the A leads. In this case, the full adders will simply add the two numbers and output the sum on the S-leads.

Subtraction Function

When a logic "1" is placed on the Control lead, the circuit functions as a 2's complement subtracter. To see this more clearly, note that the XOR gates will form the 1's complement of the number placed on the A inputs. In other words, with a "1" on the one lead of the XOR, whatever logic appears on the other lead will be inverted at the output. Every "1" will become a "0" and every "0" will become a "1."

This means that the full adders will be adding the 1's complement of the A input number. Recall that in 2's complement subtraction that we add the 2's complement of the subtrahend (number to be subtracted), to the minuend. To form the 2's complement of a number, we always:

1. Form the 1's complement
2. Add +1

By raising the Control lead to "1" we have in effect formed the 1's complement. The next step would be to *add +1*. This is exactly what the C_1 input of the first stage does. Note that the C_1 will also become "1" when the control lead is raised to "1." This is how the 2's complement is formed. This action means the circuit is adding the 2's complement when the Control lead is "1" and thus we are subtracting.

 SELF-CHECK FOR SECTIONS 3-3, 3-4

9. An XOR gate is an example of a simple _____ circuit.
10. What are the three conditions comparator circuits usually test?
11. Explain the difference between a half adder and a full adder.
12. Is it possible to connect adder circuits to perform subtraction?

SUMMARY OF IDEAS

- A shift register is a group of flip-flops arranged to temporarily store binary numbers.
- Shift registers are classified by the way in which data is loaded and removed from them.
- The four major classifications of shift registers are:

  SISO   Serial In; Serial Out
  SIPO   Serial In: Parallel Out
  PISO   Parallel In; Serial Out
  PIPO   Parallel In; Parallel Out
- The Serial-In–Serial-Out shift register is loaded or unloaded one bit at a time on each clock pulse.
- In a serial-shift register, it takes as many clock pulses as there are stages to fully load or unload the register.
- A Serial-In–Parallel-Out register is loaded one bit at a time but is unloaded or read by taking all bits simultaneously, that is, in parallel.

- A Parallel-In–Serial-Out register is loaded in parallel, all bits are input at one time. The Parallel-In–Serial-Out register is read by clocking the bits out one bit at a time in a serial fashion.
- A Parallel-In–Parallel-Out register is both loaded and read in parallel.
- A recirculating shift register uses a logic circuit that connects the output of the register back to the input. This is done so that bits are not lost if the register is loaded but not immediately read.
- Shift registers can be designed to shift one bit at a time either to the left or to the right.
- The speed with which a register can be loaded is:
  T = 1/f × number of stages.
- Parallel manipulation of data within a device is more efficient than serial. For transmission, serial methods are more efficient.
- A UART, Universal Asynchronous Receiver Transmitter, is a device for receiving data in serial form and transferring it to parallel format and for accepting parallel data and transferring it to serial format.
- Comparator circuits compare the relative magnitude of binary numbers. The comparator can detect the following conditions:
  A = B, A ≠ B, A < B, A > B.
- A half-adder circuit adds two binary bits, generates a carry, and the sum.
- A full-adder adds two binary bits, generates a carry, a sum, and provides for a carry input from a preceding stage.

CHAPTER QUESTIONS & PROBLEMS

True or False

1. The number of stages in a shift register will depend on the rate or speed with which it is clocked.
2. A serial input register contains the number 000010100; after two clock pulses it will contain the number 00010001.
3. In a shift-right, serial-shift register, the output of each stage is used to clock the succeeding one.
4. A shift of one bit position to the left in a binary number multiplies it by two and thereby forms the 2's complement.
5. By introducing XOR-gates to one of the inputs of each full adder in an array, a circuit Control lead can be used to cause the XOR's to either act as buffers or inverters.

Fill in the Blanks

6. A group of flip-flops arranged so that binary numbers may be temporarily stored is called _____ _____.
7. If the 4-bit binary number 1000 is being shifted serially to the right into a shift register, after two clock pulses the number will be

   _____.
8. Provisions for a shift register to connect the output back to the input are made so that the data may be _____.
9. If data are to be taken from a microprocessor system and transmitted over a long distance, in all likelihood a _____ _____ shift register will be used.
10. An electronic circuit capable of determining the relative magnitude of two binary numbers is called a _____ circuit.

Multiple Choice

11. The 4-bit binary number 1010 is being serially loaded (shifted right) into a shift register. If the number were to be read after three clock pulses, it would be
    a. 1010.
    b. 0101.
    c. 0100.
    d. 0010.

12. In a D-type flip-flop, the Q output
    a. is always the same as the D input.
    b. is high when the clock pulse is high.
    c. follows the D input when clocked.
    d. none of the above

13. A 4-bit serial shift register contains the binary number 1100. If the register is in a shift-left mode, two clock pulses later it will contain
    a. 0011.
    b. 1100.
    c. 0000.
    d. 0110.

14. An 8-bit serial shift register is connected in a recirculating mode. The original input number was 10101010; after twelve clock pulses the register will contain
    a. 01010101.
    b. 10100000.
    c. 00001010.
    d. 10101010.

15. A serial shift register is 4,096-bits wide. If the clock frequency is 1 MHz, how long does it take to fully load the register?
    a. 4,096 milliseconds
    b. .004069 seconds
    c. 4.096 milliseconds
    d. 4.096 microseconds

16. An exclusive-OR gate is useful in
    a. full adders.
    b. half adders.
    c. comparators.
    d. all of the above.

17. If a half-adder has A = 1, B = 1, then the S and C will be
    a. 1 0.
    b. 0 1.
    c. 1 1.
    d. 0 0.

18. If a full-adder has a C of 1, A = 1, B = 1, then the S and C leads will be
    a. 1 1.
    b. 0 1.
    c. 1 0.
    d. 0 0.

19. Which of the following groups of input/output leads is found on a half adder?
    a. S, C_1, C_0, A
    b. S, C_1, A, D
    c. A, S, B, C_1
    d. A, B, C_1, C_0

20. Which of the following statements is true?
    a. The time required to load a PISO shift register is:
       $T = 1/f \times$ no. of stages.
    b. A full-adder circuit can only add using 2's complement binary addition.
    c. Twos-complement subtraction is used because it is not possible to build a subtraction unit with logic blocks.
    d. Shifting a binary number to the right one bit position at a time is the same as dividing by 2.

CHAPTER 4
MICROPROCESSOR MEMORIES (NONVOLATILE)

OUTLINE

NEW TERMS TO WATCH FOR

Nonvolatile
Fusible-Link
Address
MOSFET ROM
Matrix
UV Erasure
Erasable PROM

Electrically Alterable PROM
Write Operation
Word Organized
Read Only Memory (ROM)
Row-Column Addressing
One-Dimensional Addressing
Two-Dimensional Addressing

Read Operation
Bit Organized
Address Decoder
Cell
Floating Gate
Bubble Memory
Access Time

After completing this chapter, you should be able to:

1. Define the three basic elements of a memory.
2. Explain the term *nonvolatile memory*.
3. Describe the *read* operation and explain how it works.
4. Describe the *write* operation of a memory.
5. Show how a Read Only Memory is constructed.
6. Demonstrate how Read Only Memories are programmed.
7. Discuss the various technologies used in Read Only Memories.
8. Determine addresses for locating information in a memory.
9. Explain address decoding and why it is necessary.
10. Recognize both one and two dimensional addressing.
11. List the methods used to *erase* data stored in memory.
12. Work with the types of programmable memories currently available.
13. Discuss *floating gate technology*.
14. Show the basic workings of a bubble memory.
15. Demonstrate how a memory is organized.
16. Identify various ROM applications.

4-1   INTRODUCTION

A microprocessor would be of very little use were it not for memory. The microprocessor depends on memory for storage of its instructions, storage of data, and for its working space. If this information could not be stored and more importantly, instantly accessed, the microprocessor could not function.

Memory exists throughout a microprocessor system. Any device that can be said to hold or store binary numbers could be classified as memory. But the classification of memory is a rather difficult task because of the many technologies available. Memories are sometimes classified as being either optical, mechanical, magnetic, or electrical. They can also be classified as to their organization, such as sequential access, random access, or fixed access.

The most general and perhaps the most useful classification is to divide memories into either **Nonvolatile** or *volatile* types. A memory device that retains (remembers) its contents when power is removed is a *nonvolatile* memory. Conversely, a memory device that loses its contents, never again to be recovered when power is removed, is classified as a *volatile* memory.

In this chapter we focus on the basics of memory circuits and their fundamental operations. We will then examine specific types of nonvolatile memories and their characteristics.

4-2   ELEMENTS OF A BASIC MEMORY

Simple Memory

The simplest electronic memory possible would be capable of storing a binary representation of either a logic-1 or a logic-0. A flip-flop, for example, has this capability. A single flip-flop could be called a 1-bit memory. As we have seen in the previous chapter, a string of flip-flops can store several bits of binary information, if only temporarily. A basic memory then, must have storage space for binary information.

In addition to the storage, however, it is necessary to have access TO and FROM the storage area. This is referred to as INPUT/OUTPUT (I/O) and simply means that there is an electrical pathway both into and out of the storage area.

An Additional Element

When the basic memory is expanded to contain several bits, an additional element will be needed. Each bit has meaning and we may wish to know the value of a given bit location. The *bit* location we are interested in will be in a specific storage area of the memory. Therefore, a method is needed to identify which location we wish to access. This is accomplished by giving all locations an identifying number called an **Address**.

An Analogy

The basic memory unit is analogous to a mini-storage warehouse. It has a place to store things, a way to get in and out of the storage area and an address or number that identifies each storage location (Fig. 4-1).

Memory Analogous to Mini-Storage Warehouse
Basic Memory Unit has: 1) place to store info
2) way to get info in and out
3) address system to locate info

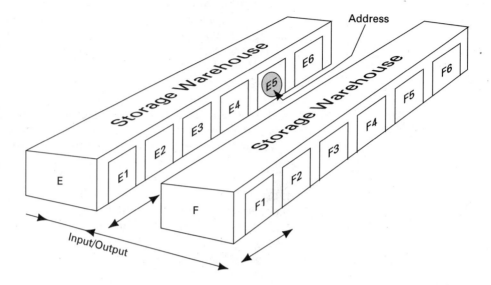

**FIGURE 4-1 Memory
is Storage**

4-3   THE BASIC MEMORY UNIT

A Cell

The storage area in a basic memory is called a **cell**. The location of a cell is referred to as an ADDRESS. Every location in a memory has a specific and unique address (Fig. 4-2).

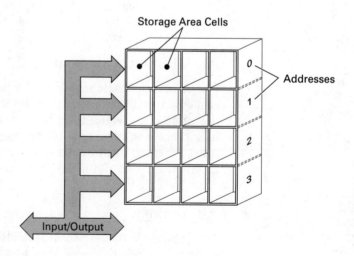

**FIGURE 4-2 Basic
Memory Unit**

Write Operation

When the input/output access is used to put information into the memory, it is called *writing to memory*. A **write operation** simply refers to the process of putting binary information into the storage area of a memory. To do this, the address of the location where the binary information is to be stored must be first specified (Fig. 4-3).

FIGURE 4-3 Write Operation

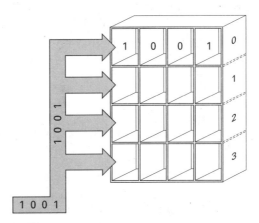

Read Operation

Conversely, using the input/output access to take information out of the storage area is called *reading from memory* (Fig. 4-4). Once again it is necessary to specify the exact address of the information to be read. We *write* TO memory or *read* FROM memory. In microprocessor language we simply refer to this as *read* or *write* operations.

FIGURE 4-4 Read Operation

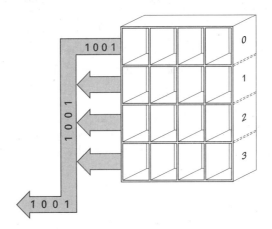

Access Time

There are certain delays involved with read and write operations. In the **read operation**, the address is presented to the input of the memory but the data does not instantly appear on the output lines, there is a delay. This time delay is called **Access Time** and is measured in seconds or parts of seconds. Access time can be thought of as the time delay between when a memory chip becomes available for reading and when the data actually appears on the output lines. Technically, it is measured from the time the memory chip receives the address to the time when the data is available on the memory output lines.

Write Cycle

The time required for a read operation is not necessarily the same as the time required for a write operation. The time lapse for a write operation is referred to as the *write cycle time*. A write cycle is measured from the time when the chip is available for the write operation to the time when the operation is finished. It is considered finished when data and address lines are again available.

Times vary widely for both read and write operations. They depend on such things as propagation delays in the active devices used, complexity of decoding or address interpreting circuits, and physical construction of the storage locations.

✔ SELF-CHECK FOR SECTIONS 4-1, 4-2, 4-3

1. Memory can be classified as either _____ or _____.
2. Name the four basic elements of a memory.
3. The storage area of a memory is called a _____.
4. Explain the meaning of a write operation.
5. Explain the meaning of a read operation.
6. Explain access time.
7. What is write cycle time?

4-4   THE READ ONLY MEMORY

Nonvolatile

Not all memories can be written to. In such memories, once the information has been put into storage, it cannot be changed. The storage area is a permanent unalterable record. The information can only be *read*. A memory like this is *nonvolatile* and is called **Read Only Memory** or **ROM**. A Read Only Memory is a memory with permanently stored data such as operating system instructions or math tables. Later in the chapter we will discuss some of the uses of ROM memories in detail.

A Matrix

ROM is usually constructed in a **matrix** type format. A matrix is a grid of mutually perpendicular lines. The intersections of lines represent storage areas or cells. At any given intersection, there is either the presence of a logic-1 or there is not. The absence of a "1" means the storage area contains logic-0. The intersection should be thought of as a cell.

Diode Matrix

A simple ROM can be constructed with diodes (Fig. 4-5). The bus bar supplies a logic-1 to all horizontal lines. The diodes determine if a logic-1 will be present at an intersection or not. In the diagram for the diode ROM (Fig. 4-5), the output is taken from points D1, D2, D3, and D4 which then represent a 4-bit binary number. When voltage is applied to the bus bar, the outputs will be:

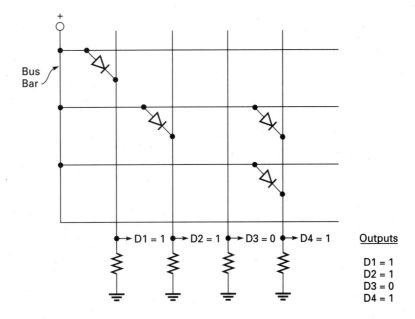

FIGURE 4-5 Diode Matrix ROM

Address Inputs

To make the ROM more useful and to expand its capacity, an *addressing* method is added (Fig. 4-6). Instead of the single bus bar, we now have the possibility of selecting one horizontal line at a time.

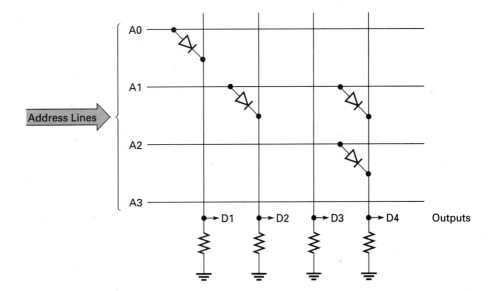

FIGURE 4-6 Diode Matrix ROM with Address Lines

If, for example, the address input is 0100 (Fig. 4-7) then the output will be:

$$D1 = 0 \qquad D3 = 0$$
$$D2 = 1 \qquad D4 = 1$$

FIGURE 4-7 Diode Matrix ROM with Input Address Lines

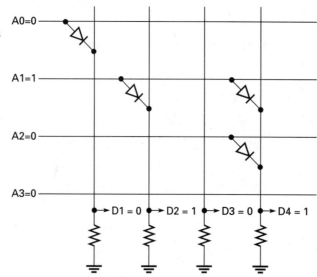

Address Input				Output			
A0	A1	A2	A3	D1	D2	D3	D4
0	1	0	0	0	1	0	1

FIGURE 4-8 (A) Address Decoder and Output Table

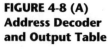
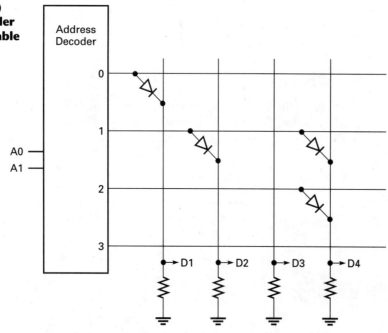

Input		Output of Decoder			
A0	A1	0	1	2	3
0	0	1	0	0	0
0	1	0	1	0	0
1	0	0	0	1	0
1	1	0	0	0	1

Address Decoding

The four lines connected to the matrix are actually derived from only two address input lines. Recall that in the binary system, two inputs can generate four combinations. That is, 2^n where "n" is the number of inputs. In other words, 2 input lines can generate $2^n = 2^2 = 4$ combinations.

The generation of four output combinations from two input lines is called *address decoding*. All memories have **address decoders** that expand the address input into the number of lines necessary to read all storage areas. The address decoder in Figure 4-8(A) has two input address lines and four decoded output lines. It is called a "1-of-4" decoder, because one of the four lines is always high or logic-1. The rest are always low or logic-0.

Decoder Output

The table in Figure 4-8(A) shows the four possible input combinations for the address lines A0 and A1. The resulting decoder outputs are shown next to them. Note that only one output at a time is high (logic-1).

For example, if the input address generated is A0 = 0 and A1 = 1, output line Pt1 of the decoder will be high. The other lines remain low (Fig. 4-8(B)).

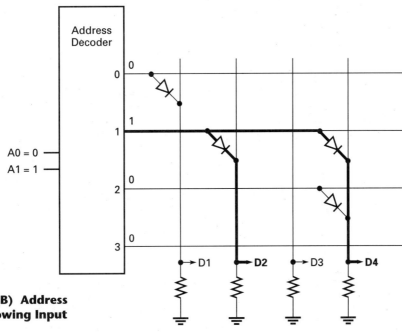

Input		Output of Decoder			
A0	A1	0	1	2	3
0	0	1	0	0	0
0	**1**	**0**	**1**	**0**	**0**
1	0	0	0	1	0
1	1	0	0	0	1

FIGURE 4-8 (B) Address Decoder Showing Input and Output

ROM Table

The ROM in Figure 4-9 is storing four different 4-bit numbers. The numbers stored at the address locations can be read as often as needed. The table shows the output of the ROM for every possible input address. Two address lines allow access to four different locations or binary numbers.

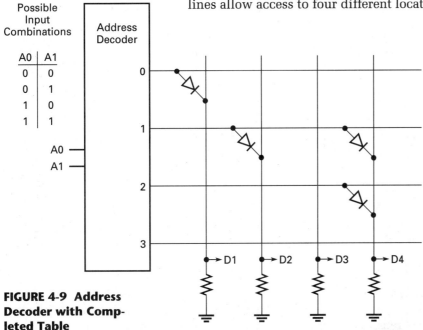

Input		Output of Decoder				Output of ROM			
A0	A1	0	1	2	3	D1	D2	D3	D4
0	0	1	0	0	0	1	0	0	0
0	1	0	1	0	0	0	1	0	1
1	0	0	0	1	0	0	0	0	1
1	1	0	0	0	1	0	0	0	0

ROM Table

FIGURE 4-9 Address Decoder with Completed Table

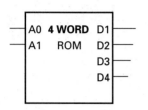

FIGURE 4-10 Symbol for ROM

Permanent Storage

It is obvious, the data stored is related to the location of the diodes. To change the output would mean to change the diodes, either moving them or adding more. On the other hand, if power is removed, the information remains. When power is applied the information can be *read* as often as needed. Figure 4-10 shows a symbolic representation of our 4-bit, 4-word diode-ROM.

4-5   BIPOLAR ROM

Using Bipolar Transistors

The diode matrix demonstrates how a ROM works, but it does have definite limitations. Loading is a problem. The output load for such a ROM would be limited by the driving capabilities of the diodes. To improve the driving capacity of the matrix, the diodes could be replaced with bipolar transistors. Figure 4-11 shows the construction of a bipolar ROM.

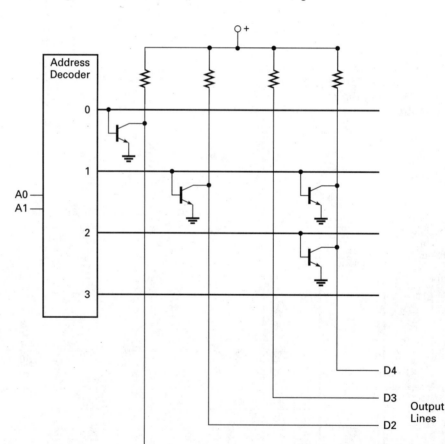

FIGURE 4-11 Bipolar Transistor ROM

How It Works

When a decoder output line is high, it provides base current to the transistor. The transistor saturates and pulls the output data line low. The other transistors remain cut off so that their output data lines are at logic-1.

✔ **SELF-CHECK FOR SECTIONS 4-4, 4-5**

8. Explain the term Read Only Memory.
9. What is meant by a matrix?
10. What is the major drawback of a diode matrix?
11. Explain address decoding.
12. What is the advantage of bipolar ROMs over diode ROMs?

4-6   MOSFET ROM

Using MOSFETs In ROM

The bipolar transistors improve the driving capability of the ROM but they do require a certain amount of current to operate. For this reason and because manufacturing techniques are somewhat simpler, the **MOSFET ROM** is more common. Figure 4-12 shows ROM construction with MOS devices. Due to their extremely high input impedance, they require little current to operate. The operation is essentially the same as the bipolar ROM; a high on the decoder line will turn on the MOSFET and cause the cell to output a low.

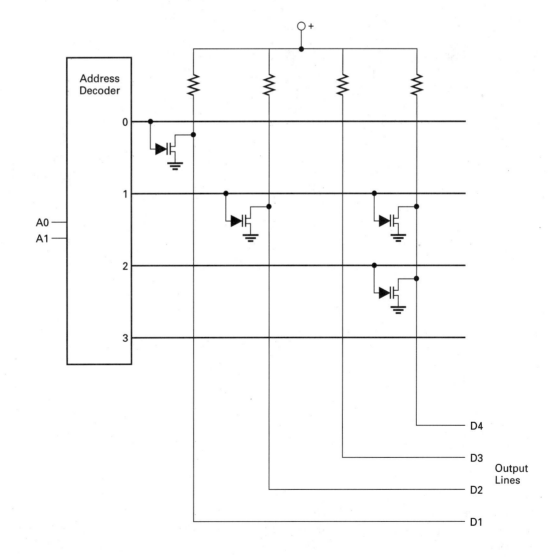

**FIGURE 4-12
MOSFET ROM**

4-7   MEMORY ADDRESSING

Addressing

Before going further, let's take a closer look at memory addressing and address decoders. There is nothing particularly mysterious about an address decoder. Simply defined, it is a device that accepts x number of input lines and produces a unique output line for every possible combination of inputs. If x is the number of input lines then 2^x unique combinations can be produced. Therefore there will be 2^x output lines on the address decoder.

The decoder in Figure 4-13 has 2 input address lines, so there are 2^2 or 4 possible input combinations. There will also be 4 output lines. What is accomplished here is that we can reach or address 4 locations with only 2 address lines. This is very important when we realize that most memories have thousands of locations. For example, a memory with 1,024 locations could be addressed with 2^{10} or just 10 address lines. In other words, 1,024 different outputs can be generated from 10 input address lines (Fig. 4-14).

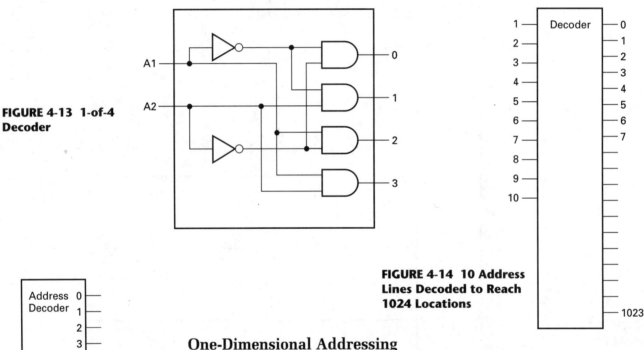

FIGURE 4-13 1-of-4 Decoder

FIGURE 4-14 10 Address Lines Decoded to Reach 1024 Locations

One-Dimensional Addressing

Using an address decoder in the way just discussed is called **one-dimensional addressing**. There are some limitations to decoding in this manner. As the number of address locations increases, so does the need for decoder output lines. The decoder in Figure 4-15 has four input address lines and there are 2^4 or sixteen output lines. Sixteen input address lines would mean 65,536 output lines. But there is a way to reduce the number of output lines yet not reduce the number of locations reached.

Two-Dimensional Addressing

A frequently used method for reducing the number of output lines is called **two-dimensional addressing**. This scheme is also referred to as X-Y addressing or **row-column addressing**. Figure 4-16(A) shows the two-dimensional addressing concept. The decoders have only 4 outputs, yet 16 locations can be reached. To address a particular cell, both a ROW and a

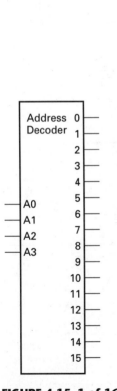

FIGURE 4-15 1-of-16 Decoder (One-Dimensional Addressing)

COLUMN address are required. For example, to reach cell number 12, a row address of 10 and a column address of 11 is generated (Fig. 4-16(B)). Two-dimensional address techniques are common and considerably reduce the complexity of memory wiring.

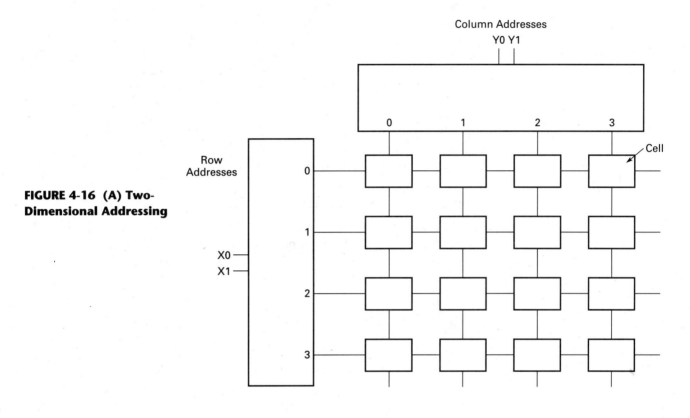

FIGURE 4-16 (A) Two-Dimensional Addressing

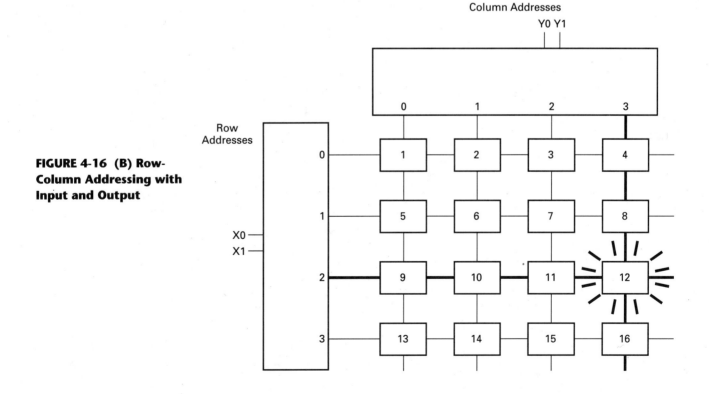

FIGURE 4-16 (B) Row-Column Addressing with Input and Output

4-8 THE PROM

Read Only Memories

Read Only Memories are built by semiconductor manufacturers. The user must supply the bit patterns or *program* that the ROM will contain. In the last step of the manufacturing process, an overlay or *mask* is applied to the matrix. The mask determines which intersections of the matrix will have a connected active device and which will not. The presence or absence of the active device will in turn, determine if the output of that intersection will be a "1" or a "0." The production of a mask is expensive and for this reason, a manufacturer demands a minimum order. This means that ROM is cost effective only when purchased in large quantities. In addition, the typical lead time for a custom mask is four to six weeks of development. These are major drawbacks, especially for prototype work in experimental or developmental stages.

Programmable Read Only Memories

Fortunately there is an alternative to custom-made ROM. The Programmable Read Only Memory or PROM is a ROM that can be programmed by the user. This is accomplished by putting a **fusible-link** in series with the active device in a memory cell, as in Figure 4-17.

FIGURE 4-17 Fusible-Link PROM

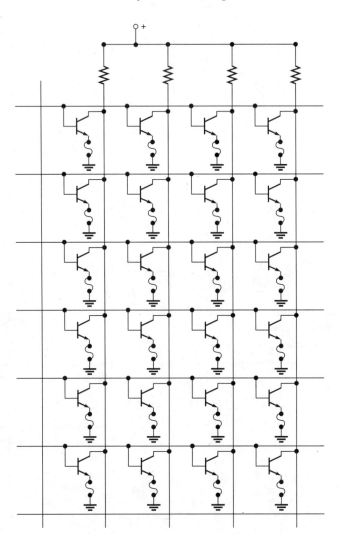

Fusible-Links

The fusible-link is usually made from nichrome or polycrystalline silicon and will *blow* just as a fuse blows when heavy current is applied.

Before the PROM is programmed, there is an intact fuse and transistor at every intersection. This means that initially all cells, when addressed, will output a logic-0. To program it, each cell is addressed and if a "1" is desired, heavy current is applied to "blow" the fuse at that intersection. If a "0" is desired no current is applied (Fig. 4-18).

Naturally care must be taken to ensure that a fuse at any given intersection *should* be fused (blown). Once blown or programmed, the links are permanently destroyed and cannot be restored.

Because of the high impedances found in MOS devices, current levels required to blow the fuse are likely to destroy the entire device. For this reason, PROMs are constructed with bipolar transistors and not MOS devices.

FIGURE 4-18 Fusible-Link PROM After Fusing

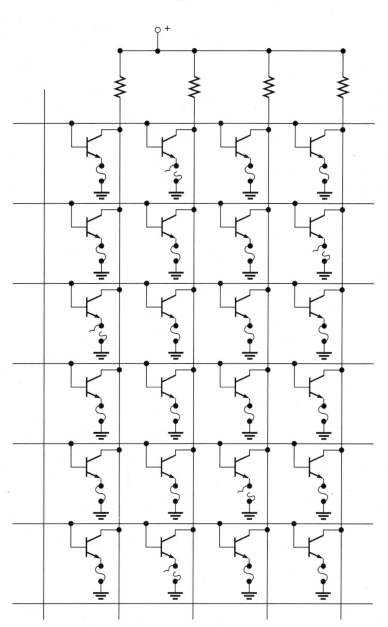

4-9   ERASING

Erasable PROMS

The drawback of course, to using PROM is that it can only be programmed once. The answer to this problem is a device called the Erasable Programmable Read Only Memory or **EPROM**. Erasing a memory means that the logic contained in all cells is rewritten or reset. After an erasure, all cells will be at the same logic level—all 1's or all 0's. There are actually two types of **erasable PROMs**.

The first type called **EEPROM** (Electrically Erasable or sometimes called EAPROM for **Electrically Alterable**) is erased with electrical energy. The other type, simply called an EPROM, is erasable with ultraviolet light.

4-10   THE EEPROM

Erasing the EEPROM

The EEPROM can be erased with the application of voltage to the erase inputs. Erasing can be focused on only one location at a time. Of course, it is also possible to erase the entire memory at one time (Fig. 4-19). The time required for an erasure is about 14 milliseconds, a relatively long time compared to a read operation that can occur in a microsecond.

FIGURE 4-19 EEPROM

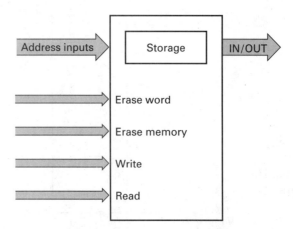

Cell Life

Each time a read/write operation occurs, the storage life of the memory cell is reduced. Earlier EEPROMs specified 10,000 write/erase cycles, but more recently released EEPROMs are specified at 100,000 write/erase cycles.

Programming

The advantage of the EEPROM is that specific memory locations can be changed while the chip remains in the circuit. The disadvantage is that they usually require multiple supply voltages. Typically ±5V, ±12V, and ±26V sources are necessary. More recent EEPROM technology, however, has introduced *on board* programming voltage generators. This means that the higher voltages required to reprogram the chip are generated inside the chip itself from a single external supply. The newer chips also include the capability to modify a single bit, thus saving the stress on the other bit cells associated with the byte to be altered.

4-11   THE EPROM

Floating-Gate Technology

The EPROM is more widely used than the EEPROM. An EPROM is man-ufactured using a special type of MOSFET called a floating-gate MOSFET (Fig. 4-20). The MOSFET is normally cut off (in a nonconducting state) when no voltage is applied to the gate. Applying a positive voltage to the gate allows current to flow in the source-drain circuit. In other words, it turns on just as the transistor does. The **floating gate** has no leads and no connections but is buried inside the silicon dioxide. If a sufficiently negative voltage is applied to the external gate lead, electrons will be injected into the floating-gate through the silicon dioxide layer. Since the floating gate has no output, the charge will remain. If a positive potential is now applied to the gate, it will no longer turn the device on. The effect of the negative charge on the floating gate keeps it in cutoff.

A charged floating gate cell contains a logic-0. It takes about 6 millisec-onds to charge a floating gate. This charge will remain after power is turned off, and has in fact been shown to remain for 10 or more years.

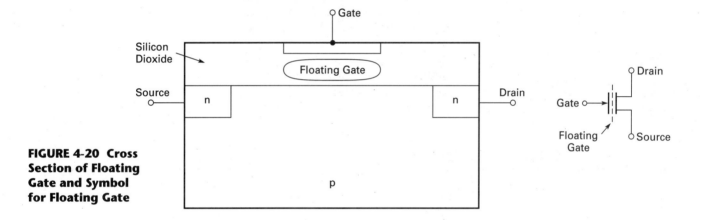

FIGURE 4-20 Cross Section of Floating Gate and Symbol for Floating Gate

EPROM Erasure

Before the EPROM can be reprogrammed, the charges from the old pro-gram must be erased. Since there is no electrical connection to the floating gate, another method must be used to discharge it.

Exposing the floating-gate MOSFET to ultraviolet light will impart enough photon energy to the trapped electrons to allow them to bleed off to the substrate material. To permit exposure to ultraviolet light, a quartz *win-dow* is manufactured into the top of the IC chip. The window is normally covered with a piece of tape to reduce accidental UV exposure. By removing the tape and exposing the chip to a strong UV lamp for 20 to 30 minutes, the entire program can be erased. Leaving an EPROM on the window sill without the tape over the quartz window will also discharge it. It would take about three weeks. Since florescent lights also emit UV, exposure to room lighting would require about three years for erasure.

The advantage of the EPROM is that erasure is simple and does not require special techniques. Programming has also become relatively easy with PROM programmers, called PROM *burners* (Fig. 4-21). A *master* ROM is inserted in the program socket and the PROM programmer will duplicate the program resident in the master ROM, in several others simultaneously, in just a few minutes.

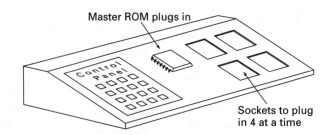

FIGURE 4-21 PROM Burner Duplicates Program in Master ROM

Many electronic companies have adopted the EPROM as a method of updating their equipment. If a customer wants to have the latest features or updated software, it is a relatively simple matter to add the new features to an EPROM chip. When a customer buys more features, or requests updates, he simply exchanges the EPROM he currently has for one that contains the updates.

SELF-CHECK FOR SECTIONS 4-6, 4-7, 4-8, 4-9, 4-10, 4-11

13. What is one feature of a MOSFET ROM?
14. Explain one-dimensional addressing.
15. Explain two-dimensional addressing.
16. What is a PROM?
17. Explain a fusible-link.
18. Name two types of erasable PROMs.
19. What is a floating gate?
20. Explain a PROM burner.

4-12   BUBBLE MEMORY

Bubbles

The latest form of nonvolatile memory is the **Bubble Memory**. Although announced as far back as 1969, the technology has been slow to develop. It is based on the presence or absence of a magnetized area on a thin film of synthetic ferrite or garnet. Exposing the garnet to a perpendicular magnetic field cause small cylindrical shaped magnetic domains to form called *bubbles* (Fig. 4-22).

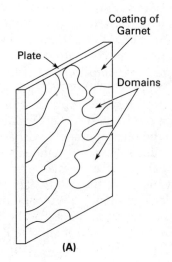
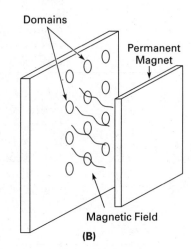

FIGURE 4-22 (A) Random Distribution of Domains Before Exposure to Magnetic Field. (B) Domains Reduced to "Bubbles" by Exposure to Perpendicular Magnetic Field.

Organization

The bubbles are moved around in serial fashion through the film in a highly controlled manner by a rotating magnetic field. The storage areas are divided into minor loops. The contents of a minor loop is injected into the major loop by duplicating the bubbles in a minor loop. This is done with a *bubble replicator*. This device splits the bubbles and thereby retains the information contained in the minor loop while outputting a duplicate of the information to the major loop (Fig. 4-23).

Bubble memories require a considerable amount of sensitive interfacing circuitry to translate domains into usable digital signals. Extensive clock circuitry is also needed for the critical timing necessary in bubble circulation. In addition, the circuitry for generating the rotating magnetic field is rather complex.

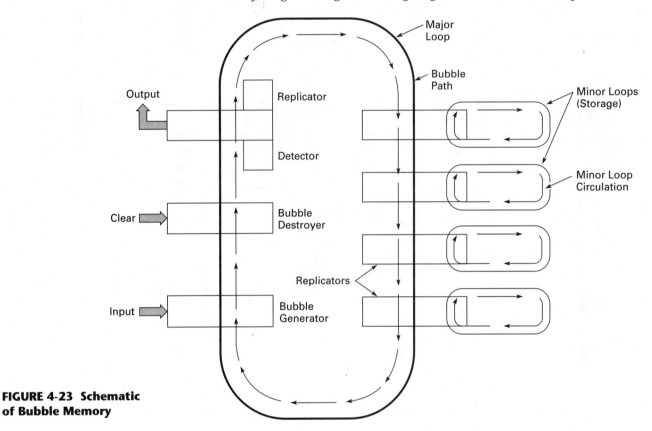

FIGURE 4-23 Schematic of Bubble Memory

The advantage of bubble memory is the extremely high density of the storage media, but it is somewhat offset by the ponderously slow access time of about 10 milliseconds. Compare this with an average of 250 microseconds to access a MOS technology EPROM.

4-13   MEMORY ORGANIZATION

Bit or Word Organized

Memories are said to be either **bit organized** or **word organized**. In a bit-organized memory each cell has an address and contains only one bit (Fig. 4-24). Such memories are small and are usually organized so the data is input and output on a single line in serial fashion. A word-organized memory has more than one bit at an address. Each address usually contains a 4-bit or 8-bit *word*. An 8-bit word is called a byte. The word is output four or eight bits at a time on parallel data lines (Fig. 4-25).

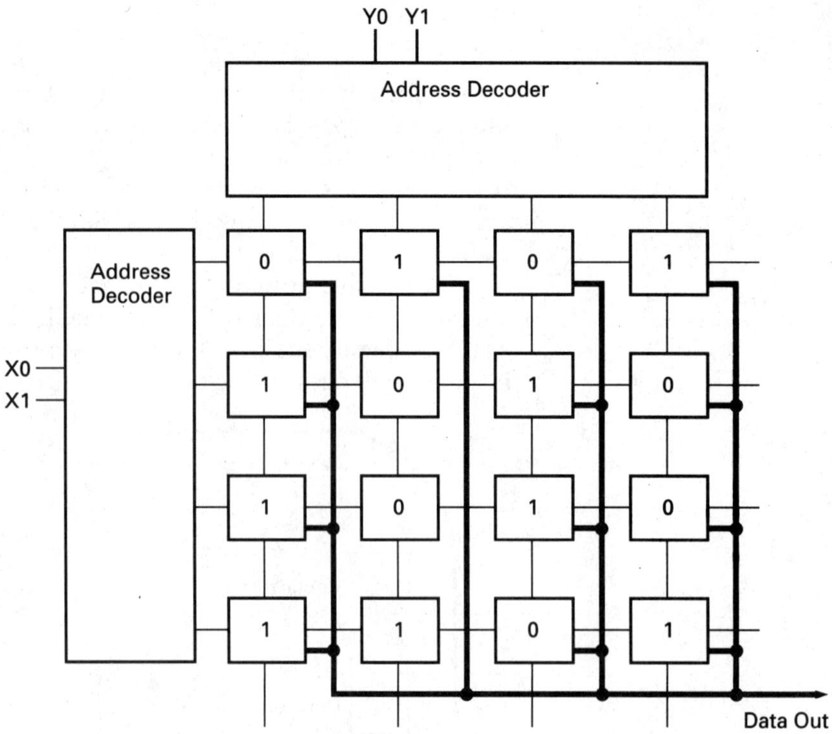

FIGURE 4-24 Bit-Organized Memory. Each Cell Has an Address and Each Location Contains One Bit.

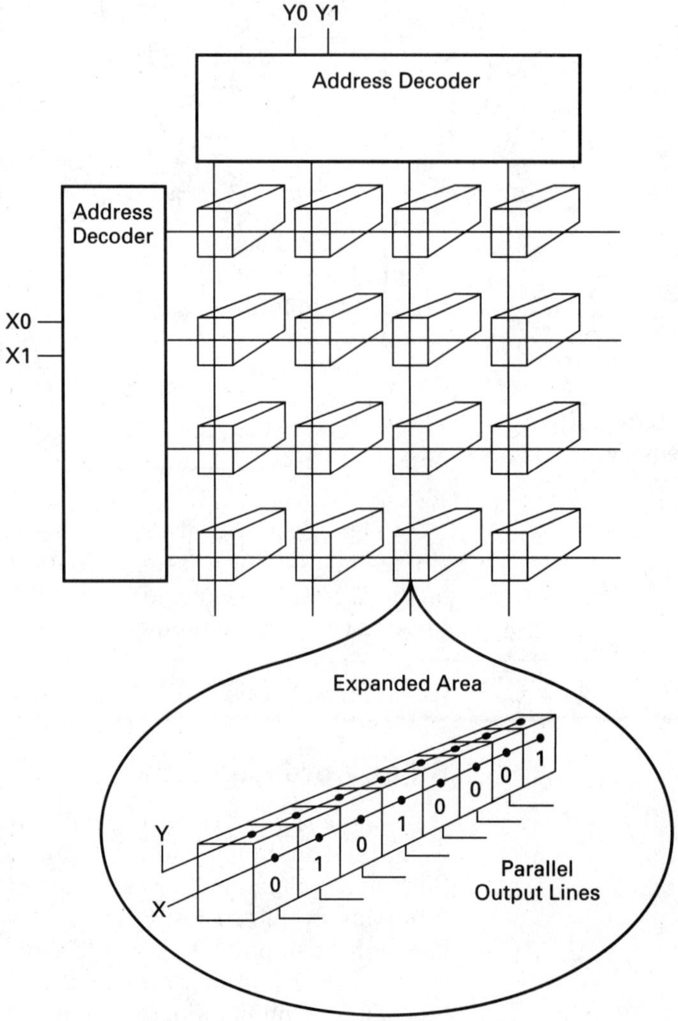

FIGURE 4-25 Word-Organized Memory

4-14   APPLICATIONS

What Can Be Stored in a ROM

The applications of ROM devices are practically endless. Any information that has a relatively permanent nature can be stored in a ROM.

Math Tables

Math tables are stored in ROM and are referred to as *look up* tables, just as though they were in a math handbook. For example, trigonometry functions are stored in ROM. When the microprocessor is doing math requiring a "trig" function, the value can be retrieved from a look-up table that contains the functions.

Personal Computer Instructions

Personal computers do not permanently store the entire operating system instructions. Yet in order for the computer to *know* how to load the operating system instructions from disk to memory it must already have these instructions available. To make these basic instructions permanently accessible, they are put into ROM. All personal computers come with ROM that contains the essential startup and operating commands. These are called BIOS (basic input/output systems).

Speech Synthesis

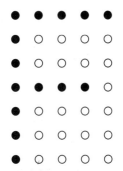

Another application of ROM is for speech synthesis. There are only a small number of basic sounds used to form all the words in a language. These sounds (about sixty for English) are called phonemes. Phonemes can be digitized and stored in ROM and used for speech synthesis. Speech is produced when a microprocessor accesses the phoneme and combines it with other phonemes to form words.

The pattern of dots for each character is stored in ROM.

FIGURE 4-26 5 × 7 Dot Matrix Character Display

Character Generators

Character generators are also a common application of ROM. The display of an alpha or numeric character on the screen of a monitor requires a character generator. Characters are made from a matrix of dots. A pattern of dots is illuminated on the screen to form the various characters. Storage in ROM of the pattern required to form a character is a perfect use of digital information. Each memory cell can retain the information for a given dot. Logic-1 stored in ROM illuminates a dot on the monitors screen; logic-0 does not (Fig. 4-26).

 SELF-CHECK FOR SECTIONS 4-12, 4-13, 4-14

21. Explain what is meant by a "bubble."
22. Explain the purpose of a bubble replicator.
23. Explain a bit-organized memory.
24. Explain a word-organized memory.
25. Name two uses for a ROM.

SUMMARY OF IDEAS

- A basic memory has a *storage area, input* and *output access,* and *address* capability.
- The *write operation* places a logic-1 or logic-0 into a memory storage area.
- The *read operation* is the process of retrieving the logic-1 or logic-0 from storage.
- The basic memory storage area is called a *cell.*
- A memory that retains its information after power has been removed is a *nonvolatile* memory.
- A memory that loses its information after power has been removed is a *volatile* memory.
- A Read Only Memory (ROM) is a permanent memory that can only be *read;* it is not possible to *write* to a ROM.
- A *matrix* memory is a set of mutually perpendicular lines. The intersections represent cells and store either a "1" or "0."
- Matrix memories can be constructed with diodes, transistors, or MOSFET devices.
- Each memory location has an address. To write or read a location, an address must be applied to the memory unit.
- Address decoding is the process of generating a unique output for every address combination that is input.
- *One-dimensional addressing* uses fewer decoder output line for each location in the memory.
- *Two-dimensional addressing* uses fewer decoder output lines to reach memory locations due to a row and column scheme for bit location.
- Programmable Read Only Memories (PROMs) use a fusible-link technology. The device at a given cell location can be permanently deactivated by *fusing* it.
- Electrically Alterable Programmable Read Only Memories (EAPROMs) are ROMs that can be erased and reprogrammed with the application of the proper voltage.
- Erasable Programmable Read Only Memories (EPROMs) are ROMs that can be erased by exposure to ultraviolet light.
- Bubble memories use a technology that creates *bubbles* or tiny magnetic domains in a ferrite material. The presence or absence of a bubble in a location indicates a 1 or 0.
- Any information of a relatively permanent nature can be stored in a ROM. Math tables, basic computer instructions, and character generators are common applications.

CHAPTER QUESTIONS & PROBLEMS

True or False

1. A basic memory has three elements.
2. A cell is defined as a 2-bit address line.
3. Read Only Memories are used to store relatively permanent information.
4. Matrix memory locations cannot be addressed.
5. Fusible-link PROMs can be erased.

Fill in the Blanks

6. EAPROM is the acronym (stands for) _____.
7. The 1-of-4 decoder has _____ output lines.
8. A PROM can be reprogrammed _____ number of times.
9. Two address line inputs will generate _____ unique addresses.
10. UV erasable PROMs use a special MOS device called a _____ gate.
11. Fusible-link PROMs cannot be constructed with _____ devices.
12. An EEPROM can be erased with _____.
13. Accessing the information at a given address to determine its value is called a _____ operation.
14. X and Y addressing is also referred to as _____ and _____ addressing.
15. The generation of a unique output from all possible input combinations is called _____.

Multiple Choice

16. An address input is 8-bits wide, that is, it has 8 separate input lines. How many locations can it access?
    a. 16
    b. 8
    c. 1,024
    d. 256

17. When power is removed, which of the following memories will lose information?
    a. bubble memory
    b. EPROM
    c. EEPROM
    d. none of the above

18. Which of the following devices is used in ROM construction?
    a. diodes
    b. transistors
    c. MOSFETs
    d. all of the above

19. A write/erase cycle in an EEPROM will
    a. require UV light.
    b. not require voltage.
    c. reduce the life of the cell.
    d. occur much faster than a read cycle.

20. A bubble memory is
    a. electrically alterable.
    b. a matrix type construction.
    c. the simplest form of ROM.
    d. not very fast.

CHAPTER 5 — MICROPROCESSOR MEMORIES (VOLATILE)

OUTLINE

NEW TERMS TO WATCH FOR

Volatile	Chip Select (CS)	Static
Refreshing	Refresh Cycle	Dynamic
Row Address Strobe (RAS)	Random Access Memory (RAM)	MOSFET
Sequential Access	Column Address Strobe (CAS)	DRAM
Hidden Refresh	Bipolar Memory Cell	ECL Cell
RAS Only Refresh	Automatic Refresh	Sense Line
Packet Charge	Charge Coupled Devices (CCD)	Potential Well

After completing this chapter, you should be able to:

1. State the difference between static and dynamic RAM.
2. Understand the operation and construction of a bipolar memory cell.
3. Determine the size and organization of a memory matrix used in a RAM chip.
4. Explain why MOS devices are chosen for the construction of RAM memory cells.
5. Describe the way in which row and column addresses are multiplexed.
6. Show the need for refresh circuitry.
7. Recognize several refresh methods.
8. Apply the chip select method in memory organization.
9. Read and understand the timing diagrams that are associated with memory circuits.
10. Demonstrate the action of a packet charge in a CCD memory.
11. Discuss the difference between the major categories of volatile memory devices.

5-1   INTRODUCTION

In the last chapter we examined nonvolatile memories, that is, memories that retain their data after power is removed. The information contained in the memory, we learned, is more or less permanent. Certain types of nonvolatile memories allow erasure but only under very specific conditions.

In this chapter, we will introduce **volatile** memories. Volatile memories are defined as those types of storage units that will lose their information if power is removed. This broad classification includes two subcategories of volatile devices called **static** and **dynamic** memories. Both categories are constructed from semiconductor devices.

5-2   RANDOM ACCESS MEMORY

Random Access

Volatile memory circuits are usually called RAM or **Random Access Memory (RAM)**. The term *random access* refers to the fact that, any data located in the memory is accessible without first having to consider any other data in memory. The data may be accessed at random. The random accessibility is the converse of sequential or serial access. In **sequential access**, a given bit of data may not be accessed without first reading all the data preceding the desired bit.

5-3   STATIC RAM

Static Device

A **static** memory is considered to be a memory that has a static or stable state. Certainly the ROM memories described in Chapter 4 are static memories. But the definition is broader and includes RAM memories constructed from circuits that exhibit a stable or static state. A flip-flop is an example of a circuit that displays a stable state. The output of logic-1 or logic-0 will not change as long as there is no outside input. The flip-flop must be triggered by a clock pulse before its static state will change. As long as power is applied and no clock pulse is input, the output remains in a stable condition.

Bipolar Static RAM

Memory cells can be constructed from flip-flops built with bipolar transistors. The advantage of bipolar transistor memories lies in the simplicity of the needed memory interface circuits. Bipolar transistors are compatible with bipolar IC logic gates. But bipolar devices tend to cost more to manufacture, they occupy more area on an IC chip, and they consume more power than other types of memory. Nevertheless, bipolar memories are desirable for the speed with which they can change states. This ultimately allows very fast read and write times.

A typical **bipolar memory cell** is shown in Figure 5-1. Recall that a memory cell is the basic memory storage unit and has a capacity of one binary bit.

In Figure 5-1, Q1 and Q2 form a flip-flop like the ones used in a TTL gate circuit. Such a circuit has two stable states. Either Q1 is *on* and saturated holding Q2 *off*, or Q2 is *on* and holds Q1 cut *off*. These are the only possible states.

**FIGURE 5-1 Bipolar
Transistor Static
Memory Cell**

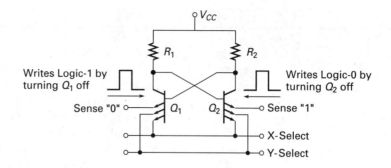

Multiple Emitters

Most transistor configurations are designed so that the emitter and collector circuits are connected to a fixed voltage. The base potential will then be varied in order to turn the transistor on or off. Multiple–emitter transistors are not actually manufactured as discrete components. But integrated circuit manufacturing technology easily permits this type of construction. In the multiple-emitter transistor, the collector and the base area are connected to fixed voltages and the emitters determine whether the transistor is to be turned on or off.

In Figure 5-1, if any of the emitters of Q1 or Q2 are at ground (logic-0) the transistor will saturate. If all the emitters are at Vcc (logic-1), or open, the transistor will be cut off. If any one emitter is at logic-1, that emitter will appear as an open circuit.

Row and Column

In Chapter 4, the concept of two-dimensional addressing was discussed. This idea requires both a row or X-address and a column or Y-address. As illustrated in Figure 5-1, one emitter from Q1 and one emitter from Q2 are tied to the X-select and form the row address. One emitter from Q1 and one from Q2 are tied to the Y-select and form the column address. This leaves one emitter from each transistor available for the *sense* leads. The Q1, sense-0 lead will detect the logic-1 condition. The sense leads constitute the read/write lines.

Static State

If the cell is not being selected for a read or write operation, then both the X and the Y lines are kept at logic-0. This means that the emitters of both transistors are properly biased for stable operation. One transistor will be on and the other will be off.

Reading the Static Cell

To select the cell for reading, both the X- and Y-select lines are brought high (logic-1). This action removes two of the emitters from each transistor electrically from the circuit. The sense emitters now become the controlling emitters.

If we assume Q2 was in conduction (on) and Q1 is cut off, then the sense-1 line will have current flow and the sense-0 line will not have current flow. The **sense lines** are connected to the sense amplifier. If the sense amplifier detects current in Q2, it will output a logic-1, indicating the cell contains a "1." If however, the sense amplifier detects current in the Q1 emitter, the output of the sense amplifier will be logic-0. Reading or *sensing* the current does not in any way affect the state of the flip-flop, it still retains the same logic and remains in a stable state.

Writing to the Static Cell

To write to or change the logic output of the static cell, it must again be selected. Selection for the write operation is accomplished in exactly the same way as it was for reading. The X- and Y-select lines are brought high. This again causes the sense emitters to become the controlling emitters.

Write "0"

For the cell to contain logic-0, Q1 must be on. Therefore, to write a logic-0, the sense-1 line is pulsed with a logic-1. The "1" pulse will turn Q2 off because, at that time, none of the three emitters will be a logic-0 or ground. Turning Q2 off forces Q1 on. When Q1 is on, the sense-0 line will have current.

Write "1"

To write a logic-1 to the cell, the sense-0 line is pulsed high. This action will cause Q1 to turn off. As Q1 turns off, Q2 turns on and current will then be available in the sense-1 line. After the write operation is complete, the X- and Y-sense lines are again returned to logic-0 and the cell remains in the new static state.

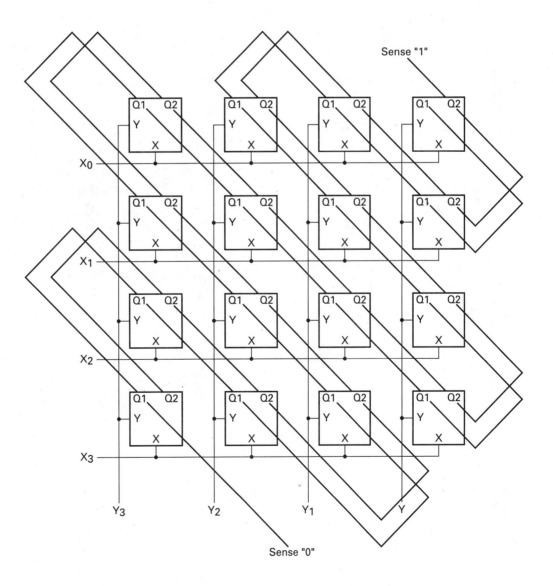

FIGURE 5-2 Bipolar RAM 6 × 1

Bipolar RAM

Figure 5-2 shows how several bipolar RAM cells could be connected together to form a simple memory. The memory is 16 × 1, that is, it stores 16 different 1-bit pieces of information. The sense amplifier is not shown, but both sense leads connect to the amplifier and the result is a single logic output. This output will reflect the status of the row and column selected cell.

A word organized 16-bit memory is shown in Figure 5-3. This introduces the concept of memory planes. There are actually 16 different 4-bit words available in this memory. Each of the 16 addresses possible activates one cell on each plane. The output word will appear on D0 through D3.

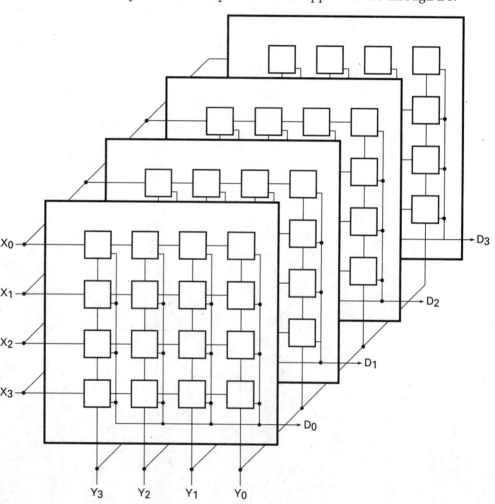

FIGURE 5-3 Word Organized 16 × 4 Bit Static RAM

ECL Static RAM

Another commonly used bipolar, static-RAM is the ECL or Emitter Coupled Logic type. A simplified **ECL cell** construction is shown in Figure 5-4.

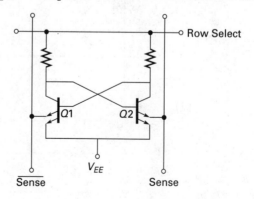

FIGURE 5-4 ECL Memory Cell

ECL transistors are operated in the nonsaturated region. When the cell is not selected, the voltage on the select line is reduced and the flip-flop is in standby with one transistor on and the other off. Raising the row select provides a large sense current for reading and writing the cell.

In ECL memory, the cell sizes are larger than they are in TTL, due to the complexity of ECL circuits. ECL chips are faster than TTL, but the speed is accompanied by increased power dissipation. Typical speeds are less than 10 nanoseconds, as in the MCM10145 16 × 4 RAM shown in Figure 5-5. Speed is probably the most important aspect of ECL RAM.

MOTOROLA
SEMICONDUCTOR ▬▬▬▬▬▬▬
TECHNICAL DATA

MCM10145

64-BIT REGISTER FILE
(RAM)

The MCM10145 is a 64-Bit RAM organized as a 16 x 4 array. This organization and the high speed make the MCM10145 particularly useful in register file or small scratch pad applications. Fully decoded inputs, together with a chip enable, provide expansion of memory capacity. The Write Enable input, when low, allows data to be entered; when high, disables the data inputs. The $\overline{\text{Chip Select}}$ input when low, allows full functional operation of the device; when high, all outputs go to a low logic state. The $\overline{\text{Chip Select}}$, together with open emitter outputs allow full wire-ORing and data bussing capability. On-chip input pulldown resistors allow unused inputs to remain open.

- Typical Address Access Time = 10 ns
- Typical Chip Select Access Time = 4.5 ns
- Operating Temperature Range = 0° to +75°C
- 50 kΩ Pulldown Resistors on All Inputs
- Fully Compatible with MECL 10,000
- Pin-for-Pin Compatible with the F10145

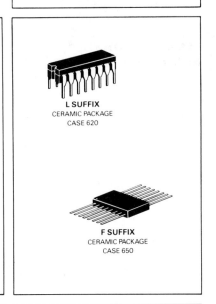

L SUFFIX
CERAMIC PACKAGE
CASE 620

F SUFFIX
CERAMIC PACKAGE
CASE 650

FIGURE 5-5 Word-Organized 16 × 4 Bit Static RAM

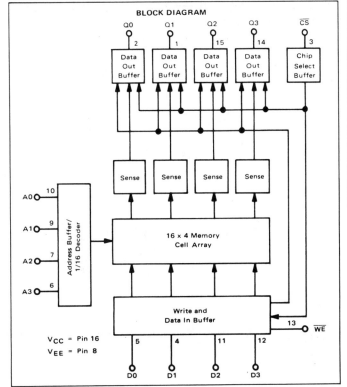

BLOCK DIAGRAM

V_{CC} = Pin 16
V_{EE} = Pin 8

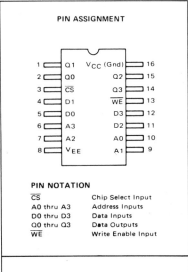

PIN ASSIGNMENT

1	Q1	V_{CC} (Gnd)	16
2	Q0	Q2	15
3	$\overline{\text{CS}}$	Q3	14
4	D1	$\overline{\text{WE}}$	13
5	D0	D3	12
6	A3	D2	11
7	A2	A0	10
8	V_{EE}	A1	9

PIN NOTATION

$\overline{\text{CS}}$	Chip Select Input
A0 thru A3	Address Inputs
D0 thru D3	Data Inputs
Q0 thru Q3	Data Outputs
$\overline{\text{WE}}$	Write Enable Input

TRUTH TABLE

MODE	INPUT			OUTPUT
	$\overline{\text{CS}}$	$\overline{\text{WE}}$	D_n	Q_n
Write "0"	L	L	L	L
Write "1"	L	L	H	L
Read	L	H	φ	Q
Disabled	H	φ	φ	L

φ = Don't Care.

MOSFET Static RAM

MOSFET or MOS Field Effect Transistors are also used extensively for static RAM. This is due to relatively uncomplicated manufacturing techniques when compared to bipolar transistors. Even more important, MOSFET ICs also consume less power than bipolar devices.

The illustration in Figure 5-6 shows a memory cell constructed with MOS devices. The Q2 and Q4 transistors are connected as a flip-flop circuit, just as the TTL cell was. The Q1 and Q3 transistors are there to provide a resistive load for Q2 and Q4. It is simpler in the manufacturing process to use the same semiconductor geometry for its resistive effects than it is to form pure resistors.

FIGURE 5-6 MOSFET Static Memory Cell

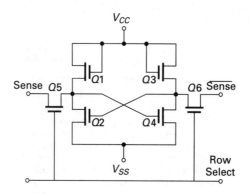

The row select signal enables Q5 and Q6 for all the cells in the given row. The output of the cells on the sense leads is then available on the column-sense amplifier outputs of all the cells of the selected row. The column select consists of choosing the column-sense amplifier output for the desired cell. In other words, a separate column select is not needed.

Figure 5-7 shows a block diagram of this arrangement. Address lines A4 through A7 select one of 16 possible rows. Address lines A0 through A3 select one of 16 possible column sense amplifier outputs. In this way, any of 256 different cells can be selected. The output of a cell will be 1 bit, available at D_{out} when the S-line is low. This is a bit-organized chip and has the capacity of 256 separate 1-bit *words*. It is referred to as a "256 × 1 memory chip."

FIGURE 5-7 Block Diagram of Static RAM 256 × 1 Memory

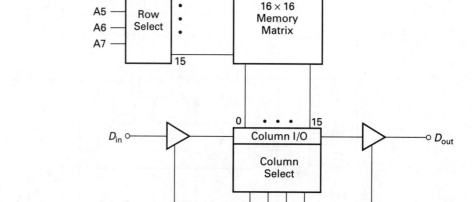

Applications

In certain applications, it is vital that the information in RAM be saved in the event of a power failure. The information in static RAM is volatile and power must be applied at all times to prevent the loss of data. Because MOS devices use little power, nickel cadmium batteries can be used to backup power supplies in the event of a power failure. When a power failure occurs, the battery takes over and can continue to operate the memory for several hours.

 SELF-CHECK FOR SECTIONS 5-1, 5-2, 5-3

1. Explain the term volatile.
2. Explain random access.
3. What is serial access?
4. What is a static RAM?
5. What is the advantage of a bipolar RAM?
6. Explain sense leads.
7. What happens when power is lost to a static RAM?

5-4 DYNAMIC RAM

Introduction

Dynamic RAM, sometimes called **DRAM**, is also volatile memory, but it needs more than just the continued application of power to retain its information. The dynamic-RAM cell depends on a capacitance to retain its logic. This capacitance, or ability to store a charge, is limited, due to the small physical size of the capacitor. For this reason, it must be recharged frequently. The recharging is called **refreshing**. The rate at which the refresh action takes place is called the **refresh cycle**. The refreshing cycle needs to take place about every 2 to 4 milliseconds or less. Offsetting the need for refreshing is the fact that a dynamic cell is smaller and less expensive to manufacture.

Dynamic Memory Cells

A simplified construction of a dynamic memory cell is shown in Figure 5-8. When the row is selected, the MOS device couples the capacitor to the sense line. If the capacitor is charged, a logic-1 is output. If it is discharged, the sense line output is logic-0.

In reality, the actual cell is somewhat more complicated than shown in Figure 5-8. A more complete example of the construction of a dynamic-RAM cell can be seen in Figure 5-9. The storage capacitor, C1, will retain the

FIGURE 5-8 Simple Dynamic Memory Cell

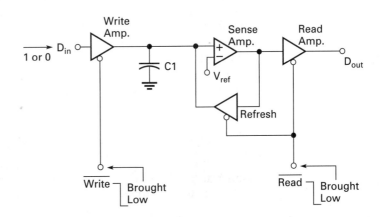

FIGURE 5-9 Dynamic RAM Cell

desired logic of the cell. It is connected to the input of the sense amplifier which has a very high input impedance. This impedance prevents the discharge of the capacitor through the amplifier.

If the capacitor is charged, its voltage will be higher than the reference voltage. In this case, the output of the sense amplifier and, therefore, D_{out}, will be logic-1. If, on the other hand, the capacitor is discharged, the input to the sense amplifier will be lower than the reference voltage and the output will be logic-0.

Writing to the Cell

To write to the cell, the WRITE-line is brought low. This enables the write input amplifier. The logic on the D_{in} line will then affect the charge on the capacitor, either charging it with logic-1 or discharging it with logic-0.

Reading the Cell

The read operation calls for the READ-line to be brought low. The READ-control line enables the read amplifier. This makes the charge status of the capacitor available, from the sense amplifier, on the D_{out} line.

Refreshing the Cell

Note that the output of the sense amplifier is also connected to the refresh amplifier. This means the READ signal will also enable the refresh amplifier. The refresh amplifier will keep the capacitor charged, if it was charged, or keep it discharged, if it was discharged. In other words, it forms a feedback circuit. Reading the cell also refreshes it by maintaining the charge on the capacitor.

A Typical RAM Chip

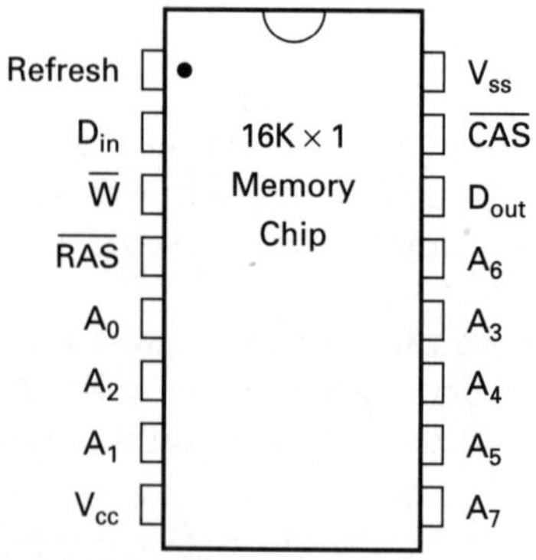

A typical RAM chip with its pin assignments is illustrated in Figure 5-10. Rather than separate the read and write inputs on two pins, chips usually make use of just one pin. The W line determines whether the chip is in the read mode, (W = high) or the write mode, (W = low). The D_{in} pin is for the data stream input and the output is labeled D_{out}.

This chip is a 16K × 1 RAM. The 16K is an abbreviated way of saying 16,384. The K means 1,000 (really 1,024 for digital work), and the number 16,384 is always rounded off to 16K. The chip has only seven address lines. We might expect that since 2^{14} = 16,384, 14 address lines, not 7, would be needed. The problem is that on a 16-pin chip, there is not enough room to use 14 pins for address inputs. The solution to this problem is to multiplex the address lines. The address is divided into two bytes, a low byte of 7 bits and a high byte of 7 bits. The same 7 address lines are used first for the low byte of the address (row input) and then for the high byte of the address (column input). In other words, only half the address is input at a time. This is accomplished with the RAS and CAS control inputs.

FIGURE 5-10 16 × 1 Memory Chip

Row and Column Address Strobe

To enter the row address, the RAS **(Row Address Strobe)** is brought low and the low byte or 7-bit row address is input on A0 through A7. Next the CAS **(Column Address Strobe)** line is brought low and the high byte or 7-bit column address is input on A0 through A7. The full 14-bit address is assembled in registers inside the chip and presented to the memory matrix. The matrix memory cells are organized in 128 rows by 128 columns. $128 \times 128 = 16,384$.

Refresh

Recall that the dynamic memory cell is built around a capacitor. The charge on this capacitor will decay rather quickly so that it needs to be refreshed about every 2 milliseconds. We have seen how reading a cell can refresh it, but it is impractical to read the entire memory this often. For this reason, other, more-efficient ways are provided. The methods are based on addressing each of the rows in the memory matrix every 2 milliseconds. Just how and when this takes place is largely explained by timing diagrams.

Timing Diagrams

The action of reading, writing to, and refreshing memory is somewhat complicated. The understanding of this action is best accomplished through timing diagrams that reflect what is happening in RAM and the time sequences involved. At first, timing diagrams can appear confusing and intimidating, but they need not be.

There are a few conventions used in timing diagrams and once they are understood, reading them is much easier.

First of all, bear in mind that timing diagrams are graphical representations. They depict time on the horizontal axis and logic levels of 1 and 0 on the vertical axis.

The waveforms drawn are a combined or consolidated waveform. This simplifies reading the diagram. For instance, there are usually several address lines to be considered, but they can all be represented on a single graph line as in Figure 5-11. It is not important, in terms of understanding the timing, to know if an individual address line is at logic-1 or logic-0 at any given time. What we are interested in is the time at which the address needs to be present on the address input pins in order to latch the address in and decode it.

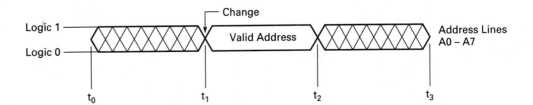

FIGURE 5-11 Timing Diagram Conventions

Note that at time t_1, a change takes place on all address lines. This change is indicated by the crossing of logic levels. The high transits toward a low and the low changes to a high and the two form a crossover point. The change at time t_1 is significant because it means that at this point, the address lines must and do contain a valid address. They may or may not have had a valid address on them before this change. But since it is not of importance before t_1 or after t_2, it does not matter. The fact that it does not matter is indicated by the cross-hatching. Note that after time t_2, the cross hatching appears once again, indicating that the address logic levels no longer matter, that is, they are not valid. Now let's examine a refresh timing diagram.

The RAS Only Refresh

There are in fact, several methods in use to refresh dynamic memory chips. A commonly used method is the **RAS Only Refresh**. In this method, each row in the matrix is addressed and the RAS line is pulsed low. This method requires an external counter to generate each of the possible row addresses. Every time an address is generated, the RAS line is pulsed. The external counter increments and the RAS line is again pulsed. This must occur at least once every 2 milliseconds for every row in the memory.

In the timing diagram in Figure 5-12, the row addresses, A0 through A7 are valid at the beginning of time t_{ASR}. They remain valid until the end of t_{RAH}. Shortly after the row address lines have valid data, the RAS line is brought low. This occurs at the beginning of t_{RC}. Once the RAS line becomes active, it remains active for the time t_{RAS}. After it is again inactive, it remains inactive for the time t_{RP}. This sequence is repeated 128 times for a 128 × 128 matrix in a 16K chip, until all rows are addressed and refreshed.

The external counter must also have the capability to lock out the microprocessor as the memory cannot be read from or written to by an external device during a refresh period.

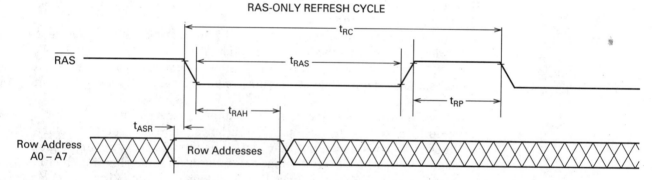

FIGURE 5-12 RAS Only Refresh Timing Diagram

Automatic Refresh

The **automatic refresh** method makes use of the refresh input pin on the chip, if the chip has provisions for this method. The RAS line is brought high while the refresh pin is pulsed low. Inside the chip, an internal counter increments the row address register every time the refresh line is pulsed. No external counter is needed. Again, the memory chip cannot be accessed during the refresh time.

The Hidden Refresh Cycle

It usually requires more time to execute microprocessor instructions than it takes to complete a memory read or write cycle. This time can be used to accomplish a refresh and is called a **hidden refresh**. In other words, the refresh can be performed while valid data is still on the output line. This is done by holding CAS low and taking RAS high. This sequence begins at t_1 (Fig. 5-13), when RAS is brought low. When RAS is brought low, the internal counter is activated for refreshing and the refresh cycle occurs.

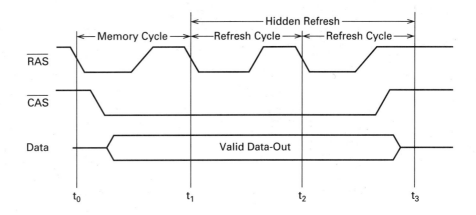

FIGURE 5-13 The Hidden Refresh Cycle

Dynamic RAM Read Cycle Timing

The Motorola MCM6256B is a 256K $\times$ 1 bit dynamic RAM chip. The data sheet appears in Figure 5-14. The diagram illustrated in Figure 5-15 is taken from the data sheet for this device. During the read operation, the main sequence of events are as follows:

1. The ROW address is input on the address pins A0 through A8. The address is valid at the beginning of time t_{ASR}.
2. The ROW Address Strobe, RAS, line is brought low at the beginning to time t_{RC}. This action strobes the ROW address into the chip address decoders. At the end of time t_{ASC} the column address is input.
3. At the beginning of t_{RCS} on the W input, the read command brings W high.
4. After a short delay, t_{RCS}, the column address is available on the address lines A0 through A8.
5. Shortly after the column address is valid, the CAS line is brought low. This strobes the column address into the chip address decoders.
6. The data has been selected but is not immediately available, because all electronic devices have some propagation delay. The data is actually not available until after delay t_{CAC}.

The entire read cycle process for this chip is t_{RC}. For the MCM6256B-10, it is given as 190 nanoseconds.

Dynamic RAM Write Cycle Timing

The write sequence does not differ greatly from the read sequence. First, the row address appears and is strobed in by RAS (Fig. 5-16). Then the W line is brought low. Next the column address appears and is strobed in by the CAS. Data for writing must be available for time t_{DS}, data setup time, and for time t_{DH}, data hold time. The entire write cycle requires time t_{RC}.

MOTOROLA
■ SEMICONDUCTOR
TECHNICAL DATA

MCM6256B

Advance Information
256K-Bit Dynamic RAM

The MCM6256B is a 262,144 bit, high-speed, dynamic random access memory. Organized as 262,144 one-bit words and fabricated using N-channel silicon-gate MOS technology, this single +5 volt supply dynamic RAM combines high performance with low cost and improved reliability. All inputs and outputs are fully TTL compatible.

By multiplexing row and column address inputs, the MCM6256B requires only nine address lines and permits packaging in standard 16-pin 300 mil wide dual-in-line packages. Complete address decoding is done on-chip with address latches incorporated. Data out (Q) is controlled by $\overline{CAS}$ allowing greater system flexibility.

The MCM6256B features "page mode" which allows random column accesses of the 512 bits within the selected row.

- Organized as 262,144 Words of 1 Bit
- Single +5 Volt Operation (±10%)
- Maximum Access Time: MCM6256B-10 = 100 ns
    MCM6256B-12 = 120 ns
    MCM6256B-15 = 150 ns
- Low Power Dissipation: MCM6256B-10 = 440 mW Maximum (Active)
    MCM6256B-12 = 396 mW Maximum (Active)
    MCM6256B-15 = 358 mW Maximum (Active)
    28 mW Maximum (Standby)
- Three-State Data Output
- Early-Write Common I/O Capability
- 256 Cycle, 4 ms Refresh
- $\overline{RAS}$-Only Refresh Mode
- $\overline{CAS}$ Before $\overline{RAS}$ Refresh
- Hidden Refresh
- Page Mode Capability

P PACKAGE
PLASTIC
CASE 648

PIN ASSIGNMENT

A8	1 ●	16	V_{SS}
D	2	15	$\overline{CAS}$
$\overline{W}$	3	14	Q
$\overline{RAS}$	4	13	A6
A0	5	12	A3
A2	6	11	A4
A1	7	10	A5
V_{CC}	8	9	A7

PIN NAMES

A0-A8	Address Input
D	Data In
Q	Data Out
$\overline{W}$	Read/Write Input
$\overline{RAS}$	Row Address Strobe
$\overline{CAS}$	Column Address Strobe
V_{CC}	Power (+5 V)
V_{SS}	Ground

BLOCK DIAGRAM

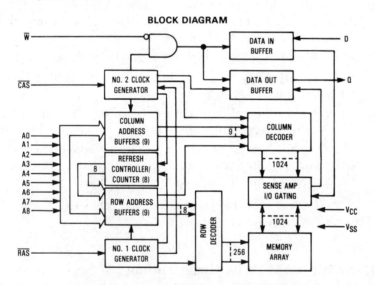

This document contains information on a new product. Specifications and information herein are subject to change without notice.

FIGURE 5-14 MCM 6256B Data Sheet

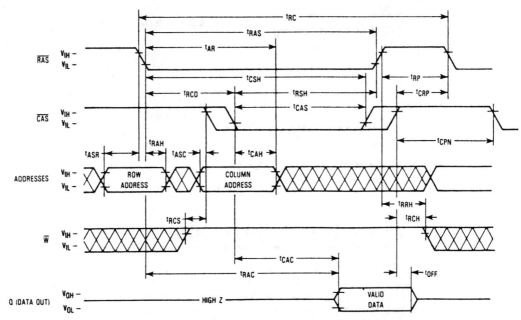

FIGURE 5-15 MCM 6256B Read Cycle Timing
Note: see Appendix for timing abbreviations.

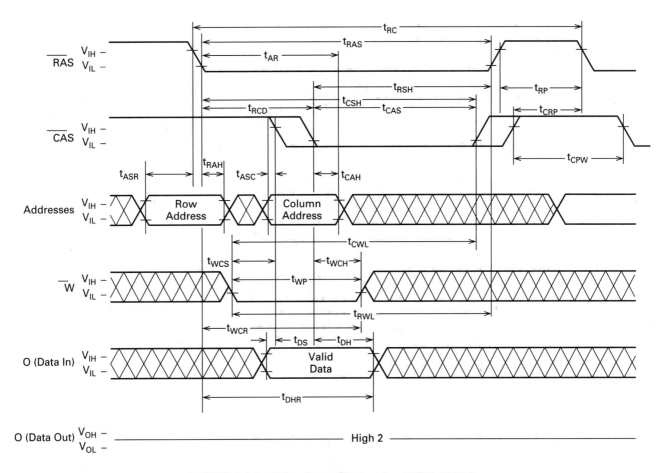

FIGURE 5-16 Write Cycle Timing for MCM 6256B

✔ SELF-CHECK FOR SECTION 5-4

8. What is the difference between a static and a dynamic RAM?
9. Explain "refresh."
10. What does a read operation do to the logic code stored in a dynamic RAM?
11. Explain the need for a multiplexed address.
12. What is RAS?
13. What is CAS?
14. Explain RAS only refresh.
15. Explain hidden refresh.

5-5 MEMORY ORGANIZATION

It is not unusual to find memory chips organized according to bits, for example the 16K × 1. As we have seen, however, serial bit organization is much less efficient than parallel organization. In fact, microprocessors are designed to accept at least eight bits at a time in parallel fashion, and the newer ones, sixteen or thirty-two bits.

A set of 16K × 1 chips can be used to generate 8-bit words when connected, as in Figure 5-17. By using the row and column scheme, the seven address input lines, A0 through A6, allow the memory to be used as a 16K × 8. In other words, by using eight 16K chips, the memory can generate 16,384 different 8-bit words.

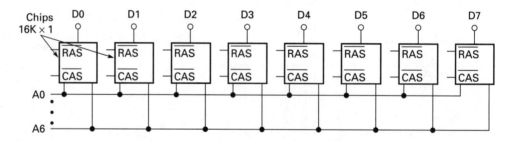

FIGURE 5-17 16K × 8 Memory Constructed with 16K × 1 Chips

Chip Expansion

It is also possible to organize a memory chip for 8-bit words by using the concept of memory planes (Fig. 5-18). Each of the 16,384 locations contains one 8-bit word. The number of address input requirements remain the same. The only change is that there are now eight parallel data line outputs.

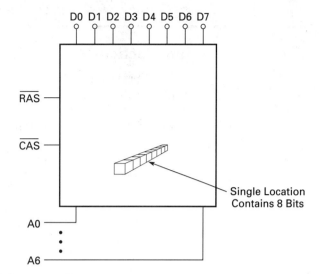

FIGURE 5-18 16K × 8-Bit Chip

Chip Select Expansion

Figure 5-19 illustrates a 64K × 8 memory. This memory uses the same number of address lines as the 16K × 8 memory. The data outputs are tied together into an 8-bit data bus.

This arrangement is made possible by the **Chip Select**, pin S, sometimes called chip enable (CE). The S-input is a sort of on/off switch. It determines whether or not the chip is *on* and available for addressing or *off*, meaning off line and not available.

Two more address lines have been added to decode the chip select. Any one of the four chips can be selected based on bits A7 and A8.

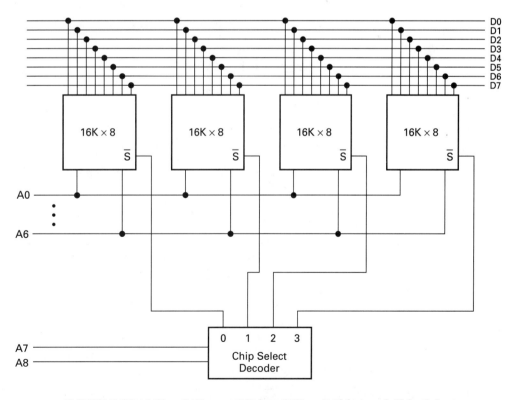

FIGURE 5-19 64K × 8 Memory Using 16K × 8 Chips and Chip Select

5-6   CHARGE-COUPLED DEVICES

Introduction

Charge-Coupled Devices, announced by Bell Labs in 1970, are a special kind of volatile device. As we have seen, dynamic RAMs require a refresh procedure to keep the capacitive storage element charged. A charge-coupled device, or CCD, uses a recirculating technique to accomplish the same thing.

The construction of a CCD is significantly less complicated than either bipolar or MOS devices (Fig. 5-20). For this reason, and because higher densities are possible, CCDs are becoming more popular.

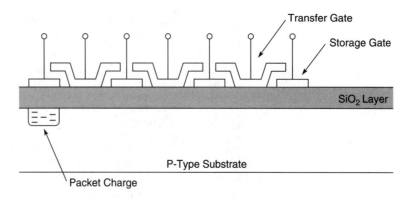

FIGURE 5-20 CCD Constructions

Continuous Shifting

The CCD is essentially a serial shift register that continuously shifts the logic information it contains. The logic is in the form of an electrical charge called a **packet charge**. The negative packet charge is injected into the first cell and shifted by a four-phase clock circuit. The injection is in a serial format and always occurs at the first cell of a given register.

Storage Cell

The storage element itself is best understood as a **potential well** or storage area. The *well* is created by a positive potential applied to the storage gate by the clock signal. The positive potential repels the majority carriers and forms a depletion area or *well* that is prepared to accept the negative packet charge. This well does have a tendency to fill back up due to thermally generated carriers. This is why the charges are continually shifted.

The Shift Mechanism

All gates or cells that operate on the same clock phase are tied together. The timing for the first shift cycle begins at time A (Fig. 5-21). During this time, a packet charge is stored under the gate connected to Ø2. The Ø2 clock is already high, storing the charge under the gate area in the substrate. At time B, the Ø4 clock is brought high, forming a potential well under the gate connected to Ø4. The well is *empty* at this time. During time C, the Ø3 clock and gate are brought high. This expands the storage area into one continuous gate connecting area 2 to area 4. The charge then begins to redistribute through all 3 gate areas.

At time D, the Ø2 gates transit is low. This eliminates the charge that was beneath Ø2 gate. The packet charge is now confined to Ø3 and Ø4 gates. At time E, the Ø3 gate is brought low. This eliminates the charge under the Ø3 gate. Now the charge is under Ø4 gate, filling the potential well and the 1st shift cycle is complete. The next shift cycle starts with the Ø2 clock transiting high. This creates the next potential well for the second shift cycle.

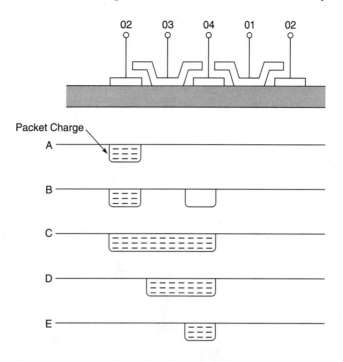

FIGURE 5-21 CCD Shift Cycle Timing

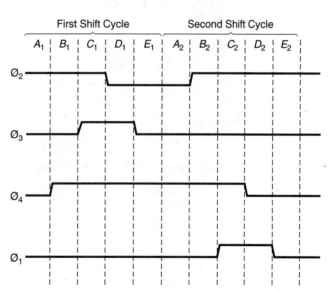

The Intel 2416 CCD

The 2416 from Intel is a 16K-CCD memory. It is organized as 16,384 × 1-bit words. It contains sixty-four 256-bit independent recirculating registers, as seen in Figure 5-22. After every shift cycle, each of the sixty-four registers are available to be selected for input or output. This is done with the 6-bit address inputs A0 through A5. The address lines select only one of the sixty-four loops and cannot track which of the 256 available bits are to be read. Therefore, external device controllers are required to track and time the input/output data for the chip.

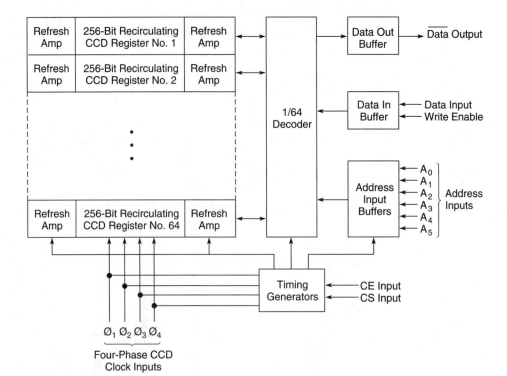

FIGURE 5-22 Block Diagram of Intel 2416 CCD

SELF-CHECK FOR SECTIONS 5-5, 5-6

16. What is the purpose of *chip select* on a memory chip?
17. What is a CCD?
18. Explain a packet charge.
19. Explain a potential well.

SUMMARY OF IDEAS

- Volatile memories are memory devices that will lose their data if power is removed.
- Volatile memories can be divided into two broad classifications, static and dynamic.
- Volatile memories are generally classed as RAM or *Random Access Memories*. This refers to the accessibility of a given piece of data. The data can be obtained without having to search through unwanted data as in sequential access.
- A static memory cell is a cell that has a static or stable state, such as a flip-flop circuit.
- Bipolar transistors can be connected to form a flip-flop circuit to serve as a memory cell. The cell will have a capacity of 1-bit.
- Row and column addressing schemes are used to access a memory cell within a memory matrix.
- MOSFETs are also used to construct static memory cells. They have the advantage of low power consumption.
- Dynamic Random Access Memories or DRAMs must be refreshed. This is because the storage element is a charged capacitance and the charge tends to decay very quickly.

- In order to reduce the number of address input pins on a chip, the address lines are multiplexed.
- The RAS signal strobes the row address input into the chip while the CAS input strobes the column address input into the chip.
- There are several common refresh methods used for DRAMs. One is called the RAS Only Refresh method. In it, each row of the memory matrix is addressed while the RAS line is pulsed low. This method requires an external counter register. Each time the counter increments, the refresh input on the chip is pulsed.
- The hidden refresh method calls for the refresh cycle to take place immediately following a microprocessor memory access. During this time, the microprocessor is carrying out instructions and the refresh process has time to occur.
- The addition of a Chip Select (CS) or Chip Enable (CE) input allows a single memory chip to be selected on a common address bus. This enhances memory size while minimizing memory bus wiring.
- A Charge Coupled Device (CCD) is a special type of volatile memory. It is based on a series of recirculating shift registers.

CHAPTER QUESTIONS & PROBLEMS

True or False
1. Bipolar RAM chips are generally slower than MOSFET static RAMs.
2. A MOSFET static RAM does not need three separate inputs for row select, column select, and data sense.
3. It is possible for a dynamic RAM cell to refresh itself during a read operation.
4. The RAS signal and CAS signal are generally timed to arrive at the chip simultaneously.
5. A CCD memory chip has characteristics similar to a recirculating shift register.

Fill in the Blanks
6. Static memory cells are usually constructed with semiconductor devices configured in a _____ circuit.
7. A dynamic-RAM cell has to be refreshed because of the _____ storage elements.
8. The logic contained in a given cell is output through the _____ amplifier.
9. When the refresh cycle occurs immediately after a memory access, (read or write) it is called _____.
10. If a memory has an on board address counter/generator that increments when the refresh input pin is pulsed, the chip is said to have _____ refresh.

Multiple Choice
11. Which of the following memory constructions is generally considered to have the fastest access time?
    a. TTL Static RAM
    b. MOS Static RAM
    c. ECL Static RAM
    d. CCD Memory

12. Which figure most closely reflects a typical refresh frequency timing?
    a. 10 microseconds
    b. 10 nanoseconds
    c. 2 milliseconds
    d. 2 microseconds

13. Which of the following statements is not true?
    a. Reading a memory cell does not cause it to need refreshing.
    b. Most refresh schemes require a row address only.
    c. Some refresh schemes require an external counter to generate refresh addresses.
    d. A memory can be written to during the refresh cycle.

14. Which of the following would be correct for a 16K row and column matrix?
    a. 128 × 128
    b. 256 × 64
    c. 512 × 32
    d. 128 × 64

15. Which of the following combinations could be used to build a 16K × 8 memory?
    a. two 8K × 8 chips
    b. four 4K × 8 chips
    c. eight 16K × 1 chips
    d. all of the above

16. During a read cycle, which of the following generally occurs first?
    a. the CAS line is brought low
    b. the RAS line is brought low
    c. the row address is input
    d. the column address is input

17. The chip select input is used to
    a. enable the read function.
    b. enable the write function.
    c. turn on the sense amplifier.
    d. make the chip available for read/write.

18. Which of the following clock phases can be used to read or write to a CCD? (refer to Figure 5-21)
    a. 1 and 3
    b. 2 and 4
    c. none
    d. all phases

19. The potential well in a CCD is best described as
    a. the storage area for refresh charges.
    b. a negatively charged area under a gate.
    c. the depletion region formed by a positive gate potential.
    d. the input storage area where the packet charge is injected.

20. Which access time would be typical for a MOS dynamic RAM?
    a. 200 milliseconds
    b. 190 microseconds
    c. 190 nanoseconds
    d. 2 milliseconds

MASS STORAGE DEVICES

OUTLINE

NEW TERMS TO WATCH FOR

Mass Storage	Formatting	Tracks
Cylinders	Indexing	Record Head
Domains	TPI	Polarized Beam
CRC	Gap	Pits and Lands
Return-to-Zero	Beam Splitter	Pick Up
Non-Return-to-Zero (NRZ)	Radial Tracking	Diskette
Frequency Modulation	Write Protect	Collimator
Constant Linear Velocity	Ferric Oxide	Modified Frequency Modulation (MFM)

After completing this chapter, you should be able to:

1. Explain the need for mass storage devices.
2. State the two main classes of mass storage units.
3. Describe how it is possible to record electrical impulses on a magnetic surface.
4. Demonstrate how a record/playback head works.
5. Discuss the various methods employed to encode digital information on magnetic media.
6. Show how digital information is organized on diskettes.
7. Explain what disk formatting is and why it is used.
8. Identify the various magnetic disk media currently in use in terms of physical size and data capacity.
9. Recognize the major differences between rigid drives and flexible disk drives.
10. Understand the technology used in optical disk media.
11. Describe the way in which digital data is recorded on an optical disk.
12. Explain how the digital data is read from an optical disk.
13. Show how radial tracking and focusing is accomplished on optical media.

6-1   INTRODUCTION

Need for Mass Storage

Both volatile and nonvolatile memories are essential to the operation of a microprocessor system. It can be said that nonvolatile memories serve to store permanent information, such as character generators or *boot* instructions. On the other hand, volatile memory, due to its temporary nature, is more useful for work space and for storing information that must be instantly available to the microprocessor. Application programs are stored in volatile memory (RAM). Both types of memory have been implemented on IC chips and in spite of their usefulness, both suffer from two major limitations, capacity and cost.

The capacity, or amount of information that can be stored in IC chip memories, and the cost of these memories are the chief reasons for development of **mass storage** technologies. The media used for mass storage must be able to store large amounts of digitized (binary) data and be less expensive than electronic memories. In addition, it must be nonvolatile, that is, permanent and easily randomly accessed.

Two Classes of Mass storage

Mass storage technologies that meet these requirements can be divided into two main classes; *magnetic* and *optical*. Magnetic storage has been with us for some time, since 3M introduced the first magnetic oxide recording tapes in 1947. This method depends on the physics of magnetism and electromagnetics. The optical method is relatively new. It was first introduced in 1984, but it has advanced at incredible speed. In 1987, world-wide standards for digital recording with optical media were established. The optical storage method uses a reflected laser beam focused on a plastic disk. Variations in the optical character of the disk surface contain the coded digital information. In this chapter, we will examine both of these storage media. Considerable space is given to the optical method in the belief that optical mass storage will be the standard of the future.

6-2   MAGNETIC MEDIA

Tape

The most familiar form of magnetic media is cassette recording tape. There is no difference between the tape used in audio recording and that used for digital recording. Recording tape is coated with a **ferric oxide** material, almost the equivalent of iron rust. These magnetic particles are distributed throughout the coating that covers one side of the tape surface. The particles tend to form clusters called **domains**. The domains can be thought of as tiny bar magnets each exhibiting a north and south pole. If a magnetic field is brought near the tape surface, the domains will align their poles in the same direction as the applied magnetic field. Figure 6-1 illustrates the magnetizing action on a tape surface.

Magnified Top View of Tape

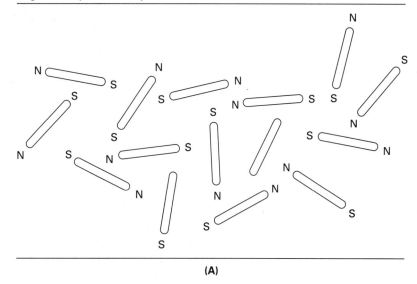

(A)

Magnified Top View of Tape

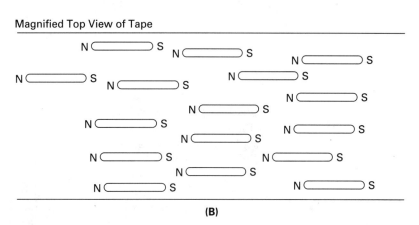

(B)

FIGURE 6-1 (A) Magnetic Tape, No Field Applied, Random Alignment (B) Alignment in Direction of Applied Field

Recording

The magnetic field used to influence the alignment of particles on tape is produced by a recording head. The recording head is an electromagnetic device that has a **gap** as seen in Figure 6-2. When an electrical potential is applied to the winding, lines of magnetic force (flux), are concentrated around the gap in the core. The purpose of the gap is to concentrate the density of the applied field. Both the intensity and direction of the flux field can be varied by the strength and direction of the electric current through the winding on the core. The tape is passed over the gap in the head while the current in the head is varied. The domains will assume an alignment that corresponds with the strength and direction of the current through the winding. The magnetized domains will remain aligned in the direction of the applied flux field after the field is removed.

Playback

If the tape is then passed over the gap again, the field created by the magnetized particles (domains) will induce an electric current through the gap and into the winding. These tiny currents can then be amplified and the tape will reproduce the exact patterns that were recorded on it.

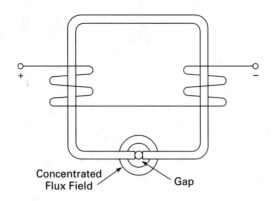

FIGURE 6-2 Recording Head

Concentrated
Flux Field   Gap

Recording 1's and 0's

The methods used to record digital signals, that is, 1's and 0's, are referred to as code or coding. A logic-1 or a logic-0 represents a steady or stable state that is more like DC than anything else. A steady state signal is not suitable for recording on a magnetic media. For this reason, coding consists of modulating data into a suitable DC-free format. Dozens of these codes have been devised and, therefore we will only discuss a few representative examples. Most other codes are variations on the basic types.

Return-to-Zero

Probably the earliest code devised was the **Return-to-Zero** method. A positive pulse represents a logic-1 while a negative pulse represents logic-0 (Fig. 6-3). The main problem here is that there are really three states. During logic-1, the recorded magnetic field is in one direction, during logic-0 the field is in the opposite direction. But between each bit, a zero state exists where the field is neither in one direction or the other. It is between the two opposite states. Among the difficulties with this is that the tape must be erased before new information can be recorded. In addition, the electrical zero state is sensitive to noise spikes which cause false 1's or 0's.

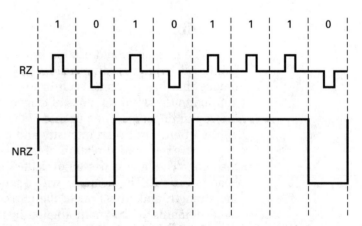

FIGURE 6-3 Recording Methods

Non-Return-to-Zero

The **Non-Return-to-Zero (NRZ)** is shown below the RZ method in Figure 6-3. In this variation, the digital signals never remain at an electrical zero. The magnetized particles are either fully saturated in one direction or the other. Current is always flowing in the head. Since the tape is always fully magnetized in one direction or the other, it is less sensitive to noise. Moreover, the old data can simply be recorded over with new data without having to erase.

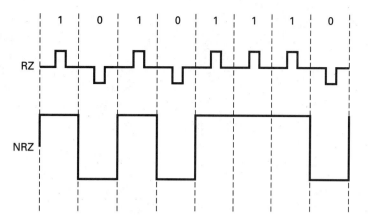

FIGURE 6-3 Recording Methods

FM

In order to encode and track each bit, a clock pulse is inserted at the beginning of each bit cell (Fig. 6-4). The clock pulse, C, is always present but the logic frame just after a clock pulse will contain a pulse only if a logic-1 is to be recorded. This frame will not contain a pulse if a logic-0 is recorded. The standard bit cell is 4 microseconds wide. Therefore, a logic-0 cell, one that has only a clock pulse present, will occur at the rate of 250 Khz. A logic-1 cell contains twice the number of transitions that a logic-0 cell contains. The logic-1 rate occurs at twice the frequency or 500 Khz, hence the name double frequency or **frequency modulation**.

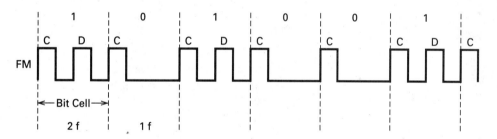

FIGURE 6-4 Frequency Modulation (FM)

MFM

The **Modified Frequency Modulation (MFM)** method is more widely used today than any other. With this method, the time for a bit cell is short-ened to 2 microseconds. To accommodate the increased density of transi-tions, excess transitions have been removed. This is done by eliminating the clock transitions altogether in logic-1 cells and inserting them only in cells where successive logic-0's are present, as in Figure 6-5. This method allows the recording of twice the amount of data as the FM method.

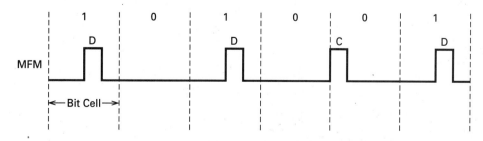

FIGURE 6-5 Modified Frequency Modulation (MFM)

Tone or Pulse Burst Methods

A further method of encoding is to assign logic-1's a certain tone frequency or burst of tone while logic-0's are assigned another. An example of this is the so called Kansas City Standard used in hobby systems. In this method, eight cycles of a 2400-Hz tone represent a logic-1. Four cycles of a 1200-Hz tone represent a logic-0 (Fig. 6-6). The waveforms are usually sinusoidal in shape.

FIGURE 6-6 Kansas City Standard

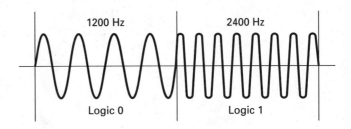

1200 Hz   2400 Hz

Logic 0   Logic 1

Additional Coding

In addition to the coding for logic-1 and logic-0, the data can be divided into *words* or strings consisting of 8 bits or some other fixed length. The words can then be grouped in blocks or *records*, also of a fixed length. A standard record length is 256 or 512 words. Moreover, several **tracks** can be recorded on a single wide band of tape using parallel recording heads. Larger computers use 7, 9, or even 18 parallel-track tape on reel-to-reel-type storage systems.

Access

Even though data is in a parallel format (recorded on parallel tracks), it still requires sequential access. If you are interested in a block of data stored at the end of a tape, you are obliged to run through all the data on the tape before reaching it. On the other hand, disk systems offer almost immediate access. Disk systems are classed as direct-access storage methods and offer a considerable advantage over tape systems.

 SELF-CHECK FOR SECTIONS 6-1, 6-2

1. Explain the need for mass storage.
2. What are domains?
3. Explain what happens to domains when exposed to a magnetic field.
4. What is the purpose of the gap in a recording head?
5. Explain how recording on magnetic tape works.
6. Explain how playback works.
7. What does *non-return-to-zero* mean?
8. Draw a diagram explaining a bit cell.
9. Explain FM as it relates to magnetic recording of digital data.
10. Explain the Kansas City Standard.
11. Explain the purpose of tracks on tape.

6-3   MAGNETIC DISKS

The Diskette

In 1970, IBM introduced an 8 inch mylar disk in a square PVC envelope (Fig. 6-7). The envelope is fairly stiff but the disk or **diskette**, as it is called, is flexible. This probably contributed to the name *floppy diskette*. The diskette has a hole in the center for placement on a rotating spindle and an oblong slot cut in the envelope that exposes the spinning diskette. The diskette is coated with the same magnetic ferric oxide as recording tape. The storage of data is on rings of concentric tracks accessed with a **record head** that moves perpendicular to the tracks. The diskette is rotated inside the envelope at a speed of 300 rpm. The head is in constant contact with the coated diskette and positioned with a stepper motor across 78 concentric tracks.

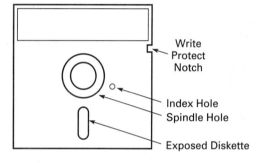

FIGURE 6-7 Floppy Diskette

Write Protection

The notch labeled **write protect** is used to prevent accidental recording of information. With magnetic media, it is possible to record over old information or accidentally record over and destroy information that is needed. By placing a piece of tape over this notch, a switch inside the disk drive is activated which prevents the disk drive circuitry from being placed in the record or write mode.

Indexing

In order to find data on the diskette, a form of **indexing** is required. An index hole near the spindle hole is used for this purpose. The arrangement uses an LED light source and a photo cell combination for the detection of an index pulse. The index pulse marks the beginning of the circular tracks. One pulse is produced for every revolution.

Sectoring

As a further method for orienting the data on a diskette, a sectoring system is used. Figure 6-8 shows a diskette divided into eight sectors by using sector holes. The same LED and photo cell arrangement used for indexing is used to detect sector holes. Figure 6-8(C) shows the pulse train of both the index and sector holes. The system of holes that divide the disk into sectors is called *hard-sectoring.* An 8 inch hard-sectored diskette usually has thirty-two sector holes.

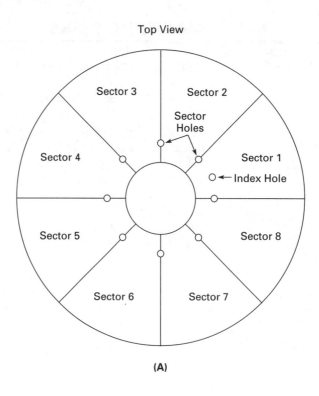

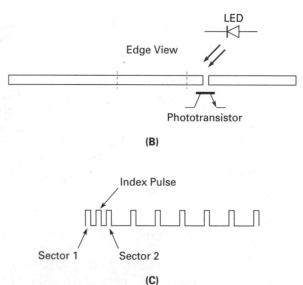

FIGURE 6-8 (A) View of Hard Sectored Diskette (B) LED/Phototransistor (C) Pulse Train Generated By Holes and Photocell

The 5 1/4 inch diskette

The 8 inch diskette quickly gave way to the 5 1/4 inch size which was introduced by Shugart and Associates in 1976. In addition, the hard sectoring has given way to the *soft* sectoring method. In soft sectoring, the beginning of a sector is marked by a recorded number. The beginning of each sector has not only the prerecorded sector number but the track number and certain other pertinent data. This prerecorded information is called the format and the action of placing this important data onto the diskette before data is recorded is called **formatting**.

Formats

Blank diskettes are prepared for use by the operating system of the computer by *formatting.* Formatting arranges the sectors and tracks and identifies them so that the microprocessor can know where a given sector starts, how long or how much data it contains and where it ends. The format also includes a directory (DIR) so that the files can be located by name. The directory also contains information regarding the location of empty sectors so that the microprocessor knows where to record new data. A look-up table is generated for this purpose called a file allocation table (FAT). The outer track is the first track and is numbered track 00 while sectors start with number one. Early versions of IBM DOS for 51/4 inch diskettes called for 9 soft sectors and 40 tracks. Later versions use 15 sectors and 80 tracks. Figure 6-9 illustrates an example format for a 51/4 inch floppy diskette.

FIGURE 6-9 Format Information Contained in a Sector

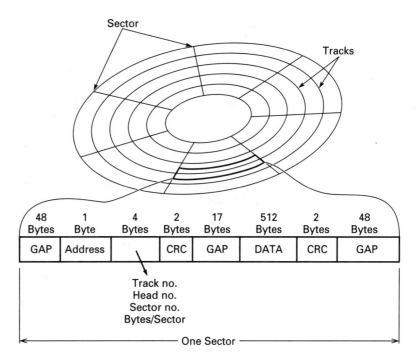

Error Detection

A very important part of recording data on a disk is the method used to detect an error in recording or playback. Part of the disk format for a sector of data includes a space set aside for the error detection procedure. The most commonly used method is called the Cyclic Redundancy Check or **CRC.** Here is basically how it works. The data recorded in any sector is taken as an uninterrupted serial string of bits. The bits in the string are used as the coefficients to generate a characteristic polynomial. This polynomial is used to generate a 16-bit number that is unique to the data stream used to generate it. The 16-bit number is calculated and then recorded in the CRC area for each sector. When the data is read, a CRC circuit again reads the data and performs the calculation. If any bit in the data stream is different, the calculation will result in a new 16-bit number. If the numbers do not match, the data must be reread. Depending on the system, if the calculation does not match what has been recorded in the CRC area for a given sector after a given number of retries, an error message is presented.

Tracks

Track density, that is, how close together the tracks are, is measured in tracks per inch or **TPI**. For a 5 1/4 inch diskette, the normal track density is 48 TPI. The rated track density figure, such as 48 TPI, is a measure of its quality, in the sense that the density measure for a diskette should not be exceeded. Recording 40 tracks on a diskette rated at 48 TPI is acceptable. A single side holds about 180 Kbytes or 180,000 8-bit words. By constructing the read-write head to contact both sides of the diskette at once, 360 Kbytes are possible. Later developments have allowed the doubling of track density to 96 TPI, and we have seen that the MFM method also effectively doubles amount of recorded information. Again, a 96 TPI diskette need not necessarily have 96 tracks. In the DOS environment, 80 tracks are common. This has led to the usage of 5 1/4 inch diskettes with a storage area of four times the standard capacity or about 1.2 Mbytes.

The 3 1/2 inch Diskette

The latest standardized modification to the disk media was the introduction of the 3 1/2 inch microfloppy from IBM. The microfloppy has a track density of 135 TPI, uses 80 tracks and stores either 720 Kbytes or 1.44 Mbytes of data. The *floppy* may have become somewhat of a misnomer. The diskette itself is still produced with flexible mylar but the protective jacket is now made of hard plastic (Fig. 6-10). This allows a sliding door to be mounted over the slot provided to access the tracks. The door protects the diskette itself from contamination. Also the write protect mechanism has been changed to a sliding plastic tab so that tape is no longer necessary to write protect a diskette. There has also been a major change in the index system. The microfloppy does not have an index hole but instead, uses a pin and slot mechanism that always engages and aligns the diskette exactly in the same way every time it is placed on the hub.

FIGURE 6-10 3 1/2 inch Minidiskette

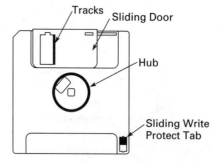

Hard Disk Drives

The IBM 350, a memory unit with rotating solid rigid disks was introduced back in 1957, long before the floppy diskette. And it was again IBM that brought to market a dual, hard-drive unit that contained two 30 Mbyte drives called a 30-30. The connection with the Winchester rifle was natural and since then, rigid drives have also been known as Winchesters.

Rigid Platters

Hard disk drives are made with aluminum platters stacked much like a juke box record player. The platters are from 3 1/2 to 14 inches in diameter and coated with the same ferric oxide material used on tapes and diskettes. There are at least two or more platters mounted on a common spindle as seen in Figure 6-11. The rotation speed is considerably faster than floppy diskettes, ranging from 2400 rpm to 6000 rpm. Unlike the floppy, which rotates only during an access, the rigid platters rotate constantly while the drive is powered up.

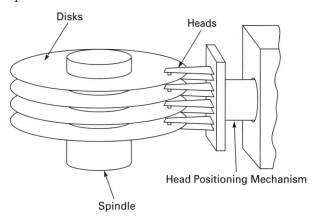

FIGURE 6-11 Rigid Disk Drive Assembly

The Heads

If the head were to come into contact with the platter at these speeds, it could be disastrous. The heat and friction would destroy both the head and the disk surface with a resulting loss of the data. For this reason, heads are aerodynamically designed to actually *fly* above the surface in the air pressure created from disk rotation. The head to surface clearance is very small, about .1 mil, much smaller than the diameter of a human hair. Safety mechanisms are built in so that the heads cannot be inserted until the rotation speed is correct. By the same means, the heads are immediately retracted should the speed drop for any reason. A *landing area* is provided outside the recording area where the heads come to rest when the drive is turned off.

Head Positioning

There are two methods commonly used to position the heads over the tracks. The older method is a voice coil arrangement and is shown in Figure 6-12. This system is more likely to be found in larger drives. The voice coil mechanism is similar to the magnet and coil in a large loudspeaker. The inductive motor develops considerable power and speed which greatly enhances access time for a given track. The other method, more commonly found in newer smaller drives is the rotating head positioner arm. The pivot arm rotates through a mechanical linkage driven with a stepper motor (Fig. 6-13).

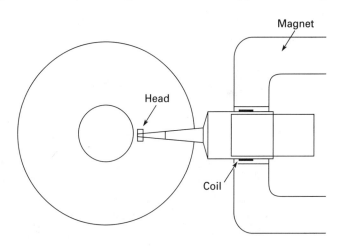

FIGURE 6-12 Voice Coil Head Positioner

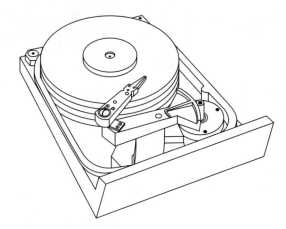

FIGURE 6-13 Pivot Arm Head Positioner

Tracks and Cylinders

Hard drive platters can have up to 2,000 tracks. Because the multiple heads are connected to a common drive, the same track is accessed simultaneously on all platters (Fig. 6-14). The columns of coincidental tracks are called **cylinders**. An address for data is based on the head number and on a cylinder number.

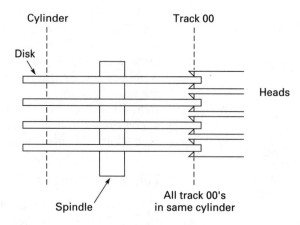

FIGURE 6-14 All Tracks With the Same Number Are in the Same Cylinder.

Capacity

Obviously the capacity of a hard drive is much greater than that of a diskette. Portability is the main advantage of the diskette, but when greater capacity is needed, there is no substitute for a hard drive. Capacities have been constantly growing while the size of hard drives has been decreasing. A 40-Mbyte drive that fit into a PC was quite new in 1986. But today, a 5 1/4 inch floppy slot accommodates drives with a capacity of 1.2 Gbytes (1×10^9) and 40 Mbyte 3 1/2 inch rigid drives are common place.

✔ SELF-CHECK FOR SECTION 6-3

12. What principle is used for recording on diskettes?
13. Explain the purpose of a write protect notch.
14. Explain indexing.
15. What is a sector on a disk?
16. What is a format?
17. What is the purpose of CRC?
18. Track density is measured in _____.
19. What recording principle is used on hard disks?
20. Explain a cylinder on a hard disk.

6-4   OPTICAL STORAGE

Introduction

Optical disk storage technology is relatively new but holds much promise for the future. Originally conceived for the audio industry as an alternative to records, it became the fastest growing consumer electronic device in history. The computer industry has also been quick to adopt it as a storage media.

The compact disk or CD disk is a 4 3/4 inch polycarbonate (an extremely hard form of plexiglass) disk that uses an optical method to store up to 660 Mbytes of information. At least one encyclopedia company is already offering their entire set of volumes on this medium. The CD-Audio disk is physically identical to the CD-ROM and both contain over 3 miles of storage track.

Optical Pickup

The optical pickup unit of the compact disk drive is analogous to the record head in a magnetic device. Its job is to transform optical information from the disk into electrical impulses. This is accomplished by shining a highly focused laser beam onto the disk and sensing the strength of the reflected light. The intensity of the reflected light is affected by **pits and lands** on the surface of the disk. The depth of a pit is 1/4 the wavelength of the laser beam light frequency. This ultimately causes the refraction of the pit to be different from the refraction of a land area by shifting the phase of the light beam. This shifting causes a destructive interference in the refracted beam reducing its intensity.

Since the laser beam is larger than the pit area, the resultant reflected light will consist of light from the pit and light from the adjacent land area, or it will consist of light from a land area alone. Note that in the illustration, Figure 6-15, the laser spot overlaps the pit. The pit and land areas are the cause of the difference in intensity of the reflected beam. This difference in the reflected beam is read with photo diodes that detect its strength and convert it into electrical signals.

FIGURE 6-15 Section of Track Area on CD-Disk

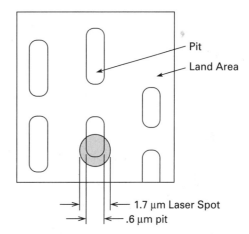

Optical Pickup Structure

The laser beam is generated with a semiconductor PN junction device that emits coherent light at 790 nanometers in wavelength and at about 5 mw of power (Fig. 6-16). Due to the very small tolerances necessary, an intricate focusing and tracking mechanism must be used. Two small side beams are created in the diffraction grating plate. They are used for radial tracking. The three beams are then passed together through a **collimator** lens that adjusts the three beams so that they are parallel. Next the light is focused through a **polarized beam** splitter. The **beam splitter** allows the light from the collimator to pass, but it will redirect reflected light 90 degrees down to the photodiode. The polarized beam splitter passes horizontally polarized light from the laser, but it eliminates the vertical component. Then the light passes through a quarter-wave plate that shifts it 90 degrees. The light then reflects off the disk and again passes through the quarter-wave plate. This shifts it once more by 90 degrees, so that it has been shifted a total of 180 degrees and is vertically polarized. It can no longer pass back through the polarized beam splitter that admits only horizontally polarized light. It is, therefore, reflected by 90 degrees to a focusing lens and into the photodiode.

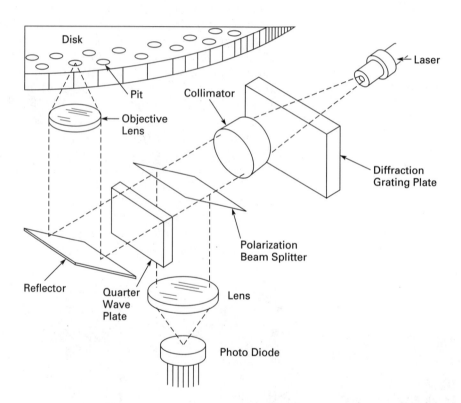

FIGURE 6-16 Optical Pickup Diagram

Disk Surface

The beam focused on the transparent surface of the disk is a round spot .8 mm in diameter. The transparent layer of the disk is 1.2 mm deep and has a refractive index of n = 15. This reduces the laser spot down to 1.7 micrometers (Fig. 6-17) and helps to compensate for dirt on the disk surface. Any dirt particles are reduced in effective size because of the refractive index of the 1.2 mm transparent thickness.

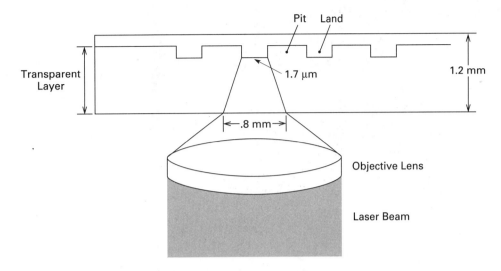

FIGURE 6-17 Transparent Layer Reduces Laser Beam Spot

Radial Tracking

The two side beams generated in the diffraction grating plate follow the main beam throughout the entire pickup device. They end up focused to either side of the photodiode on two additional photodiodes. The side beams are aimed somewhat to the side of main beam on the disk surface, as in Figure 6-18. If the main beam is centered, the reflected intensity from both side beams will be equal and the photodiodes will have an equal output. In this case, no radial correction in tracking is necessary. If the main beam is off track to the right, as in Figure 6-19(A), the photodiode currents will be unequal and a correction signal will be generated. If the main beam is off track to the left, as in Figure 6-19(C), the left photodiode will have more light and a left correction signal will be generated.

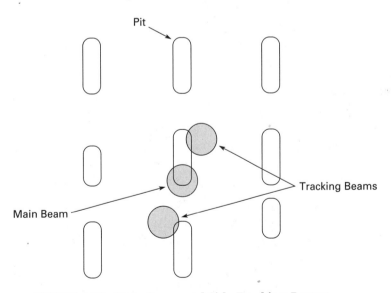

FIGURE 6-18 Main Beam and Side Tracking Beams

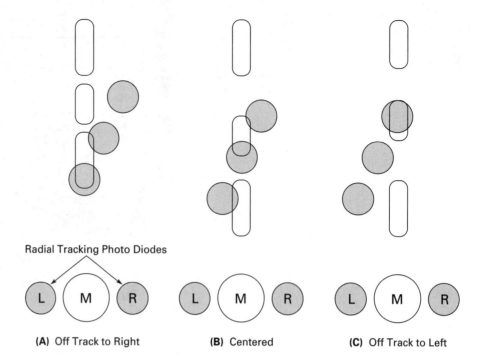

FIGURE 6-19 Radial Tracking Photo Diodes

Radial Tracking Photo Diodes

(A) Off Track to Right   (B) Centered   (C) Off Track to Left

Focusing

Variations in disk-to-lens heights due to irregularities or warping must be compensated for in the focus mechanism. This is accomplished in the main photodiode itself, giving it a dual purpose. The photodiode is divided into 4 quadrants. If the reflected beam is perfectly round, as in Figure 6-20(B), all four quadrants will have the same output and the beam is focused. If the laser spot is too close to the disk surface, Figure 6-20(A), an elliptical spot is formed. In this case, quadrants A and C receive more light which activates the servo to increase the distance from the lens to the disk. If the disk surface is too far, a spot such as shown in Figure 6-20(C) is formed. In this instance, the quadrants B and D receive more light and generate a signal to decrease the surface to lens distance.

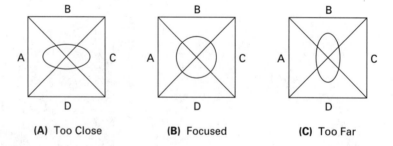

FIGURE 6-20 Four Quadrant Photo Diode and Focus Spot

(A) Too Close   (B) Focused   (C) Too Far

Tracks

The optical pickup must search for and find up to 20,000 tracks on the disk. Due to the heavy track density, the speed control assembly on optical media is quite different from magnetic media. Magnetic disks rotate at a constant angular velocity. In other words, the disks rotate at a fixed speed. CDs rotate at a **constant linear velocity**. This means the speed of the disk depends on where the **pick up** head is located. The constant linear velocity is 1.3 meters per second. In this way, when the pick up head is located at the innermost tracks, the disk spins at about 500 rpm. When the pick up head is at the outer tracks, the speed is reduced to about 200 rpm.

The rotating optical pick up arm for accessing tracks is illustrated in Figure 6-21. The mechanical assembly is such that extremely small steps are possible in the positioning of the optical pickup head.

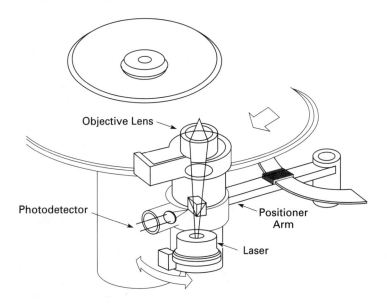

FIGURE 6-21 Optical Pickup Positioner

Recording on Optical Media

The technology for recording and then rerecording (called rewritable) lags somewhat behind the *read only* capability. No doubt, this technology will come into its own in the next few years. Presently, there are three main contenders for *erasable* CD-ROM, reversible dye, magneto-optic and phase-change techniques. Tandy Corporation is working with a dye method, but both dyes and phase-change modes are based on polymer technology that does not currently meet the number of read/write cycles necessary.

Magneto-Optics

The magneto-optic method is a combination of both new and old technologies. A laser is used as a tiny heating element to heat the disk surface coated with a film of rare earth metals. The heat of the beam causes the coercivity of the coating to change. Coercivity is the measure of reverse magnetic force necessary to reduce the magnetic flux of a magnet to zero. In other words it indicates the strength of an opposing magnetic field necessary to demagnetize a metal. The spots that have been changed by the laser heat can be easily magnetized by the field surrounding a coil. The coil magnetizes the spots in the opposite direction of the areas that have not been heated. The spots that were not heated retain their original magnetic character.

Kerr-Faraday Effect

This technology has been around for a while. Its basic principle is that the polarization of reflected light is affected by the magnetic property of the reflecting surface. Now that we have changed the property of the surface by heating and magnetizing, we need only to detect the phase change in the reflected light. This, of course, is exactly what the optical pickup head does in the CD-ROM. The intensity of the laser is reduced in order that a read operation can take place without altering the disk.

Erasing

The erasure is accomplished by realigning the domains in the rare earth material, so that the entire surface is aligned with the same magnetic polarity. The surface is again heated and a realigning field is applied from the coil.

Erasable CD-ROM

The technology that is ultimately adopted as a standard will undoubtedly use a combination of some of the techniques we have discussed. The limitations currently seem to lie in the chemical composition of the disk material and not the electronics available. In addition, economics of the right combination are of major importance. The solution that works will be the one that brings the most cost-effective mass-storage unit to market.

✔ SELF-CHECK FOR SECTION 6-4

21. What is the purpose of a pick-up head on an optical system?
22. Explain pits and lands.
23. Explain the function of a collimator.
24. Explain radial tracking of the beam.
25. CD disks rotate at a constant _____ velocity.

SUMMARY OF IDEAS

- Mass storage devices meet the need for large capacity, nonvolatile digital storage methods.
- The two most widely used media for mass storage are magnetic and optical media.
- Magnetic recording media uses ferric oxide coatings to render the media sensitive to magnetic fields.
- Varying the current in the winding of the record head varies strength of the flux field formed in the head gap.
- Record and playback of digital signals take place through the same head.
- The main drawback of tape as a storage medium is its sequential access limitation.
- Standard floppy diskette sizes are 8 inch, 5 1/4 inch, and 3 1/2 inch.
- The system of using a hole through which a photo cell and LED indicate the beginning of the disk is called indexing.
- The method of dividing a disk into several pie shaped slices is called sectoring.
- Hard-sectored disks use punched holes to indicate sectors while soft sectoring uses a recorded binary number to indicate sectors.
- Formatting refers to the prerecorded housekeeping information on a disk that helps organize and label the data storage areas.
- Coding refers to the way in which digital data is modulated to encode the logic-1's and 0's.
- The standard 5 1/4 inch floppy holds about 360 Kbytes but 1.2 Mbyte capacities are not uncommon.
- The 3 1/2 inch mini-floppy has a capacity of 720K or 1.44 Mbytes.
- Hard drives use rigid aluminum platters that constantly rotate. The head assembly accesses a vertical cylinder of tracks simultaneously.

- Hard drives that have a capacity of 1.2 Gbytes and fit into a PC are commercially available. Standard sizes though are more modest at about 40 Mbytes.
- CD-ROMs are plastic disks that use an optical encoding method for storage of data.
- Data on the surface of an optical disk is encoded in a series of pits and lands. The refractive property of a pit is different from the land area.
- The optical pick-up head focuses a laser beam on the CD-ROM tracks and senses the difference in the refractive character of the disk surface.
- The capacity of a 4 3/4 inch CD-ROM is about 660 Mbytes.

CHAPTER QUESTIONS & PROBLEMS

True or False
1. Because of the large capacity of a mass storage device, the recorded data need not be digitized.
2. In a Non-Return-to-Zero recording code, the logic-0 level is eliminated.
3. The density of recorded bits is doubled by doubling the number of recorded tracks on a diskette.
4. Radial tracking on optical media is accomplished by sensing the shape of the reflected laser spot.
5. The CD-ROM disk is rotated at a constant linear velocity.

Fill in the Blanks
6. Lines of magnetic flux are _____ around the gap in the core material of the record head.
7. In the FM method of coding digital information on diskettes, the beginning of every bit cell contains a _____.
8. A 5 1/4 diskette has a small hole near the spindle hole that is used for_____ the diskette.
9. The 3 beams generated in the CD-ROM optical pick up are made parallel by a _____.
10. A four-quadrant photodiode is used to _____ the CD-ROM laser beam.

Multiple Choice
11. A double-sided, double-density 5 1/4 inch diskette with a recording capacity of 1.2 Mbytes probably has
    a. 48 tracks.   c. 135 tracks.
    b. 40 tracks.   d. 80 tracks.

12. Which of the following is not included in the format of a diskette?
    a. the CRC
    b. sector number
    c. track number
    d. data block

13. Which of the following is not true.
    a. Tracks on a diskette pass the head at a constant linear velocity.
    b. The diskette need not be in constant rotation if no access is requested.
    c. Magnetic diskettes are sensitive to any magnet or strong electrical field.
    d. Hard disk drives also have sectors.

14. The elimination of excess transitions in recording data is most characteristic of
    a. tone modulation.
    b. MFM.
    c. FM.
    d. Non-Return-to-Zero.

15. Which statement is true?
    a. Hard sectoring methods eliminate the use of an indexing hole.
    b. The mini-floppy (3 1/2") uses soft sectoring and no index hole.
    c. The mini-floppy no longer has a write protect mechanism.
    d. all of the above

16. Which of the following groups would be the most logical to use in order to locate data on a hard disk?
    a. Sector, Format, Track, Head
    b. Cylinder, Head, Sector, Index
    c. Index, Track, Head, Sector
    d. Cylinder, Head, Sector, Track

17. The polarized beam splitter
    a. creates three parallel beams.
    b. rejects horizontally polarized light.
    c. shifts the laser beam 90 degrees.
    d. rejects vertically polarized light.

18. Radial tracking is accomplished by
    a. a 4-quadrant photodiode circuit.
    b. measuring the intensity of the two side beams.
    c. detecting the shape of the reflected laser spot.
    d. collimating the laser beams before they are shifted.

19. Focusing the laser is accomplished by
    a. a photo cell and LED arrangement.
    b. detecting the shape of the reflected laser spot.
    c. collimating the laser beams before they are shifted.
    d. a 180-degree phase shift between the laser and the reflected light.

20. Which of the following most accurately describes the transparent layer on the CD-ROM disk?
    a. It causes a horizontal polarization of the reflected light.
    b. It causes a 180 degree phase shift in the laser beam.
    c. It shifts the light by 90 degrees.
    d. It reduces the laser spot to about the width of the recorded pits.

BINARY REVISITED

OUTLINE

NEW TERMS TO WATCH FOR

Binary-Coded Decimal
Floating Point
Octal
Normalize

Fixed Point
Gray Code
Exponent
Fixed Length

Excess-3
Mantissa
Hexadecimal

After completing this chapter, you should be able to:

1. Recognize and use the binary encoding systems for decimal representation.
2. Convert decimal numbers to BCD and BCD representations to decimal.
3. Use the special methods necessary for BCD math operations.
4. Understand what a microprocessor does to make use of BCD arithmetic.
5. Describe the excess-3 binary method for encoding numbers.
6. Name the advantage of excess-3 encoding.
7. Explain the need for Gray-coded binary and how it is used.
8. Define the octal number system and name its main advantage.
9. Convert from octal to decimal, octal to binary, and convert in the reverse direction.
10. Describe and use the hexadecimal number system.
11. Convert decimal and binary to hexadecimal numbers and convert hexadecimal numbers to either binary or decimal.
12. Explain the difference between fixed- and floating-point numbers.
13. Normalize numbers for use in a floating-point system.
14. Show how a fixed length binary number is apportioned for use as a floating-point number.

7-1   INTRODUCTION

Learning the binary number system and the theory of different number bases is only a beginning. With this background, you are now prepared to study several other useful formats that have their basis in the binary system. These additional methods of number representations are used chiefly because they are, in certain applications, more convenient than binary itself. Of course, they are designed to help us, not the microprocessor, because the microprocessor has no need for anything but binary numbers.

In Chapter 2, we discovered the way in which binary math operations are carried out. In addition, we saw the method for representing both positive and negative binary numbers. The drawback to binary numbers is that they require considerably more positions. To represent large binary numbers, long strings of 1's and 0's must be dealt with. As a result of the unwieldy length of binary numbers and codes, methods have been developed to solve the problem and to make binary easier to manage. In this chapter, we will discover two more number base systems and some shortcuts to binary representation.

7-2   BINARY-CODED DECIMAL

Weighted Code

As we have stated, binary numbers are not generally useful in the world outside of computer systems. In the outside world, we will continue to use the decimal system. For this reason, we have developed shortcuts or ways to quickly get from a binary value to a decimal value and back again. One of the most commonly used methods is the **Binary-Coded Decimal** or BCD. The BCD is a 4-bit encoding method for representing all decimal digits from 0 to 9. It is also called the 8, 4, 2, 1-weighted code. This is because the *weights* or values of the positions in a 4-bit number correspond to this sequence.

$$2^3 \; 2^2 \; 2^1 \; 2^0$$
$$8 \quad 4 \quad 2 \quad 1$$

The BCD code is as follows:

BINARY	DECIMAL
0000	0
0001	1
0010	2
0011	3
0100	4
0101	5
0110	6
0111	7
1000	8
1001	9

Notice that with 4-bits, we could represent 16 decimal numbers. BCD is, however, only valid for 10 decimal digits, 0 through 9. The other six numbers are considered illegal.

Decimal to BCD

The conversion of a decimal number to a BCD number is simple. Each digit in a decimal number will require 4-bits. For example, the number 47_{10} requires 8 bits.

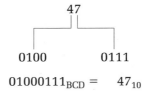

$01000111_{BCD} = 47_{10}$

The more digits a decimal number has, the larger the BCD number.

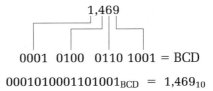

$0001010001101001_{BCD} = 1,469_{10}$

A four-position decimal number requires 16 bits.

BCD to Decimal

Conversion from a BCD number to a decimal number is equally simple:

$$0110 \quad 0010$$
$$\downarrow \quad \downarrow$$
$$6 \quad 2$$

$$62_{10} = 01100010_{BCD}$$

Starting at the LSB, count 4 bit positions to the left. Each 4-bit group represents a decimal from 0 to 9.

It is important to understand that a BCD number is an encoded decimal and *not* a pure binary number.

$$01100010_{BCD} = 62_{10} = 00111110_2$$
$$\text{BCD} \qquad\qquad \text{BINARY}$$
$$01100010_{BCD} = 00111110_2$$

Although a given bit string in BCD looks just like a binary number, because it is all 1's and 0's, its value is different. For example, the bit string 00010001_{BCD}, if it is considered to be a BCD representation will be 11_{10}. If 00010001_2 is considered to be a pure binary number, it will be 17_{10}.

BCD Arithmetic

Conversion from decimal to BCD and from BCD to decimal is easy and convenient. But math operations using BCD present a small problem. This is due to the fact that six of the possible 4-bit combinations are considered unusable or *illegal*.

What happens if a math operation generates one of the illegal combinations?

4	0100	BCD
+6	0110	BCD
10	1010	= illegal code

The binary addition is correct but the representation of 10_{10} in BCD is 00010000_{BCD} and not 00001010.

The way around this problem is to add 6 to any of the five illegal binary numbers.

$$
\begin{array}{cl}
4 & 0100 \\
+6 & 0110 \\
\hline
10 & 1010 \\
& +0110 \\
\hline
& 10000 \; = \; \text{BCD} \\
1 \qquad 0 & = \; \text{Decimal}
\end{array}
$$

Here is another BCD addition problem:

$$
\begin{array}{cll}
& \text{BCD} & \\
47 & 01000111 & \\
+26 & 00100110 & \\
\hline
73 & 01101101 & \text{illegal BCD code} \\
& +\;0110 & \text{add} +6 \\
\hline
& 01110011 & \text{BCD} \\
& 7 \quad 3 &
\end{array}
$$

In microprocessors, subtraction is usually done by adding complements. Recall that to form the 1's complement, all 1's are changed to 0's and all 0's are changed to 1's.

$$
\begin{array}{l}
32_{10} \; = \; 00110010_{\text{BCD}} \\
11001101 \; = \; \text{1's complement}
\end{array}
$$

However, 11001101 contains two illegal BCD numbers.

One way around this difficulty is to use the 10's complement. This is because BCD is a decimal representation.

For example, $52-32 = ?$

$$
\begin{array}{r}
52 \\
-32 \\
\hline
20 \;\; \text{using decimal subtraction}
\end{array}
$$

To subtract by adding, we form the 10's complement of -32 by first forming the 9's complement and adding 1.

$$
\begin{array}{rl}
99 & \\
-32 & \\
\hline
67 & = \; \text{9's complement} \\
+1 & \\
\hline
68 & = \; \text{10's complement}
\end{array}
$$

$$
\begin{array}{cccll}
52 & & 52 & 01010010_{\text{BCD}} & \\
-32 & & +68 & 01101000_{\text{BCD}} & \\
\hline
20 & 1 & 20 & 10111010 & \text{illegal} \\
& & & 01100110 & \text{add six to each BCD no.} \\
\text{discard} \longrightarrow & 1 & & 00100000 & \\
& & & 2 \quad 0 &
\end{array}
$$

Adding six to correct any illegal BCD number is the way in which many microprocessors do BCD arithmetic.

BCD is not the only binary-coded system to represent decimal numbers. There are other weighted codes such as 2421, 5421 and **excess-3**.

✔ SELF-CHECK FOR SECTIONS 7-1, 7-2

1. What is BCD?
2. How many bits in BCD would be required to encode the decimal number 144?
3. Are BCD numbers the same as binary numbers?
4. Explain how illegal BCD numbers are corrected.
5. Convert 459 to a BCD number.

7-3   EXCESS-3

The excess-3 code is another 4-bit binary code used to represent decimal numbers. Here is the excess-3 code:

EXCESS-3	DECIMAL
0011	0
0100	1
0101	2
0110	3
0111	4
1000	5
1001	6
1010	7
1011	8
1100	9

The interesting thing about this code is that it is *self-complementing*. The 9's complement of the decimal digit is obtained by complementing each bit of the excess-3 code.

Example:

DECIMAL		EXCESS-3	
Number	9's	Number	9's (in excess-3)
6	3	1001	0110
2	7	0101	1010

This makes the excess-3 code easy to use for the 10's complement subtraction.

EXCESS-3 SUBTRACTION

52	10000101	excess-3
−32	01100101	excess-3
	10011010	9's in excess-3
	+1	
	10011011	10's in excess-3

Now restating the problem by adding the 10's complement of 32:

52	10000101	excess-3
−32	10011011	10's in excess-3
20	00100000	
	2 0	

Although there are other codes possible that are self complementing, the excess-3 is the most commonly used one.

7-4   GRAY CODE

The **Gray code** is also a binary code. It is mainly used to encode binary numbers produced mechanically. This is because in mechanical design, there always exists the possibility that a mechanical contact will straddle two coded areas and produce an error. In pure binary, an error in one bit position could cause an error in magnitude as large as the MSB. Additionally, in pure binary, the coded areas used sometimes have to change as many as all four bit positions at one time, such as the change from 0111 (7_{10}) to 1000 (8_{10}). An instance such as this multiplies the possibility of error.

The characteristic feature of the Gray code is that only one bit position ever changes for any given sequential number. The Gray code is as follows:

GRAY CODE	DECIMAL
0000	0
0001	1
0011	2
0010	3
0110	4
0111	5
0101	6
0100	7
1100	8
1101	9
1111	10
1110	11
1010	12
1011	13
1001	14
1000	15

The disk in Figure 7-1 is a Gray-coded disk. As the disk rotates, electrical contacts placed on the four concentric tracks generate the Gray-coded binary numbers. Math operations with Gray code are possible, but complicated. For this reason, Gray code is rarely used to perform math. Conversion to binary is more practical.

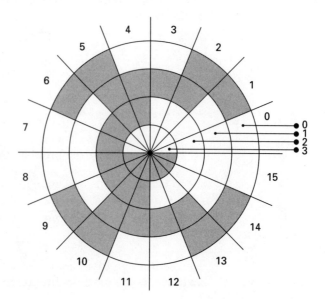

FIGURE 7-1 Gray-Coded Disk

7-5   OCTAL NUMBERS

The **octal** number system is a number system using the base of 8. In other words, this numbers system has only 8 possible unique symbols. They are:

OCTAL SYMBOLS

0
1
2
3
4
5
6
7

After the symbol "7" is used, we have to begin using the symbols over. This, we discovered in Chapter 2, is done with positional notation. Since it is the base 8 system, all positional values are a power of 8.

8^5	8^4	8^3	8^2	8^1	8^0
5th	4th	3rd	2nd	1st	Units
Position	Position	Position	Position	Position	Position

The powers of 8 for these positions are:

$$8^0 = 1$$
$$8^1 = 8 \times 1 = 8$$
$$8^2 = 8 \times 8 = 64$$
$$8^3 = 8 \times 8 \times 8 = 512$$
$$8^4 = 8 \times 8 \times 8 \times 8 = 4,096$$
$$8^5 = 8 \times 8 \times 8 \times 8 \times 8 = 32,768$$

This establishes the positional values for the octal system. In order to represent 8_{10} in octal, we need two positions, 10_8.

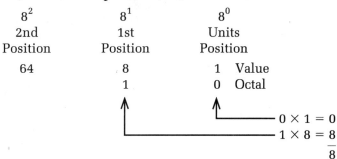

8^2	8^1	8^0
2nd	1st	Units
Position	Position	Position
64	8	1 Value
	1	0 Octal

$$0 \times 1 = 0$$
$$1 \times 8 = 8$$
$$\overline{8}$$

So that $8_{10} = 10_8$.

As another example, here is how we determine the decimal value of 507^8:

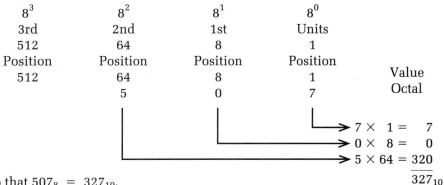

8^3	8^2	8^1	8^0
3rd	2nd	1st	Units
512	64	8	1
Position	Position	Position	Position
512	64	8	1 Value
5	0	7	Octal

$$7 \times 1 = 7$$
$$0 \times 8 = 0$$
$$5 \times 64 = 320$$
$$\overline{327_{10}}$$

So that $507_8 = 327_{10}$.

At first glance, this system would appear to have little if any advantage over the decimal system. Its true value is seen only in relation to binary numbers. Here is a table of octal numbers:

DECIMAL	BINARY	OCTAL
0	0000	0
1	0001	1
2	0010	2
3	0011	3
4	0100	4
5	0101	5
6	0110	6
7	0111	7
8	1000	10
9	1001	11
10	1010	12
11	1011	13
12	1100	14
13	1101	15
14	1110	16
15	1111	17

Note that the first 8 digits in octal can be represented with a 3-bit number. We don't need the fourth place. This means that octal can be used for directly encoding binary numbers, similar to the way it is done with BCD. For example,

5	0	7	Octal/Base 8
101	000	111	Binary/Base 2

Once more, the significance of this is not obvious until we realize that 101000111 is the binary number 327_{10}. The difference between this sort of code and BCD is now obvious. We can go directly from octal to a true binary number with a 3-bit encoding method. In addition, the process is also reversible, that is, we can go directly from binary to octal.

Octal-to-Binary Conversion

To convert the octal number 64 to binary:

	64		Octal
110		100	Binary

To check this, note that both the binary number and octal number convert to the same base-10 number, but note also how easy it is to convert from octal to decimal.

Convert 110100 to base 10

$$32 + 16 + 0 + 4 + 0 + 0 = 52$$

Convert 64_8 to base 10

$$4 \times 1 = 4$$
$$6 \times 8 = 48$$
$$\overline{52}$$

Binary-to-Octal Conversion

To convert a binary number to octal, we begin at the least significant bit position and form 3-bit groups. For example, convert the binary 001011011 to octal.

Begin by forming 3-bit groups:

001	011	011	Binary
1	3	3	Octal

To check this:

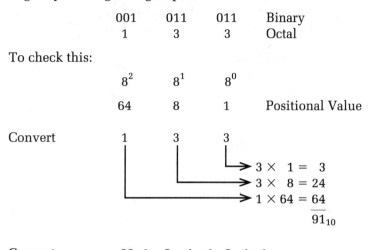

8^2	8^1	8^0	
64	8	1	Positional Value

Convert   1   3   3

$$3 \times 1 = 3$$
$$3 \times 8 = 24$$
$$1 \times 64 = 64$$
$$\overline{91_{10}}$$

Convert   00 1 0 1 1 0 1 1

$$64+0+16+8+0+2+1 = 91_{10}$$

Many computer systems have been designed using the octal number base because of the ease of transferring from octal to binary. Nevertheless, a base-8 system still requires more positions than the decimal or base-10 system. There is another system that has found widespread popularity because it has even fewer positions. In addition, like the octal or base-8 system it will also convert directly to binary. This system is called **hexadecimal**.

7-6   HEXADECIMAL

The hexadecimal number system, or *hex* as it is called, uses the base 16. This means that in hexadecimal there are 16 unique symbols.
They are:

DECIMAL	HEX
1	1
2	2
3	3
4	4
5	5
6	6
7	7
8	8
9	9
10	A
11	B
12	C
13	D
14	E
15	F

The positional values of each symbol are based on the powers of 16.

16^5	16^4	16^3	16^2	16^1	16^0
5th	4th	3rd	2nd	1st	Units
Position	Position	Position	Position	Position	Position

The value of these positions are:

$$
\begin{aligned}
16^0 &&&= 1 \\
16^1 &= 16 \times 1 &&= 16 \\
16^2 &= 16 \times 16 &&= 256 \\
16^3 &= 16 \times 16 \times 16 &&= 4{,}096 \\
16^4 &= 16 \times 16 \times 16 \times 16 &&= 65{,}536 \\
16^5 &= 16 \times 16 \times 16 \times 16 \times 16 &&= 1{,}048{,}576
\end{aligned}
$$

Hexadecimal Numbers

A hex number representing a 16-bit memory address might look like this, $1A2E_{16}$.

There are two ways to approach a hex representation if we need to know the decimal value. We could convert it using the positional values to find the decimal equivalent or we could convert it to binary and then find the decimal value. Here's how it works:

Convert 1A2E to decimal.

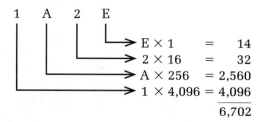

$$
\begin{aligned}
E \times 1 &= 14 \\
2 \times 16 &= 32 \\
A \times 256 &= 2{,}560 \\
1 \times 4{,}096 &= \underline{4{,}096} \\
&\ 6{,}702
\end{aligned}
$$

We can also convert a hex number directly to binary. In hex, we use all 4 bits in a 4-bit group to represent the symbols 0 to F. Using Table 7-1 or your memory, convert each 4-bit group, beginning at the LSB, to the binary equivalent:

1	A	2	E
0001	1010	0010	1110

$$1A2E_{16} = 0001101000101110_2$$

If needed, we can convert this binary number into a decimal:

000 1 1 0 1 0 0 0 1 0 1 1 1 0
↓ ↓ ↓ ↓ ↓ ↓ ↓ ↓ ↓ ↓ ↓ ↓ ↓
$$4096 + 2048 + 0 + 512 + 0 + 0 + 0 + 32 + 0 + 8 + 4 + 2 + 0 = 6{,}702_{10}$$

But in many cases, it is not necessary to know the decimal value of a binary number. We simply go back and forth between hex and binary.

Hexadecimal Math

There are several approaches to hexadecimal arithmetic. One way is to convert the hex number to its 4-bit, binary equivalent, use binary addition and convert back to hexadecimal.

Below is an example of hex addition using this idea.

$$
\begin{array}{rl}
1\,D\,6\,4_{16} & \quad 0001\ 1101\ 0110\ 0100_2 \\
+\,2\,3\,F\,E_{16} & \quad 0010\ 0011\ 1111\ 1110_2 \\
\hline
& \quad 0100\ 0001\ 0110\ 0010_2 \\
& \qquad 4 \quad\ \ 1 \quad\ \ 6 \quad\ \ 2_{16}
\end{array}
$$

Hexadecimal numbers can also be added directly. Since the decimal addition values, such as 2 + 2, are learned at a very early age, simply substitute in your head for the hex symbols A through F. A_{16} plus 2_{16} is simply 10_{10} plus 2_{10} or 12_{10}.

For example:

$$
\begin{aligned}
A_{16} &= 10_{10} \\
+\ 2_{16} &= +\ 2_{10} \\
\hline
C_{16} &= 12_{10}
\end{aligned}
$$

If the sum turns out to be greater than 15_{10}, subtract 16_{10} and carry a 1 to the next position. In all number systems, a carry is generated when the addition of two numbers exceeds the number of available symbols.

For example:

$$
\begin{aligned}
A_{16} &= 10_{10} \\
+\ 6_{16} &= +\ 6_{10} \\
\hline
10_{16} &= 16_{10}
\end{aligned}
$$

Note that because A_{16} plus 6_{16} exceeds the number of symbols, (only 15 are possible), a carry is generated and the next position is used.

For example:

$$
\begin{aligned}
C9_{16} \\
+\ 9_{16} \\
\hline
D2_{16}
\end{aligned}
$$

Adding 9 and 9 we get 18 and therefore a carry is required. Then subtract; 18 minus 16 is 2. The 2 is placed in the first position and a carry is added to C_{16}.

The operation of the carry is shown here:

$$
\begin{aligned}
&\overset{1\ 1}{B7FF_{16}} \\
+\ &2_{16} \\
\hline
&B801_{16}
\end{aligned}
$$

There is little doubt that hexadecimal is the premier code for use with microprocessors. The reason is that microprocessors work with 8-bit or multiples of 8-bit bytes. Hex readily transfers 2 place hex representations to 8-bit bytes or 4 place representations to 16-bit bytes. In addition, 7 segment displays can represent all 16 symbols.

TABLE 7–1 Table of Number Codes

DECIMAL SYSTEM	BINARY	8421 BCD		EXCESS-3		GRAY CODE	OCTAL	HEXA-DECIMAL
0	0000		0000	0011	0011	0000	0	0
1	0001		0001	0011	0100	0001	1	1
2	0010		0010	0011	0101	0011	2	2
3	0011		0011	0011	0110	0010	3	3
4	0100		0100	0011	0111	0110	4	4
5	0101		0101	0011	1000	0111	5	5
6	0110		0110	0011	1001	0101	6	6
7	0111		0111	0011	1010	0100	7	7
8	1000		1000	0011	1011	1100	10	8
9	1001		1001	0011	1100	1101	11	9
10	1010	0001	0000	0100	0011	1111	12	A
11	1011	0001	0001	0100	0100	1110	13	B
12	1100	0001	0010	0100	0101	1010	14	C
13	1101	0001	0011	0100	0110	1011	15	D
14	1110	0001	0100	0100	0111	1001	16	E
15	1111	0001	0101	0100	1000	1000	17	F

✔ SELF-CHECK FOR SECTIONS 7-3, 7-4, 7-5, 7-6

6. Name one advantage of the excess-3 code.
7. What is the chief characteristic of the Gray code?
8. Octal numbers use the base _____.
9. If the decimal number 9 is converted to octal, how many places will the octal number have?
10. If 56 is an octal number, what is the decimal value of the 5?
11. Write the octal number 24 in binary.
12. Hexadecimal uses the base _____.
13. If 10 is a hex number, what is the value of the 1 in decimal?
14. Convert the hex number FF to binary.

7-7　FLOATING-POINT NUMBERS

Introduction

The methods of representation shown so far are used to facilitate the use of binary numbers. We could say that BCD, octal, hexadecimal, and the Gray code all exist so that binary systems can be more easily implemented. Ultimately, however, the microprocessor will be doing math operations with pure 1's and 0's. This leaves us with two problems. The larger the number, the more positions it will require. In addition, we have to make some provision for placing the decimal point.

For example, if we multiply:

$$
\begin{array}{r}
1423.6 \\
\times\ \ .21 \\
\hline
14236 \\
28472\ \ \\
\hline
298956\ =\ 298.956
\end{array}
$$

We manually count the number of decimal places in each of the numbers, add them up, count off the number of places required in the answer and position the decimal. This is perfectly right and expresses the correct answer. It would be a bit much, however, to expect this of the microprocessor.

Fixed-Point Numbers

The numbers 1423.6 and .21 are said to be **fixed-point** numbers. In other words, the point or decimal is fixed immediately to the right of the least significant digit. When a microprocessor is programmed to do math with fixed-point numbers, the programmer must deal with the decimal. The microprocessor will multiply 14236 times 21 and the result will be 298956. The programmer must then place the decimal in the correct position. This process is called *scaling* and is usually done with a multiplier called the scaling factor. The scaling factor is a multiplier that is used to change a number into a range that can be expressed by the microprocessor. Scaling factors are commonly powers of 10 or powers of 2. For example, 1423.6 can be represented as $.14236 \times 10^4$ and .21 as $.21 \times 10^0$. Now both numbers are between .1 and 1. The **exponent** of each number is used to keep track of the magnitude. The microprocessor will multiply the numbers, and the programmer will have to scale them by placing the decimal after the operation is complete.

In business applications, where math operations are usually with currency, each number would be assumed to have only two decimal places, such as $142.36. In this case, tracking the decimal may not present a problem but in other applications, where there is a large variation in magnitudes, placing the decimal point can be cumbersome.

Floating-Point Numbers

Floating-point arithmetic means that the decimal is *floated* to the correct position both before and after the math operation is complete. The scaling of the number is done automatically, because the microprocessor keeps track of the exponent. This is accomplished by using a **fixed-length** binary number to represent all possible magnitudes. All numbers are **normalized,** that is, changed to a value between .1 and 1. (The proper math expression for this is .1 sf < 1, where f = the fraction and s is the sign of the fraction). This part of the number is called the **mantissa** or fraction. The other part, representing the magnitude, is called the characteristic or exponent. Here are some examples of normalized numbers:

NUMBER	NORMALIZED	ALTERNATE FORM
1423.6	$.14236 \times 10^{4}$	.14236 E+4
−7.894	$−.7894 \times 10^{1}$	−.7894 E+1
.0479	$.479 \times 10^{-1}$	.479 E−1
.000732	$−.732 \times 10^{-3}$	−.732 E−3

Each normalized number has two parts, a fraction and an exponent. Note also that both the fraction and the exponent can be positive or negative. The sign of the fraction is the sign of the original value. The sign of the exponent will depend on whether the original value was less than or greater than .1. The technique of normalizing a number is the same for binary or any other number base. For example, binary numbers are normalized:

BINARY	NORMALIZED
1001.10	$.100110 \times 2^{4}$
.0001101	$.1101 \times 2^{-3}$
1.101	$.1101 \times 2^{1}$

or hexadecimal

HEX	NORMALIZED
2B6.7	$.2B67 \times 16^{3}$
4CD79	$.4CD79 \times 16^{5}$
.00B29	$.B29 \times 16^{-2}$

Floating-Point Words

Floating-point representations are fixed in length. For example, in a binary floating-point system, all numbers will be changed to a binary word with a constant or fixed number of bits. A 32-bit word length is common.

31		24	23	0
S	Exponent	S	Fraction	

The first 3 bytes, bit 0 to bit 23, are used for the fraction. Bit 24 is available for the sign of the fraction, that is, the sign of the original number. The next 6 bits are used to represent the exponent and bit position 31 is for the sign of the exponent. The 6-bit exponent will allow numbers ranging from 2^{-64} to 2^{+63}. These binary numbers represent decimal numbers with about 20 places, more than sufficient for most applications.

Floating-Point Systems

All numbers in a floating-point system are contained in a fixed-length word. This greatly increases the efficiency and speed of the processor. A floating-point computer system is designed with hardware that normalizes all numbers, calculates the fractional part and the exponent separately and presents the output in a normalized form.

✔ SELF-CHECK FOR SECTION 7-7

15. What is a fixed-point number?
16. Explain scaling.
17. What is a fixed length?
18. Explain normalizing.
19. Are floating-point representations fixed length?
20. Normalize 5325.1.

SUMMARY OF IDEAS

- Binary-Coded Decimal (BCD) is a 4-bit encoding method for representing decimal digits 0 through 9.
- BCD numbers are subject to error if the six *illegal* numbers are not compensated for.
- Most microprocessors use a system of adding +6 to all illegal BCD numbers.
- BCD subtraction is done with 10's complements.
- Excess-3 code is formed by adding 3 to binary numbers 0 through 9.
- The excess-3 code is self complementing, that is, the 9's complement of the decimal digit is obtained by complementing each bit.
- The Gray code is used in mechanical systems. Each sequential binary number differs from the next in only one bit position.
- The octal number system is constructed from the base of 8.
- Octal is convenient because each octal digit can be directly converted to a 3-bit binary number.
- Hexadecimal is a number system constructed on the base of 16.
- Each hex number is directly convertible to a 4-bit binary number. Thus a 4-position hex number is directly translatable to a 16-bit binary number.
- Fixed-point numbers are integers with the binary or decimal point immediately to the right of the least significant bit or digit.
- In floating-point numbers, the point *floats* to the correct position after the calculation.
- Fixed-point math requires scaling, that is, the programmer must deal with the decimal or binary point.
- Floating-point numbers are normalized or adjusted so that they consist of a fraction of a limited value, usually .1 to 1, and an exponent.
- Floating-point systems normalize all numbers, calculate the fraction and exponent separately and normalize the result.

CHAPTER QUESTIONS & PROBLEMS

True or False

1. The correct BCD representation for the number 12 is 1100.
2. A binary number can be converted to an octal number by grouping the bits, starting at the least significant bit, into groups of four and applying the octal code.
3. A hex number can be converted to a binary number by translating each hex digit into a 4-bit binary number.
4. The excess-3 code was designed for use in mechanical systems.
5. A fixed-point number cannot be normalized or changed to a floating-point representation.

Multiple Choice

6. Which is the correct BCD form for $1,578_{10}$.
   a. 0001010101110100
   b. 001101111111
   c. 0001010101111000
   d. 0001010111111000

7. The BCD number for 001000100011_2 is
   a. 113
   b. 212
   c. 123
   d. 223

8. The Hex number FEED is
   a. 1111111011101100
   b. 1111111011101001
   c. 1111111011011101
   d. 1111111011101101

9. The octal number 47 is decimal
   a. 51
   b. 47
   c. 39
   d. 37

10. The hex number 47 is decimal
    a. 47
    b. 51
    c. 71
    d. 77

Problems

11. Change the following BCD numbers to decimal.
    01110000
    10010101
    010100000011

12. Write the following BCD numbers as binary.
    10010111
    00010101
    01000111

13. Convert the following octal numbers to binary.
    50
    134
    702

14. Convert the binary numbers to octal.
    1010111
    111111111
    0101001001

15. Convert the hex numbers to decimal.
    AE
    18
    42

16. Convert the hex numbers to binary.
    AE14
    1478
    E0FA

17. Convert the following binary numbers to hex.
    101011110000
    101011110001
    1000010101011010

18. Do the additions in hex.

    AF   CD
    +F   +1

    BC11   149A
     +F   +711B

19. Write the normalized expression for the following decimal numbers.
    .123789
    −732.3891
    .0000012

20. Write the fixed-point expression for these floating-point expressions.
    .342 E+3
    $.1523 \times 10^{-2}$
    $-.76 \times 10^{4}$

21. Write the floating-point expression for the following binary numbers.
    1101
    11.11
    1010.1010

CHAPTER 8

ELEMENTS OF A MICROPROCESSOR

OUTLINE

NEW TERMS TO WATCH FOR

Central Processing Unit (CPU)

Buses

Arithmetic Logic Unit (ALU)

Accumulator

Zero-Address Instructions

Single-Address Instructions

Clear

Fetch

Decode

Execute

Program Counter

Address Bus

Comparator

Shifter

Status Register

Flags

Data Registers

Load

Data Bus

Load And Store

Address Registers

Instruction Cycle

Machine Cycle

Instruction Decoder

Architecture

Single, Double And Triple Bus

Multiplexer

Control Unit (CU)

Microcode

Sequencing

Control Bus

After completing this chapter, you should be able to:

1. Name the basic parts of a microprocessor.
2. Understand the functioning of each of the elements of a microprocessor.
3. Describe how a microprocessor does arithmetic.
4. Explain how each part of the microprocessor is interconnected.
5. Define accumulator-based microprocessors.
6. Discuss basic microprocessor bus structure.
7. Demonstrate how a microprocessor is controlled.
8. List the instruction sequence of a microprocessor.
9. Predict microprocessor timing and event-sequencing.
10. Explain how each phase of the instruction cycle works and how it affects the microprocessor.
11. Describe how a microprocessor generates addresses.
12. Identify basic microprocessor architecture.

8-1   INTRODUCTION

All modern computers, regardless of their size and complexity, have only three basic parts:

1. *Memory* for storage of instructions, storage of data, and for working space.
2. *Input/output* devices such as keyboards, screens, and disk drives that allow input of data and output of results.
3. **CENTRAL PROCESSING UNIT** (CPU) that controls the action, performs the calculations, and manipulates the data.

The heart of the computer is the CPU because it controls, calculates and generally determines what the computer can do and how well it can do it.

With the advent of integrated circuit technology, the complicated construction of the CPU was miniaturized and placed on a silicon chip no bigger than a half inch square. Today the entire CPU resides in a *micro chip*. This intricate miniature silicon structure now replaces what used to be separate modular units that made up the central processing unit. It seems fitting that the shrinking of the central processing unit itself has shrunken the words as well to simply, "microprocessor."

The microprocessor has become the heart of the computer. It does all the things the CPU does but uses practically no real estate. The size of a microprocessor in no way indicates simplicity. There is no simple solution to the control of something as complex as a computer.

Disagreement as to the best solution or the best way to construct a microprocessor chip has given rise to several generations of incompatible devices from a variety of manufacturers. Each manufacturer has developed a unique way of connecting and using the basic elements of a microprocessor.

The implementation of computer control on a microprocessor chip may be at issue but nevertheless, there is a common denominator among the elements used. These common parts are found on most microprocessor chips manufactured today. Understanding what the common elements are and how they work will provide the basis for understanding all microprocessors.

This chapter discusses these basic elements and how they work. We will then connect them together in a simple model and see step-by-step, how a microprocessor functions.

8-2   BUS STRUCTURE

Definition

All of the elements to be discussed must be connected together in a system. The means of interconnection is called a *bus structure*. A bus is simply parallel electrical lines or paths connecting a source to a destination (Fig. 8-1). It is a common path used for specific exchange of data between various block functions. They are analogous to highways that connect cities. **Buses** can be on printed circuit boards (Fig. 8-2), or parallel-connected wires in a *ribbon cable* or conductive paths etched on the microprocessor chip.

FIGURE 8-1 Buses

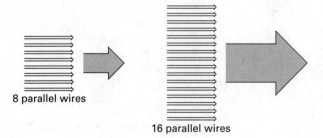

8 parallel wires

16 parallel wires

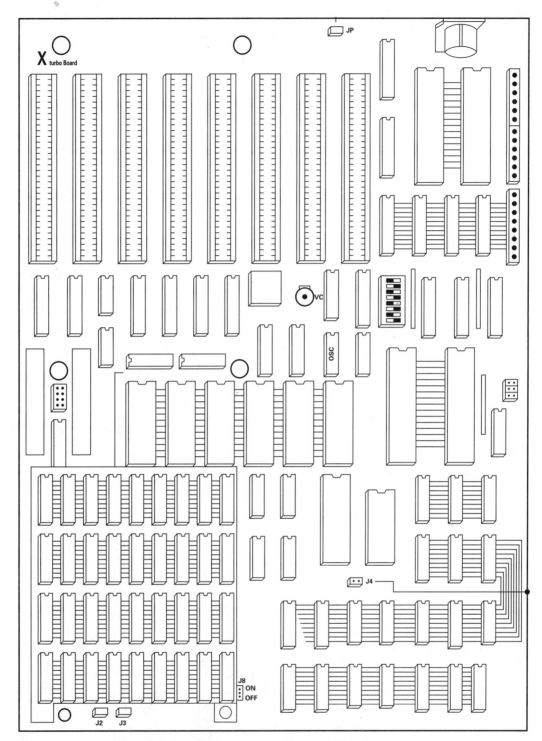

FIGURE 8-2 Bus Circuits on a Printed Circuit Board

8-3   ELEMENTS OF A MICROPROCESSOR

Arithmetic Logic Unit

Just as the microprocessor is the heart of the computer, the **Arithmetic Logic Unit**, abbreviated ALU, is the heart of the microprocessor. Its basic function, as the name implies, is to carry out arithmetic and logic operations. Since all computation performed by the microprocessor is done by the ALU, it is easy to see its importance. In addition, logic operations are also an integral part of data manipulation and decision-making. A very large part of what the microprocessor does occurs in the ALU.

ALU Structure

Figure 8-3 shows a simple block diagram of a typical ALU. The blocks represent circuits made from basic digital gates that perform the functions. The structure of a digital adder, can be found in any good text on digital electronics. The adder circuit can perform both addition and subtraction by 2's complement, as we learned in Chapter 2.

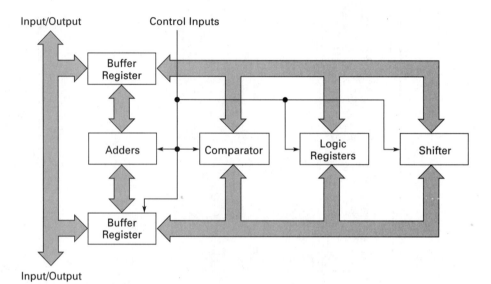

FIGURE 8-3 Block Diagram of ALU

The Comparator

The **comparator** block contains digital gate circuitry that compares the magnitude of two numbers placed in the buffer registers. The comparator, used in conjunction with another specialized register (the **Status Register**), will output the results of a comparison.

Logic Registers

The block labeled *Logic Registers* contains those digital gates that perform such logic operations as AND, OR, XOR, etc. Reference is made to any good digital text where these fundamental gates are discussed.

Control of the ALU

The operation of the ALU must be controlled. This is accomplished through the control leads shown in Figure 8-3. These leads provide the input path for control signals and facilitate the **sequencing** and operation of each individual block of circuits.

Shifter

The block labeled **SHIFTER** is a special function register. The logic circuitry in this block will move the contents of a register one or more positions left or right. Used with the *status register*, it can also perform a unique operation called *rotate*. The ability to do this is very important for certain arithmetic operations, as we shall see in later chapters. Shifting and rotating will be discussed in detail in the chapter on microprocessor instructions.

ALU Symbol

The actual structure of an ALU, showing all the circuitry involved and the control leads, is not normally published by the microprocessor manufacturer. Instead, the ALU is represented as the V-shaped block shown in Figure 8-4. The arrows on the data input bus indicates that data may be input to both sides of the ALU. For example, when two bytes of data are to be added, they each have separate input paths. After the ALU has completed an operation, the result is output on the data output bus (Fig. 8-4). It is understood that this V-shaped block performs:

1. Arithmetic operations such as add and subtract. Some ALU's have divide and multiply functions as well.
2. All logic operations, such as AND, OR, XOR, etc.

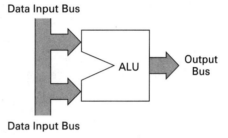

FIGURE 8-4 ALU Symbol

SELF-CHECK FOR SECTIONS 8-1, 8-2, 8-3

1. Name the three main parts of a computer.
2. Explain the concept of an electronic bus.
3. What is an ALU?
4. What is the purpose of an ALU?
5. Name two parts of the ALU.

8-4   THE ACCUMULATOR

A Special Register

The **ACCUMULATOR** is a shift register with a special function. The name is derived from the fact that after arithmetic operations are complete, this register *accumulates* the results.

Zero Address Instructions

The ALU in early microprocessors had to perform arithmetic operations on numbers that were located outside of the microprocessor. The numbers had to be in a special area of the memory called the *stack*. If, for example, the addition of two numbers was required, the implicit location of the numbers was the top two locations on the *stack* (Fig. 8-5(A)). The numbers were brought to the ALU, added, and the result was placed in the top location of the stack (Fig. 8-5(B)). Processors using this sort of method are said to have a **zero-address instruction** set.

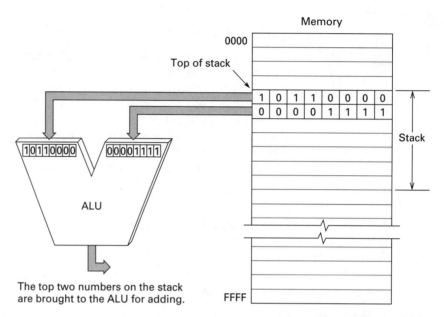

FIGURE 8-5 (A) Zero-Address Instruction Set

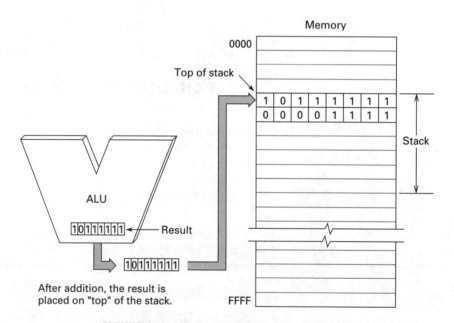

FIGURE 8-5 (B) Zero-Address Instruction Set

Single-Address Instructions

A *single-address instruction* set refers to a microprocessor that has an accumulator register. In an arithmetic operation, one of the numbers, called the operand, is always placed in the accumulator. The address location of the other number is all that need be given in an accumulator system, hence the term *single address* (Fig. 8-6(A)). The command to *add*, carries the implicit information that one of the numbers is in the accumulator register. After the operation is complete, the result is always placed in the accumulator (Fig. 8-6(B)).

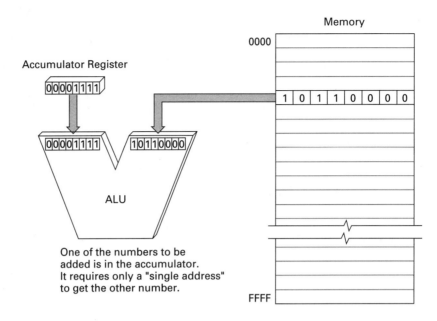

FIGURE 8-6 (A) Single-Address Instruction Set

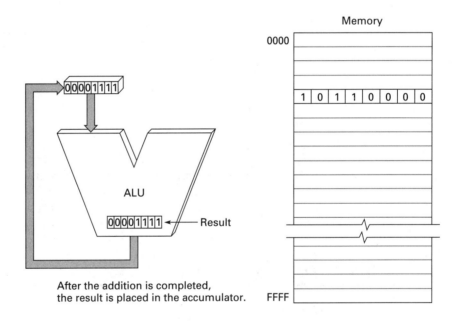

FIGURE 8-6 (B) Single-Address Instruction Set

Load and Store

Single address instruction set microprocessors are also called **LOAD AND STORE** types. This is because to do any arithmetic operation, the operand must first be *loaded* into the accumulator register. After the operation is complete, the result appearing in the accumulator must be *stored* (put into another location) (Fig. 8-7).

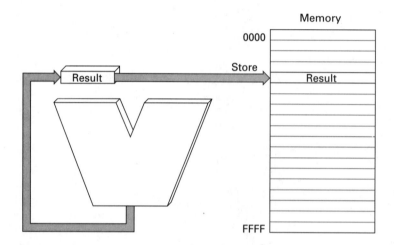

FIGURE 8-7 Load And Store

Option

In microprocessors built today, there is an option to perform arithmetic operations either with the accumulator or on two locations outside the microprocessor. Arithmetic operations performed with the accumulator are generally faster than operations done in other registers or memory.

8-5 DATA REGISTERS

General Purpose

Data registers, sometimes called general purpose registers, are defined as registers that do not have dedicated functions. They are used for a variety of operations and as temporary storage areas for data before processing. They are also used to hold the source address of an operand or the destination address of a result. They serve as extremely-fast, short-term memory which can be accessed in as little as 50 nanoseconds or less.

Working Space

Data registers can be thought of as working space or temporary storage areas that help the microprocessor to be more efficient in handling data. The number of general purpose registers available depends on the manufacturer's design. Figure 8-8 shows an arrangement with eight such registers.

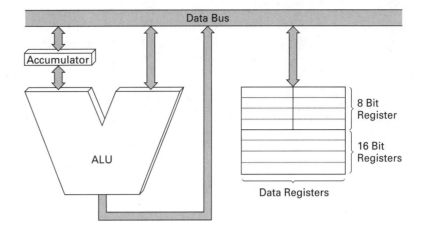

FIGURE 8-8 Data Registers

✔ SELF-CHECK FOR SECTIONS 8-4, 8-5

6. Describe the function of the accumulator.
7. What is a zero address instruction set?
8. What is a single address instruction set?
9. Name one of the uses for a data register.

8-6   ADDRESS REGISTERS

Address Registers and Bus

This grouping of registers, as the name indicates, is specifically for addressing. As we saw in the chapter on memory, all storage locations have addresses. When data is read from memory, the address of the data must be placed on the **address bus**. The address bus is a collection of lines that carries the addresses needed to the various memories used in a microprocessor system. It is said that the **address registers** create the address bus (Fig. 8-9).

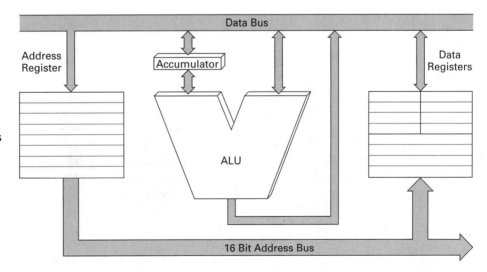

FIGURE 8-9 Address Registers

Address registers are usually at least 16 bits wide. This is necessary to provide numbers large enough to access vast numbers of memory locations. There are several types of address registers. They are categorized according to the specific type of addressing technique used when employing the register. Discussion of addressing techniques is reserved for a later chapter in the book. For informational purposes, index registers, page registers, and stack registers are all forms of address registers.

8-7   CONTROL UNIT (CU)

The CU

If a microprocessor can be said to have a heart, like the ALU, it might also be said to have a head or *brains*. The **Control Unit** could be considered the brains (Fig. 8-10). It contains all that the microprocessor *knows*, in what is called the *microprogram*.

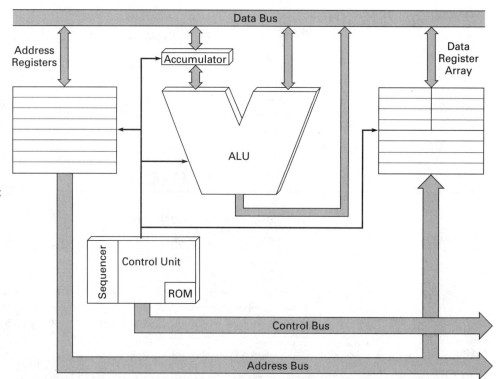

FIGURE 8-10 Control Unit

Microprogram

The microprogram resides in an internal ROM that cannot be accessed by the user. The microprogram contains the entire *instruction set*. The only instructions that the microprocessor can carry out are contained in this ROM, permanently imbedded by the manufacturer. These are the operations that the designers of the microprocessor chip have decided to build into the chip. An 8-bit microprocessor usually has only sixty to eighty instructions. We will cover instruction sets in later chapters.

Sequencing

In addition to issuing the signals necessary to control the operations of the microprocessor, the control unit is also responsible for sequencing these actions. In other words it controls what registers and devices are to be enabled and when they are to function. This control is achieved through a bus structure called the **control bus**.

8-8   INSTRUCTION DECODER

Decoding

The **Instruction Decoder** is properly part of the Control Unit. Decoding of the instruction, however, is a separate and distinct phase of microprocessor operations. You may well ask why the instruction needs to be decoded if the microprocessor already has its entire instruction set in the microprogram. The answer is that the microprocessor *"knows" how* to add for example, but does not know· *when* to add or even *what* to add. The command for the microprocessor to *"add"* is sent in from memory because the user has decided when it should add. The word or instruction to "add" is then "decoded," that is, interpreted. This means it is time to issue those control signals that cause addition.

The instruction to *add* is first sent to the instruction decoder (Fig. 8-11). The process whereby the microprocessor interprets the bit pattern appearing in the instruction decoder register is called *instruction decoding*.

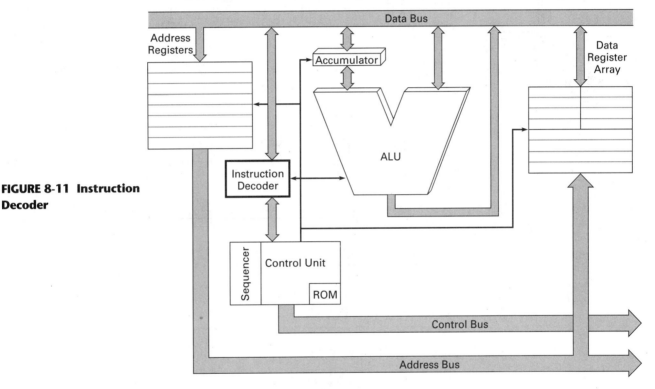

FIGURE 8-11 Instruction Decoder

8-9   PROGRAM COUNTER

A Counter and a Register

The **program counter** is really both a counter and a register (Fig. 8-12). The register portion is 16 bits wide, because it must be able to hold an address. The address in the program counter register is always the address of the next instruction to be executed. Since programs are normally carried out sequentially, the counter portion of the device generates sequential address numbers.

FIGURE 8-12 Program Counter Block Diagram

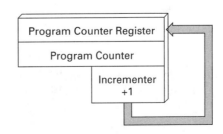

Incrementing

The program counter generates an address and places it on the address bus. It then increments, that is, adds 1 to the address it just generated and puts that number in the counter register. When the current instruction is finished, it places the new address on the address bus and again adds 1 to the register. In this way the program counter continually generates sequential addresses (Fig. 8-13).

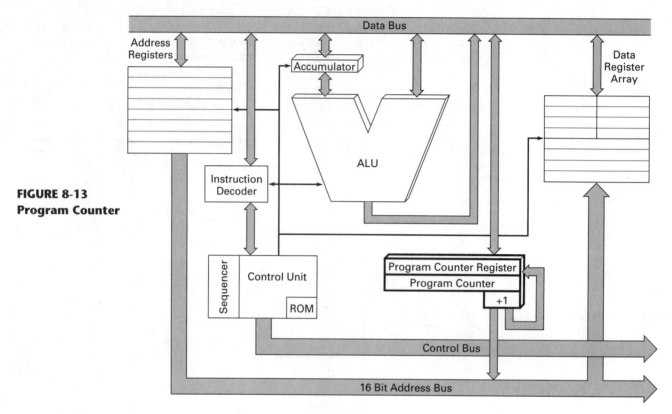

**FIGURE 8-13
Program Counter**

8-10   STATUS REGISTER

Connection to the ALU

The *status register* is sometimes called the *flag register* or *condition-code register*. This register is connected directly to the ALU (Fig. 8-14) and monitors its status. The *status* of the ALU is monitored after an ALU operation and refers to the character of the result. Each bit in the 8-bit status register has a specific meaning in relation to the result in the ALU. If a bit position in the status register is "1," then it is said to be *set*, or we say a "flag bit is set." If it is not "set," then it is "0" or **clear**.

$$\text{SET} = 1$$
$$\text{CLEAR} = 0$$

There is some variation from microprocessor to microprocessor as to the assignment of bit positions and what they monitor. There is, however, always a bit position to monitor negative results. If the result in the ALU after an operation is negative, the corresponding bit position in the status register will be *set*. Similarly, another bit position is assigned to be *set* when the result is zero. By *testing* or checking these bit positions after an ALU operation, the microprocessor can make decisions. In later chapters we will study these **flags** in more detail.

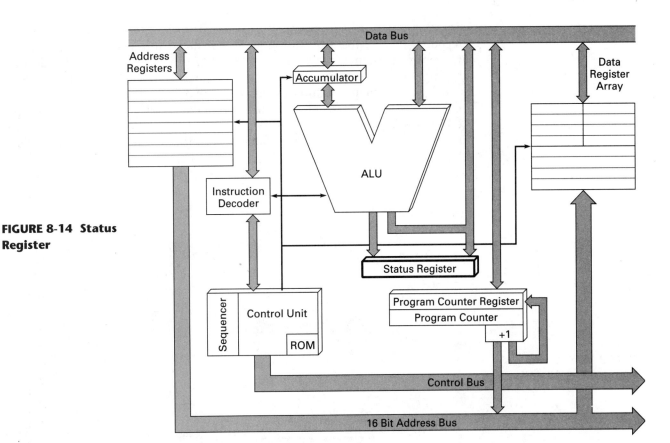

FIGURE 8-14 Status Register

✔ **SELF-CHECK FOR SECTIONS 8-673, 8-7, 8-8, 8-9, 8-10**

10. When data is called for from memory, the address of the data must be placed on the _____.
11. What is the control unit of a microprocessor?
12. Explain the "microprogram."
13. Explain the need for an instruction decoder.
14. What is the need for a program counter?
15. What is another name for the flag register?
16. If a bit position is at logic-1, the bit is said to be _____.
17. If a bit position is at logic-0, the bit is said to be _____.

8-11   PUTTING IT ALL TOGETHER

Fetch-Decode-Execute

A microprocessor carries out instructions in a three-step process. It simply repeats the three-step operation with almost no variation, as long as power is applied to it. These three steps are called **fetch, decode,** and **execute**.

Fetch

Fetching, in a microprocessor, is the term used to indicate that the microprocessor is retrieving an instruction from memory. The program or group of instructions that the microprocessor is to carry out resides in memory. The microprocessor gets or fetches these instructions from memory, one at a time, and brings them into the instruction decoder register where they are decoded. The fetch action is a series of small steps.

In the first step of the fetch process, the program counter register places an address on the address bus (Fig. 8-15(A)). This address appears almost simultaneously at the memory unit. Inside the memory, the address is decoded, that is, the 16-bit number is translated into a location in memory where the instruction resides (Fig. 8-15(B)). At the same time that the address is placed on the address bus, a control signal is sent to the memory. This signal puts the memory into the *read* mode of operation.

The instruction, located at the address that has been sent, is then output to the data bus. The instruction is propagated along the data bus and arrives inside the microprocessor to be latched into the instruction decoder register (Fig. 8-15(C)).

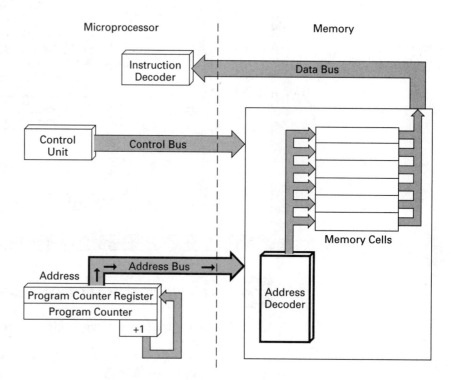

FIGURE 8-15 (A) Address Placed on Address Bus

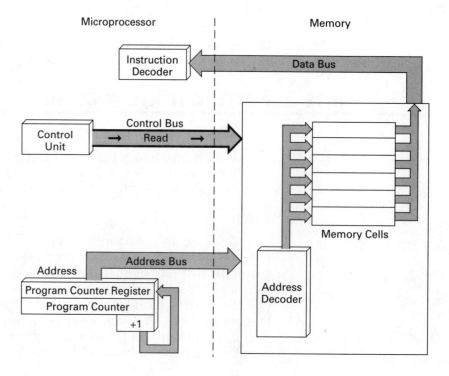

FIGURE 8-15 (B) Read Signal P149

The fetch phase of operation is measured from the time that the address appears on the address bus to the time it is placed into the instruction decoder register.

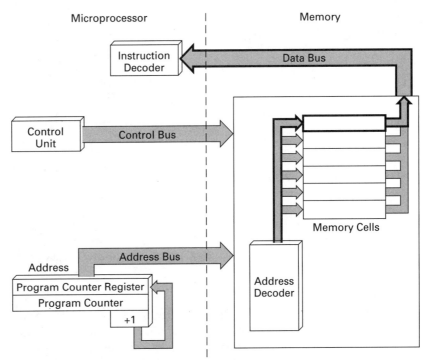

FIGURE 8-15 (C) Instruction Placed on Data Bus

Decode

The *decode* phase of the cycle begins as soon as the instruction, in the form of an 8-bit byte, appears in the instruction decoder register. The decoding is done via a PLA (Programmable Logic Array). The array will output the control signals necessary to carry out the instruction. The PLA is designed with the **microcode** to recognize only those bit patterns contained in the instruction set. Upon recognition of a bit pattern the PLA or microcode then generates the internal and external control signals necessary to carry out the given instruction.

Execute

The execution phase begins as soon as the microcode outputs the control signals necessary to carry out the instruction. The length of time needed to complete the execution phase varies considerably with the type of instruction involved. Some instructions are several bytes long. Each byte is fetched and decoded one at a time. After each byte is decoded, the necessary control signals are executed.

8-12 MICROPROCESSOR TIMING

Clock Cycles

Microprocessors must perform all operations under a very strict timing sequence. Exact timing is achieved by using a crystal controlled oscillator (Fig. 8-16). The times required for fetching, decoding, and executing are measured in the number of elapsed clock cycles.

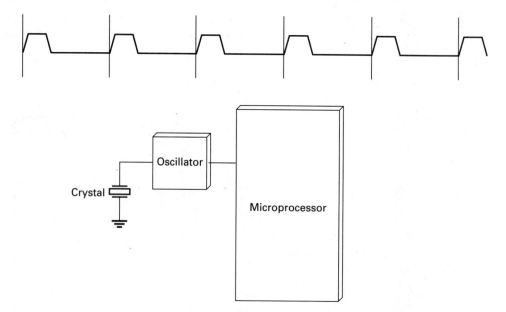

FIGURE 8-16 Clock Cycles Generated From Crystal Controlled Oscillator

Instruction Cycle

The time beginning when the address for retrieving an instruction from memory is placed on the address bus for a *fetch*, and ending when the execution phase is completed, is called the **Instruction Cycle**. Even the fastest microprocessors require at least one clock cycle to complete a fetch operation, and a minimum of one more cycle is required to decode and execute the instruction (Fig. 8-17). Fetching, decoding, and executing, then, comprise an instruction cycle.

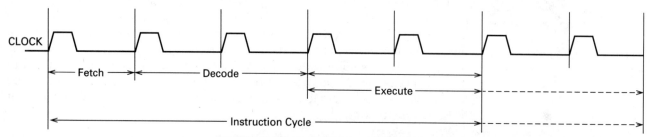

FIGURE 8-17 Instruction Cycle Timing

Some microprocessors need several clock cycles to do each of the three phases— fetch, decode, and execute. The clock cycles are broken up into **machine cycles**. An example of machine cycle timing is seen in Figure 8-18. The first five clock cycles, during which the fetch operation is completed, is called machine cycle 1, or M1. The next four cycles needed to decode the instruction are called machine cycle 2, or M2. The last four to eight cycles are called machine cycle 3, or M3. This is the execution phase. Depending on the length of the instruction, the execution phase will require four to eight cycles.

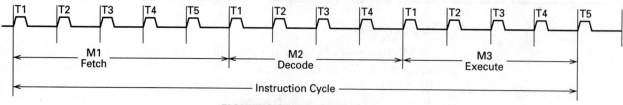

FIGURE 8-18 Machine Cycles

8-13   EXAMPLE OF THE INSTRUCTION CYCLE

One of the simplest instructions that the microprocessor performs is loading a byte of data into the accumulator register. We will assume for our example, that the instruction to **load** a byte into the accumulator is contained in the very first memory location 0000H (Fig. 8-19).

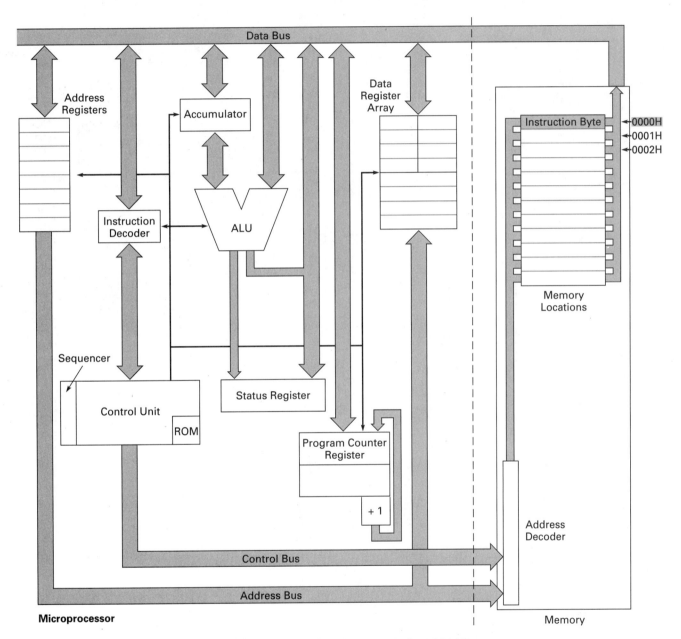

FIGURE 8-19 Instruction Located at 0000H

Reset

When power is applied to the microprocessor chip, a reset pulse is generated. This pulse resets the value in all registers, including the program counter, to zero. As a result, the first address that the program counter generates and places on the address bus is 0000H. We will use a capital "H" to indicate that the number given is in *hex* or base 16 (Fig. 8-20).

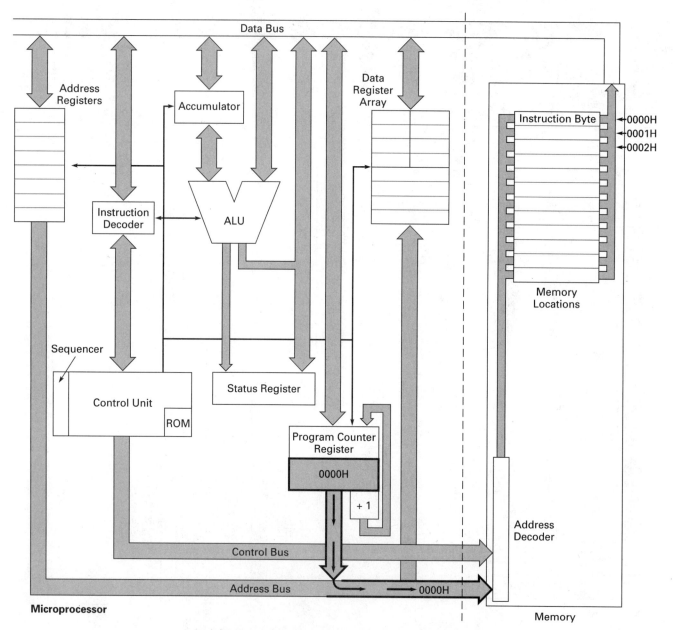

FIGURE 8-20 Address 0000H Placed on Address Bus

Read Signal Output

At the same time that the address is being placed on the address bus, the control unit generates a read signal on the control bus. The read signal is propagated along the control bus to the memory unit. This signal places the memory in a *read* mode. The contents of the address 0000H is then placed on the **data bus** (Fig. 8-21).

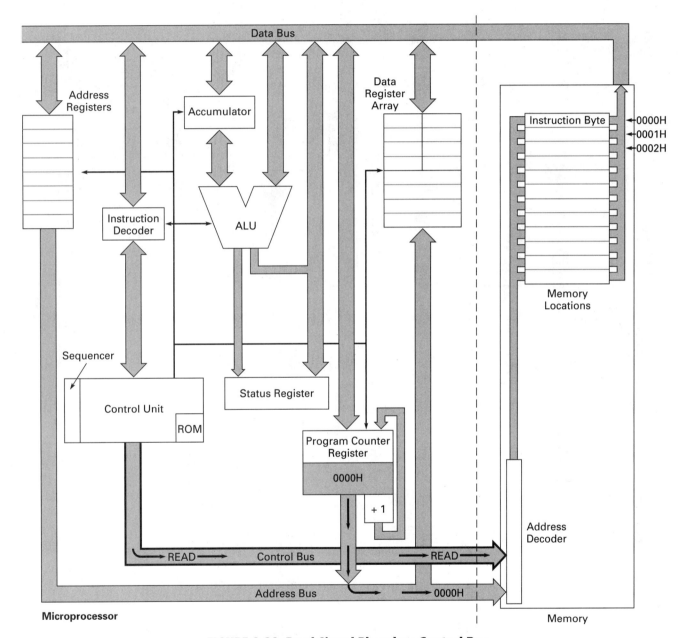

FIGURE 8-21 Read Signal Placed on Control Bus

The First Memory Location

Location 0000H contains the instruction for loading the accumulator. The instruction, in the form of an 8-bit byte, is sent down the data bus to the instruction decoder register. Here it is interpreted (decoded) by the microcode (Fig. 8-22).

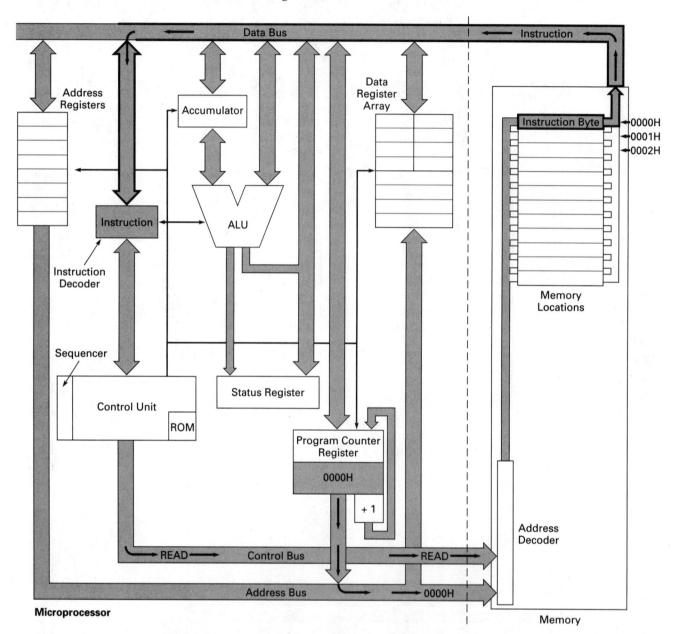

FIGURE 8-22 Instruction Loaded into Instruction Decoder

Variations on the LOAD Instruction

The microcode usually contains several variations of the *load accumulator* instruction. The variations of the instruction have to do with the location of the data to be loaded. The accumulator is capable of loading data from other registers or from memory. The data may be at the next location in memory or it may be elsewhere in the system. The 8-bit pattern received by the instruction decoder will be the exact pattern necessary for the microprocessor to *know* what it must do to load the data and where to find it.

Data in the Next Memory Location

If the load accumulator instruction is in the form that indicates the data to be loaded is in the next sequential location, the processor will cause the program counter to increment. In other words, +1 is added to the address in the program counter. The program counter will then contain 0001H (Fig. 8-23).

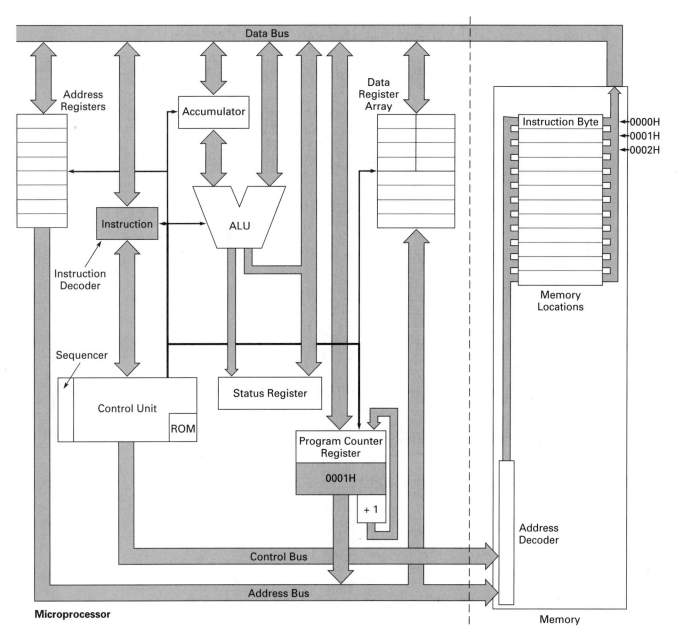

FIGURE 8-23 Program Counter Increments

Address 0001H Sent to Memory

This address is sent to memory, via the address bus, and is decoded by the memory unit. At the same time that address 0001H is sent, the control unit again generates a read signal for the control bus, putting the memory unit in the read mode (Fig. 8-24). The contents of location 0001H are placed on the data bus. The byte contained at 0001H is the data to be loaded into the accumulator.

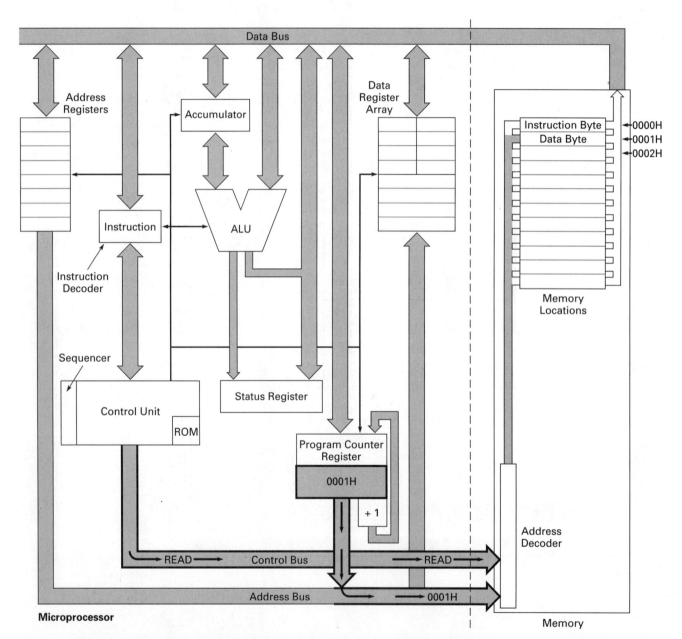

FIGURE 8-24 Address 0001H Placed on Address Bus and Read Signal Placed on Control Bus

Data Loaded into Accumulator

The microprocessor control unit then generates a control signal to enable the accumulator register to receive the data now on the data bus (Fig. 8-25). Once the data is present in the accumulator, the instruction cycle is complete. The program counter will then increment once more and begin a new fetch operation that is part of the next instruction cycle.

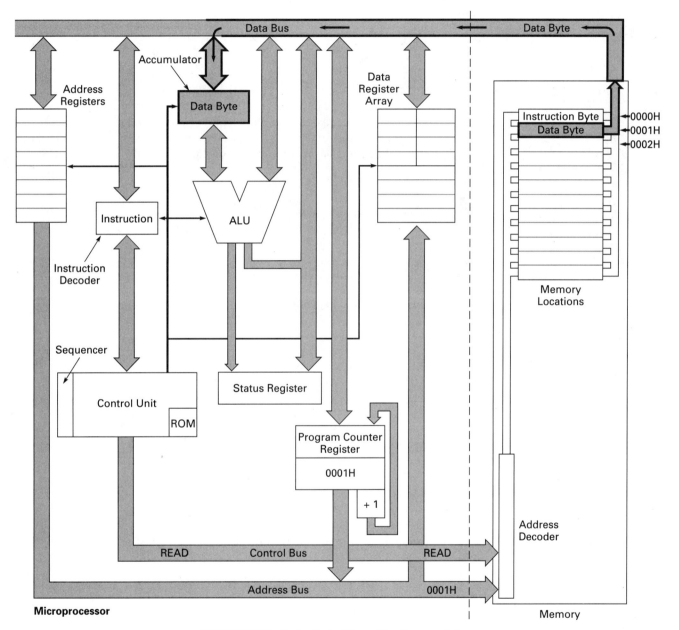

FIGURE 8-25 Data Byte Placed in Accumulator

8-14   MICROPROCESSOR ARCHITECTURE

Architecture

The term **architecture**, as applied to computer systems, refers to the various hardware devices that make up the computer and their interconnections. The architecture of a microprocessor includes the various registers and devices and the way in which they are connected. More specifically, architecture in a microprocessor is a direct reference to the internal bus structure.

Single Bus Architecture

A **single bus** microprocessor system is illustrated in Figure 8-26. The data from an external source or from an internal register must travel along a single bus. The obvious problem is that each operation requires sole access to the bus system. For example, if the data in register R0 is to be added to the data in register R1, three separate transfers of data must take place.

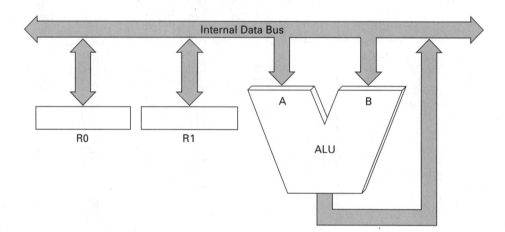

FIGURE 8-26 Single Bus Architecture

How Data is Transferred

First, data in R0 is transferred to input A of the ALU. Then data from R1 must be transferred to the B input of the ALU. After the numbers have been added, the result must also be transferred via the same data bus.

Double Bus Architecture

An example of a **double bus** architecture is shown in Figure 8-27. Bus I is the input bus. All data to be input travels on this bus. The R bus is the result bus. After an operation, the results appear on this bus to be transferred to the appropriate register. With the help of the buffer registers, it is possible to input to the ALU at the same time that results are being sent to output.

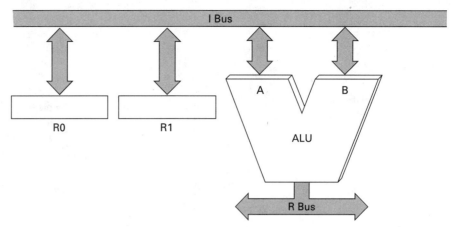

FIGURE 8-27 Double Bus Architecture

Triple Bus Architecture

An example of **triple bus** structure is seen in Figure 8-28. With a triple bus system, it is possible to input two numbers simultaneously into the ALU, one on the A bus and another on the B bus. The R or result bus is the third bus in this architecture.

More buses may add to the speed with which a microprocessor can execute instructions but they also take up space. Since space is at a premium in microprocessors, most processors built today use a single data bus system.

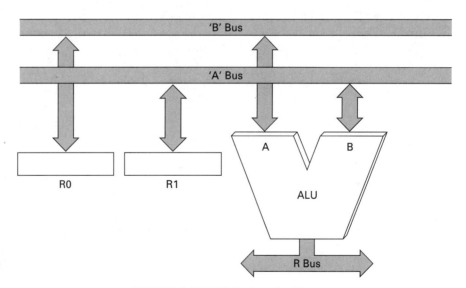

FIGURE 8-28 Triple Bus Architecture

Register Access

All registers have access to the data bus. In order to save space, the registers are usually arranged in an array (Fig. 8-29). A **multiplexer** is part of the array and it allows all registers to use the bus in a multiplexed fashion. That is to say, each register shares access to the bus at a different time determined by the multiplexer.

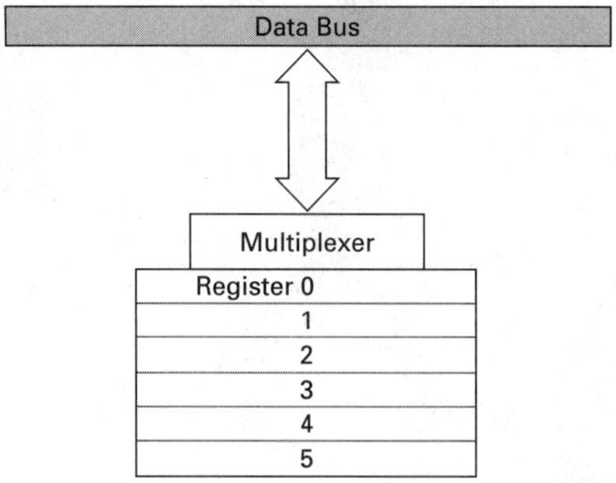

FIGURE 8-29 Register Array with Multiplexer

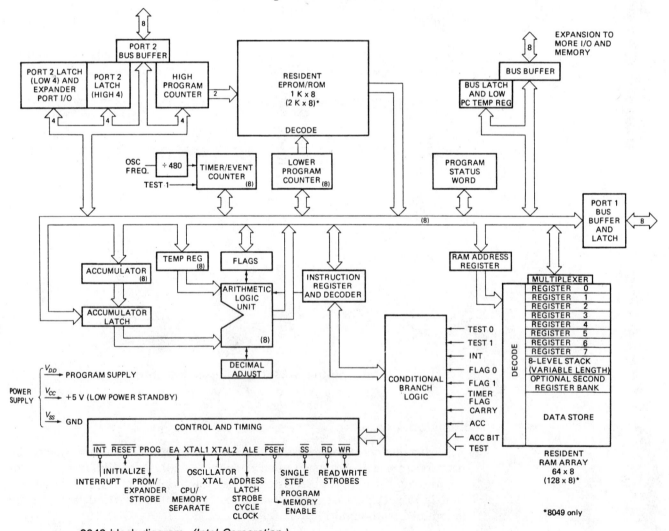

Standard 8-Bit Architecture

Figure 8-30 shows a standard 8-bit microprocessor with all the necessary components. As mentioned, the majority of microprocessors on today's market are single bus architecture.

8048 block diagram. *(Intel Corporation.)*

FIGURE 8-30 Standard 8-Bit Microprocessor

✔ SELF-CHECK FOR SECTIONS 8-11, 8-12, 8-13, 8-14

18. Name the three steps a microprocessor carries out to process instructions.
19. When does the fetch phase of the sequence begin?
20. Explain how the decode phase is related to microcode.
21. When does the execution phase begin?
22. Explain the difference between a clock cycle and a machine cycle.
23. What happens during reset?
24. Which part of the microprocessor holds the address of the next instruction to be executed?
25. Explain double-bus architecture.

SUMMARY OF IDEAS

- All microprocessor chips have certain elements in common.
- The Arithmetic Logic Unit (ALU) is the heart of the microprocessor and performs all arithmetic and logic functions.
- The ALU has the ability to compare the magnitude of two numbers. It also has a device called a *shifter* which can move the contents of a register one or more positions to the left or right.
- The accumulator is a special function register. It is used to contain bytes of data to be operated upon, called the *operands.* It also will contain the result of an ALU operation.
- Zero-address instruction sets do not use an accumulator. Operations are performed in the stack.
- Single-address instruction sets refer to microprocessors using accumulators.
- Load and store operations are initiated by first loading the data into the accumulator and then storing the result that has been placed in the accumulator.
- Registers which have no specific functions are called data registers. They can be used to contain addresses or data.
- Address registers are 16-bits wide and contain the memory locations necessary for microprocessor operation.
- The control unit (CU) of the microprocessor implements the microcode or microprogram. It generates the signals necessary to enable the other blocks within the processor. It also sequences or determines the timing of the various elements.
- The microprogram is the instruction set for the microprocessor and is contained in an internal ROM.
- The instruction decoder is the register that interprets the 8-bit bytes sent in from memory to initiate the activity of the processor.
- The microprocessor uses a program counter to generate the addresses necessary for instruction fetching. The program counter generates sequential numbers and places them on the address bus.
- The status register works in conjunction with the ALU to indicate the character of a result. It monitors such things as negative results or zero results.
- The instruction cycle consists of three distinct phases of operations: fetching, decoding, and executing.
- Fetching refers to the retrieval of an instruction from memory and placing it in the instruction decoder.
- Decoding is the process whereby the instruction is interpreted and the attendant control signals are issued.

- Execution is the phase during which the action demanded by the instruction is carried through.
- Microprocessors operate with a crystal-controlled clock signal that is responsible for the timing. Each phase of the instruction cycle requires a given number of clock cycles.
- Microprocessor architecture is a reference to the way in which the various elements inside the microprocessor are interconnected.
- If a microprocessor has only one internal bus for data transfers, it is said to be *single bus architecture*. Most microprocessors built today have single bus architecture.
- With the understanding of the basic elements given in this chapter, it is possible to analyze the microprocessors on the market today.

CHAPTER QUESTIONS & PROBLEMS

True or False
1. The ALU cannot perform logic operations.
2. The accumulator performs the arithmetic operations in a microprocessor.
3. Data registers are registers with specific functions.
4. The program counter register always contains the address of the next instruction to be executed.
5. If the result of an ALU operation is zero, a flag will be set in the status register.

Fill in the Blanks
6. The ALU is the element in a microprocessor that performs all _____ and _____ operations.
7. The device that has the ability to move the contents of a register left or right one or more bits is called a _____ .
8. After an arithmetic operation has been performed, the accumulator will contain the _____ .
9. In a zero-address instruction set, the data to be operated upon is always located _____ .
10. Data registers can be used to store either data or hold a _____ address or _____ address.
11. The control unit in a microprocessor generates _____ signals.
12. The internal ROM of the microprocessor is used to store the _____ .
13. The program counter automatically _____ to next the address after the instruction is completed.
14. When a bit position in the status register is logic-0, we use the term, the bit is _____ .
15. The fetch operation begins when the address in the program counter is placed on the address bus and finishes when the instruction is placed in the _____ register.

Multiple choice
16. The decoding phase begins when
   a. the execution phase ends.
   b. an instruction is placed in the accumulator.
   c. an instruction is placed on the data bus.
   d. none of the above

17. The instruction cycle consists of
    a. one machine cycle.
    b. the execution phase.
    c. retrieving an instruction, interpreting it, and carrying it out.
    d. none of the above

18. The architecture of a microprocessor includes
    a. the buses found in a microprocessor.
    b. the ALU and the control unit.
    c. the arrangement of the elements.
    d. all of the above

19. The machine cycle
    a. is always equal to the instruction cycle.
    b. consists of one or more clock cycles.
    c. is the fetch phase of operation.
    d. is always shorter than a clock cycle.

20. A single bus architecture
    a. is always faster.
    b. uses one external bus system.
    c. uses one data bus.
    d. cannot use accumulator addressing.

MICROPROCESSOR STATUS

OUTLINE

NEW TERMS TO WATCH FOR

The Carry

Overflow

Hit Positions

Sign Bit

Zero Bit

Half Carry

HOLD

Negative Bit

Parity

Odd Parity

Even Parity

Parity Bit

HALT

WAIT

READY

After completing this chapter, you should be able to:

1. Explain the purpose of the status register.
2. Describe the action of the carry bit, C, during *ALU* operation.
3. Predict the value of the carry bit for any given math operation.
4. Recognize an overflow condition.
5. State the two conditions that create an overflow.
6. Name the function of the sign bit.
7. Demonstrate the action of the zero bit.
8. Identify the H-flag and describe its use.
9. Explain the use of parity.
10. Correctly represent the parity bit.
11. Determine the difference between odd and even parity.
12. Discuss the need for WAIT and HALT states of the microprocessor.

9-1   INTRODUCTION

The microprocessor, while designed to be as independent as possible, is not truly a *stand alone* device. It not only needs to be instructed, but it must also have a means to communicate the status of the instruction process. It is necessary to know if the instruction is finished and the character of the result obtained. In many instances, what the microprocessor should do next depends on the result of the current instruction.

The status register is one of the most important ways of checking the character of a result. Recall that the status register is connected to the ALU and monitors its status. In this chapter we will examine the status register in detail.

In addition to the status register, the microprocessor has several other ways of communicating its condition. It has wait or hold states and a variety of other circumstances and situations that must be known and accounted for. We will examine how the various status signals from the microprocessor are generated and used.

9-2   THE STATUS REGISTER

The Carry

An 8-bit microprocessor is restricted to number representations that cannot exceed 8-bits. The size of the ALU and most of the other registers in the microprocessor is 8-bits. Obviously, the microprocessor will generate numbers that require a ninth bit, even if the two numbers to be added are only 8-bits. For example,

$$
\begin{array}{rcl}
+127 & = & 01111111 \\
+131 & = & 10000011 \\
\hline
+258 & = & (1)\,00000010
\end{array}
$$

Several **carry** bits were required to do this addition. In fact, nearly every bit addition generated a carry. In the microprocessor world, however, only one type carry is called *the carry*, abbreviated "C." The carry "C" is specifically the carry generated between bit position number 7 and bit position number 8.

We have, in earlier chapters, been illustrating binary numbers in this way:

8 7 6 5 4 3 2 1 Decimal numbering of **bit positions**

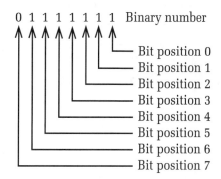

As you can see, the number above is indeed an 8-bit number, but the bit positions are referred to as bit position 0 to bit position 7. Be sure to understand this convention before going further. The eighth bit in an 8-bit number is placed in bit position number **7**.

The carry C needs special attention as we see in the example,

$$
\begin{array}{rcl}
+127 &=& 01111111 \\
+131 &=& 10000011 \\
\hline
+258 &=& (1)\,00000010
\end{array}
$$

The carry from bit position number 7 to bit position number 8 caused the number to exceed 8-bits. A 9-bit number needs special attention to be handled by an 8-bit microprocessor architecture. Of course, when 8-bit numbers are added, a carry is not always generated.

$$
\begin{array}{rcl}
+127 &=& 01111111 \\
+127 &=& 01111111 \\
\hline
+254 &=& (0)11111110
\end{array}
$$

In this case, no carry from bit position 7 to bit position 8 was produced.

When 9-bit numbers are generated, we need a way of recognizing them. A carry from bit position 7 to bit position 8 is always created when a 9-bit number is generated. Detecting this condition is a function of the status register. The status register, sometimes called the condition register or the flag register, is attached to the ALU (Fig. 9-1).

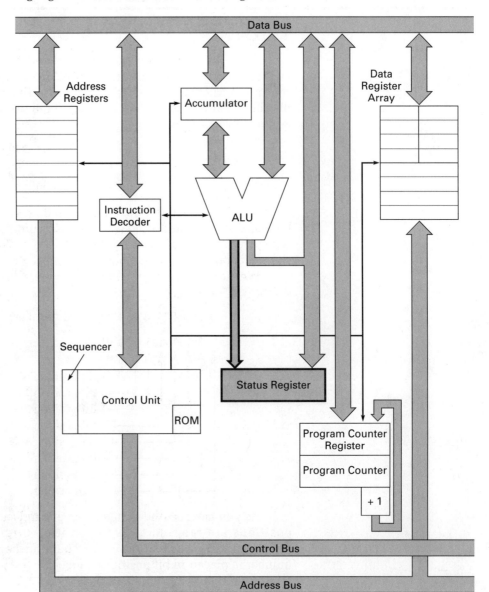

FIGURE 9-1 Status Register

One of the bit positions in the 8-bit status register is assigned to monitor the carry from position 7 to position 8. This bit or *flag* in the status register is called the C-bit. If an addition or any other math operation calls for a carry from bit position 7 to bit position 8, the C-flag is set to "1." If an operation does not result in a position-7-to-position-8 carry, the C-flag remains clear and holds a zero bit. After every math operation, the C-bit position in the status register will contain either a "1" or a "0" depending on what happened between bit position 7 and bit position 8. Figure 9-2(A) shows a math operation that results in a carry of zero. The carry or C-bit in the status register remains "0." Figure 9-2(B) shows a math operation that causes the C-bit to be equal to "1" which sets the status register carry flag to logic-1.

FIGURE 9-2 (A) Carry Clear (B) Carry Set

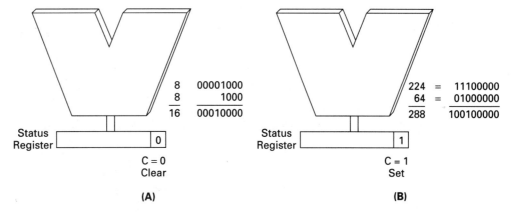

Usually, we think in terms of a C-carry from position 7 to position 8. In fact, when we subtract a larger number from a smaller one, a *borrow* occurs from position 8 to position 7. The carry bit in the status register is also set to "1" when a borrow occurs.

There are program instructions which check the status of the C-bit in the status register when the ALU performs math operations. This is necessary to enable the microprocessor to deal with numbers that exceed eight bits.

The Overflow

Microprocessors most often use the 2's-complement form for representing negative values. This means that bit position 7, the sign bit, is used to indicate the sign of the number.

$$01111111 \ = \ +127$$

The **sign bit** is 0, indicating a positive number.

$$10000001 \ = \ -127$$

The sign bit is 1, indicating a negative number.

Microprocessors, however, do not "know" a positive number from a negative number. The addition circuits simply combine the bit patterns present in the ALU registers according to instructions in ROM. It is up to us to determine the nature of the bit patterns. For example, the microprocessor can add two signed numbers such as:

$$
\begin{array}{rcl}
+64 & = & 01000000 = +64 \\
+96 & = & 01100000 = +96 \\
\hline
+160 & = & 10100000 = -96
\end{array}
$$

The result, 10100000_2, is correct from the microprocessor's point of view, and the sum would be correct if we were adding 8-bit binary numbers.

However, we have decided to work with signed numbers. The "1" in the 7th bit position means that our result would be −96, rather than +160.

Check this: 10100000 = −96

01011111   forms the 1's complement
_____+1_   add +1
01100000   forms 2's = +96

By forming the 2's complement, we get +96, which means that the result must have been −96. An error or **overflow** has occurred. The cause of the error was the carry from bit position 6 to bit position 7. This carry changed the sign of the result.

01000000
01100000
_____
10100000
7 ⎏⎎ 6

Now let's look at another signed addition.

11000000 = −64
11111100 = −4
_____
(1) 10111100 = −68
⎸
⎣ Disregard

The rules for 2's complement math call for us to disregard any carry greater than the original number. The result, (10111100) if it is −68, should yield +68 as the 2's complement.

Check: 10111100 = −68

01000011   forms 1's complement
_____+1_   add +1
01000100 = 2's complement = +68

In this case, although we did have a position-6 to position-7 carry, the sign, and, therefore, the result was correct. It is clear we can't simply use the position-6-to-position-7 carry, by itself, as an indicator of an overflow error.

To detect an overflow error, it is necessary to monitor not only the position-6-to-position-7 carry but also the position-7-to-position-8 carry, the C-flag in the status register.

The rules or conditions for overflow are stated like this:

An overflow error exists when *either* of two conditions are met.
Condition 1: When a carry *is* generated from bit position 6 to bit position 7, but there is no carry from bit position 7 to bit position 8, an overflow error has been created.

OR

Condition 2: When there is *no* carry from bit position 6 to bit position 7, but there *is* a carry from bit position 7 to bit position 8, an overflow error has been created.

It may seem a little complicated when stated in words, but it really is quite simple. There are only four possibilities for these two types of carries.

They are:

Carry from Bit 6 to Bit 7	Carry from Bit -7 to Bit 8
yes	*yes*
no	*no*
yes	*no*
no	*yes*

No other combinations can exist. Two of the combinations cause an overflow error and the other two do not.

Carry from Bit 6 to Bit 7	Carry from Bit 7 to Bit 8	Answer is:
yes	*yes*	*correct*
no	*no*	*correct*
yes	*no*	*incorrect*
no	*yes*	*incorrect*

All we need do is examine the results in carry positions seven and eight to know if an error is generated. We cannot correct the error without first knowing that it exists.

Another function of the status register is to examine the result for these conditions. The overflow error is called "V" in many systems. If the V-bit is set, an error or overflow occurred. In other words, one of the two conditions for an overflow error was encountered.

Example:

$$
\begin{array}{r}
11111000 = -8 \\
11111000 = -8 \\
\hline
(1)\ 11110000 = -16
\end{array}
$$

In this example, there has been a carry from bit position 6 to bit position 7 and from position 7 to position 8.

$$
\begin{array}{r}
1\,1\,1\,1\,1\,0\,0\,0 \\
1\,1\,1\,1\,1\,0\,0\,0 \\
\hline
(1)\ 1\,1\,1\,1\,0\,0\,0\,0
\end{array}
$$

This does not meet either *condition-1* or *condition-2*. In terms of the chart:

Carry from Bit 6 to Bit 7	Carry from Bit 7 to Bit 8	Answer	V-bit	C-bit
yes	*yes*	*correct*	*0*	*1*
no	*no*	*correct*	*0*	*0*
yes	*no*	*incorrect*	*1*	*0*
no	*yes*	*incorrect*	*1*	*1*

In this case, V=0. In the status register, the V-bit will be clear. However, the C-bit will be set (Fig. 9-3).

FIGURE 9-3 Carry Set, Overflow Clear

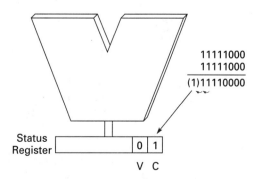

Example:

$$00010000 = +16$$
$$00001100 = +12$$
$$\overline{00011100} = 28$$

In this addition, no carry takes place from position 6 to position 7, and no carry is generated in the carry bit of the status register (C).

$$00010000$$
$$00001100$$
$$(0)\ \overline{00011100}$$

Again, neither of the conditions for an overflow are met. The chart indicates that the answer is correct (Fig. 9-4).

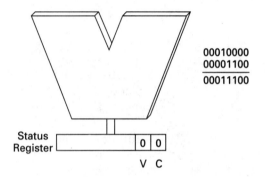

FIGURE 9-4 Carry Clear, Overflow Clear

Example:

$$01111111 = +127$$
$$00000001 = +1$$
$$\overline{10000000} -128$$

Here we meet *condition-1*. A position-6-to-position-7 carry occurred.

$$01111111$$
$$00000001$$
$$\overline{10000000}$$

Condition-1 A carry *is* generated from bit position 6 to bit position 7 but there is *no* carry from bit position 7 to bit position 8.

The chart indicates:

Carry from Bit 6 to Bit 7	Carry from Bit 7 to Bit 8	Answer	V-bit	C-bit
yes	yes	correct	0	1
no	no	correct	0	0
yes	no	incorrect	1	0
no	yes	incorrect	1	1

Example:

$$10000001 = -127$$
$$11000010 = -62$$
$$(1)\ \overline{01000011} = +67$$

In the example, *Condition-2* has been met.

Condition-2 There is *no* carry from bit position 6 to bit position 7, but there *is* a carry from bit position 7 to bit position 8. '

$$10000001$$
$$11000010$$
$$(1)\ \overline{01000011}$$

The chart shows:

Carry from Bit 6 to Bit 7	Carry from Bit 7 to Bit 8	Answer	V-bit	C-bit
yes	*yes*	*correct*	*0*	*1*
no	*no*	*correct*	*0*	*0*
yes	*no*	*incorrect*	*1*	*0*
no	*yes*	*incorrect*	*1*	*1*

It should now be obvious that when the microprocessor works with signed binary numbers, the possibility of generating an error must be taken into consideration. This is usually done by the programmer, who must write something into the program to check for an error. It is relatively simple to do, because it is only a matter of checking the V-bit position in the status register to see if an error flag is present.

If the V-bit is set (V=1), the program must execute an error-correcting routine. Of course, the V-bit will set or clear when ALU operations occur, regardless of whether we choose to call a number signed or unsigned. In unsigned arithmetic, the V-bit is ignored.

The Sign Bit

The sign bit or "S" bit, in the status register is used to indicate the sign of the binary result in the ALU. Some microprocessors call it the N-bit for **negative bit**. It is set if the sign of the result is negative and clear if the result it positive. Obviously, this is accomplished by monitoring bit position 7, the most significant bit (Fig. 9-5).

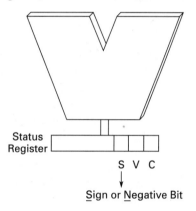

FIGURE 9-5 Status Bit Monitors Bit Position 7

The sign bit in the status register also has other uses. For example, devices that are connected to the microprocessor must have a method for notifying the microprocessor of their status, that is, busy or ready. Bit position 7 is very often used for this purpose. The external device will *condition* bit 7, that is, set or clear it based on its status. The byte is then loaded into the ALU and the sign bit checked. In this way, the processor can read the status of external devices.

The Zero Bit

The **zero bit** or Z-flag indicates that the result of an ALU operation is zero. This flag will be set whenever a result is equal to zero. If a result is anything other than zero, the flag is clear or "0." For example, if the

$$\begin{array}{r} 10 \\ -10 \\ \hline 0 \end{array}$$

subtraction, is performed, the result is zero. This would cause the Z-bit to be set, Z=1.

In some processors, the Z-bit can also be used to test a single bit position. For example, if the value of bit position 3 needs to be known, the byte can be transferred into the microprocessor and the instruction to test this bit position given. The Z-bit will then be set or clear, depending on the value of bit position 3.

It is worth noting that some microprocessor instructions transfer data without changing it. Data is moved in and out of various locations within the processor system. Many of these instructions also effect the status register, even though they are not math operations. The instruction set for the microprocessor needs to be checked to see if a transfer operation will effect the status bit of interest.

The Half-Carry Flag

The **half carry** or H-flag monitors for a carry from bit position 3 to bit position 4. In other words, from the first 4 bits of a byte to the most significant 4 bits. Incidently, a half byte or 4 bits, is called a *nibble*. The H-flag is intended for use in BCD operations. It will be set whenever a carry from bit position 3 to bit position 4 occurs. The H-flag is clear if no carry is generated between these two positions, and, just as the C-bit will also be set if a borrow is necessary, the H-bit is set if a borrow occurs from position 4 to position 3.

✔ SELF-CHECK FOR SECTIONS 9-1, 9-2

1. The carry, C, in an 8-bit microprocessor refers to the carry from bit position ____ to bit position ____.
2. The eighth bit in an eight-bit number is referred to as bit position ____.
3. If the C-flag is set, we can assume a carry occurred from bit position ____ to bit position ____.
4. What does an overflow indicate?
5. Can a carry from bit position 6 to bit position 7 always be used to indicate an overflow?
6. Name the two conditions that indicate an overflow.
7. If the V-bit is set, an _____ occurred.
8. If the microprocessor did not work with negative numbers, would there be a need to worry about overflow?
9. Explain the function of the sign or negative bit.
10. What is the zero bit used for?
11. The half carry indicates a carry between bit position _____ and bit position _____.

9-3   PARITY

Error Checking

The **parity bit** or P-bit is commonly found in microprocessor status registers. First, however, we need to understand what **parity** is. Simply put, parity is an error checking method. Huge numbers of bytes are constantly being transferred in and out of the microprocessor. Data flows from disk drives, in and out of memory and even between computers. There is always the possibility for an error to occur. An error would mean a logic-1 is changed to a logic-0 or a logic-0 is inadvertently changed to a logic-1. Parity checking is designed to detect such errors.

Odd or Even

The parity check consists of simply counting the number of logic-1's in a byte. The number of logic-1's present in any given byte will either be odd or even. A parity checking system provides a choice between two procedures. A microprocessor uses either **odd parity** or **even parity** checking, and when devices are connected to each other, they must be set to use the same odd or even parity.

The seventh bit position in a byte is usually used to store the parity bit.

1 0 1 0 1 0 1 0
↑
Parity bit

Use of a parity system means that signed numbers must be transmitted in another way.

Odd

The parity generator counts the number of 1's in each byte before it is transmitted. In an odd parity scheme, if the number of 1's in a given byte is even, a "1" is inserted into bit position 7. The job of the parity generator is to make sure that every byte to be transmitted contains an odd number of 1's.

Example:

Byte to be Transmitted	Parity bit inserted	Byte after parity generation
00001111	1	10001111
01100001	0	01100001

Even

In an even parity scheme, the parity generator counts the number of 1's in each byte and inserts a parity bit that assures that every byte transmitted contains an even number of 1's.

Example:

Byte to be Transmitted	Parity bit inserted	Byte after parity generation
00001111	0	00001111
01100001	1	11100001

Checking

On the receiving end, each byte is checked for parity. If the parity sent has been odd, the number of 1's in each byte are counted to be sure that the number is still odd. If an error has occurred, that is, if any 1 is changed to a 0 or any 0 is changed to a 1, the number of 1's will no longer be odd. An even number would indicate an error. This raises the question of what would happen if *two* bits within an 8-bit byte were accidentally changed? The odd or even status of a byte would not change, in which case, the error could go undetected. However, the possibility of two errors occurring within a byte is so small that parity checking is quite effective for small block transfers.

The Parity Bit

The parity or P-bit in the status register is used to detect the parity of a given byte. If the number of 1's in a byte is odd, then the parity flag is cleared, that is, "0." If the byte contains an even number of 1's, the P-flag is set. Testing the parity bit is part of an error checking program. When an error in parity is detected, another part of the program must be called to handle the event. Figure 9-6 shows a status register that indicates parity, half carry, zero, sign, overflow, and carry flags.

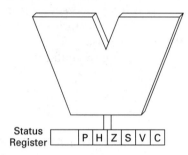

Status Register | P | H | Z | S | V | C |

FIGURE 9-6 Status Register with Parity, Half Carry, Zero, Sign, Overflow, and Carry

9-4   STATUS SIGNALS

Although there is wide variation in the type and use of microprocessor status signals, there are some commonly used forms. Any microprocessor is sure to have one or more of the following features, **HALT, WAIT, HOLD,** or **READY.** To clearly understand just what the microprocessor is doing during any of these conditions, it is necessary to look at the timing diagrams. It is also necessary to understand that the bus connections in a microprocessor system are shared. Shared buses mean that other devices will want to use the buses for their own purposes. Many of the microprocessor status signals are for the express purpose of allowing other devices to use the bus system while the microprocessor waits.

Halt

All microprocessors have the ability to halt or suspend operation. Some microprocessors, however, can only enter a halt state through a software instruction. When a halt or suspend operation is called for, the microprocessor finds a convenient place to stop, usually at the end of an instruction cycle. An output pin on the microprocessor chip indicates the halt. Sometimes the microprocessor must be halted or *interrupted* in order to complete a higher priority task. We'll look more closely at interrupts in a later chapter.

Wait

The suspended operation of a microprocessor is sometimes called a *wait* state. When the microprocessor is halted it has to wait for an appropriate input signal before continuing.

During a halt or wait state, the bus connections on the microprocessor are *floated*. This is referred to as tri-state logic. The microprocessor is usually connected to the bus system through tri-state buffers. From digital logic, you will recall that the third logic state is a high impedance state. When the buffers that connect the processor to the bus system enter this third state, they effectively disconnect the microprocessor from the bus system. The microprocessor is said to *float* the bus outputs. During this state, other devices can use the bus without interfering with microprocessor operations.

Instruction Status

In some instances, it is useful to know just what phase of the instruction cycle is taking place. That is, we need to know if it is beginning or ending a cycle. Recall that the instruction cycle consists of the three operations, fetch, decode, and execute. Some processors provide an output pin that indicates when the device enters the M1 phase. M1 or machine cycle 1 is always the fetch phase. Other processors provide an output pin that indicates when the microprocessor enters the last cycle of an instruction.

Accommodating Memory

The speed with which a microprocessor operates may be faster than the memory circuits. So there must be a way to make the microprocessor wait until data is output from memory and can be found on the data bus. One way this is accomplished is through an output pin from the microprocessor that warns the clock circuitry that it is about to access memory. The clock circuits can then extend the timing until the memory access is complete. Another way to accommodate a slow memory is through an input pin to the microprocessor that is connected to the memory. The memory can then indicate when it has output a valid byte and the microprocessor can extend its machine cycle until the byte is ready.

The various status and control signals are generally provided by control bus signals. Although some of the signals do indeed control what the processor does, that is, HALT, WAIT, etc., many of them are only output signals that indicate what the microprocessor is doing. These signals are used by peripheral, input/output devices as indicators for their actions.

 SELF-CHECK FOR SECTIONS 9-3, 9-4

12. What is the purpose of parity checking?
13. In an odd-parity scheme, the number of 1's transmitted will always be an _____ number.
14. In an even-parity scheme, the number of 1's received should always be _____.
15. Explain what happens if 2-bit positions change during a parity checking procedure.
16. Why would a microprocessor need to stop or halt operation?
17. Does memory always operate at the same speed as the microprocessor?

SUMMARY OF IDEAS

- The essential function of the status register is to check the nature of the result of a microprocessor instruction.
- The carry-C in an 8-bit number is the carry generated between bit position 7 and bit position 8.
- In a math operation, if a carry is generated from bit position 7 to bit position 8, the C-bit in the status or flag register is set (1). If no carry is generated, the C-bit is clear (0).
- The C-bit is also set if a borrow occurs.
- The overflow condition causes an error in signed-number math and can exist under two conditions:
Condition 1: A carry *is* generated from bit position 6 to bit position 7

but there is *no* carry from bit position 7 to bit position 8.

or

Condition 2: There is *no* carry from bit position 6 to bit position 7, but there *is* a carry from bit position 7 to bit position 8.

- The V-bit in the status register is set if an overflow occurs.
- Most status registers have an S- or N-bit to indicate the sign of the number.
- The Z-bit or zero bit is used to indicate that the result of an ALU operation is zero.
- The half carry or H-flag monitors the status of a bit-3-to-bit-4 carry. It is used most often in BCD arithmetic operations.
- Parity is an error-checking procedure which tests to see if any bit position in a number has changed. The parity bit, when used, is the MSB.
- Odd parity uses the parity bit to assure that the sum of 1's occurring in a number is odd.
- Even parity uses the parity bit to assure that the sum of 1's occurring in a number is even.
- The P-bit in a status register is used to determine if a given byte has an odd or an even number of 1's.
- Microprocessors have the ability to halt or suspend their operations. The output pins relating to a halt or wait state are for indicating the microprocessor condition to other devices. The input pins for halt or interrupting processing enable other devices to control the microprocessor.

CHAPTER QUESTIONS & PROBLEMS

True or False

1. The carry or C-bit, refers to a binary carry from any bit position to the next higher bit position.
2. If there is a carry from bit position 6 to bit position 7 and the C-bit is set, there is an overflow error.
3. An overflow error can be determined independently from the carry C.
4. The sign bit S and the negative bit N are both found in the flag register.
5. The flags in the status register are sometimes effected by operations other than math instructions.

Fill in the Blanks

6. The value of the C-bit will be _____ (1,0) when there is no carry from bit position 7 to bit position 8.
7. The half carry, or H-flag, is set if there is a carry from bit position _____ to bit position _____.
8. The unsigned binary result of an ALU operation is 1000000 or +128. The N-bit will be _____(set, clear).
9. The parity bit occupies the _____ bit position in an 8-bit number.
10. If the Z-bit is set, the result of an ALU operation is _____.

Multiple Choice

11. In an odd-parity system, if the byte to be sent is 01100011 the byte sent will be
    a. 01100011   c. 10011100
    b. 11100011   d. none of the above

12 Which of the following statements are true?
a. If both C and V are 1, the result is in error.
b. If C is set and there is a position-6-to-position-7 carry, the result is correct.
c. If there is a position-6-to-position-7 carry, but the C-bit in not set, then V=1.
d. all of the above

13 If the S-bit in the status register is set, we can assume that
a. the result of the ALU operation was zero.
b. an ALU operation produced a positive result.
c. parity is even.
d. none of the above is true.

14 If the half carry (H-bit) is set, then we can assume that
a. the ALU operation produced a carry from bit position 6 to bit position 7.
b. the V-bit will be set.
c. the information necessary for BCD math is available.
d. none of the above is true.

15 Select the statement that is *not* true.
a. An ALU operation that results in zero will cause the Z-bit to be set.
b. In an odd-parity system, each byte contains an odd number of bits, excluding the parity bit.
c. The S-bit monitors the MSB position.
d. An overflow error always sets the V-bit.

16. Fill in the correct parity bit in each of the following (an even-parity system is assumed).
___ 1010100
___ 1001010
___ 1100110
___ 1111111

Problems

For the next four problems, do the binary addition and fill in the value of C and V.

17. 1010010
0100000
$\overline{}$
          C=
          V=

18. 11001101
11110000
$\overline{}$
          C=
          V=

19. 01100000
00111111
$\overline{}$
          C=
          V=

20. 10101010
10010001
$\overline{}$
          C=
          V=

MICROPROCESSOR INSTRUCTIONS AND PROGRAMMING

OUTLINE

NEW TERMS TO WATCH FOR

Algorithms	Subroutine
Flowcharts	Process
Object Code	Decision
Source Code	Mnemonics
Label	Assembly Language
Op Code	Assembler Program
Operand	Generalized Op Code
Comment	

After completing this chapter, you should be able to:

1. Define and use programming algorithms.
2. Explain the concept of a flowchart.
3. State the difference between machine language programs and assembly language programs.
4. Show how a mnemonic is related to a microprocessor instruction.
5. List the four fields in an assembly language program.
6. Identify the level of computer languages as they relate to the microprocessor.
7. Recognize the difference between source and object code.
8. Represent a program as it appears in memory.
9. Follow the instruction cycle for a microprocessor command.
10. Explain in detail how a microprocessor handles an instruction.
11. Explain the need and uses for subroutines.

10-1   INTRODUCTION

Up to this point, we have discussed the main elements of a microprocessor from a functional perspective. We have seen how memory serves as storage and how the elements within the microprocessor work together.

In this chapter, we begin to look at microprocessor instructions in a general way. Communicating with and getting the processor to function in a planned way is a matter of speaking its language. Learning this language requires an understanding of the form and format of its structure. The microprocessor is a machine that works exclusively with binary numbers. This means that it works in a very formal way with very specific rules and restrictions. Unlike human communication, there is no room for ambiguity or double meaning. This makes learning how the processor is instructed a matter of learning the rules and conventions.

A Word about Programming

Many beginning microprocessor students feel that programming is somewhat of a mystery. Others are inclined to believe that the subject of programming belongs strictly to a course in programming.

Both programs and programming can be very simple, but at an advanced level, they become extremely complex. Anyone, however, can learn to write and understand simple microprocessor programs. The truth is, to become competent in working with microprocessors at any level, it is necessary to understand very simple programs.

In this chapter, we will introduce some programming terminology and concepts. With this, you will gain the background necessary to work with simple microprocessor programs.

10-2   ALGORITHMS

Problem Solving

The microprocessor is used to solve specific problems. The problem might be simple, like keeping a room at a given temperature, or it may be more complex, like tracking a satellite. The program or set of instructions that operates the microprocessor is divided into procedures written in a form called **algorithms**. Algorithms, simply put, are a set of procedures, laid out in logical steps, to solve a problem.

Everyday Example

Algorithm for opening a combination lock:

1. Turn dial two full turns clockwise.
2. Turn dial counterclockwise to 10.
3. Turn dial clockwise to 20.
4. Turn dial counterclockwise to 5.
5. Pull lock open.

We all work with algorithms every day. When a procedure like opening a lock is written down step-by-step, we can call it an algorithm. We are of course, more interested in the algorithms that apply to microprocessors. Math procedures are good examples of algorithms that can be applied to the microprocessor.

Recall that it is possible to multiply by repeated addition. For example, 4×4 can be solved by adding 4 to 4, four times. The group of instructions telling the microprocessor to multiply like this is called a multiplication algorithm. Just think of an algorithm as a procedure.

10-3   FLOWCHARTS

A Schematic

Microprocessors execute long programs and they perform complicated tasks. Programming them requires organized thought and planning. A program can contain hundreds of algorithms—each different and each solving or carrying out some aspect of the overall program.

Every program is carried out in an orderly and planned sequence of events. Planning the sequence is done in a schematic form called a **flowchart**. The flowchart uses graphic symbols to represent the entire sequence of steps the microprocessor will perform. On a smaller scale, even a single algorithm can be represented with a flowchart.

Symbols

Flowcharts are drawn with a set of geometric symbols like those shown in Figure 10-1. These standard symbols are available on plastic templates universally-used by programmers to plan algorithms and write programs. You may encounter slight variations in the symbols used.

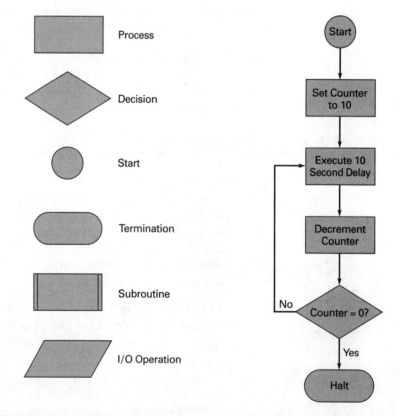

FIGURE 10-1 Flowchart Symbols   **FIGURE 10-2 Time Delay Flowchart**

Figure 10-2 is a flowchart illustrating a time-delay algorithm. The first **process**, in the rectangle, is to set the counter to 10. Then a 10-second delay is executed, after which the counter is decremented. To *decrement* means to subtract 1. The diamond shape indicates a **decision** is made. If the counter is not 0, the delay sequence is executed again. The delay sequence will be executed ten times before the counter is 0, making the algorithm a 100-second timing delay. After the tenth time, because the counter registers 0, a decision will be made to halt the program.

A Tool

The flowchart is a very useful tool to help a programmer solve a problem. In fact, defining the problem and developing the solution have been called the most difficult parts of the entire programming process. Once this is done and a flowchart is prepared, the next step is to write the instructions in the microprocessor language. This is commonly called coding. Writing code becomes an easy task once the procedures, instructions, and rules become familiar. This familiarity comes exclusively through practice. There simply is no other way.

✔ SELF-CHECK FOR SECTIONS 10-1, 10-2, 10-3

1. A set of step-by-step procedures to solve a problem is called an
_____.
2. Name one of the differences between machine language and human language.
3. Create an algorithm for unlocking a door.
4. Explain a flowchart.
5. Draw a flowchart for the algorithm in question 3.

10-4   LANGUAGE

Hierarchy

The languages of the computer world form a sort of hierarchy at the very bottom of which lies the microprocessor. The binary language, that is, the 8-bit numbers that the microprocessor understands, is called machine code. The next level up is **assembly language**. As we go up the hierarchy, the languages become more and more like English. The next level above assembly would include languages such as BASIC, COBOL, or any of the more than one hundred higher–level computer languages. Because the higher-level languages use English-like commands, they are somewhat easier to use than assembly or machine language. On the other hand, the programmer is farther removed from the actual microprocessor instruction. In higher level languages, the programmer is limited to the commands and procedures that the developer of the language has decided are important. With assembly language or machine code, the programmer is limited only by the instructions that have been built into the microprocessor.

Machine Code

The machine code is the lowest level language possible. It consists of the binary instructions that are input to the microprocessor instruction decoder. A machine code program might look like this:

Memory Address	Machine Code
0000	10000110
0001	00000010
0002	10001011
0003	00000010
0004	10010111
0005	00000110

These binary numbers are ultimately all that the microprocessor can cope with, but as we have seen, binary numbers can be represented in several different forms in order to make them easier to deal with.

Assembly Language

For the smaller 8-bit microprocessors there are only about sixty to eighty machine-code instructions, although the more sophisticated ones may have as many as two hundred codes. To make microprocessors easier to work with, assembly language was developed. It is the first step up from machine language. Assembly language is easier to use because it makes use of **mnemonics**. Mnemonic codes are English-like abbreviations that sound similar to the action the instruction performs.

The mnemonic codes and instructions found in this chapter are intended to be introductory examples. Some are derived from Motorola products while others are more like those used in Intel products. The intent of the selections is to enable you to become familiar with basic assembly language concepts, not to learn assembly language programming. Once the basic concepts are learned, programming in a specific assembler becomes easier.

For example, in some systems, LDA is the mnemonic for *load accumulator*. Another example is MOV for *move*. CLR is the mnemonic for the *clear* instruction. In other words, instead of writing 10000110 to instruct the microprocessor to load the accumulator, we can write LDA. This makes assembly language not only easier than machine language to write, but it is also easier to read and learn than machine coding.

There is, however, a slight catch. The microprocessor cannot deal with LDA or anything not binary. So there must be something to translate mnemonics into binary. This is the job of the **assembler program**. An *assembler* is a special program developed so that you can write a program using mnemonics. The assembler program will work through each line of the program and translate the mnemonic into a binary machine code that corresponds to the instruction to be executed by the microprocessor.

Assembly Language Format

The assembler program can only translate into machine code assembly programs written in strict conformance to the rules and format of assembly language. This can be thought of as analogous to using correct grammar and spelling to write an intelligible algorithm.

An assembly language program has a four-part form. Each of the parts is called a field. The four parts are:

Field 1	Field 2	Field 3	Field 4
Label:	Op Code	Operand;	Comment

Label Field

The first field, called the **label** field, is used to represent the address. It is usually separated from the next field by a colon. Symbols can be used in the label field and it should be noted that the address need not be specifically known. Only the order in which it appears is critical. This will become clear when we examine the address field in detail. The assembler program usually limits the number of symbols or characters that can be used to represent the address.

Operation Code Field

The operation code field or **Op Code** is where the actual mnemonic appears. The op code is an instruction and comes from the table of instructions provided with the microprocessor.

Operand Field

The **operand** field is the register, data, or address upon which the instruction is performed. The operand can be thought of as that which is *operated* on. When the operand is followed by a **comment**, a semi-colon is used to separate the operand from the comment. If a comment is not provided, there is no need for the semi-colon.

Comment Field

This area is reserved for brief comments about the instruction. Comments, often called "documentation," are not part of the program and are used to clarify a program instruction. Comments benefit the programmer and those who may be trying to understand the program. Programs that have been put aside get "cold" and they can become hard to understand when they are referred to at some future date. For this reason, it is always a good idea to thoroughly "comment" a program.

Assembly Language Program

Example 1: Here is how a line of an assembly language program might look:

Label:	Op Code	Operand;	Comment
0000:	LDA	$A4;	Load accumulator with Hex A4H

Figure 10-3 shows a memory with the instruction LDA and the hex value A4 loaded into the first two memory locations.

The comment, "Load accumulator with Hex A4H" is illustrative. In practice, a more meaningful comment is recommended, such as a description as to what the Hex A4H is actually used for or what it represents. For example, "load accumulator with the temperature constant A4H."

This line of code will load the accumulator with the binary number 10100100.

The hex number A4H is 10100100_2. The $ sign is used to tell the assembler that we are using hexadecimal. This can be done in different ways. Some systems use the capital "H" behind the hex number to indicate hexadecimal, for example, 04BAH. This tells the assembler to translate the hexadecimal number into binary. You should be aware that different methods are used, so that you can adapt to the conventions of the particular assembler you happen to be working with. In this chapter, we will use the $ symbol when the hex appears in a line of code. In the text, we will use the capital "H" after hex numbers.

Translation

After it is *assembled* the program instruction would look like this:

Address	Machine Code
0000	10000110
0001	10100100

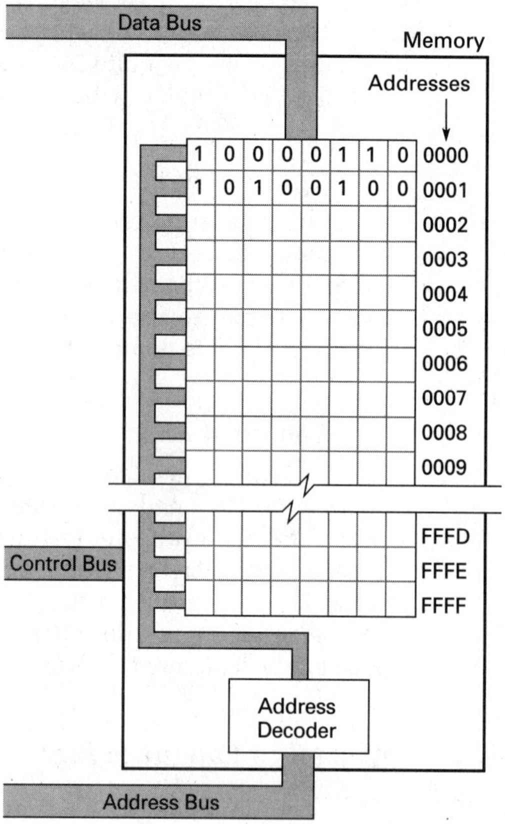

FIGURE 10-3 Memory with LDA (A4H) in the First Two Locations.

Figure 10-4 shows how the assembled instruction would look after it is loaded in memory. The assembler has translated LDA into 10000110_2 and A4H into 10100100_2. Note that while the assembly language statement took only one programming line, two addresses will be required—one for the instruction op code and one for the operand.

The assembled code is also called **object code**, assembly language being the source or **source code**.

Source Code:

Label:	Op Code	Operand;	Comment
0000:	LDA	$A4;	Load accumulator with Hex A4

Object Code:

Address	Machine Code
0000	10000110
0001	10100100

Figure 10-4 shows a microprocessor and a memory. The memory contains the object code for loading the accumulator with A4H.

When power is applied, the microprocessor will execute the instruction. Recall that the microprocessor instruction cycle consists of three steps— fetch, decode, and execute. So, the first thing that the microprocessor does is a *fetch*.

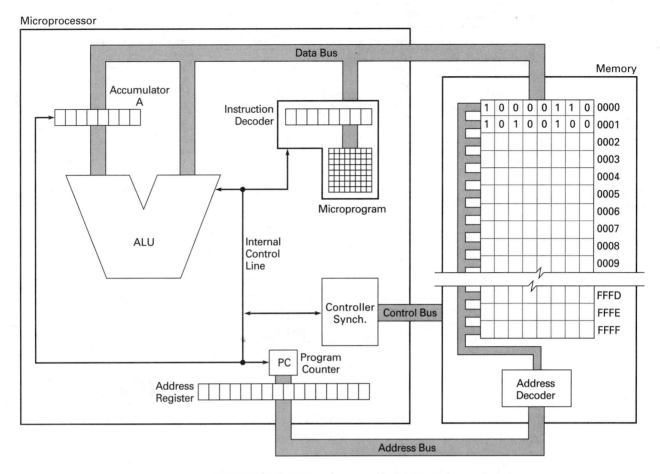

FIGURE 10-4 Microprocessor and Memory

Figure 10-5 illustrates the fetch step. A fetch step consists of:

1. The program counter generates the first address, 0000H (hexadecimal) and places it on the address bus.
2. The microprocessor places a *read* signal on the control bus. The read signal is sensed by the memory and signals it to enter its output mode.
3. The address decoder in the memory decodes the address and after a short delay, the contents of location 0000H appears on the data bus.
4. We can assume that there is no delay on the bus itself, so that whatever is on the data bus, is instantaneously everywhere on the bus. The contents of location 0000H, which is the instruction LDA, is latched into the instruction decoder. This ends the fetch phase.

The *knowledge* of what to do when LDA or 10000110 appears in the instruction decoder is permanently designed into the microprogram of the chip. When LDA appears, the microprogram calls for the contents of the next memory location to be loaded into the accumulator.

Therefore, as in Figure 10-6, during the next clock cycle, the microprocessor increments the program counter. In other words, +1 is added to the address. The address now appearing on the address bus is 0001H. At the same time, the processor again places a *read* signal on the control bus.

After the memory address decoding delay, the contents of memory location 0001H appears on the data bus. The microprocessor then latches this data into the accumulator. This completes the execution phase. Note that the execution actually consisted of fetching another byte from memory and loading it into the accumulator.

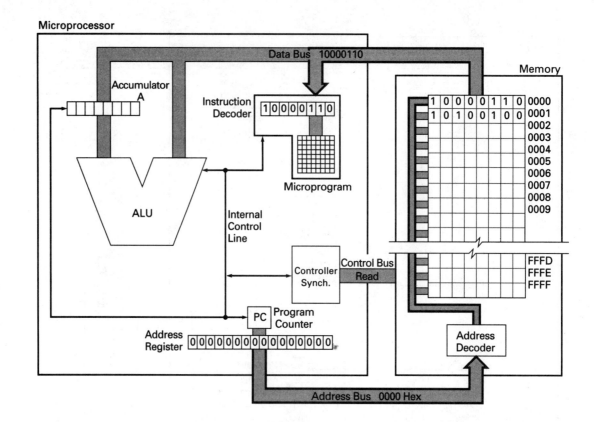

**FIGURE 10-5
The Fetch**

**FIGURE 10-6
Accumulator A
Loaded**

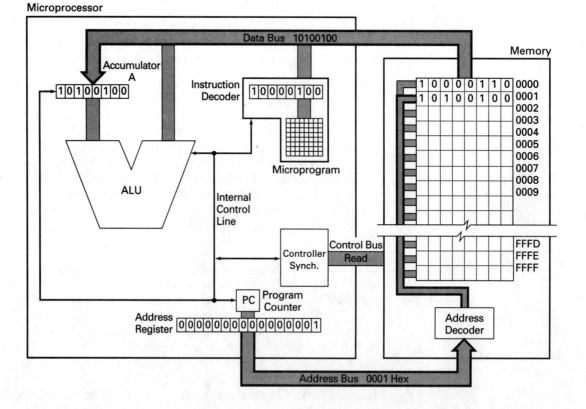

Example 2: This is a simple addition algorithm. Bear in mind that the mnemonics are only examples and that each microprocessor manufacturer has developed a set specifically for their own processor.

Label:	Op Code	Operand;	Comment
ADDPROG:	LDA	$02;	Load Acc. with 00000010
	ADDA	$02;	Add 00000010 to Acc.
	STA	$0007;	Store result

After assembly, the program looks like this:

Hex Address	Machine Code
0000	10000110
0001	00000010
0002	10001011
0003	00000010
0004	10010111
0005	00000000
0006	00000111

This is how the addition algorithm would look translated into machine code and loaded in memory. As in Figure 10-7, each of the binary numbers is loaded into a sequential memory location.

As soon as power is applied, the instruction cycle begins. The three steps—fetch, decode, and execute—will simply repeat as long as the microprocessor is on.

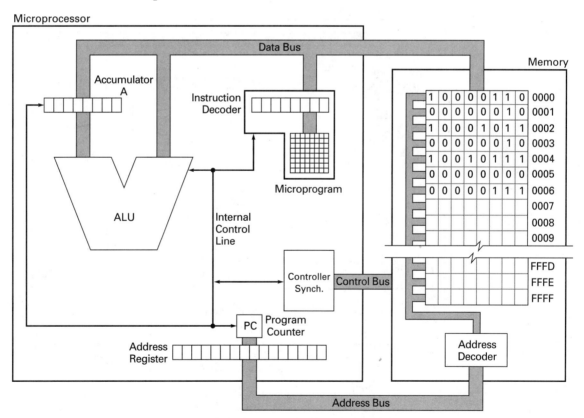

FIGURE 10-7 Program Loaded in Memory

The first step in the addition algorithm is the *fetch*. In Figure 10-8, the program counter generates the first address, 0000H, and at the same time the microprocessor issues a *read* signal on the control bus. After a short memory-decoding delay, the first instruction LDA (10000110) will appear on the data bus and will be latched into the instruction decoder in the microprocessor. The fetch phase is then complete.

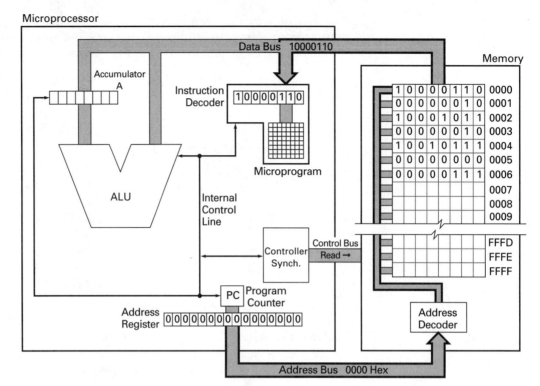

FIGURE 10-8 First Instruction Fetched

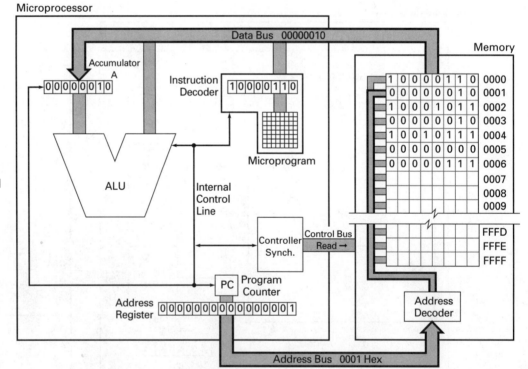

FIGURE 10-9 Load Instruction Executed

The microprocessor then decodes LDA. The microprogram built into the microprocessor knows that this instruction means to load the next byte found in memory into the accumulator.

In Figure 10-9, the program counter increments and the next sequential address 0001H, appears on the address bus. At the same time, the processor issues another read signal on the control bus. After the memory-decoding delay the first number to be added, 00000010, appears on the data bus. The microprocessor takes the byte into accumulator A. Recall that it already knows to do this from the decode phase. This completes the execution phase for the first instruction.

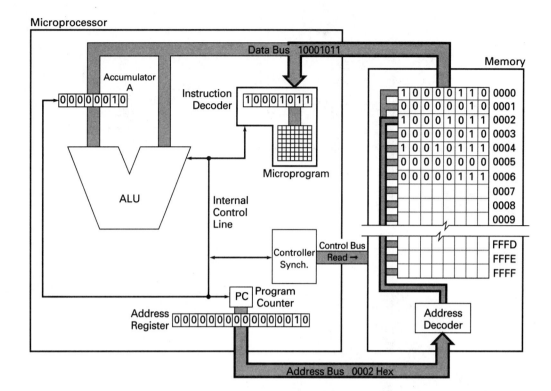

FIGURE 10-10
Second Instruction
Fetched

In Figure 10-10, the program counter increments again and issues the next address, 0002H. The processor places a *read* signal on the control bus. The byte at location 0002H is the instruction for adding. This byte is latched into the instruction decoder at the end of the fetch phase.

When ADDA is decoded, the microprocessor knows that the next byte in memory is the number to be added to the byte in the accumulator.

Therefore, as in Figure 10-11, the program counter increments and issues the next sequential address, 0003H. The byte at this location, 00000010, is then loaded into the ALU.

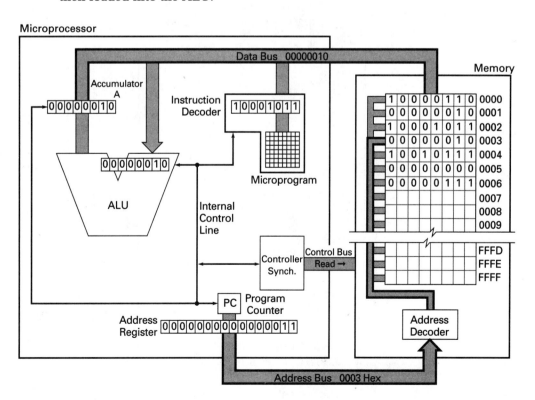

FIGURE 10-11
Second Number to
be Added Loaded
into ALU

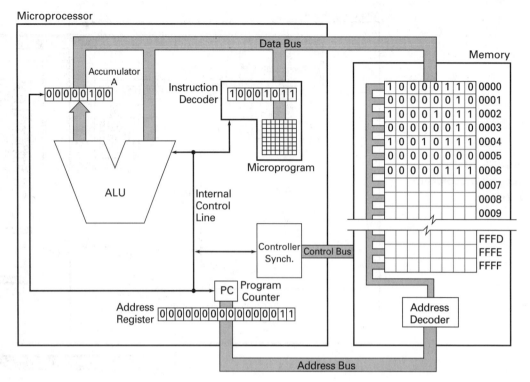

**FIGURE 10-12
Result Placed in
Accumulator A**

In Figure 10-12, the ALU adds this number (00000010) to the number in the accumulator and places the result in the accumulator. In other words, the microprocessor added the 2 in the accumulator and the 2 found at location 0003H and placed the result, 4, in the accumulator. The accumulator now contains 00000100. This is the end of the execution phase of the second instruction cycle.

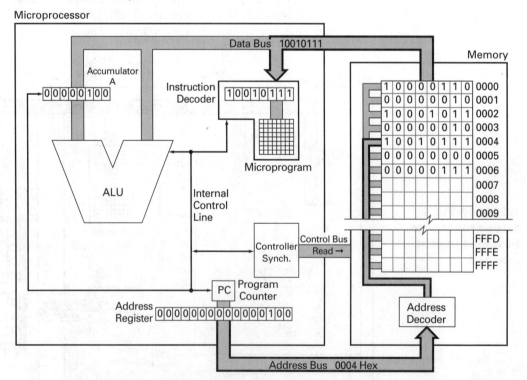

**FIGURE 10-13 Third
Instruction Fetched**

As in Figure 10-13, the program counter increments and issues address 0004H. The microprocessor places a *read* signal on the control bus. The contents of address 0004H are then placed on the data bus and latched into the instruction decoder.

This instruction, STA, means store the contents of accumulator in memory. When STA has been decoded, the microprocessor knows that the byte in the accumulator is to be stored at the address specified in the next two memory locations. We need two, 8-bit locations for an address. Memory addresses are 16-bits or two bytes. This means the microprocessor must read the next two memory locations to find out where to store the byte in the accumulator.

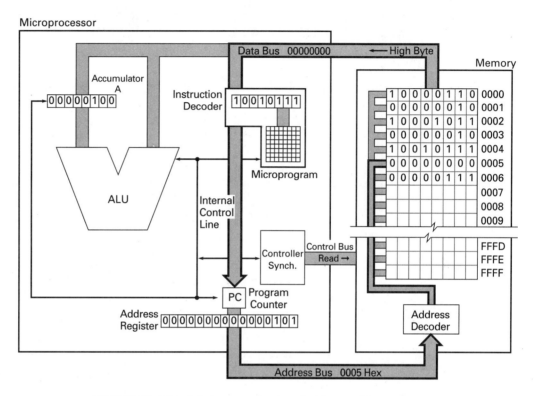

FIGURE 10-14 High Byte to be Loaded into Address Register

The program counter, Figure 10-14, issues the next sequential address, 0005H, and the processor places a *read* signal on the control bus. The byte at location 0005H is 00000000, the high byte of the address where data is to be stored. This byte is fetched first and the next address generated fetches the low byte. The microprocessor has the means to assemble the address and place it in the address register. Putting together an address is accomplished in different ways in different processors. Most microprocessors have an internal connection between the data bus and the address register, as seen in Figure 10-14. The assembling of the address can also take place in the register array, where a temporary register may be available. This means the next address issued will be the storage address.

In Figure 10-15, the assembled address, 0007H, is placed on the address bus. The microprocessor then issues a *write* signal and it is placed on the control bus. The byte in the accumulator is then taken from the accumulator, moved along the data bus and latched into location 0007H of the memory. This is the end of the addition algorithm. Normally a HALT or END instruction would be placed at the end of the last byte in a program, or the microprocessor would continue to increment the program counter and try to execute non-existent instructions.

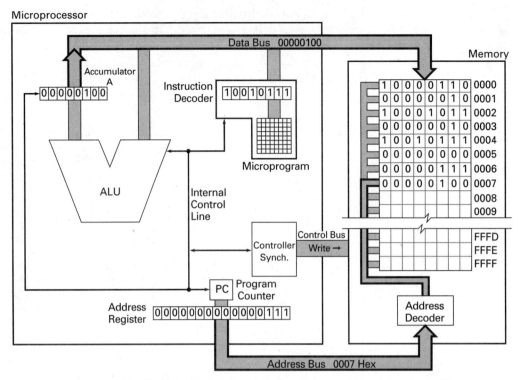

Microprocessor

Data Bus   00000100

Memory

Accumulator A

Instruction Decoder

Microprogram

ALU

Internal Control Line

Controller Synch.

Control Bus   Write →

PC   Program Counter

Address Register   00000000000000111

Address Decoder

Address Bus   0007 Hex

FIGURE 10-15 Byte in A Accumulator Stored at Location 0007H

Instruction Format

Instructions for 8-bit microprocessors are 8-bit *words*. The instruction itself is always one byte.

Mnemonic	Hex Op Code	Binary
LDA	86	10000110

But note that when we wrote the line of code to actually load the accumulator, we also specified what to load it with. This included the operand.

Label:	Op Code	Operand;	Comment
	LDA	$02	

In other words, the instruction was to load accumulator with the byte 00000010. The complete instruction actually occupied two memory locations. Including the operand as part of the instruction is called **Generalized Op Code**. For 8-bit processors, this means instructions can be formatted to be 1, 2, or 3 bytes long. Addresses are actually 16-bits long so that a generalized op code instruction that includes an address will be three bytes long and occupy as much memory.

✔ SELF-CHECK FOR SECTION 10-4

6. Would you consider assembly language to be a low level language? Why?
7. What is machine code?
8. _____ are English-like abbreviations that sound similar to the action an assembly language instruction performs.
9. Explain what an assembler program does.
10. Name the four parts or fields used in assembly language.
11. Which field is used to write the mnemonic?
12. What is object code?
13. What is source code?
14. Some assemblers use a $ sign symbol. What is the purpose of this?

10-5   SUBROUTINES

Assembly language programs are assembled and written with an assembler program. The resulting object code is then loaded into memory in sequential locations, just as we have seen in the examples. When the program is run, the microprocessor begins executing instructions in sequence.

At times there may be parts of the program that are repeated. For example, an accounting program might be expected to do addition at several places in the program. It would be wasteful and inefficient to write the same math algorithm in more than one place in the program. Since the microprocessor does everything sequentially, how can the math algorithm be accessed out of sequence? The answer lies in special microprocessor instructions called jumps or call-instructions.

Figure 10-16 shows how a group of instructions can be accessed out of sequence. The main program has been loaded from memory address 0100H to 0200H (Fig. 10-16). At address 0120H, the program encounters a need for the subgroup or **subroutine** and a subroutine call is executed. The main sequence is then left and the program begins executing instructions in the subroutine. At the end of the subroutine, the program is returned to the point where it left off. The actual mechanics of this operation will be taken up in more detail in a later chapter.

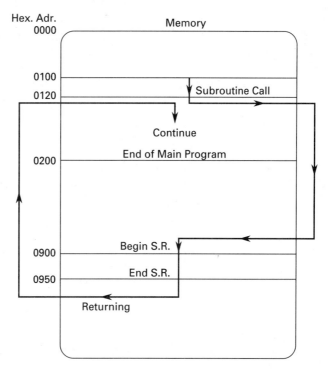

FIGURE 10-16 Subroutine Execution

The purpose of a subroutine-call instruction is to allow a subgroup of instructions within the main program to be executed out-of-sequence. For example, in an accounting program, whenever a math function is required, the program can *jump* to the subroutine algorithm, execute the math function, and return to the main program's sequence of execution. Most programs contain several subroutines that are accessible through jumps or calls.

Programmers usually keep a collection of subroutines already written on file. These routines can be inserted in a program whenever necessary, without having to go to the trouble of rewriting them. But there are limits to the usefulness of this practice. A program consisting entirely of *canned* subroutines would not always address a given programming problem in an efficient way.

Working with Assemblers

There are a few *directives* or *pseudo-instructions* that are used in an assembly language program. These directives are not part of the microprocessor instruction set, but are specifically for the assembler. For example, most assemblers have an *EQU* or *equivalent* statement. This allows us to name things like address locations or subroutines. We might want to name address 0A6BH = MYSUB. Whenever we want to refer to the address, we need only type MYSUB. This is why we mentioned earlier that the label field can be symbolically indicated. The assembler reads these directives first and translates them. This helps the programmer eliminate some errors that can occur due to transposing or mistyping numbers.

Development Kits

Program development kits are available from microprocessor manufacturers. The kits are intended to make it easy for engineers and programmers to write microprocessor routines for specific professional applications. The basic kit will usually include the microprocessor, a RAM memory, a CRT screen, a keyboard, and a disk drive. The software will consist of some sort of text editor and an assembler program. The assembly language program is typed with the text editor and stored to disk in a file. These source code files are then run through the assembler program to create object code. The object code is then loaded into the RAM and the program is debugged.

Debugging

Debugging is an important and essential step in writing programs. Due to the literal way in which machines interpret a command, unwanted results occur, even when the programmer is an experienced expert. Assembler programs have become increasingly sophisticated and can perform some degree of debugging while the program is being written.

In longer more complex programs, debugging takes place at many levels and continues even after a program is sold. Naturally, everyone tries to find and correct all the bugs or defects possible before the program is released, but there are always a few minor bugs that appear when a program is being used by the customer. The bugs that are found by customers are no longer referred to as bugs, but they are euphemistically called *features.* Software developers have an obligation to continue to maintain and correct their software and provide defect-free revisions after it is released to a customer.

✔ SELF-CHECK FOR SECTION 10-5

15. What is a subroutine?
16. Explain the need for a subroutine.
17. What is a "jump?"
18. What is an EQU or equivalent statement?

SUMMARY OF IDEAS

- An algorithm is a step-by-step procedure written to solve a given problem.
- A flowchart is a symbolic diagram of a program.
- The binary number instructions that are designed into a microprocessor chip are called machine language instructions.
- Only machine code can be input to the microprocessor.
- Assembly language is one step above machine language.
- Assembly language makes use of *mnemonics*, which are English-like abbreviations that represent machine language, binary-coded instructions.
- An *assembler* is a program that translates assembly language into machine code.
- Assembly language format consists of four fields:

  Label: Op Code   Operand;   Comment

- Assembly language code is sometimes referred to as *source code.*
- After a program is assembled into machine code, it is called *object code.*
- Subroutines are algorithms that may need to be repeated or executed several times within a program.
- Subroutines are written only once within the program and are accessed as needed by jumps or calls.

CHAPTER QUESTIONS & PROBLEMS

True or False
1. Algorithms are the symbols used to produce the flowchart.
2. Flowcharts are necessary only when the program is long and complicated.
3. Machine code is binary code, but can be represented in hexadecimal.
4. An assembler program cannot read pure binary numbers.
5. Assembly language programs are written in object code.

Fill in the Blanks
6. The _____ symbol in a flowchart represents a process or computation.
7. In a flowchart, the _____ symbol indicates that a decision must be made.
8. An English-like abbreviation representing a microprocessor instruction is called a _____.
9. In assembly language, the second field in the format is reserved for the _____.
10. The last field in assembly language format is reserved for _____.

Multiple Choice
11. How many memory locations will be occupied when a 16-bit memory address is stored in memory?
    - a. 1
    - b. 3
    - c. 16
    - d. 2

12. Which of the following words is not the same as the others?
    - a. Object code
    - b. Machine code
    - c. Binary code
    - d. Source code

13. Which of the following statements is not true?
    a. A mnemonic can be written in an assembly-language program and understood by the microprocessor.
    b. An assembled program can be loaded into memory and run.
    c. Hex numbers can be written in an assembly program.
    d. Assembled programs are called object code.

14. The fetch phase of microprocessor operation is finished when
    a. the memory address decoder finishes decoding the address location.
    b. the program counter increments.
    c. the data is available on the data bus.
    d. the data is latched into the accumulator.

15. Which statement is true?
    a. Mnemonics are used because the microprocessor cannot interpret English commands.
    b. The programmer can create mnemonics for the microprocessor as long as certain rules for form and format are followed.
    c. Mnemonics are translated by the microprocessor instruction decoder.
    d. Mnemonics are translated to object code.

16. Generalized op code is
    a. not used for assembly language.
    b. available only in some microprocessors.
    c. limited to the op code and the operand.
    d. always used to include the address with the instruction.

17. Memory locations contain
    a. addresses.
    b. op Codes.
    c. operands.
    d. all of the above

18. An operand can be
    a. an address.
    b. a register.
    c. data.
    d. all of the above

19. Subroutines are
    a. used by the microprocessor to interpret instructions.
    b. not useful in long complicated programs.
    c. called and executed from the main program.
    d. small groups of instructions that are called by the microprocessor to produce object code.

20. Assembly language programs can be
    a. written by hand.
    b. typed with a text editor.
    c. translated into machine code.
    d. all of the above

ADDRESSING TECHNIQUES

OUTLINE

NEW TERMS TO WATCH FOR

Inherent	Direct	Implied
Extended	Immediate	Based
Relative	Effective	Register
Offset	Indexed	Direct Page
Absolute	Zero Page	Base Page
String	Memory Mapped	Program Controlled

 After completing this chapter, you should be able to:

1. Recognize the basic forms of addressing used in 8-bit microprocessors.
2. Explain how registers are employed in various addressing techniques.
3. Show how the same instruction can be used with different addressing modes.
4. Demonstrate how the program counter address register is used to locate operands not in the normal memory sequence.
5. Follow a microprocessor instruction based on the form of addressing used.
6. Predict the final result of an operation by understanding how the microprocessor locates the operand.
7. Correctly determine the location of an operand based on the addressing form used.
8. Use addressing to reach all parts of the microprocessor memory.
9. Write simple instructions using basic addressing modes.
10. Apply the basic addressing techniques of this chapter to specific microprocessors.

11-1   INTRODUCTION

The methods and procedures that a microprocessor uses to manipulate data are critical to its performance. When we go about evaluating the effectiveness or desirability of a given microprocessor, a crucial point will be to examine how the microprocessor retrieves data. The single, most-influential procedure for data retrieval is addressing.

Addressing is the general term applied to the way in which a microprocessor fetches operands from memory and from internal registers. More specifically, the address refers either to the source or to the destination of an operand.

The ways in which an operand can be located or referred to—that is, addressed—are limited. There are, however, at least fifteen possible address modes or procedures used in 8-bit microprocessors. No one processor can employ them all. In fact, most processors use only about half the number possible. The set of addressing modes that a microprocessor uses are unique to that model. In general, the more addressing modes a microprocessor has available, the more powerful it is.

It would be a mistake, however, to evaluate a microprocessor simply by counting the address modes it uses. The absence of a given mode may not seriously hinder its operation. There are other things to consider too, for example the clock speed, the number of internal registers, and the organization of registers, to name a few.

In this chapter, we will examine *all* of the basic addressing modes and *a few* of the more complex modes available. With an understanding of these modes, you will be prepared to work with any variations found among different microprocessors on the market today.

11-2   MICROPROCESSOR ADDRESSING

Addressing

An address can only refer to three things:
1. A register
2. A memory location
3. An input/output device

This considerably simplifies things.

Registers are usually referred to by their name. They are named with letters of the alphabet, such as the X or Y register. A memory location must be a binary number. In a 64K memory, all addresses will be 16-bits long. This ordinarily requires two bytes. Some addressing modes refer to locations by using only one-byte addresses. An I/O or input/output device, such as a printer, is connected to the microprocessor through a *port*. Just like a memory location, the I/O port is assigned an address. When the microprocessor needs to refer to the printer, the printer port is addressed.

11-3   THE ADDRESS FIELD

The address is written in the operand field. A quick review of the *operand* is in order here. Recall that in assembly language, the grammar of an instruction consists of four fields.

<table>
<tr><td>Label</td><td>Operation Code</td><td>Operand</td><td>Comment</td></tr>
</table>

              ↑   ↑ That which is operated

    The instruction or command   on by the instruction

An example:

LDA = mnemonic for LoaD Accumulator

B   = internal register B in the register array

Label	Operation Code	Operand	Comment
	LDA	B;	Load Accumulator with the contents of B

The op-code mnemonic LDA means that the accumulator is to be loaded. The operand supplies the register address from which the data is to be fetched. That is, the operand names the register where data is located.

✔ SELF-CHECK FOR SECTIONS 11-1, 11-2, 11-3

1. _____ is the general term applied to the way in which a microprocessor fetches operands from memory and from internal registers.
2. Name the three things an address can refer to.
3. How many bits are normally contained in an address for a 64K memory?
4. Is the address normally found in the operand field or the op code field?

11-4   SIMPLE ADDRESSING MODES

Implied or Inherent Addressing

The first and most common addressing mode is called, **implied addressing**. It is also called **inherent** addressing by some manufacturers. It simply means that the address is implied or inherent within the instruction itself. The operand is contained in the Op Code. It is also referred to as **register addressing**, as it works exclusively on registers internal to the microprocessor.

TECHNICAL FACT

Implied instructions are the shortest and fastest instructions in a microprocessor.

EXAMPLE I

CLRA = mnemonic for CLeaR register A

CLRA is assembly language but the assembled machine code for CLRA will be an 8-bit byte.

Mnemonic	Hex	Machine Code
CLRA	4F	01001111

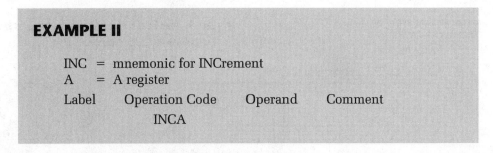

FIGURE 11-1 The Instruction CLRA Loaded in First Memory Location

The way it appears in the memory is shown in Figure 11-1.
The assembly language program would look like this:

Label	Operation Code	Operand	Comment
	CLRA		

This instruction tells the microprocessor to clear or *zero* register A. There is no more to it than that. This instruction is only one 8-bit byte. It doesn't need the operand field at all because the operand is implied or inherent IN the instruction.

Here is another example,

EXAMPLE II

INC = mnemonic for INCrement
A   = A register

Label	Operation Code	Operand	Comment
	INCA		

When this instruction is executed, the microprocessor will add +1 to register A. Again, no operand field is needed; the operand is implied within the instruction.

Register Addressing

Closely related to implied addressing is register addressing. In this addressing mode, the instruction names the action *and* the internal registers that are the source or destination of the action. An example of register addressing is illustrated in Figure 11-2(A,B).

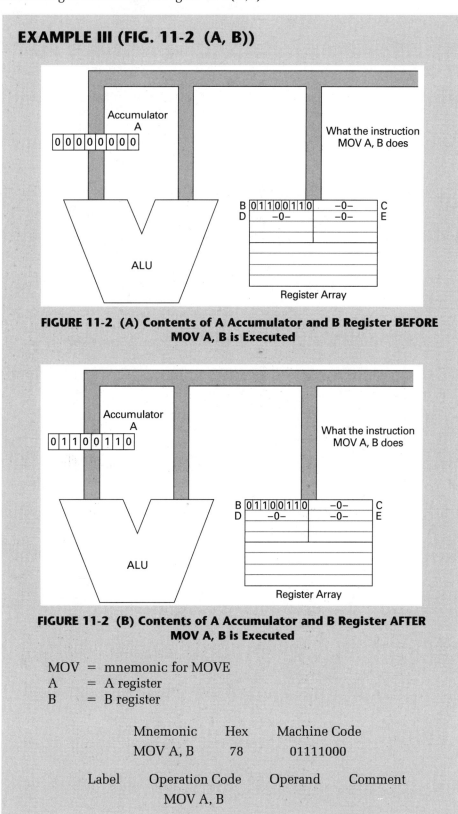

EXAMPLE III (FIG. 11-2 (A, B))

FIGURE 11-2 (A) Contents of A Accumulator and B Register BEFORE MOV A, B is Executed

FIGURE 11-2 (B) Contents of A Accumulator and B Register AFTER MOV A, B is Executed

MOV = mnemonic for MOVE
A   = A register
B   = B register

Mnemonic	Hex	Machine Code
MOV A, B	78	01111000

Label	Operation Code	Operand	Comment
	MOV A, B		

This register addressing mode instruction can be written with one 8-bit byte. It means that the contents of register B is to be MOVed to register A.

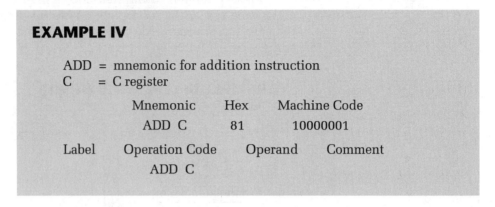

EXAMPLE IV

ADD = mnemonic for addition instruction
C   = C register

Mnemonic	Hex	Machine Code
ADD C	81	10000001

Label	Operation Code	Operand	Comment
	ADD C		

In Figure 11-3(A), the A register or accumulator contains binary 00000111, (7_{10}) and the C register contains 00000001, (1_{10}). When the instruction is performed, as in Figure 11-3(B), the contents of C register is added to the contents of A and the result appears in A. This is a very efficient instruction as it requires only one byte of memory. In addition, instructions performed exclusively with internal registers are faster than instructions which set up binary op codes in RAM.

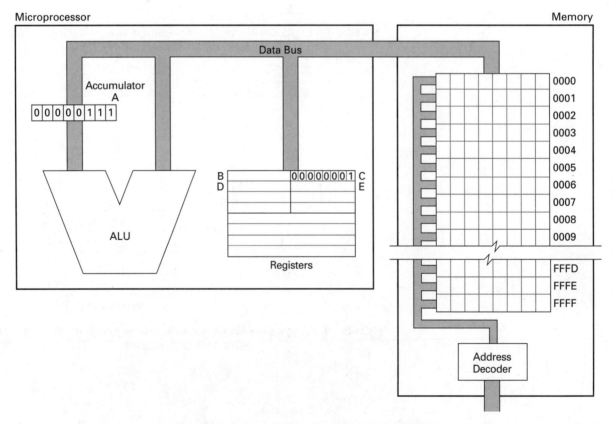

FIGURE 11-3 (A) Before ADD C is Performed

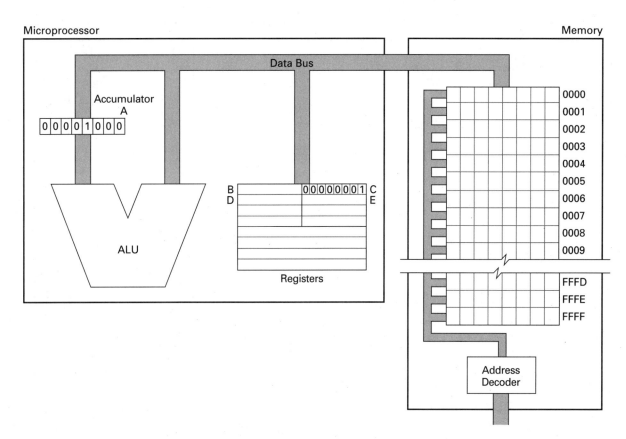

FIGURE 11-3 (B) After ADD C is Performed

Immediate Mode Addressing

The **immediate** mode addressing form takes its name from the fact that the byte immediately following the op code is to be taken literally as a value. The processor is to assume the next byte or next two bytes are a number to be acted upon. Whether the processor uses the next byte or the next two bytes will depend on the exact instruction. This is perhaps best understood by using an example.

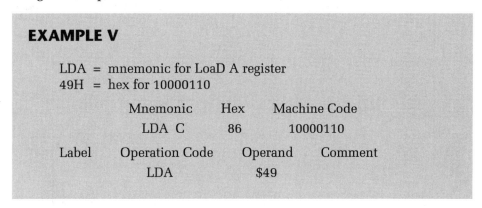

EXAMPLE V

LDA = mnemonic for LoaD A register
49H = hex for 10000110

Mnemonic	Hex	Machine Code
LDA C	86	10000110

Label	Operation Code	Operand	Comment
	LDA	$49	

The mnemonic, LDA, tells the microprocessor that the A register is to be loaded. When LDA is written in the immediate form, the processor will load the byte found in the next (immediate) memory location into register A.

Figure 11-4(A) shows how this instruction will look when loaded into memory, and Figure 11-4(B) shows how things look after the instruction is executed.

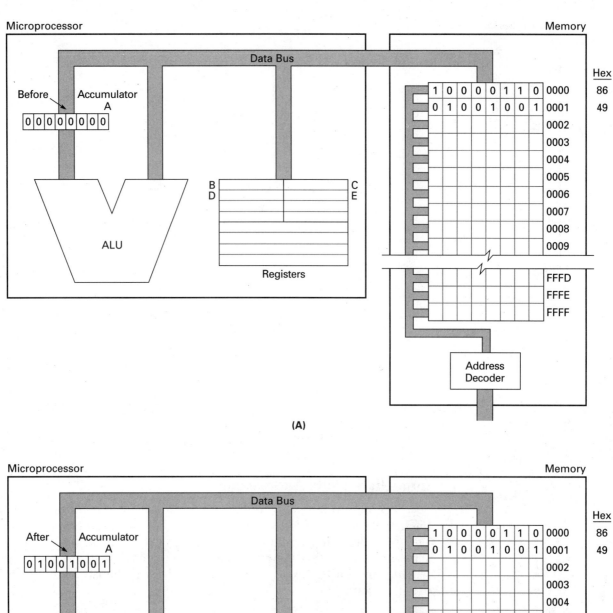

(A)

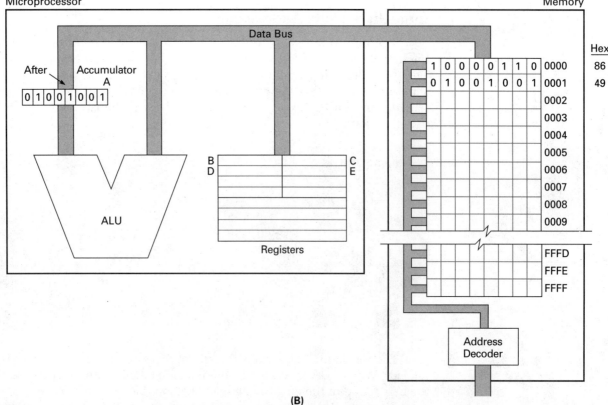

(B)

FIGURE 11-4 (A) LDA Instruction, Written in Immediate Mode, is in Memory Location 0000H. Before Execution (B) After LDA is Executed, Accumulator A is Loaded with 49H, the Byte Immediately After LDA.

Here is another immediate addressing mode example,

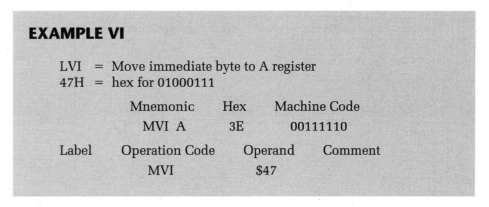

EXAMPLE VI

LVI = Move immediate byte to A register
47H = hex for 01000111

Mnemonic	Hex	Machine Code
MVI A	3E	00111110

Label	Operation Code	Operand	Comment
	MVI	$47	

Figure 11-5(A) shows this instruction loaded into memory. When the microprocessor executes the instruction, the byte 47H will be loaded into the A register. Figure 11-5(B) shows the way the microprocessor looks after execution of MVIA.

The easiest way to remember how immediate addressing works is to recall that the byte *immediately* following the instruction is literal and not to be interpreted as anything other than a number.

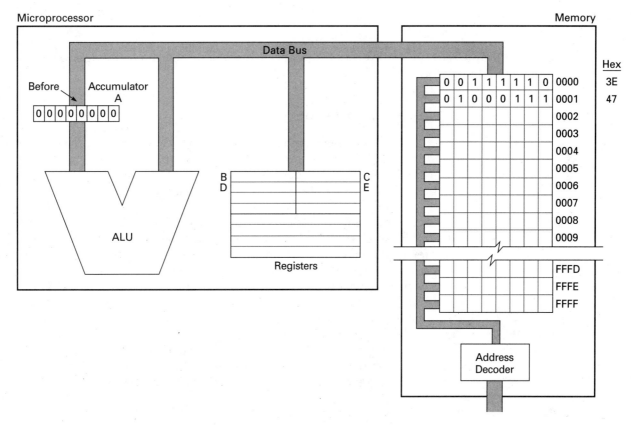

FIGURE 11-5 (A) Before MVI A is Executed, the Instruction 3E has been Loaded in Location 0000H

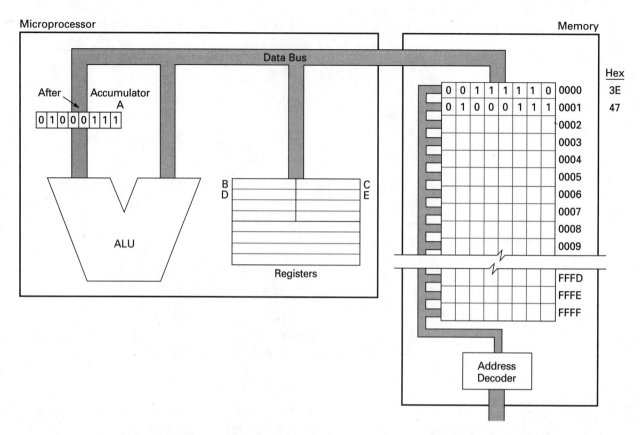

FIGURE 11-5 (B) After MVI A is Executed, the Byte Immediately Following the Instruction has been Loaded into A Accumulator.

Direct Page Addressing

The **direct page** mode of addressing is also called **zero page** or **base page** addressing. There is some slight variation in the way it operates from processor to processor, but the basic principles are the same. The principle is that an 8-bit byte can be used to supply the address.

Recall that normally we would expect to have to supply a full 16-bit number to specify an address. The assumption in direct page addressing is that the address of the operand lies on the base or zero page. A page would refer to the amount of memory that can be addressed with an 8-bit byte, namely 256 locations. So the zero page refers to the first 256 locations, all of which can be specified by an 8-bit number (00H to FFH). Not all microprocessors are capable of this mode. And there is one important variation on this mode that we'll cover later.

At this point, it is worth noting that not all microprocessors use unique mnemonics for every instruction. For example, LDA means load register A but it can be written in several addressing modes. The letters LDA are always the same, since they always mean, *load accumulator*. But LDA can be written:

LDA = 86 = immediate mode

LDA = 96 = direct mode

For assemblers that do not use unique mnemonics, symbols are used to indicate whether LDA is to be interpreted as the immediate, direct, or some other mode. The # symbol indicates the immediate mode while no symbol usually means direct.

For example, LDA #$FF; Load FFH in the immediate mode.

EXAMPLE VII

LDA = LoaD register A
04H = hex for 00000100

Mnemonic	Hex	Machine Code
LDA	96	00000100

Label	Operation Code	Operand	Comment
	LDA	$04	

Figure 11-6(A) illustrates the before and after effects of this instruction. The direct mode form of LDA tells the microprocessor that the next byte in memory is the 8-bit (zero page) address of the operand. In other words, this memory location contains the number to be loaded into the A register.

As in Figure 11-6(B), the microprocessor goes to address location 04H and fetches the byte FFH contained there. The byte FFH is loaded into the A register.

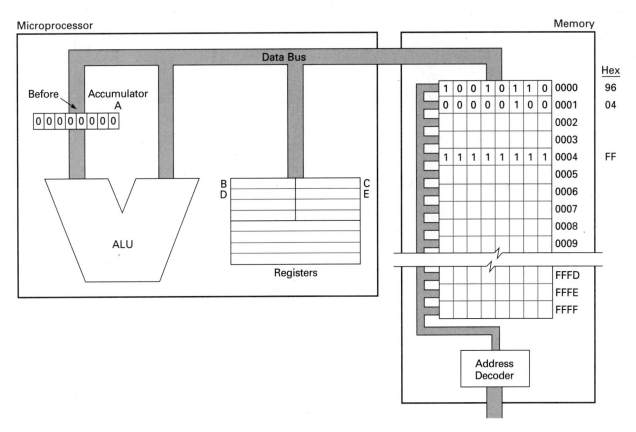

FIGURE 11-6 (A) The LDA Instruction is Contained in Memory Location 0000H. The Next Location, 0001H, Tells the Microprocessor to Load the Byte at Address 04H.

Microprocessor

Memory

Data Bus

After ➤ Accumulator A

| 1 | 1 | 1 | 1 | 1 | 1 | 1 | 1 |

ALU

B D

C E

Registers

Hex

1	0	0	1	0	1	1	0	0000	96
0	0	0	0	0	1	0	0	0001	04
								0002	
								0003	
1	1	1	1	1	1	1	1	0004	FF
								0005	
								0006	
								0007	
								0008	
								0009	

FFFD
FFFE
FFFF

Address Decoder

FIGURE 11-6 (B) After LDA in the Direct Mode is Executed, the A Accumulator is Loaded with FF, the Byte Located at 04H.

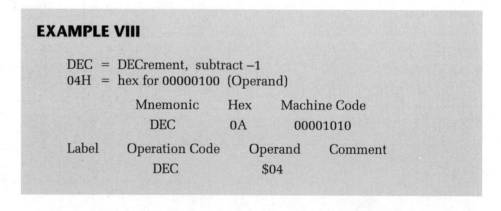

EXAMPLE VIII

DEC = DECrement, subtract −1
04H = hex for 00000100 (Operand)

	Mnemonic	Hex	Machine Code
	DEC	0A	00001010

Label	Operation Code	Operand	Comment
	DEC	$04	

Figure 11-7(A) shows this instruction loaded into memory as it appears before it is executed. Note that memory location 04H contains FFH. After the instruction is executed, Figure 11-7(B), the location 04H has been decremented. In other words FFH is now FEH.

In zero page or direct page addressing, we have assumed the supplied 8-bit byte to be one of the first 256 addresses in memory. Some microprocessors, however, have an 8-bit internal register that can be used to hold the upper or high byte of a 16-bit address. By pre-loading this page register, any location in a 64K memory can be reached. The low byte of the address is supplied in the instruction and the high byte is supplied by the 8-bit page register.

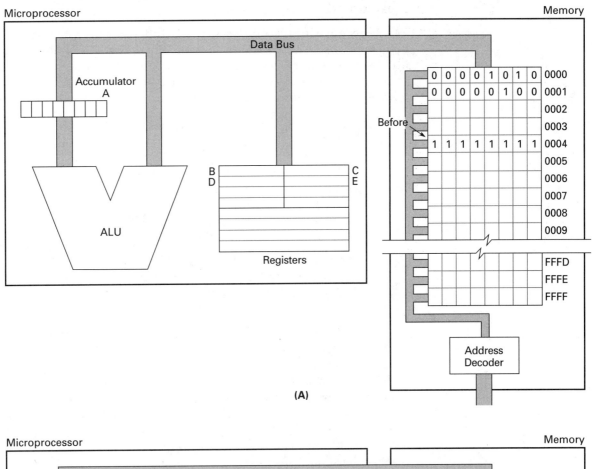

(A)

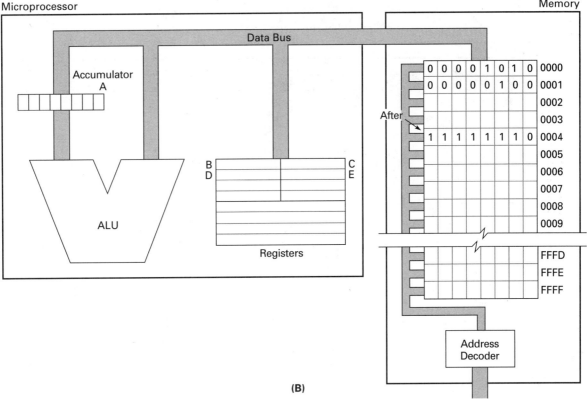

(B)

FIGURE 11-7 (A) Before DEC is Executed, Location 04H Contains FFH. (B) After DEC is Executed, Location 04H Contains FEH.

Absolute Mode Addressing

The **absolute mode** is also called the **extended mode** by some manufacturers. The absolute address refers to the full 16-bit address. Clearly all absolute mode instructions will occupy a minimum of three memory locations. One is needed for the instruction and two for the address. But with an absolute address, the exact location in memory can be named.

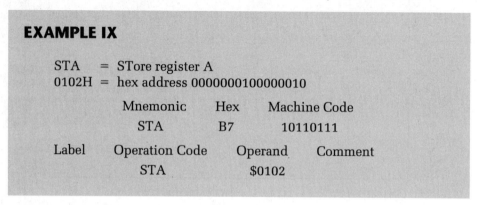

EXAMPLE IX

STA = STore register A
0102H = hex address 0000000100000010

Mnemonic	Hex	Machine Code
STA	B7	10110111

Label	Operation Code	Operand	Comment
	STA	$0102	

The STA or STore A register instruction means that the microprocessor is to store the contents of the A register. The processor will look at the next two sequential bytes in memory to assemble the address where the byte is to be stored. Figure 11-8(A) shows the state of the microprocessor and memory before the instruction is executed. The first byte after the instruction is 02H, the low byte of the address. The second byte after the instruction is the high byte of the address, 01H. Note the byte in the A register is FFH. In Figure 11-8(B) we see that after the instruction is executed, the byte in the A register has been stored at location 0102H.

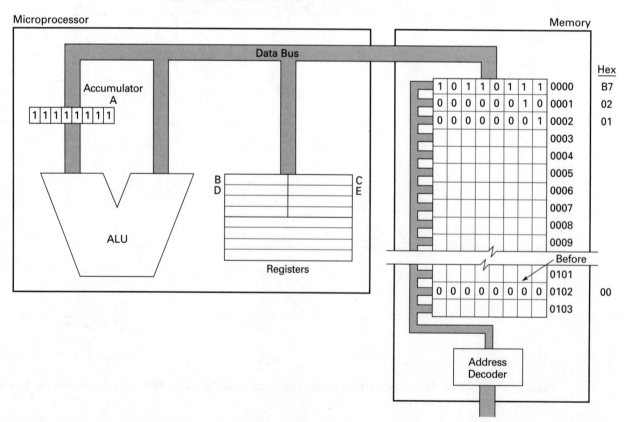

FIGURE 11-8 (A) Before STA is Executed, the Accumulator Contains FFH and Location 0102H Contains 00H.

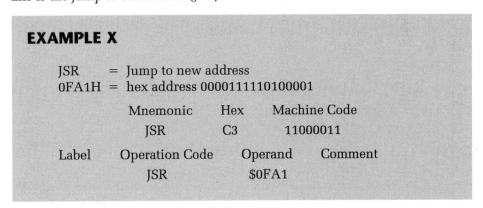

FIGURE 11-8 (B) After STA is Executed, the Byte in A Accumulator is Stored in Location 0102H.

Recall that the microprocessor has the ability to move to a new location in memory to execute a subroutine. One of the instructions to accomplish this is the *jump to subroutine* (JSR) instruction.

EXAMPLE X

JSR   = Jump to new address
0FA1H = hex address 0000111110100001

Mnemonic	Hex	Machine Code
JSR	C3	11000011

Label	Operation Code	Operand	Comment
	JSR	$0FA1	

In Figure 11-9(A), the jump instruction is in location 0003H. The absolute address for the jump instruction is the next two bytes in memory. When the Jump instruction is executed, Figure 11-9(B), the microprocessor will load the absolute address given in locations 0004H and 0005H into the program counter. In this way, the next instruction to be executed will be the subroutine located at 0FA1H.

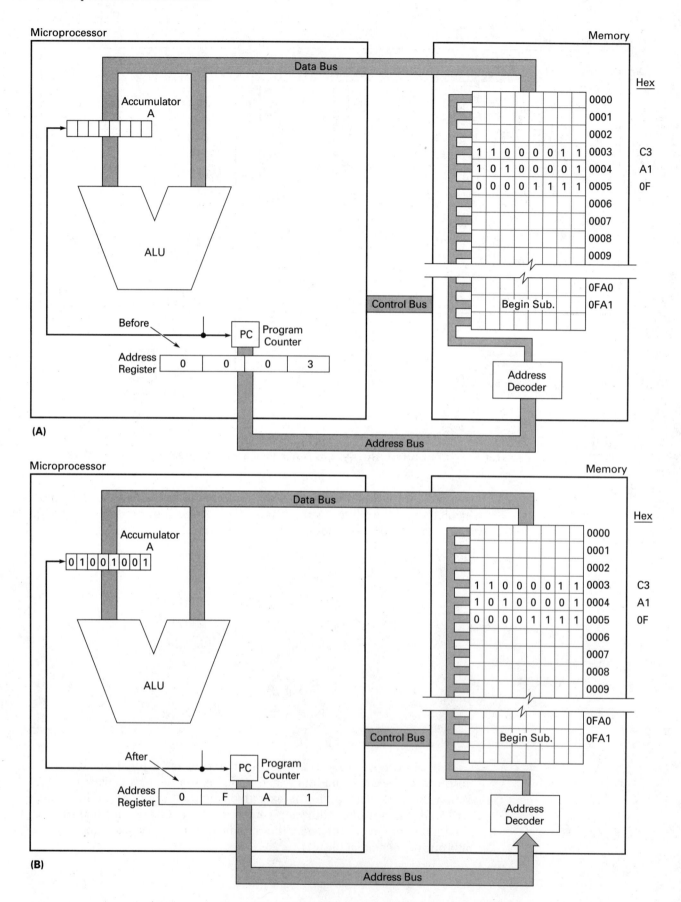

FIGURE 11-9 (A) Before JMP is Executed, the Program Counter is Working at 0003H. (B) After JMP is Executed, the Program Counter has been Loaded with Subroutine Address

✔ SELF-CHECK FOR SECTION 11-4

5. Explain inherent-mode addressing.
6. What is register addressing?
7. What does it mean to "clear" a register?
8. Does incrementing add 1 or subtract 1?
9. Explain immediate-mode addressing.
10. With direct- or base-page addressing, how many bits are required for an address?
11. Explain absolute or extended mode addressing.

11-5   ADVANCED ADDRESS MODES

Relative Addressing

Relative addressing means that the location of the new operand will be found *relative* to where the current instruction is located. This form of addressing is used to find data that is out of sequence or in addresses relative to where the instructions are taking place.

As in the jump instruction, the program counter is loaded with a new address. This is also called *branching*. In relative addressing, an 8-bit byte called the *displacement byte* is added to the current address in the program counter thereby forming a new address relative to the current one. The byte following the instruction will be in the 2's complement form, −128 to +127. The minus indicates a branch backward in memory and a plus means a branch forward.

The advantage of branching or relative addressing is that with this form of addressing, only one byte is needed to specify an address.

Here is an example of relative addressing,

BRA = Program Branch
06H = hex for 00000110

Mnemonic	Hex	Machine Code
BRA	20	00100000

Label	Operation Code	Operand	Comment
	BRA	$06;	displacement byte

The byte following the instruction is called the displacement byte. Figure 11-10 (A) shows the branch instruction loaded at location 0100H.

TECHNICAL FACT ■■■■■■■▰▰▰▰▰

IMPORTANT: It is important to remember that the microprocessor always increments the program counter to the location of the next instruction. For this reason we say that the program counter address register always contains the address of the next instruction. In fact, this means that the relative branch range extends not from 2128 to 1127 but from 2126 to 1129.

In the present example, after the microprocessor encounters the BRA instruction, the program counter will increment to address 0101H. This is where the next instruction would normally be (see Fig. 11-10(A). In the case of the branch instruction, the displacement byte of 06H will be added to the program counter which contains 0101H. The new address then will be 0107H. It is 6 locations forward relative to where the program counter was (Fig. 11-10(B).

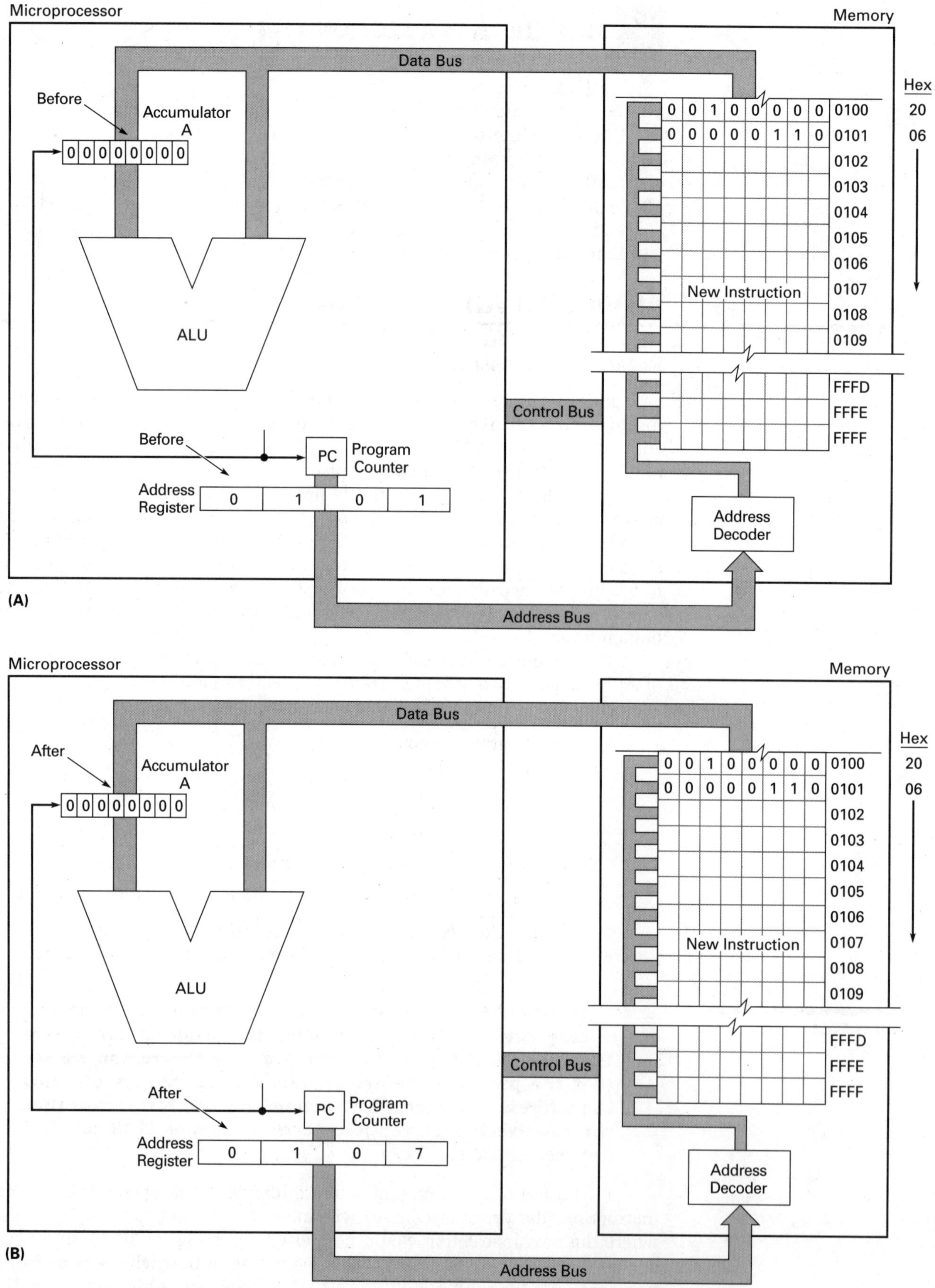

FIGURE 11-10 **(A) Before JMP is Executed, the Program Counter is Working at Location 0101H. (B) After JMP is Executed, the Program Counter "Jumps" the Microprocessor to the Displacement Address 0107H.**

Some microprocessors have a version of the branch instruction that allows a longer branch, that is, a full 16-bit relative branch. With a two byte displacement address, the branch range extends from −32768 to +32767.

Register Indirect Addressing

In register indirect addressing, a register pair is used to "point" to the memory location of an operand. In other words, a register is used to contain the address of the operand. The processors that use this mode usually have a pair of 8-bit multipurpose registers that can be employed for this purpose. Because 16 bits are needed for an address, it does require that the register pair first be loaded with a proper address.

Microprocessors employ several variations on this idea. The principle is to use an internal, on-board microprocessor register to contain the address, rather than an external memory location.

EXAMPLE X

ADD M = mnemonic for addition instruction using memory
H   = H register for high byte of address
L   = L register for low byte of address

Mnemonic	Hex	Machine Code
ADD M	89	10001001

Label	Operation Code	Operand	Comment
	ADD M		

The key to the ADDM mode of addition is that the H and L register pair will contain the address of the byte to be added to the byte in the A accumulator. This means that before the instruction is executed, one of the numbers to be added has to be in the accumulator. And the address of the other number must be in the HL register pair. This is illustrated in Figure 11-11(A).

In Figure 11-11(A), the A accumulator contains a binary 00000111 and location 0006H contains a binary 00000001. The H register holds the high byte (00000000) of the address and the L register holds the low byte (00000110). Figure 11-11(B) shows that after the ADD instruction is executed, the byte at location 0006H has been added to the byte in the A accumulator. The result then appears in the A accumulator.

Indexed Addressing Mode

Indexed addressing is somewhat more complicated than the modes discussed so far, but it is extremely efficient for certain operations. It is used to retrieve large blocks of data from memory, manipulate the data, and return it to other locations.

The indexed mode always requires a special register called the index register. Some processors have more than one index register. The index register is 16-bits wide because it is intended for memory addresses. This form of addressing is called based addressing by some manufacturers and therefore the index register is called the base register in those microprocessors. A base register, therefore, serves the same purpose as an index register.

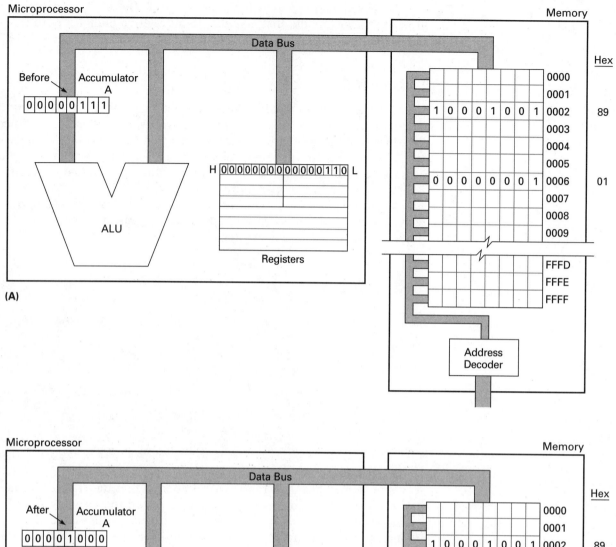

(A)

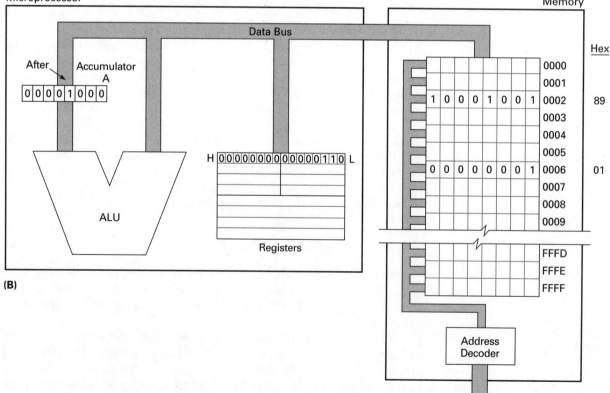

(B)

FIGURE 11-11 (A) Before ADD M is Executed, the Accumulator A Contains 00001000 (7_{10}) (B) After ADD M is Executed, the Accumulator Contains 00001000 (8_{10})

There are two numbers used to form the indexed address. The two numbers are calculated and form what is called the **effective** address. The first number used is the number contained in the index register itself. This number is called the *base address.*

The second number is found in the byte following the instruction. This displacement or **offset** byte, is added to the base address in the index register to form the effective address.

EXAMPLE XIII

LDA = Load A register
05H = hex for offset byte 00000101

Mnemonic	Hex	Machine Code
LDA	A6	10100110

Note: Clearly, unless the assembler uses unique mnemonics, a symbol must be used to indicate indexed addressing. At this point, it is better to concentrate on what indexed addressing is rather than learning symbols.

Label	Operation Code	Operand	Comment
	LDA	$05	

When the microprocessor encounters LDA in the indexed address form, it knows the next byte in memory is the offset byte. The microprogram of the processor will add this byte to the base address in the index register NX . This calculation takes place in order for the microprocessor to find the address of the byte of data to be loaded into register A. In Figure 11-12(A), the index register, NX, contains the base address 0010H and the A register is clear.

After the instruction is executed, Figure 11-12(B) the program counter has been loaded with the calculated effective address, 0015H. Note that the base address, the address in the index register NX has *not* changed. The effective address is loaded into the program counter address register. The data byte (FFH) located at the effective address, 0015H, has been loaded into register A.

Indirect Addressing Mode

There are cases when blocks of data must exist in the program that vary in size. These blocks may need to be used by various subroutines each of which may have an affect on the size of the block. The block could be large at times and shrink to almost nothing at other times. For this reason, it is not efficient to place the block of data at a fixed or absolute address. The location and size of the block may vary. This is the rationale behind indirect addressing.

In indirect addressing, a fixed location in memory is used to contain the address of a block of data. The fixed location might be thought of as *the address of the address*, and the assembly language codes for indirect addressing automatically know it.

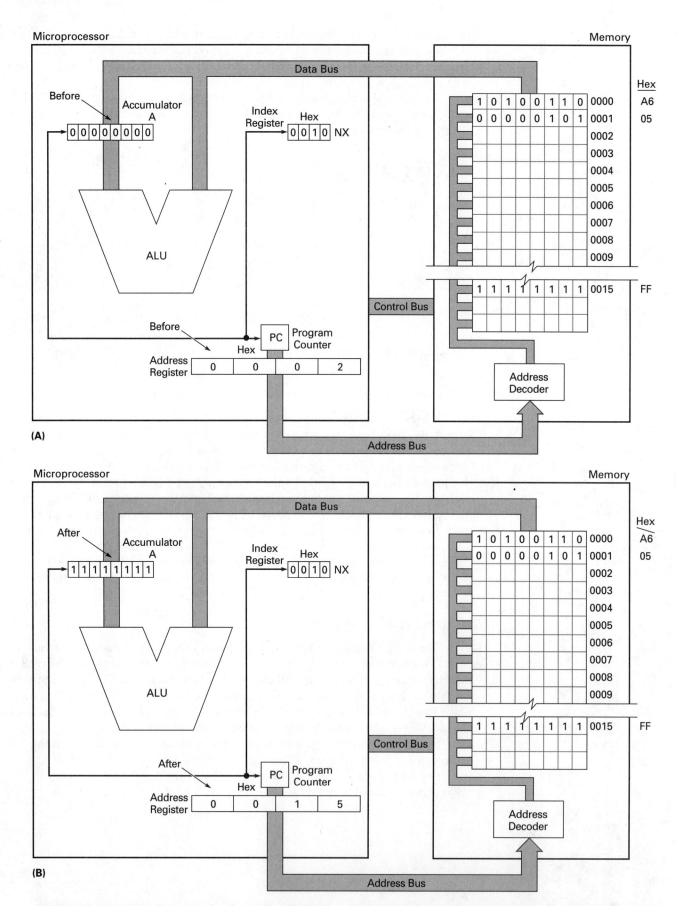

FIGURE 11-12 (A) Before LDA in the Indexed Mode is Executed, the Accumulator Contains 00H. The Byte to be Loaded is at Location 0015H. (B) After LDA in the Indexed Mode is Executed, the Program Counter has been "Indexed" to 0015H. This is so that the Byte at 0015H can be Loaded into the A Accumulator.

EXAMPLE XIV

LDA   = mnemonic for Load the A register
0A   = hex for low byte of address 00001010
0F   = hex for high byte of address 00001111

Label	Operation Code	Operand	Comment
	LDA	[$0F0A]	

In our example, the brackets, [], indicate to the assembler that we are using indirect addressing.

Figure 11-13(A) illustrates the way in which indirect addressing works. Before the instruction is executed, the A register is empty. The block of data to be accessed is at address 0FFAH. The first byte of the data block is 1001100l.

When the microprocessor finds the indirect mode instruction, LDA, it knows the next two bytes in memory will contain the address of the address it is to load the accumulator from. The bytes in the two locations immediately following the instruction are 0A, hex for the low byte; and 0F, hex for the high byte. The processor looks to this address for the address of the first byte of data in the block.

Location 0F0AH contains the low byte of the address where the byte to be loaded is stored. The microprogram has been designed so that both 0F0AH and 0F0BH will be used to assemble the address of the first byte of the data block. Figure 11-13(B) shows the accumulator loaded with the first byte of the data block. The idea is that whenever this block of data is needed, the program can check the permanent address 0F0AH to see where the first byte is located.

String Addressing

A **string**, in the microprocessor world, means any sequence of bytes stored in memory, regardless of their meaning, that have a specific beginning and end. In many cases, it is desired to move a string from one location in memory to another. This implies a source address where the string begins, and a destination address or the new area where the string is ultimately relocated.

The principle behind string addressing is that one 16-bit address register in the microprocessor serves to hold the source address of the string and another 16-bit register is chosen to hold the destination address for the string. Each time a byte is moved, the source and destination address registers decrement. This continues until the last byte of the string is in the new location.

11-6   INPUT/OUTPUT ADDRESSING

Input/output addressing is used by the microprocessor to address various peripheral devices. Data is either flowing out to the peripheral device or flowing in from it.

Input/output addressing can be divided into two types, **program-controlled** and **memory-mapped**.

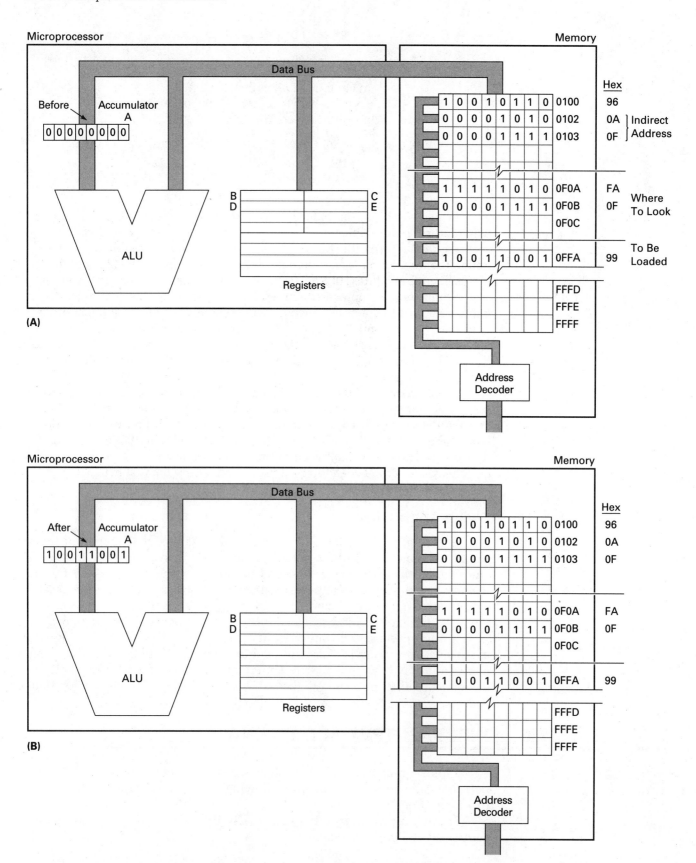

FIGURE 11-13 (A) Before the LDA in the Indirect Mode is Executed, Accumulator A is 00H. (B) After LDA in the Indirect Mode is Executed, the Byte at Location 0FFAH is Loaded into the Accumulator A.

To use program-controlled I/O, the instruction set of the microprocessor must have specific instructions for the direction of data flow. In addition, a register is usually designated to hold the I/O address. For example, to read data from a peripheral device, the I/O register is loaded with the address of the device and an *in* instruction is written into the program.

Memory-mapped I/O addressing simply means that a block of memory addresses is specifically assigned for addressing peripheral devices. The microprocessor, then, treats a peripheral device like a memory location. For example, to read an input from a peripheral, such as a keyboard, the microprocessor outputs the keyboard address on the address bus and a *read* signal on the control bus. It should be noted that the memory-mapped technique can be used by any type microprocessor.

11-7 ADDRESSING MODE SUMMARY

The basics of addressing have been covered. The variations on these basic forms are many, but an understanding of the examples discussed in this chapter will equip you to understand the variations you may encounter. It is hard to overemphasize the importance of understanding basic addressing techniques. The instruction set of a microprocessor cannot be understood without an understanding of the addressing techniques employed. Should you desire to work with 16 and 32-bit processors at some future point, you will find even more complex addressing routines. With your understanding of this chapter, you have built the foundation for learning more sophisticated forms of addressing.

 SELF-CHECK FOR SECTIONS 11-5, 11-6, 11-7

11. In relative addressing the location of the new operand will be found _____ to where the current instruction is located.
12. Explain the term displacement byte.
13. What is indexed addressing?
14. Explain the term "effective address."
15. What is an offset byte?
16. What does a string refer to?
17. Explain the difference between program–controlled microprocessors and memory mapping.

SUMMARY OF IDEAS

- Inherent- or implied-mode addressing means that the operand is contained within the instruction.
- The immediate mode of addressing means that the byte immediately following the instruction is the operand and is not an address or a register.
- In direct-page addressing, an 8-bit byte can be used as the address.
- The *zero page* refers to the first 256 memory locations.
- Absolute- or extended-mode addressing specifies the entire 16-bit memory address.
- A relative address is a memory location that has an address relative to the address contained in the program counter register. It is a jump forward or backward from the current address.

- The register-indirect mode uses a register pair to hold the address of the operand.
- Indexed addressing requires an index register to contain a base address. The byte following the instruction is used with the base address to calculate the effective address.
- The indirect mode of addressing uses a fixed location in memory that is always used to contain *the address of the address* where the operand is to be found.
- Input/output addressing is either program controlled or memory-mapped.
- Program-controlled I/O addressing requires that the microprocessor have specific I/O instructions.
- Memory-mapped I/O addressing treats peripherals just like memory locations.
- String addressing employs source and destination address registers.

CHAPTER QUESTIONS & PROBLEMS

True or False

1. Inherent-mode addressing in an instruction means that the instruction and the address require only two bytes.
2. Absolute- or extended-mode addressing requires an offset byte.
3. Treating a peripheral device like a memory location is referred to as memory mapping.
4. In register addressing, the address of the operand is found in the register named in the instruction.
5. The zero page address is contained within the 8-bit instruction mnemonic.

Fill in the Blank

6. When the byte following the instruction is added directly to the program counter address register it is called _____ addressing.
7. An absolute address instruction will require a minimum of _____ memory locations.
8. The byte added to the base address in indexed addressing is called the _____ byte.
9. In an indirect address mode instruction, the two bytes following the instruction are the address of the _____ .
10. A string address mode will require a source and a _____ address.

Multiple Choice

11. If the LDA, load register A, instruction is used in the immediate mode, the operand
    a. is located from the next byte.
    b. is located from the next two bytes.
    c. is the next byte.
    d. cannot be determined.

12. If the microprocessor instruction is written in the inherent mode, the instruction and the location of the operand require how many bytes?
    a. 2
    b. 1
    c. 3
    d. cannot be determined

13. If the high byte of an address is assumed to be zero, the addressing technique is probably
    a. inherent.
    b. register.
    c. implied.
    d. direct page.

14. Which of the following modes would most likely be used to execute a program branch?
    a. inherent
    b. direct page
    c. relative
    d. register

15. Which of the following address modes could be used for a branch instruction?
    a. indexed
    b. relative
    c. absolute
    d. all of the above

16. Where would you expect to find the address of the operand in an indexed mode instruction?
    a. in the byte following the instruction
    b. in the two bytes following the instruction
    c. in the A register
    d. none of the above

17. The effective address is found by
    a. adding offset to byte following instruction.
    b. adding the offset to the effective.
    c. adding the offset to the base.
    d. adding the base to the relative.

18. The instruction LDA, load register A, is written in the indirect mode:
    Label   Operation Code   Operand   Comment
              LDA   [$A00F]
    The address of the operand
    a. is A00FH plus base address.
    b. is A00FH.
    c. is A00FH plus offset.
    d. cannot be determined.

19. Which statement is true?
    a. Memory-mapped I/O ports are accessed only with *in* or *out* type instructions.
    b. Memory-mapping I/O ports frees up memory space.
    c. An I/O device cannot have an address with a program controlled microprocessor.
    d. none of the above

20. Which is the following is *not* true?
    a. String addressing cannot be used unless the beginning and end of a string are taken into account.
    b. Regardless of meaning, a string is a sequence of bytes stored in memory having a specific beginning and end.
    c. A string-address technique automatically moves an entire string from one location in memory to another.
    d. String addresses need only specify the destination of a string.

CHAPTER 12

INTERRUPTS AND STACKS

OUTLINE

NEW TERMS TO WATCH FOR

Polling	Priority
Interrupt	Vectoring
Call	Stack
JSR	Stack Pointer
Masking	Nesting
Maskable	Nonmaskable
Return	

After completing this chapter, you should be able to:

1. Describe polling and its limitations.
2. Explain the need for and the advantages of an interrupt.
3. Name the four general steps of an interrupt process.
4. Discuss interrupt priority.
5. Show how masking can change the status of an interrupt signal.
6. Demonstrate the action of a vectored interrupt.
7. Determine the location of the subroutine used in a vectored-interrupt scheme.
8. Explain the need for the microprocessor stack.
9. Represent the contents and construction of a microprocessor stack.
10. Correctly determine the location of the top of the stack.
11. Define the function of the stack pointer register.
12. Apply the concept of stacks as it relates to subroutine execution.
13. Demonstrate the possibility of one subroutine calling another.

12-1   INTRODUCTION

Microprocessors are designed to execute instructions in sequence. Yet much of what occurs in external or peripheral devices connected to the microprocessor is random. By random, we mean in the sense that peripheral devices demand the attention of the microprocessor at various and unpredictable times during normal program execution.

The best example of the random need for attention is the use of the keyboard on a computer. Every time a key is pressed, the microprocessor must deal with an activity. Other peripheral devices such as disk drives, CRT's, and printers also need to interact with the microprocessor. Just how the microprocessor accomplishes the task of working with these devices is the subject of this chapter.

12-2   SERVICING PERIPHERALS

Polling

One approach to taking care of peripheral devices is for the microprocessor to test each device in turn to see if it needs *service*. This is called **polling**. It is clear that in this system, a good portion of the activity of the microprocessor is simply circling through the series of peripherals asking if service is necessary. This is not particularly efficient when the processor needs to perform other tasks. In addition, some of the peripherals may rarely need attention yet must be kept in the polling sequence. This is because when they need service is not predictable. A better system would allow the processor to be free to continue normal sequential execution and only stop to deal with a peripheral when it specifically needed attention. This is exactly what the **interrupt** system has been designed to do.

12-3   THE INTERRUPT

The interrupt function is the result of the need to connect external devices to the microprocessor without increasing its normal burden. These external units *interrupt* the normal routine of sequential program execution. The interrupt is a **call** for the microprocessor to interact or service the interrupting unit. The action taken by the processor is called *servicing the interrupt.*

The main criteria of an interrupt service is speed. Speed is an absolute necessity in *real time* operation. In other words, when the operator hits a key on the keyboard, the interrupt to handle the keystroke must be acknowledged and finished in the fastest possible time.

How the Interrupt Occurs

The microprocessor controller/synchronizer contains the logic necessary to handle an interrupt. The action taken by the processor when an interrupt occurs is called an *interrupt routine*. Obviously, the procedures must be quite flexible in order to allow for the variety of peripheral devices and their needs. The flexibility is accomplished through subroutines. In other words, the interrupt service routine can be written by the programmer and placed in memory. When an interrupt occurs, the processor will then execute the interrupt routine called for.

The controller circuitry is connected to the outside world via pins on the microprocessor chip. It is fair to say that the interrupt pins are a hardware feature but that the interrupt service routines are software.

There are a limited number of interrupt input pins available on the microprocessor chip, due to size constraints. For this reason, peripheral devices often share the interrupt control lines, necessitating a priority system of some type.

Steps in an Interrupt

The way in which a microprocessor handles an interrupt is part of the chip design. There are four distinct steps that a microprocessor takes after an interrupt that are common to all processors.
They are:

1. The microprocessor finishes the current instruction. It would be chaotic for the processor to interrupt itself or stop in the middle of a fetch, for example. Waiting until the end of an instruction cycle is not a problem. Instructions are never more than a few bytes long and last only microseconds. The interrupt signal will not be acknowledged until the current instruction is carried out.

2. Normal operation is suspended. Most of what the processor does is carried out in short 3 or 4 byte instructions. So it is unlikely that any given instruction would be finished when the interrupt occurs. The various registers in the microprocessors may contain pieces of information that relate to the algorithm being carried out when the interrupt occurred. The contents of these registers and the status of the microprocessor in general must be preserved so that it can again resume operation when the interrupt has been serviced. In addition, the interrupt routine itself may require one or more of the microprocessor registers. This is another reason to preserve their contents. The suspension of the normal program sequence includes the preservation of the current status of the microprocessor in memory. The information is placed in a **stack.** We will examine how this is done later in the chapter.

3. The microprocessor jumps to the location in memory where the interrupt service routine has been stored and executes the routine. The address of the routine may be fixed in the microprocessor design. An interrupt request on certain pins of the chip will always cause the microprocessor to jump to this same fixed address for the interrupt routine. This address is designed into the microprocessor and cannot be changed. Other types of interrupts allow the programmer to supply an address for the routine.

4. The processor returns from an interrupt. The return to the normal sequence of execution is signaled at the end of the interrupt routine. This is done with a *return* instruction. Some processors include a *return from interrupt* instruction in the instruction set. The return includes restoring the microprocessor to its exact condition before the interrupt occurred. This means the contents of the registers as they were just before the interrupt must be restored. The information they contained must be retrieved form memory and placed back in their respective registers. Finally, the program counter register is loaded with the retrieved address of the instruction that would have been executed if an interrupt had not occurred.

Figure 12-1 is a diagram of the steps in an interrupt. Note that this is a diagram of events and not a flowchart.

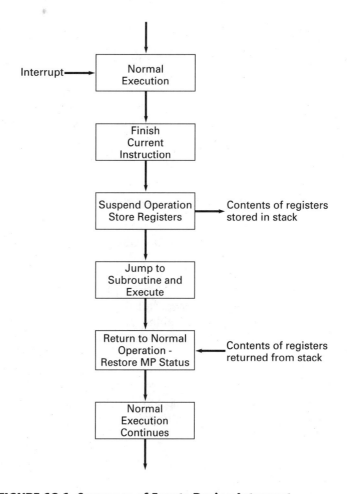

FIGURE 12-1 Sequence of Events During Interrupt

Interrupt Priority

Microprocessors have a limited number of interrupt input pins. The **priority** establishing which of the pins has precedence if simultaneous interrupts occur is fixed. This is called a *fixed priority system.* The priority of the input pins is established by the manufacturer. The system designer has the responsibility for connecting the most critical devices to the interrupt pins with the highest priority. In the event of a simultaneous request, the device connected to the highest priority input will be serviced first. The other priorities are serviced in turn.

There are also chips available that perform a prioritizing function. All peripheral devices are connected to the interrupt controller chip. The controller chip is programmable and the program determines the priority of the interrupting device. The interrupt controller chip sends the interrupt on to the microprocessor along with the address of the interrupt routine to execute. When the address of the routine is supplied at the time of the interrupt, it is called interrupt **vectoring**.

✔ SELF-CHECK FOR SECTIONS 12-1, 12-2, 12-3

1. Explain the term polling.
2. How is polling different from an interrupt?
3. The action taken by the processor when an interrupt occurs is called an _____ _____.

4. The interrupt signal will not be acknowledged until the current instruction is _____.
5. Describe the purpose of a *return* instruction.
6. Explain how the condition of the microprocessor is preserved while an interrupt is occurring.
7. What is a fixed priority interrupt system?
8. When the address of the routine is supplied at the time of the interrupt, it is called interrupt _____.

12-4 MASKING

Interrupts can be divided into two categories, **maskable** and **nonmaskable**. Masking an interrupt means that it will not be accepted. A nonmaskable interrupt is one that will always be acknowledged and accepted. A power failure routine is an example of a nonmaskable routine.

Other interrupts might not have a very high priority and should not be accepted during certain critical algorithms. These interrupts can then be disabled or *masked* so that the microprocessor does not accept them. The various interrupts can be masked by assigning each interrupt possible a bit position in an interrupt mask register.

Figure 12-2 shows an interrupt mask register. The register can be loaded by issuing an instruction designed to load the interrupt mask register. The instruction is followed by a byte that clears or sets the appropriate bit position in the register.

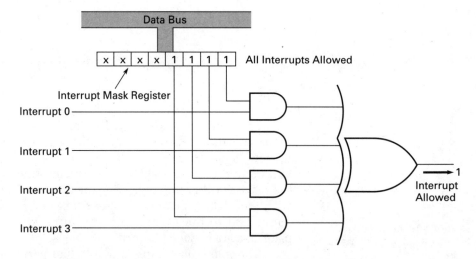

FIGURE 12-2 Interrupt Mask Register Loaded to Allow All 4 Interrupts

For example, if the bit following the instruction to load the register is 00001111, then any interrupt arriving on interrupt input lines Interrupt 0 through Interrupt 3 will cause the output of the OR gate to go high. This in turn, causes the microprocessor to service the interrupt. The X's in the register indicate that whether they are 1 or 0 is immaterial. Those bit positions are not connected to the interrupt system.

If the programmer wishes to mask Interrupt 0, 1, and 2, then the byte following the instruction would be 00001000. This byte is also called the *interrupt mask*. The mask would disable the first three interrupt inputs and allow only Interrupt 3. See Figure 12-3.

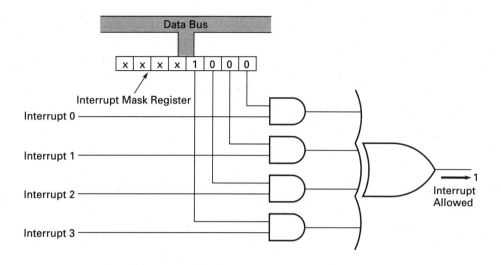

FIGURE 12-3 Interrupt Mask Register Loaded to Mask Interrupts 0, 1, and 2

12-5   VECTORED INTERRUPTS

A **vectored** interrupt means that a memory assignment has been made to which the microprocessor is *vectored* during an interrupt. In the case of some microprocessors, these memory assignments are permanent. When the interrupt request appears, the microprocessor will automatically load the program counter with the assigned address. This assigned address contains the address of the routine to be executed. In this way, the programmer is free to write the necessary routines, specify their length, and choose the best location of the routine by assigning the address. The interrupt will then check the assigned address move to the vectored address to get the interrupt routine.

Figure 12-4 illustrates the vectored interrupt. For this illustration, we assume that the assigned interrupt address is FFFAH and FFFBH. That means the interrupt *Interrupt 1* will always cause the microprocessor to check this address. In 12-4(A), the microprocessor is executing the normal program sequence. While working on the instruction located at 1003H, an interrupt request *Interrupt 1* is received. In Figure 12-4(B), the vectored request is acted upon. The interrupt caused the microprocessor to check the assigned address for the vector, FFFAH, and FFFBH. This location contains the address of the interrupt routine. The address of the routine, 2000H, is loaded into the program counter address register and the routine is executed.

At the end of the subroutine, Figure 12-4(C), the processor returns to the next sequential address in the normal routine.

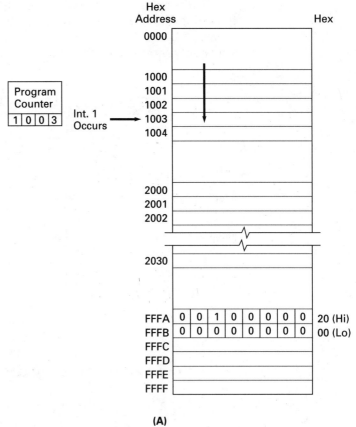

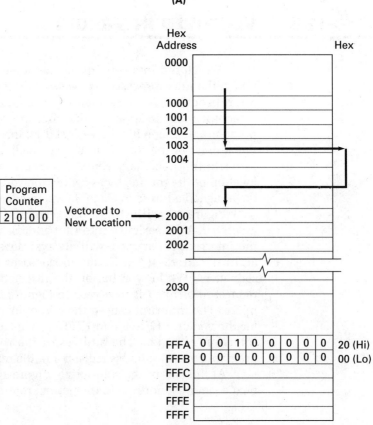

**FIGURE 12-4 (A) Program
is Interrupted While
Working at Location
1003H (B) Vectored
Interrupt Has Sent
Program to Execute at
New Location**

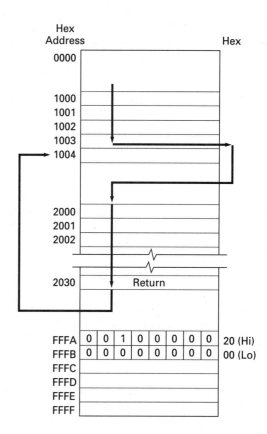

FIGURE 12-4 (C) After the Routine is Finished (at Location 2030H) the Program is Returned from the Interrupt.

✔ **SELF-CHECK FOR SECTIONS 12-4, 12-5**

9. What is a maskable interrupt?
10. What is a nonmaskable interrupt?
11. Explain an interrupt mask register.
12. What is meant when it is said that an interrupt is vectored?

12-6   THE SOFTWARE INTERRUPT

Up to this point, all the interrupts discussed could be classified as hardware interrupts. They are hardware driven and originate from hardware devices external to the microprocessor.

Software interrupts behave very much like hardware interrupts except that software interrupts are written into the main program and executed in the course of sequential operation. They are often used to jump to other programs in memory. Software interrupts, if the processor has such instructions, are vectored interrupts. The instruction will send the processor to check the assigned address for the vectored location of the interrupt service routine.

It is worth noting that many interrupts use fixed locations for vector addresses. These locations in memory are specified by the manufacturer of the microprocessor chip. Such locations should not be used or occupied with other data because this will interfere with normal microprocessor operation.

12-7   STACKS

During an interrupt routine, some or all of the microprocessor registers may be used. This would destroy the data previously in the registers if their contents were not saved in some way. Obviously, to return the microprocessor to its pre-interrupt status requires a procedure to accomplish this.

The location where the contents of the registers in the microprocessor are temporarily stored is called the *stack*. Some specialized microprocessors have a given number of registers set aside within the processor to serve as the stack location. This is known as a hardware stack. It has the advantage of rapid access and, therefore, speed. But the size of the stack is limited by the number of registers that can be provided. Limiting the size of the stack tends to restrict the flexibility of a microprocessor and, for this reason, software stacks are usually implemented.

The software stack is generally defined as an area in RAM for temporary storage of data and register contents. Building this stack is an inherent part of the interrupt signal. However, stacks can also be built independently of an interrupt request. In fact, stacks are used just about any time a subroutine is called.

The software stack is almost unlimited in size and can reside anywhere in memory. This implementation causes the need for a special register in the microprocessor called the **stack pointer** register. The sole job of the stack pointer register is to hold the address of the stack. Whenever a stack is required, the stack pointer register will track its location by holding the 16-bit stack address.

The stack is built, one byte at a time, each entered or stacked on the last entry. It is analogous to the way plates are stacked at a salad bar. Figure 12-5. The first plate put on the stack is at the bottom. The last plate put on the stack is at the top. Each plate pushes the next one down. The first plate off the stack is the last plate placed on the stack. This system has taken the inventory term from accounting called LIFO, for Last In First Out. In other words, the last byte put on the stack will be the first byte retrieved from the stack, when an interrupt is completed, for instance.

The stack will be built whenever an interrupt, a subroutine call, or a stack instruction occurs. Stack instructions use assembly language mnemonics like PUSH, to push a byte onto the stack and PULL or POP to take a byte off the stack.

FIGURE 12-5 (A) Stack of Plates Illustrating First-In Concept (B) Stack of Plates Last-Out Concept

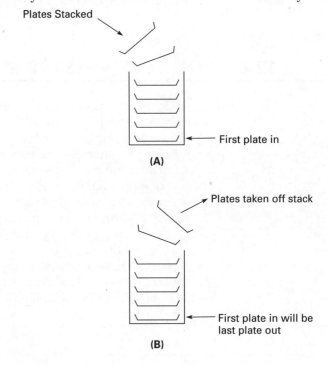

Plates Stacked

First plate in

(A)

Plates taken off stack

First plate in will be last plate out

(B)

Most stack operations are, however, automatic. That is, the entire process of saving the contents of registers is done automatically whenever a subroutine call is encountered. Figure 12-6 illustrates the sequence of building a stack. In 12-6(A), the contents of all registers at the instant of the interrupt is shown. Note that the stack pointer register contains the address F00AH. This will be the first address location in the stack. The stack builds downward. Direction is relative but in the sense that the occupied addresses are moving toward lower addresses, we can say it is building downward.

In Figure 12-6(B), the contents of the A register is stored in location F00AH. This occurs because the stack pointer register issues the address F00AH via the address bus. After the A register is stored, the stack pointer register decrements. The next register to be stored is the B register. The contents of the stack pointer register is again placed on the address bus and the byte in the B register is transferred to memory location F009H.

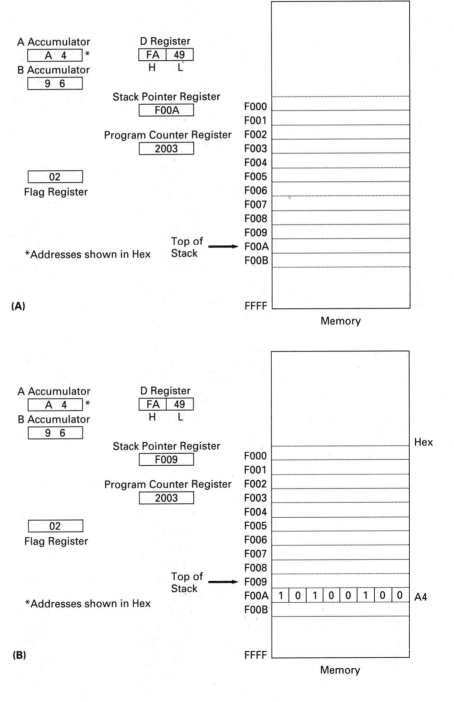

FIGURE 12-6 (A) Contents of Registers Before Stack is Built and at the Time the Interrupt Occurs (B) Stack is Begun. First Register to be Stored is the A Accumulator. The Stack Pointer Decrements.

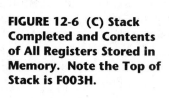

FIGURE 12-6 (C) Stack Completed and Contents of All Registers Stored in Memory. Note the Top of Stack is F003H.

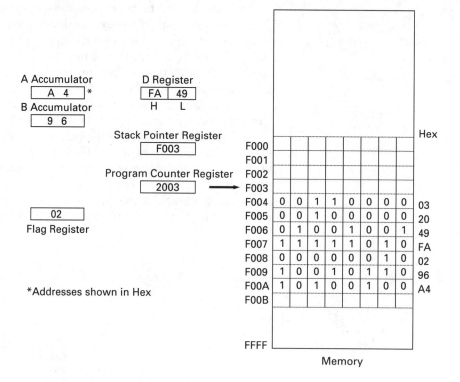

The stack continues to build in this way until, finally, the contents of the program counter register byte are stored, Figure 12-6(C).

Now the subroutine has free access to all registers without fear of destroying data. The stack pointer register, however, must remain untouched. The address it contains is the only way the stack can be located.

To indicate that a subroutine is finished, a special **Return** instruction is programmed as the last instruction in the subroutine. The return instruction initiates the rebuilding of the microprocessor's preinterrupt status.

The content of each register is restored, starting with the last stack entry. A PULL or POP is the reverse of the PUSH action and the stack pointer will now increment to reload each register. This means that at the end of the restoring action, the microprocessor is in exactly the same condition as it was before the subroutine. The program counter will again direct the processor to the next sequential instruction as the normal sequence resumes.

Stack Building

In our example, we followed a certain sequence in loading the registers on the stack. The sequence may vary from processor to processor, but whatever it is, it cannot normally be changed. The interrupt instructions usually save the entire microprocessor status in some given order. The individual stack instructions, however, do sometimes allow a choice as to which registers to save. There may be no point in saving the status of the entire microprocessor for some short operations. By specifying only those registers whose content is important to us, we save valuable processor time.

Naming the registers to be saved is accomplished within the byte following a PUSH instruction. Each bit position can be assigned to a register.

BYTE

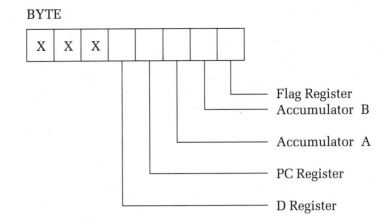

If a bit is set, the register is saved. If a bit position is clear, the register is not saved.

For example, if the byte:

$$XXX10011$$

follows the PUSH instruction, then the D register, accumulator B, and the flag register would be pushed or saved to the stack. This is because the bit corresponding to those registers is set. The others are clear, indicating that the registers they represent will *not* be saved to stack.

12-8   SUBROUTINE CALLS

In Chapter 10 we learned that a subroutine is an out-of-sequence part of the program that can be accessed by the *jump to subroutine* (**JSR**) or a *call* instruction. A math algorithm is a good example of a subroutine. It need only be written once, placed in memory and then accessed by a JSR or *call* instruction as needed.

The *call* or JSR instruction always saves the contents of the program counter. Whether other registers are saved will depend on the microprocessor manufacturer. Now that we have seen how the status of the microprocessor can be preserved, we can look more closely at the workings of a subroutine.

Figure 12-7 shows the main program loaded in memory from location 0200H to 0350H. As the program executes, it encounters a JSR instruction at location 0210H. The instruction occupies three bytes of memory, one for the instruction and two for the address of the subroutine to be executed. The next instruction that would have been executed is at location 0213H. The microprogram knows that the JSR instruction requires 3 bytes and, therefore, places address 0213H on the stack.

The JSR instruction then causes the program counter address register to be loaded with the address of the subroutine. The top address of the stack is F00AH and will contain the high byte 02H and F009H will contain the low byte, 13H.

The microprocessor then begins executing instructions at location 1000H. At location 1015H, another subroutine is required, this time at location 2000H. The JSR instruction occupies 3 bytes as before. Again the microprocessor places the address of the next instruction to be executed on the stack. Note that the top of the stack is now address F009H, where the last in address is stored.

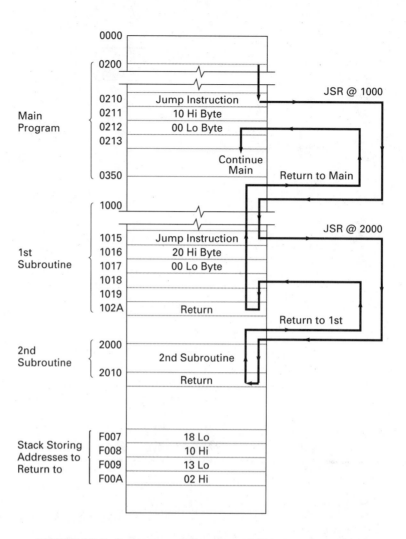

FIGURE 12-7 Sequence of Events and Memory Locations

Now the microprocessor begins executing the second subroutine. If another subroutine is required, it is also possible to call it. When subroutines call on other subroutines, the programs are said to be *nested*. One routine is nested in another.

The second routine finishes at location 2010H when the RETURN instruction is reached. The RETURN instruction does not need an address because the address to return to has been stored on the stack. The RETURN instruction POPs the address off the top of the stack and loads it into the register of program counter.

The address on the top of the stack, location F007H, is 1018H. This is where the program was executing the first subroutine when the second call instruction was encountered.

The first routine then continues until the RETURN instruction is found. Now the top address in the stack is 0213H. This address is loaded into the program counter register. 0213H is the address of the next instruction in the main program.

As mentioned before, subroutines can be called at any time and as often as needed. One subroutine can call another and this routine can call a third, etc. While there is no real limit to **nesting**, from a practical point of view, when too many subroutines are nested there may be something amiss in the overall structure of the program.

✔ SELF-CHECK FOR SECTIONS 12-6, 12-7, 12-8

13. Why would it be a good idea not to use certain address locations specified by the microprocessor manufacturer?
14. The location where the contents of the registers in the microprocessor are temporarily stored is called the _____.
15. Where is the software stack located within a microprocessor system?
16. What is a stack pointer?
17. Explain a LIFO stack.
18. Is it possible to save only some of the registers in a microprocessor when building a stack?
19. What is the purpose of a *call* or JSR instruction?
20. When subroutines call on other subroutines, the programs are said to be

    _____.

SUMMARY OF IDEAS

- In the polling process, the microprocessor constantly interrogates each peripheral to see if service is required.
- The four steps to the interrupt are:
  1. Microprocessor finishes current instruction.
  2. Microprocessor operation suspended and stack built.
  3. Microprocessor executes the interrupt routine.
  4. Microprocessor returns from interrupt routine and restores the microprocessor registers.
- In a fixed-priority interrupt system, each peripheral is assigned a priority. The one with the higher priority always has precedence. The lower priority interrupts are serviced in turn.
- Masking refers to disabling an interrupt so that the processor does not acknowledge it.
- Masking can be accomplished by assigning bit positions in a masking byte to each interrupt.
- A nonmaskable interrupt cannot be disabled.
- Vectored interrupts are interrupts that seek out a fixed location in memory to find the address of the routine to be serviced.
- A software interrupt is an interrupt that occurs due to a software instruction.
- The stack is a location in RAM for temporary storage of register contents or data.
- An interrupt causes the microprocessor to build a stack where the pre-interrupt status of the microprocessor is stored.
- Information in the stack is stored in a Last In First Out (LIFO) configuration.
- The stack pointer is an address register that is used to contain the current address of the stack.
- The stack pointer register always points to the last entry on the stack.
- When a subroutine is called, the address of the next instruction is stored in the stack.
- A *return* instruction uses the stack to find the address that is to be returned to.

CHAPTER QUESTIONS & PROBLEMS

True or False

1. A peripheral device is polled only when it is in need of service.
2. Interrupt subroutines are fixed and cannot be changed.
3. The priority of an interrupt is established by the peripheral system designer.
4. The interrupt signal establishes the *return* address.
5. A subroutine can be called from anywhere in the program.

Fill in the Blanks

6. A byte of data used to disable an interrupt is called a _____.
7. When an interrupt causes the microprocessor to check a fixed address for the location of a subroutine, it is called a _____ interrupt.
8. When two interrupts are requested at the same time, the interrupt that has the highest _____ is serviced first.
9. The end of a subroutine is indicated with a _____ instruction.
10. An interrupt signal written into the program is called a _____ interrupt.

Multiple Choice

11. Which of the following operations would require the stack?
    a. JSR
    b. RETURN
    c. Software interrupt
    d. All of the above

12. Select the statement that is not true.
    a. The stack can be in different RAM locations at different times.
    b. The contents of the stack pointer register is not placed in the stack.
    c. The stack cannot be constructed without a subroutine.
    d. The first address placed in a stack will be the last one out.

13. A vectored interrupt
    a. cannot be accomplished with a software interrupt.
    b. eliminates the need for an interrupt service subroutine.
    c. always follows a hardware interrupt.
    d. can be either hardware or software generated.

14. If address FFFAH and FFFBH have been assigned as the location of vector addresses
    a. the programmer should not use them.
    b. they can be changed by the programmer.
    c. they will contain the first instruction of the interrupt routine.
    d. they will point to the interrupt routine.

15. A stack is needed because
    a. there is no other place to store interrupt instructions.
    b. during an interrupt routine, microprocessor registers may be needed.
    c. the RETURN instruction is followed by the address to be returned to.
    d. during an interrupt, the microprocessor may need to store the instructions for the subroutine.

CHAPTER 13

DATA TRANSMISSION AND COMMUNICATIONS

OUTLINE

NEW TERMS TO WATCH FOR

Asynchronous	Null Modem	Synchronous
FSK	Start Bit	PSK
Stop Bit	CCITT	ASCII
Bit Framing	EBCDIC	Biphase
Half Duplex	Simplex	Current Loop
Full Duplex	Bisync	Baud Rate
SDLC	RS-232	Centronics
DTE	Trellis Encoding	DCE
Bit Stuffing		

After completing this chapter, you should be able to:

1. Name the two major classes of data transmission methods.
2. Explain how the ASCII code represents alpha-numeric characters.
3. Describe the method for determining the rate of data transmission.
4. Recognize common transmission speeds.
5. Show how data is synchronized during synchronous transmission.
6. Represent the contents of a frame in an asynchronous transmission.
7. Predict line conditions during RS-232 communication.
8. Discuss current loop transmission.
9. Illustrate the need for a modem.
10. Explain duplex operation.
11. Demonstrate the difference between frequency shift keying and phase shift keying.
12. Identify parallel interfaces and parallel transmission connections.

13-1   INTRODUCTION

The subject of communication and data transmission actually stands alone as a field of study and a discipline. This chapter serves as an overview to this area and, as such, covers a wide range of topics in an introductory way.

With the advent of the personal computer and sophisticated phone systems, communication between computers of all sizes and types has proliferated. Naturally, the microprocessor has been part of this growth, for it is used not only to run the computers, but to control and enhance the communication abilities of the computer.

A complete array of computer hardware exists whose sole function is to facilitate communication between computers. Much of it is designed with microprocessor controllers. With the view that microprocessors play a major role in communications, a thorough examination of the terms and standards of basic communication is essential.

13-2   CODES

ASCII

In order for computers or any other two electronic devices to communicate, there must be an agreement as to the symbols used and exchanged. In other words, there must be a convention established so that when the letter "A" is sent, the letter "A" is received and understood as an "A."

As you are well aware, microprocessors are best suited to operate *and* communicate in binary. Since humans have a need to communicate in English (or other languages), some common method for translating English to binary is necessary.

The most commonly used code for translating English into binary is called **ASCII** (American Standard Code for Information Interchange).

The ASCII code is a 7-bit code. This means that each ASCII character uses 7 binary bits. Using a 7-bit binary number allows, 2^7 or 128 different ASCII characters. This is more than enough for the alphabet (both upper and lower case letters), the numbers 0 through 9, the punctuation marks, and some special control characters. Table 13-1 details the ASCII code.

To send the letter "a," the binary number would be, 01100001. Note that an entire 8-bit byte is used. Each letter of a word requires a full byte.

ASCII AND PARITY

The ASCII code is considered a 7-bit code yet an ASCII character occupies a full 8-bit byte. The reason for this is that the eighth bit can be used, optionally, as a parity bit. The letter "a," using an even parity, would be represented in ASCII as, 11100001.

EBCDIC

The **EBCDIC** code is another commonly used alphanumeric code and is customarily used in IBM machines, mostly mainframe computers. EBCDIC, Extended Binary Coded Decimal Interchange Code, is an 8-bit code. If parity is required for EBCDIC, a ninth bit must be added.

TABLE 13–1 The ASCII Code

DECIMAL	HEX	ASCII	DECIMAL	HEX	ASCII	DECIMAL	HEX	ASCII	DECIMAL	HEX	ASCII
0	00	NUL	32	20		64	40	@	96	60	'
1	01	SOH	33	21	!	65	41	A	97	61	a
2	01	STX	34	22	"	66	42	B	98	62	b
3	03	ETX	35	23	#	67	43	C	99	63	c
4	04	EOT	36	24	$	68	44	D	100	64	d
5	05	ENQ	37	25	%	69	45	E	101	65	e
6	06	ACK	38	26	&	70	46	F	102	66	f
7	07	BEL	39	27	'	71	47	G	103	67	g
8	08	BS	40	28	(	72	48	H	104	68	h
9	09	HT	41	29	)	73	49	I	105	69	i
10	0A	LF	42	2A	*	74	4A	J	106	6A	j
11	0B	VT	43	2B	+	75	4B	K	107	6B	k
12	0C	FF	44	2C	,	76	4C	L	108	6C	l
13	0D	CR	45	2D	-	77	4D	M	109	6D	m
14	0E	SO	46	2E	.	78	4E	N	110	6E	n
15	0F	SI	47	2F	/	79	4F	O	111	6F	o
16	10	DLE	48	30	0	80	50	P	112	70	p
17	11	DC1	49	31	1	81	51	Q	113	71	q
18	12	DC2	50	32	2	82	52	R	114	72	r
19	13	DC3	51	33	3	83	53	S	115	73	s
20	14	DC4	52	34	4	84	54	T	116	74	t
21	15	NAK	53	35	5	85	55	U	117	75	u
22	16	SYN	54	36	6	86	56	V	118	76	v
23	17	ETB	55	37	7	87	57	W	119	77	w
24	18	CAN	56	38	8	88	58	X	120	78	x
25	19	EM	57	39	9	89	59	Y	121	79	y
26	1A	SUB	58	3A	:	90	5A	Z	122	7A	z
27	1B	ESC	59	3B	;	91	5B	[	123	7B	{
28	1C	FS	60	3C	<	92	5C	\	124	7C	¦
29	1D	GS	61	3D	=	93	5D	]	125	7D	}
30	1E	RS	62	3E	>	94	5E	^	126	7E	~
31	1F	US	63	3F	?	95	5F	_	127	7F	DEL
127	7F	DEL									

13-3   RATE OF TRANSMISSION

Baud

Tribute is paid to the telegraph pioneer Emile Baudot by naming the transmission rate, *baud*, in his honor. The rate or speed of transmission is simply called the *baud* or **baud rate** although attaching the word *rate* is actually redundant. In keeping with tradition, we will use the convention and speak of the *baud rate*.

The baud rate refers to the number of symbols transmitted per second. If the symbols happen to be bits, then the baud rate would mean the number of bits-per-second. That is to say, baud rate in this case, would be the same as bps (bits-per-second).

$$\text{Baud} = 1/\text{time period for one bit}$$

If one bit has a duration of 3.33ms then,

$$\text{Baud} = 1/3.33 \text{ ms}$$
$$\text{Baud} = 300$$

At this rate, an 8-bit byte could be transmitted in 26.6 ms and thus 1,000 characters (an average business letter) would theoretically require about 26 seconds to transmit. This gives you some idea of the speeds involved.

The most commonly used baud rates used are: 75, 110, 300, 600, 1200, 2400, 4800, 9600, and 19,200. Frankly, however, speeds below 1200 do not find much use in today's computer world. The trend is for ever faster rates and 9600 baud modems are becoming very popular.

13-4   SYNCHRONOUS TRANSMISSION

The Need for Methods

Now that we have an idea of what is being sent and at what rate, we can now look at *how* it is sent. Recall that a PISO shift register can change a parallel byte into a serial string of eight bits. Each 8-bit byte could contain an ASCII character. Yet a string of bits flowing out of a computer has to be defined and coordinated. There must be a method for distinguishing which bits belong with which character and for that matter, where a single bit starts and ends.

There are two basic methods for coordinating the serial string of bits, **synchronous** and **asynchronous**.

Synchronous

The synchronous method of bit transmission is characterized by one clock source. In other words, there is a single origin for the clock pulse which synchronizes both the transmitter and receiver. This insures that both transmitter and receiver are locked in step with each other. This synchronizing of the timing is critical for the reception of coherent data. (Fig. 13-1).

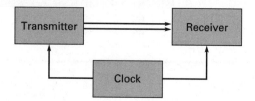

FIGURE 13-1 Synchronous Transmission

In synchronous transmission, the transmitting unit usually takes responsibility for providing the timing signals. For this reason, synchronous transmission requires a lot of *overhead*. Overhead is a term used to describe any information that must be transmitted to coordinate and organize the data—such as timing pulses. Each bit of data sent requires that timing be included to keep the data bytes discrete.

Biphase Synchronous

Several schemes have been devised for sending the synchronizing signals. Figure 13-2 illustrates one method. The **biphase** method insures that a signal change takes place at the end of each bit, regardless of whether the data sent changes or not. A "1" data bit consists of a dual transition during the bit time period. A "0" data bit has no transition during the bit time. In this method, the logic-1 or logic-0 level bears no relation whatever to the data logic sent. As you can see, this method, as with all synchronous procedures, carries overhead. This type of overhead requires a level of complexity that can be seen in the hardware needed.

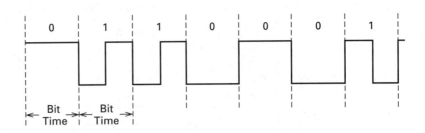

FIGURE 13-2 Biphase Synchronizing

Block Operation

Synchronous operation lends itself to sending large batches or blocks of information at one time. This considerably reduces overhead. For example, a message in a block of 512 characters would begin with a couple of synchronizing signals, indicating to the receiver that a block of data is about to be sent. After that, the block of 512 characters would proceed uninterrupted. Synchronous transmission such as this is also used by the microprocessor to transfer blocks of data from one area to another, for example, from disk to memory. Synchronous transmission is analogous to a freight train. Each box car represents a character and the entire train is sent from one point to another, in one long sequence.

Bisync

Bisync or *binary synchronous* protocol was developed and used extensively by IBM. A diagram of a typical bisync block is shown in Figure 13-3. The word *bisync* refers to the two sync characters sent with each block.

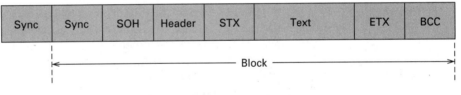

FIGURE 13-3 Typical Bisync Message Block

Sync –   Synchronizing character
SOH –   Start of header
Header – Control codes, addresses, etc.
STX –   Start of text
Text –   Data sent
ETX –   End of text
BCC –   Block character check

When the line is idle, a series of 1's are sent. If a block is ready, the sync characters are transmitted, followed by an ASCII control character called SOH for start of header. The header contains control codes, which are the labels and addresses necessary to define what is being sent. The STX (start of text) character ends the header and is followed by the block of text. The text will be a 256-byte block ending with an ETX (end of text) character.

The last two bytes of the message block are a block character check. This is, in most cases, a cyclic-redundancy error check for the entire block. After the message block is sent, the transmitter waits for an ACK or acknowledge character to be returned by the receiver. Reception indicates the block was successfully transmitted.

The send and wait procedure is a sort of *ping pong* protocol, introducing even more delay when a block must be retransmitted due to errors. This whole procedure is somewhat inefficient and has been largely replaced with **SDLC.**

SDLC

Synchronous Data Link Control, SDLC, is also an IBM development. Instead of being byte-oriented, like bisync with codes like SOH, STX, and ETX, SDLC is bit-oriented. In other words, each bit has meaning. Figure 13-4 is a diagram of an SDLC frame.

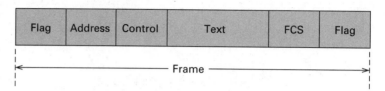

FIGURE 13-4 SDLC Message Frame

Flag –   8-bit character between frames
Address – 8-bit byte identifying the intended receiver
Text –   Data sent
FCS –   Frame check sequence = 16-bit CRC check

Each block of data, called a frame, begins and ends with a *flag byte*. The flag byte is 01111110. Note there are six 1's sent successively. The text field can contain any number of bits and is sent in 8-bit multiples. It may contain as many as 20,000 bits. The data is followed by an FCS, Frame Check Sequence. A Frame Check Sequence is a 16-bit CRC error detection signal. In addition, the transmitter does not pause between frames but sends them in batches. At the end of the frame, the flag is sent again. This marks both the end of the last frame and the beginning of the next.

It is important to prevent the receiver from reacting to a false flag in the midst of the text stream. This is accomplished by a method called **bit stuffing**. During text transmission, a sequence of five 1's will be detected and a zero inserted. A *stuffed* zero will follow every sequence of five 1's, regardless of whether the sixth bit is a 1 or a 0. This totally eliminates the possibility of having six bits in a row and thus eliminates the possibility of a false flag. Naturally, this zero is detected and removed by the receiver. The procedure is actually a hardware implementation and easily accomplished in a chip. At the end of the message, a polling bit is sent with the flag that indicates it is time for the receiver to respond.

SDLC protocol transmits several frames at a time and has error checking within each frame. This makes SDLC not only faster than bisync but more reliable, too.

✔ SELF-CHECK FOR SECTIONS 13-1, 13-2, 13-3, 13-4

1. The most commonly used code for translating English into binary is called _____.
2. With a 7-bit binary number, how many ASCII characters are possible?
3. Is it possible to use parity with ASCII?
4. What is EBCDIC?
5. The rate or speed of transmission is called the _____.
6. Would 300 baud be considered very fast?
7. There are two basic methods for coordinating the transmission of a serial string of bits, _____ and _____.
8. How is timing accomplished with synchronous transmission?
9. Synchronous transmissions are usually sent in large _____ of information.
10. What is bisync?
11. Explain the need for bit stuffing in SDLC.

13-5   ASYNCHRONOUS TRANSMISSION

Clocks

Asynchronous operation does *not* mean that the transmission and reception are not synchronized. Both the transmitter and receiver have their own synchronizing clocks. (Fig. 13-5). The receiving clock is capable of being locked to the transmitter clock by a prearranged signal. But this means that both clocks must already be running at a prearranged rate. This is accomplished by using one of the standard baud rates. For example, to communicate at 1200 baud, both transmitter and receiver must be set to 1200 baud.

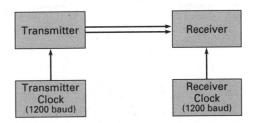

FIGURE 13-5 Asynchronous Transmission

Bit Framing

Recall that each character usually occupies a single 8-bit byte. In asynchronous transmission, each character sent will be preceded by a **start bit** and ended with a **stop bit**. When no characters are being sent, the transmission line is kept at logic-1 or high. In this condition the line is said to be *marking*, that is, held high. When a character is to be sent, the line is brought to a logic-0 for the duration one bit. The logic-0 bit is called a *space*. This is the start bit and it alerts the receiver that a character is to follow. The next eight bits will be the character itself, followed by the stop bit. The duration of a stop bit is usually 1 1/2 to 2 bits long. Surrounding a character with a start and a stop bit is known as **bit framing**. (Fig. 13-6).

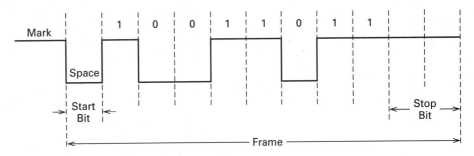

FIGURE 13-6 Asynchronous Transmission. Bit Framing Shows 2-Bit Wide Stop Bit.

Asynchronous transmission does require more overhead than synchronous transmission of data. It is analogous to using a fleet of trucks to deliver a product instead of a train. Each truck would represent a character. The trucks would travel in convoys but the convoys would vary in size. Figure 13-7 compares the two methods of data transmission.

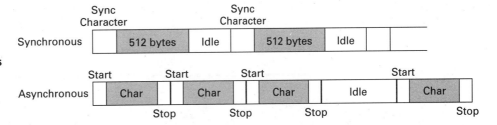

FIGURE 13-7 Synchronous v. Asynchronous

✔ SELF-CHECK FOR SECTION 13-5

12. How is timing accomplished with asynchronous transmission?
13. When no characters are being sent during asynchronous transmission, the line is kept at logic-1 or high. In this condition the line is said to be _____.
14. Explain bit framing.

13-6   RS-232

The **RS-232** standard was a response by the Electronic Industries Association (EIA) to the need for standard signals between **DTE** and **DCE** devices. DTE refers to Data Terminal Equipment and DCE refers to Data Communication Equipment. The standard defines the signal voltage levels and the *handshake* signals. The latest revision of the standard also includes the definition for the 25-pin connector to be used, a DB25. The term *handshake* refers to the fact that two devices are in communication. The sending device sends a handshake signal that is acknowledged by the receiving device. The existence of a handshake means communication may proceed.

Table II is the complete listing of pin functions for the 25-pin connector used in RS-232 linkages. Not all twenty-five pins are used. In fact, normally only the first eight, as seen in Table II below are commonly used.

TABLE II

PIN #	DESCRIPTION	SOURCE	COMMON NAME
1	Ground		
2	Transmitted Data	DTE	TxD
3	Received Data	DCE	RxD
4	Request to Send	DTE	RTS
5	Clear to Send	DCE	CTS
6	Data Set Ready	DCE	DSR
7	Signal Ground (return)		GND
8	Received Line Signal	DCE	CD
9	Reserved for testing		
10	Reserved for testing		
11	Unassigned		
12	Secondary CD	DCE	
13	Secondary CTS	DCE	
14	Secondary TxD	DTE	
15	Transmitter Signal Timing	DCE	
16	Secondary RxD	DCE	
17	Receiver Signal Timing	DCE	
18	Local Loop testing	DTE	
19	Secondary RTS	DTE	
20	Data Terminal Ready	DTE	DTR
21	Remote Loop testing	DCE	
22	Ring Indicator	DCE	
23	Data Signal Rate	Both	
24	Transmitter Signal Timing	DTE	
25	Test Mode	DTE	

In examining these definitions, it is well to keep in mind that they are designed for communication between a DTE device like a terminal or computer and a DCE device like a modem.

TxD   The Transmitted-Data pin, sometimes called **TD** is the pin used to transmit the text or data. It is the one way direction of outgoing data.

RxD   The Received-Data pin, sometimes called **RD** is for received data. This is the data input pin.

DSR   Data Set Ready refers to the DCE equipment. It is the line used to signal the DTE that the DCE is connected to the communication link and ready to operate.

DTR   The Data-Terminal-Ready pin is reserved for the terminal or computer to indicate it is ready for business.

RTS   The Request-to-Send pin is used by the terminal (DTE) to signal that it is ready to transmit data.

CTS   Clear-To-Send is used by the DCE to signal the terminal that it is OK to send data. It is expected by the terminal right after it sends a RTS.

CD   The Carrier Detect, also called Received-Line-Signal Detector, is used by the DCE to indicate that it senses the carrier or connection to a remote device. In other words a connection exists with the intended receiver.

RI   The Ring Indicator is used exclusively on a telephone line connection. This line is turned on whenever the incoming phone line rings, signaling the terminal that a call is present.

Null Modem

Frequently, two data terminals or computers are physically close enough to be connected directly together. All that is required in this case is that both be equipped with an RS-232 port and a **null modem**. Modems will be covered in the next section—in any case, a null modem is not truly a modem. It is simply a connector that cross couples the essential RS-232 signals to the two computers. Figure 13-8 shows how a null modem is constructed.

FIGURE 13-8 Null Modem

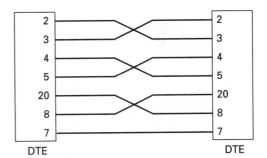

Voltage Levels

The RS-232 standard requires logic-1 signals that range from -3 to -25 volts. Logic-0 signals are specified at $+3$ to $+25$ volts. (Figure 13-9). In practice, voltages from 10 to 12 volts are used.

FIGURE 13-9 RS-232 Signal Levels

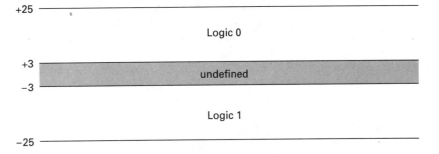

Limits

The RS-232 standard also specifies that a maximum rate of 20,000 baud can be used when the distance between DTE and DCE is 50 feet. Here again, in practice, lower baud rates are used and lengths of 2,000 feet are possible.

The maximum length of the RS-232 connection is a function of cable capacitance, the limit being about 2,500 picofarads. But good cable today is usually less than 12 picofarads per foot which means about 200 feet, not 50 feet., of cable is actually permitted. For distances beyond this, it is well to test such installations before a major commitment is made.

RS-232 and Personal Computers

It should be noted that the RS-232 standard includes both synchronous and asynchronous definitions. However, PC's equipped with RS-232 ports, as most are, are designed to work in an asynchronous mode only. What it amounts to is that the serial RS-232 port is now almost a de facto asynchronous standard. A typical arrangement in a PC is shown in Figure 13-10.

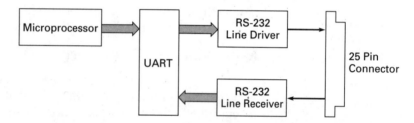

FIGURE 13-10 Typical RS-232 Arrangement

✔ SELF-CHECK FOR SECTION 13-6.

15. Explain the term "handshaking."
16. What is a DTE device?
17. What is a DCE device?
18. Explain a null modem.

13-7   CURRENT LOOPS

Current is sometimes used to send and receive logic-1's and 0's. There are two ways of using current to indicate logic levels. In *polar-working* loops, a logic-1, or mark, is indicated by current in one direction, while logic-0 is indicated by current in the reverse direction. In *neutral-working* loops (Fig. 13-11), a logic-1 is the presence of current while a logic-0, or space, is simply the absence of current. The most commonly used currents are 20 ma and 60 ma.

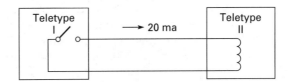

FIGURE 13-11 Current Loop

Current-loop devices are best suited for electromechanical equipment. The most common application of current loops is in teletype machines. Teletype usually operates at less than 300 baud and typically 110 baud. While the fax machine has just about replaced the teletype in this country, they are very much in use in other parts of the world.

13-8   MODEMS

Much of today's computer communication takes place between remotely-located computers networking over the phone lines. Phone lines were originally designed purely for transmitting audio signals, not for the rapid reversals and on–off nature of digital signals. In fact, regular phone lines only have a bandwidth capable of passing 300 to 3,300 Hz. (Fig. 13-12). This is a situation unsuitable for transmitting and receiving digital signals. To get around the phone line limitations, *modems* are used.

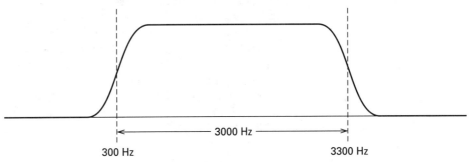

FIGURE 13-12 Phone Line Bandwidth

The word *modem* is an acronym for *MOD*ulator–*DEM*odulator. This is in reference to the fact that to transmit over the phone lines, high-frequency digital signals must be changed to lower frequency audio signals or *modulated*. At the receiving end, the signal must be *demodulated*, that is, changed back into a digital signal. When digital signals are translated into the audio-frequency bandwidth, they can be sent over the phone lines as easily as voice.

Duplex Operation

Before we look at the methods of modulating signals for modems, there is some customary terminology that needs to be understood. It has to do with the direction of the traffic flow or direction of the flow of the data in telecommunications links.

When data flows in one direction only—from a PC to a printer, for instance—the linkage is referred to as **simplex** operation. If data can flow in both directions, but not at the same time, the linkage is referred to as **half**

duplex operation. In other words, both ends can transmit and receive, but not at the same time. The set-up resembles a one-lane country bridge. **Full duplex**, on the other hand, is like a two-lane bridge, traffic can flow in both directions at the same time. (Fig. 13-13).

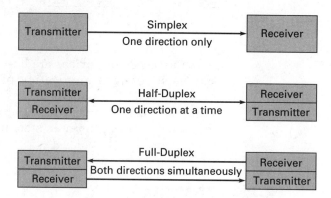

FIGURE 13-13 Data Flow Definitions

Frequency-Shift Keying (FSK)

The simplest scheme for modulation entails using two different frequencies, one to represent a mark (logic-1) and the other to represent a space (logic-0). For example, 1,000 Hz could be a logic-0 and 2,000 Hz would be a logic-1.

In practice, the Bell 103A type modem uses this basic idea. The 3,000 Hz bandwidth is divided into two channels. (Fig. 13-14). One modem uses the lower channel where a mark is 1070 Hz and a space is 1270 Hz. The other modem uses the upper channel where a mark is 2025 Hz and a space is 2225 Hz.

A convention has been established where the *originating* modem transmits on the high channel while the *answering* modem is assigned the low channel. This scheme permits full duplex operation, but it has limitations. The bandwidth of the phone lines necessitates the packing of the mark and space frequencies fairly close together. This situation coupled with the normal noise and signal degradation of the phone system limits the speed to less than 600 baud.

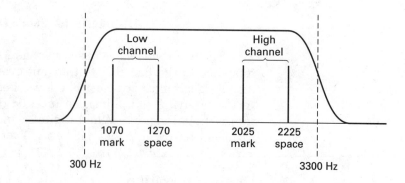

FIGURE 13-14 Bell 103A Standard

Phase-Shift Keying (PSK)

Phase-shift keying is designed to overcome the speed limitation inherent in **FSK**. The only real way to pack more information into the bandwidth is to increase the number of symbols used. FSK is limited to either a "1" or a "0—" two symbols. How many symbols can be transmitted within a 3000-Hz band? Henry Nyquist, a Bell Labs researcher, determined this number for us back in the 1920's. The theory, called the Nyquist Limit, says that for bandwidth BW, only 2BW symbols per second are possible. So when BW = 3,000, only 6,000 symbols per second are theoretically possible. The secret to obtaining higher speeds is to put more information in the symbols. This concept will become clearer as we look at the following real examples.

One method of **PSK** uses four symbols:

Symbol 1 = 00
Symbol 2 = 01
Symbol 3 = 10
Symbol 4 = 11

With these four symbols, two bits can be transmitted at a time. Look at it this way, if we are using a binary code, there are no other combinations for two sequential bits. We have covered all possibilities with the four symbols given above.

Now we have to decide how to transmit four, 2-bit symbols. It is relatively simple to assign each symbol a phase angle. Since a sine wave tone has 360^0, four points of the phase angle can be chosen. A 00 is assigned a 0 degree phase shift, 01 is assigned 90 degrees, 10 assigned 180 degrees, and 11 assigned 270 degrees. (Fig. 13-15).

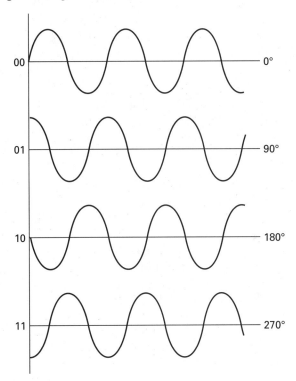

FIGURE 13-15 Phase Shifted Signals

Each phase shift encodes two bits of information. During one bit period, two bits are actually sent. These symbols are called *dibits*. And yes, there are also *tribits* and even *quadbits*. Encoding three bits, creates eight possible combinations, $(2^3 = 8)$. The *tribit* phase code simply uses four more phase angles in addition to the original four, namely, 45, 135, 225, and 315-degree phase shifts. With eight combinations, three bits can be sent during one bit period. If we extend the idea to encoding four bits, we acquire 16 possible symbols. Beyond this, we use what is called **trellis encoding**. In trellis encoding, several carriers are used, all within the 300 to 3300-Hz band. Each carrier uses some form of PSK encoding. With PSK, the speed limit is definitely raised, but trellis-encoded systems are not widely available at the moment.

The Bell 212A standard includes the 103A method combined with phase encoding two bits in four phase-shifted angles:

212A Operation:

Phase Shift	Symbol
90°	00
0°	01
180°	10
270°	11

Even while using PSK encoding, the 212A type modem is designed to operate at a mere 1200 baud. It is worth noting here that in phase shift keying, two bits are encoded at a time. This means 600 symbols-per-second are sent at the 1200-bits-per-second baud rate. As you can see, then, bits-per-second does not equate to the baud rate.

Modems operating at 2400 baud are now easily-available and widely-used. Credit for this is largely due to the work of **CCITT** (Consultive Committee of International Telephone and Telegraph). The introduction of the V.22 international standard into the US has led to the availability of full-duplex modems operating at 2400 baud.

The current standards list:

Standard	**Duplex**	**Speed**	**Type**
Bell 103A	Full	0-300	Async
CCITT V.21	Full	0-300	Async
Bell 202A	Half	600-1200	Async
Bell 212A	Full	1200	Both
CCITT V.22	Full	2400	Both
Bell 201B	Both	2400	Sync
CCITT V.26	Both	2400	Sync
Bell 208	Full	4800	Sync
CCITT V.27	Full	4800	Sync
Bell 209	Full	9600	Sync
CCITT V.29	Full	9600	Sync
CCITT V.32	Full	9600	Sync
CCITT V.33	Full	14,400	Sync

This table tells us that while a variety of standards are employed, most of them feature only synchronous operation. Synchronous transmission requires hardware not generally available in PC's.

On the other hand, manufacturers like Hayes Microcomputer have done well in establishing standards of their own. Hayes, for example, sells a 9600-baud, asynchronous/synchronous modem, the Ultra. (Fig. 13-16). It works as a half-duplex system but it has a sophisticated line-reversal procedure.

Hayes also is responsible for the so called *smart modem*. A smart modem uses a microprocessor to perform various duties, such as dialing the phone, storing phone numbers, and even recognizing and dealing with busy signals. Smart modems respond to a command language and have become an industry standard influenced by the popularity of the Hayes modem.

FIGURE 13-16 Hayes V-Series ULTRA Smartmodem 9600

13-9   PARALLEL COMMUNICATION

Serial vs Parallel

Up to this point, we have been speaking of serial transmission and communication of data. Serial communication requires serial hardware, methodology, and standards. RS-232 is the universal serial standard. In many instances, however, parallel transmission of data is the method of choice. The main advantage of parallel communication is the capacity to transmit eight or more bits at one time. This capacity brings about a marked increase in the amount of data that can be exchanged in a given period of time. Parallel communication of data is achieved with the expense of considerably more wire. Wire alone does impose a reasonable limit on distance, but it is not just the amount of wire that concerns us, but the additional electrical problems associated with the additional wire. Electrical noise, capacitance problems, and the power required to drive the lines limit parallel interfaces to an average of twenty-five feet. When phone lines are used, parallel transmission, of course, is not an option.

Centronics

Parallel communication is most commonly used between computers and printers. The industry standard was developed by **Centronics** Data Computer Corporation for their line of printers. It requires a 36-pin connector. Eight of the pins are used for the transmission of 8-bit bytes. The other pins are used for control signals. It should be mentioned that the transmission of data from computer to printer is actually one way. There is essentially no need for a printer to transmit data back to a computer.

IEEE-488

Centronics is by no means the only parallel interface employed. There are several other interface standards employed; the one that has found the most acceptance is the IEEE-488 bus, developed by Hewlett-Packard. It uses a 24-pin connector with eight pins for data, eight for control signals, and several grounds. Its working length is specified at twenty meters. It is in fact, a bus *system*, because up to fifteen devices can be interconnected at one time, and each is allowed to both transmit and receive.

✔ SELF-CHECK FOR SECTIONS 13-7, 13-8, 13-9

19. Explain the difference between polar-working and neutral-working loops.
20. What is an example of a current-loop machine?
21. Explain simplex operation.
22. Explain half-duplex operation.
23. Explain full-duplex operation.
24. What is FSK?
25. What is PSK?
26. Explain a DIBIT.
27. Does bits-per-second always equate to baud? Why or why not?
28. Is RS-232 a serial or a parallel standard?

SUMMARY OF IDEAS

- ASCII is a 7-bit binary code used to represent alpha-numeric characters for data transmission.
- EBCDIC is an 8-bit alpha-numeric code widely used by IBM.
- The rate of transmission is called *baud*. The baud rate can be found: Baud = 1/time period for one symbol.
- The two main methods for transmission of binary data are classified as *synchronous* and *asynchronous*.
- The synchronous method requires that the transmitter and receiver share a common clock.
- The asynchronous method does not require a common clock. Instead, the transmitted data is *framed* with start and stop bits.
- Synchronous data transmission is characterized by the sending of blocks of data.
- The biphase-synchronous method insures that a signal change takes place at the end of each bit, regardless of whether the data sent changes or not.
- Bisync transmission is the protocol developed by IBM. It specifies exactly what form the blocks of synchronous data are to have.
- SDLC is the synchronous protocol that is replacing bisync. It is faster and more efficient that bisync.
- The RS-232 standard is the most widely used interface between Data Terminal Equipment and Data Communication Equipment.
- RS-232 is a serial data transmission standard that specifies the assignments of a 25-pin connector.
- Current-loop transmission uses the presence or absence of current in a loop to indicate logic level changes.
- A modem is Data Communications Equipment (DCE) used to interface computers and terminals to telephone lines.
- Modems translate digital signals into audio signals suitable for phone line transmission.
- Frequency-Shift Keying (FSK) is a method whereby the modem converts logic-1's into one frequency for transmission and logic-0's into another.
- Phase-Shift Keying (PSK) makes use of the sinusoidal shape and phase relation of audio signals to encode data logic.
- Parallel transmission of data takes place along parallel wires defined by standards employed by Centronics and IEEE-488.

CHAPTER QUESTIONS & PROBLEMS

True or False
1. The ASCII code does not have room to encode both parity and alpha-numeric characters in 8-bit bytes.
2. Baud rate means the number of bits-per-second that are transmitted.
3. In synchronous transmission, data is sent in blocks rather than one byte at a time.
4. In biphase-synchronous transmission, the line logic levels bear no direct relation to the data logic.
5. Asynchronous transmission takes place one byte at a time.

Fill in the Blanks
6. In asynchronous transmission, a start bit followed by 8-data bits and ending with a stop bit is called a _____.

7. When two computers with RS-232 ports are connected directly together, they will most likely use a _____ modem.

8. When a modem encodes digital signals by changing them to different frequencies it is called, _____ _____ _____.

9. If phase shift keying encodes two bits at a time, each symbol is called a _____.

10. The standard for connections between Data Terminal Equipment (DTE) and Data Communication Equipment (DCE) is called the

    _____.

Multiple Choice

11. For a direct connection, the RS-232 standard has a practical distance limit of
    a. 20 feet.   c. 2 miles.
    b. 200 feet.   d. 25 feet.

12. When communication over a phone line takes place in only one direction at a time, the line is said to operate at
    a. full duplex.   c. multiplex.
    b. half duplex.   d. simplex.

13. Which of the following statements about RS-232 is *not* true?
    a. RS-232 uses a negative voltage to represent logic-1 and a positive voltage to represent logic–0.
    b. Most of the lines in the 25-pin RS-232 are not normally used.
    c. Either serial or parallel transmission is permitted.
    d. Either synchronous or asynchronous transmission is permitted.

14. Which of the following does *not* apply to synchronous transmission?
    a. bisync   c. SDLC
    b. PSK   d. biphase

15. A Centronics connector has
    a. 25 pins.   c. 24 pins.
    b. 9 pins.   d. 36 pins.

16. How many phase shifts are required to encode two bits at a time?
    a. 2   c. 8
    b. 4   d. 16

17. If the time for one bit is 0.833 ms, what is the baud rate?
    a. 300   c. 1200
    b. 600   d. 2400

18. In a bit-stuffing circuit, the flag is 01111110. Which of the following bytes would need a zero insertion (bit stuffing)?
    a. 11110111   c. 00000001
    b. 11111000   d. 11001111

19. The standard phone line has bandwidth of
    a. 1070 Hz.
    b. 20,000 Hz.
    c. 300 Hz.
    d. 3000 Hz.

20. Which of the following statements apply to asynchronous data transmission?
    a. Each byte is preceded by a start bit and ends with a stop bit.
    b. Characters can appear at odd intervals on the transmission line.
    c. The transmit and receive clocks are not in continuous synchronization.
    d. all of the above

CHAPTER 14

THE MOTOROLA MC6800 MICROPROCESSOR

OUTLINE

NEW TERMS TO WATCH FOR

PIA	DMA	Bidirectional
Three-State Bus	Nonoverlapping Clocks	Base Page
Displacement Byte	Effective Address	Pipelining
Relative Addressing	Offset Byte	Memory Mapped
Memory Oriented	Scratch Pad	Virtual Memory
Indirect Addressing	Extended Indirect	Cache Memory

After completing this chapter, you should be able to:

1. Describe the clock signals needed for synchronizing the MC6800 operation.
2. Name the major units or parts required to build a basic MC6800 system.
3. List the control bus functions of the MC6800 and explain their use.
4. Explain the hardware interrupts on the MC6800 and describe how they operate.
5. Discuss the methods of bus control and the associated signals both to and from the MC6800.
6. Describe the RESET process.
7. Discuss a memory-mapped system.
8. Work with the MC6800 register array.
9. Interpret and use the seven different address modes available to the MC6800.
10. Define the four groupings of the MC6800 instruction set.
11. Recognize the various series of microprocessors that Motorola has developed since the MC6800.

14-1   INTRODUCTION

Up to this point, we have discussed microprocessors in a generic way; all that was said applies in general to microprocessors. In this chapter, we will specifically discuss the Motorola MC6800 microprocessor. You will be able to apply all that you have learned about microprocessors to the MC6800.

The MC6800 was one of the first competing microprocessors introduced after Intel brought out the 8080 in 1974. The MC6800 has been almost as popular as the Intel 8080, and, like the 8080, it has spawned entire generations of successors, including the 68040 chip and beyond.

The MC6800 is easy to learn, and by understanding the 6800, you will have built the solid foundation necessary to learn the more advanced microprocessors.

14-2   THE BASIC SYSTEM

The MC6800 needs a +5V supply and an external clock. Recall that microprocessor timing depends on crystal-controlled oscillators. The MC6800 requires a crystal-controlled, two-phase clock input. Figure 14-1 shows the clock and a basic MC6800 system.

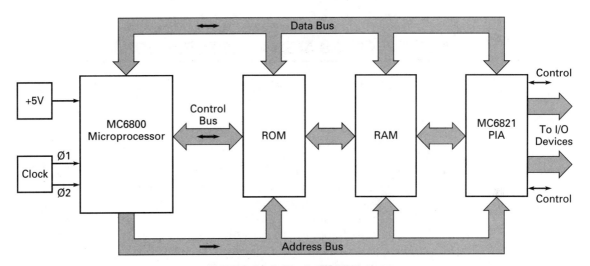

FIGURE 14-1 Basic 6800 System

In addition to the ROM and RAM memory, the MC6800 system employs a special chip called a **PIA**—Peripheral Interface Adapter. The MC6821 PIA has two, 8-bit output buses for connecting to peripheral devices. The peripherals will be the devices that the MC6800 is controlling. The 6821 contains temporary storage registers and its main purpose is to serve as an interface between the 6800 and the outside world. It has four control lines, two for each I/O bus.

The address bus is 16-bits wide, making it possible for the MC6800 to directly address up to 64K of memory. The data bus is 8-bits wide and **bidirectional**. There are nine different control signals used. This arrangement fits into a 40-pin chip package as shown in Figure 14-2.

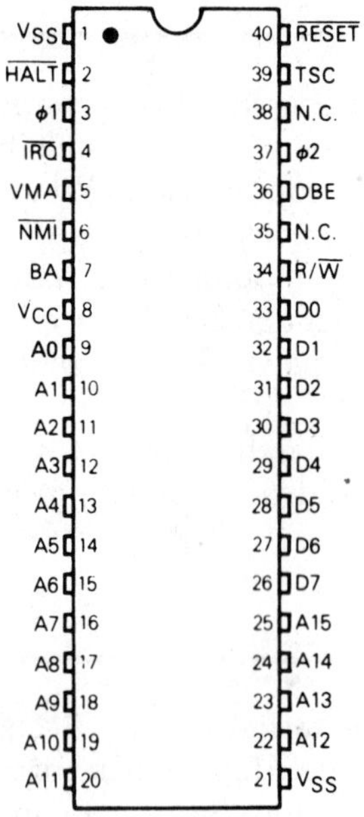

Pin	Signal	Pin	Signal
1	V_{SS}	40	$\overline{RESET}$
2	$\overline{HALT}$	39	TSC
3	φ1	38	N.C.
4	$\overline{IRQ}$	37	φ2
5	VMA	36	DBE
6	$\overline{NMI}$	35	N.C.
7	BA	34	$R/\overline{W}$
8	V_{CC}	33	D0
9	A0	32	D1
10	A1	31	D2
11	A2	30	D3
12	A3	29	D4
13	A4	28	D5
14	A5	27	D6
15	A6	26	D7
16	A7	25	A15
17	A8	24	A14
18	A9	23	A13
19	A10	22	A12
20	A11	21	V_{SS}

ORDERING INFORMATION

Package Type	Frequency (MHz)	Temperature	Order Number
Cerdip	1.0	0°C to 70°C	MC6800S
S Suffix	1.0	−40°C to 85°C	MC6800CS
	1.5	0°C to 70°C	MC68A00S
	1.5	−40°C to 85°C	MC68A00CS
	2.0	0°C to 70°C	MC68B00S
Plastic	1.0	0°C to 70°C	MC6800P
P Suffix	1.0	−40°C to 85°C	MC6800CP
	1.5	0°C to 70°C	MC68A00P
	1.5	−40°C to 85°C	MC68A00CP
	2.0	0°C to 70°C	MC68B00P

FIGURE 14-2 MC6800 Pin Assignment

14-3   MC6800 SIGNAL DESCRIPTIONS

For the following signal descriptions, refer to the block diagram of the MC6800 shown in Figure 14-3.

Clock Signals

As mentioned, the MC6800 requires a two-phase clock to synchronize its operation. The minimum clock frequency is .1 MHz and the maximum is 1 MHz. This means the duration of the clock signal must be a minimum of 1 microsecond to a maximum of 10 microseconds. If the processor is operated at speeds below 10 microseconds, the internal registers will lose data. If operated above 1 microsecond, the processor would not have time to properly access the peripherals.

Figure 14-4 shows the relation of the phase-1 and phase-2 clock pulses. The clock waveforms are **nonoverlapping**, that is, when phase-1 is high, phase-2 is low, and vice versa. Note, in Figure 14-4, there are some variations on the MC6800 chip. For example, the MC68B00 is designed to operate up to 2 MHz.

The rise and fall times are very specific. If the pulse width timing t_{ut} is not met, the ability of the processor to access the peripheral devices cannot be guaranteed.

Address Bus

There are 16 address bus pins labeled A0 though A15. The buffers shown in Figure 14-3 are actually **three-state bus** drivers. When activated to the third state, they cause an open circuit (high impedance state) to exist between the MC6800 and the 16 bus lines. This frees the bus for use by other devices in the system.

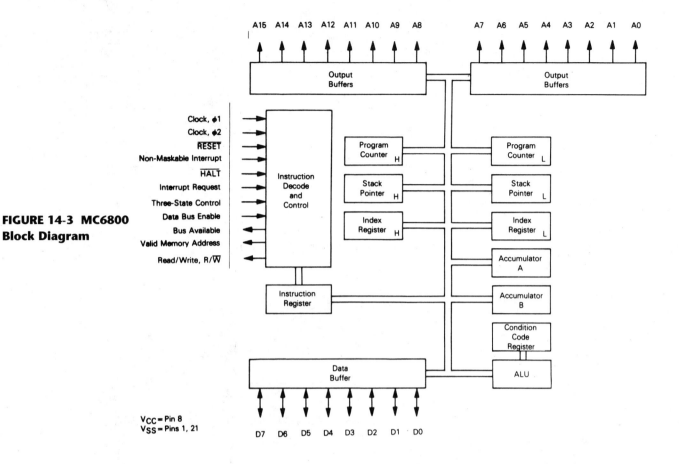

FIGURE 14-3 MC6800 Block Diagram

Data Bus

The 8-pin data bus, labeled D0 through D7, is also connected to a tri-state bus driver. The bidirectional data bus is used to transfer data to and from memory and peripherals.

RESET

The RESET is an input pin that is activated whenever the microprocessor is powered up. It can also be used to reinitialize or restart the processor while it is in operation.

When the RESET line is pulsed low for a specified time, the reset sequence will begin. The RESET pulse causes the program counter register to be loaded with address FFFEH. This vectored memory location (FFFEH) must contain the high order byte of the reset routine address. Next the program counter is automatically loaded with FFFFH, the address of the low order byte for the reset routine. In other words, the last two locations in memory are reserved for the address of the reset routine. In this way, the reset routine can be located anywhere in memory. For this reason, many practical applications place ROM memory at the highest addresses. (Fig. 14-5).

CLOCK TIMING ($V_{CC}=5.0$ V, $\pm5\%$, $V_{SS}=0$, $T_A=T_L$ to T_H unless otherwise noted)

Characteristic		Symbol	Min	Typ	Max	Unit
Frequency of Operation	MC6800		0.1	—	1.0	
	MC68A00	f	0.1	—	1.5	MHz
	MC68B00		0.1	—	2.0	
Cycle Time (Figure 1)	MC6800		1.000	—	10	
	MC68A00	t_{cyc}	0.666	—	10	µs
	MC68B00		0.500	—	10	
Clock Pulse Width	$\phi1, \phi2$ — MC6800		400	—	9500	
(Measured at $V_{CC}-0.6$ V)	$\phi1, \phi2$ — MC68A00	$PW_{\phi H}$	230	—	9500	ns
	$\phi1, \phi2$ — MC68B00		180	—	9500	
Total $\phi1$ and $\phi2$ Up Time	MC6800		900	—	—	
	MC68A00	t_{ut}	600	—	—	ns
	MC68B00		440	—	—	
Rise and Fall Time (Measured between $V_{SS}+0.4$ and $V_{CC}-0.6$)		t_r, t_f	—	—	100	ns
Delay Time or Clock Separation (Figure 1)						
(Measured at $V_{OV}=V_{SS}+0.6$ V@$t_r=t_f\leq100$ ns)		t_d	0	—	9100	ns
(Measured at $V_{OV}=V_{SS}+1.0$ V@$t_r=t_f\leq35$ ns)			0	—	9100	

FIGURE 1 — CLOCK TIMING WAVEFORM

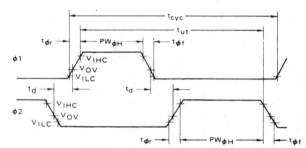

NOTES:
1. Voltage levels shown are $V_L\leq0.4$, $V_H\geq2.4$ V, unless otherwise specified.
2. Measurement points shown are 0.8 V and 2.0 V, unless otherwise noted.

READ/WRITE TIMING (Reference Figures 2 through 6, 8, 9, 11, 12 and 13)

Characteristic	Symbol	MC6800			MC68A00			MC68B00			Unit
		Min	Typ	Max	Min	Typ	Max	Min	Typ	Max	
Address Delay											
C = 90 pF	t_{AD}	—	—	270	—	—	180	—	—	150	ns
C = 30 pF		—	—	250	—	—	165	—	—	135	
Peripheral Read Access Time $t_{acc}=t_{ut}-(t_{AD}+t_{DSR})$	t_{acc}	530	—	—	360	—	—	250	—	—	ns
Data Setup Time (Read)	t_{DSR}	100	—	—	60	—	—	40	—	—	ns
Input Data Hold Time	t_H	10	—	—	10	—	—	10	—	—	ns
Output Data Hold Time	t_H	10	25	—	10	25	—	10	25	—	ns
Address Hold Time (Address, R/$\overline{W}$, VMA)	t_{AH}	30	50	—	30	50	—	30	50	—	ns
Enable High Time for DBE Input	t_{EH}	450	—	—	280	—	—	220	—	—	ns
Data Delay Time (Write)	t_{DDW}	—	—	225	—	—	200	—	—	160	ns
Processor Controls											
Processor Control Setup Time	t_{PCS}	200	—	—	140	—	—	110	—	—	
Processor Control Rise and Fall Time	t_{PCr}, t_{PCf}	—	—	100	—	—	100	—	—	100	
Bus Available Delay	t_{BA}	—	—	250	—	—	165	—	—	135	
Hi-Z Enable	t_{TSE}	0	—	40	0	—	40	0	—	40	ns
Hi-Z Delay	t_{TSD}	—	—	270	—	—	270	—	—	220	
Data Bus Enable Down Time During $\phi1$ Up Time	t_{DBE}	150	—	—	120	—	—	75	—	—	
Data Bus Enable Rise and Fall Times	t_{DBEr}, t_{DBEf}	—	—	25	—	—	25	—	—	25	

FIGURE 14-4 MC6800 Clock Frequency

The RESET routine itself will vary according to the job the processor is doing and is highly dependent on the application. The routine is also used to tell the microprocessor, via the program counter, where to start executing instructions.

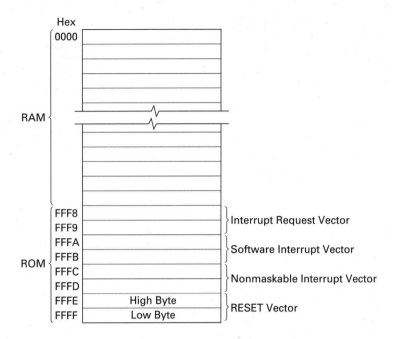

FIGURE 14-5 64K Memory for MC6800

Nonmaskable Interrupt

The nonmaskable interrupt input is one of the two interrupts available on the MC6800. The nonmaskable interrupt is just that, it cannot be masked and will be serviced whenever it occurs. Recall from the chapter on interrupts and stacks that a maskable interrupt can be ignored or rejected by the microprocessor.

The nonmaskable interrupt (NMI) is also a vectored interrupt. When the NMI input pin is pulsed low, the processor will finish the instruction it is currently executing, because the processor has set the interrupt mask bit. This is a bit position in the *condition code register as* seen in Figure 14-6.

The condition code register is connected to the ALU and monitors the status of the ALU. In the MC6800, the condition code register also has a bit position dedicated to the interrupt mask. This "I" bit, when set, prevents any further interrupts from affecting the microprocessor.

The MC6800 automatically builds a stack. Remember, the stack consists of the register contents as they exist at the time of the interrupt. The registers that are placed on the stack are the program counter, index register, the A and B accumulators, and the condition code register. Figure 14-7 flowcharts the nonmaskable interrupt sequence.

Finally, the MC6800 automatically loads the program counter with the vector address FFFCH. This address will contain the high order byte of the interrupt routine to be executed. (Fig. 14-5). Then the low order address is fetched from FFFDH. After the interrupt routine is completed, the processor returns to normal operation. (Fig. 14-7).

FIGURE 14-6 The Condition Code Register for MC6800

```
7  6  5  4  3  2  1  0
1  1  H  I  N  Z  V  C
```

H = Half Carry
 I = Interrupt Mask
N = Negative Flag
Z = Zero Flag
V = Overflow
C = Carry

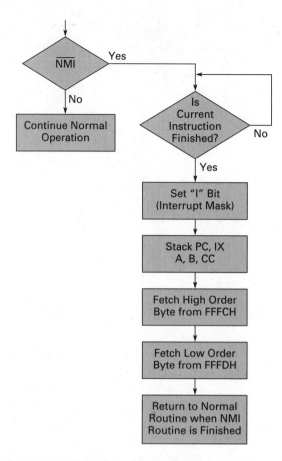

FIGURE 14-7 The Nonmaskable Interrupt Sequence

Interrupt Request

The interrupt request input (IRQ) is a hardware interrupt, very much like the NMI. The difference is that this interrupt is maskable. The processor will accept IRQ interrupt only if the interrupt mask is *not* set. Recall that the interrupt mask is the "I" bit in the condition code register.

If the mask is not set, the processor will place the contents of the program counter, index register, A and B accumulators, and the condition code register in the stack. The 6800 then sets the interrupt mask bit to prevent further interrupts. Next it loads the vectored IRQ address FFF8H into the program counter. FFF8H contains the high order byte of the interrupt routine to be executed. FFF9H contains the low order byte. After the interrupt routine is complete, the processor resumes normal operation. Figure 14-8 illustrates the Interrupt ReQuest sequence.

There is an instruction called the *software* interrupt, SWI, that is also a vectored interrupt. It is in contrast to the *hardware* interrupts in that it is part of the instruction set and will occur only when encountered within a program.

We mention the software interrupt (SWI) here because the vector addresses used are also at the top of the memory, namely, FFFAH and FFFBH. (Fig. 14-5).

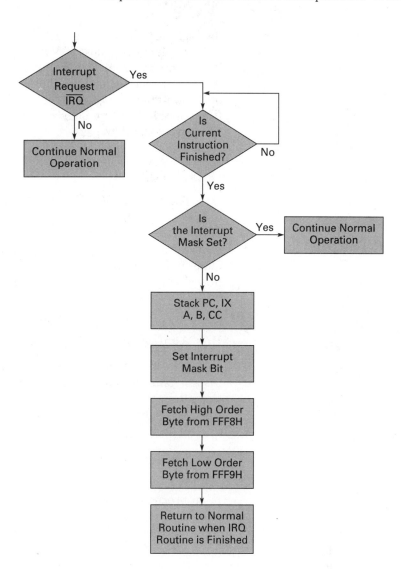

FIGURE 14-8 The Interrupt Request Sequence

[Flowchart content:]

Interrupt Request IRQ — Yes → Is Current Instruction Finished?

No → Continue Normal Operation

Is Current Instruction Finished? — No (loop back); Yes ↓

Is the Interrupt Mask Set? — Yes → Continue Normal Operation

No ↓

Stack PC, IX A, B, CC

Set Interrupt Mask Bit

Fetch High Order Byte from FFF8H

Fetch Low Order Byte from FFF9H

Return to Normal Routine when IRQ Routine is Finished

HALT

The HALT input is to allow program execution to be controlled from an outside source. When the HALT input is high, program execution proceeds. When the HALT is brought low, the processor finishes the instruction it is executing and goes into a suspended or idle state. During this state, it will not execute instructions nor will it execute an interrupt request.

The signal to halt also frees the address and data buses for other use. Both of these buses will go to the open circuit state (tri-state) when the HALT pin is brought low. In addition, the Read/Write pin will be in the high-impedance state.

When a HALT input is received, the microprocessor outputs a signal to indicate that its buses are now in the high-impedance state. This condition is signaled by a high on the Bus Available (BA) output line. When the microprocessor is using the buses, the BA output is low. The HALT signal causes the BA output to go high. This indication is used as a signal to external devices desiring to use the data and address buses. The high on the BA output means the buses are now available.

Three-State Control

The Three-State Control input (TSC) is active when high, that is, TSC = 1. It causes the address bus and the Read/Write control line (R/W) to change to the high-impedance state. This pin is for use with an external device that has a Direct Memory Access **(DMA)** capability. A DMA operation is only possible if there are external devices present that can utilize a Direct Memory Access and if a device for controlling the access is present. An example of a DMA operation might be the transfer of data from a disk drive directly to memory. It is possible to move large blocks of data like this more efficiently when the microprocessor is bypassed.

Data Bus Enable

The Data-Bus-Enable input (DBE) is the three-state control line for the data bus. When DBE is high, the bus is active. Bringing the DBE line low disables the data bus by putting it in the high-impedance state. Data transfers to and from memory or peripherals occur during the time that the phase-2 clock is high. For this reason, the DBE pin is sometimes connected to the phase-2 clock signal. If a DMA is required, the Data-Bus-Enable input should be held low.

Bus Available

The Bus Available (BA) is used, as mentioned during the HALT discussion, to signal the status of the address and data buses. During normal execution, the BA line is low. When the HALT or TSC is activated, the BA line is brought high, indicating the high-impedance state for the buses.

Valid Memory Address

The Valid Memory Address (VMA) is an output signal. It is used by the microprocessor to signal that there is a valid address available on the address bus. This signal is used to enable devices like the PIA. A high on the VMA indicates that a valid address is currently present on the address bus.

Read/Write

The Read/Write (R/W) is an output pin used to signal memory or peripherals that the microprocessor is in the read or the write state. When the output is high, the processor is the read condition. It is in the write condition when R/W is brought low. This three-state output is placed in the high-impedance state when the microprocessor is halted.

✔ SELF-CHECK FOR SECTIONS 14-1, 14-2, 14-3

1. Does a 6800 need and external clock circuit?
2. What is the purpose of a PIA?
3. The data bus is 8-bits wide and _____.
4. How many pins on the 6800 package?
5. What is the maximum clock frequency of the 6800.
6. What is a three-state bus?
7. Is the RESET routing always the same?
8. What is the NMI pin for?
9. Which bit in the status register is assigned to the interrupt mask?
10. What are SWI instructions?
11. Describe the purpose of the HALT input.
12. What is DMA?

14-4   MC6800 REGISTERS

The 6800 has three 16-bit registers and three 8-bit registers available to the programmer. Figure 14-9 is the programming model of the 6800. The interconnection of the various registers is better illustrated, however, in the block diagram in Figure 14-3.

FIGURE 14-9 MPU Registers

The MPU has three 16-bit registers and three 8-bit registers available for use by the programmer (Figure 14-9).

Program Counter — The program counter is a two byte (16 bits) register that points to the current program address.

Stack Pointer — The stack ponter is a two byte register that contains the address of the next available location in an external push-down/pop-up stack. This stack is normally a random access Read/Write memory that may have any location (address) that is convenient. In those applications that require storage of information in the stack when power is lost, the stack must be nonvolatile.

Index Register — The index register is a two byte register that is used to store data or a sixteen bit memory address for the Indexed mode of memory addressing.

Accumulators — The MPU contains two 8-bit accumulators that are used to hold operands and results from an arithmetic logic unit (ALU).

Condition Code Register — The condition code register indicates the results of an Arithmetic Logic Unit operation: Negative (N), Zero (Z), Overflow (V), Carry from bit 7 (C), and half carry from bit 3 (H). These bits of the Condition Code Register are used as testable conditions for the conditional branch instructions. Bit 4 is the interrupt mask bit (I). The unused bits of the Condition Code Register (b6 and b7) are ones.

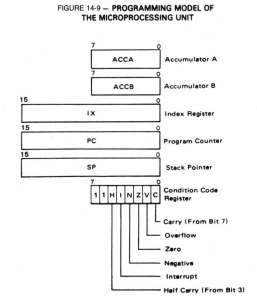

FIGURE 14-9 — **PROGRAMMING MODEL OF THE MICROPROCESSING UNIT**

Program Counter

The program counter (PC) is a 16-bit register that always contains the address of the next instruction to be executed. (Strictly speaking, it is used to point to the *current program address* which in fact may or may not contain an instruction.)

Stack Pointer

The stack pointer (SP) register is also a 16-bit register but it is used to contain the current address of the stack. It will always contain the address of the next available location. The stack is built in a Last-In-First-Out fashion. The stack for the MC6800 can be located anywhere in RAM.

Index Register

The index register (IX) is a 16-bit register used for indexed addressing. It can also be used as a temporary storage location for any 16-bit word. We will learn more about this register when we discuss indexed addressing for the 6800.

Accumulators

The 6800 has two 8-bit accumulators, A and B, which are used for various microprocessor operations. The MC6800's accumulators perform as described in the chapter on microprocessor elements.

Condition Code Register

The condition code register (CC) is an 8-bit register containing the various flags listed in Figure 14-9. The function of each flag (with the exception of the I flag) has already been covered in the chapter on microprocessor status. The first two positions in the register are not used.

 SELF-CHECK FOR SECTION 14-4

13. How large is the program counter register?
14. How large is the stack pointer register? Why?
15. Where is the stack located for the 6800?
16. How are the accumulator registers referred to (what are their names)?

14-5   MC6800 ADDRESSING MODES

The MC6800 has seven addressing modes. We have in fact covered most of them in the chapter on addressing techniques. Nevertheless, the actual application and use of these techniques can now be seen in a *real world* example.

Accumulator Addressing

This mode of addressing is really a subset of *inherent* or *implied* mode addressing. Instructions using this mode are listed by Motorola under the *implied* mode. The operand is always one of the two accumulators and is contained within the opcode. An example is CLRA or CLRB which calls for the appropriate accumulator to be cleared to hold all zeros. Such instructions are the shortest and fastest instructions for the microprocessor. They require only one byte.

Implied Addressing

There are several other implied-mode instructions that do not involve the accumulators. They are also only one byte long and imply the register or action to take place, within the opcode. The CRC instruction, meaning to clear the carry bit in the condition code register, is an example. DES is another example, meaning to decrement the stack pointer register. Again the key feature is that inherent-mode instructions are all written in one byte.

Immediate-Mode Addressing

Immediate-mode addressing indicates that the operand will be in the next byte or the next two bytes. The mode means that the operand is to be taken *literally* and not interpreted as an address. The assembler form looks like this:

Label	Opcode	Operand	Comment
	ADDA	#$46;	add 46H to value in A Accumulator

In this example, ADDA (8B) is written in the immediate mode. It means "add Hex 46 to whatever value is in the A accumulator." The # sign in assembler language means that the immediate addressing mode is indicated. The $ sign means the number is written in hex.

Direct-Mode Addressing

In direct-mode addressing, the byte following the instruction is the address of the operand. With only 8-bits possible, the operand must be stored in one of the first 256 locations of memory. This is sometimes called the **base page** and addressing the base page is called base-page addressing. In the 6800, the main feature of this address mode is that the operand must be somewhere in the first 256 locations. The advantage is that only two bytes are needed for a direct mode instruction.

The instruction ADDA written in the direct mode is shown here:

Label	Opcode	Operand	Comment
	ADDA	$FE;	add contents of location FE to the A Accumulator

Extended-Mode Addressing

The extended mode of addressing is just like the direct mode, except that a full, 16-bit address is made available by using the *two* bytes immediately following the instruction. The first byte after the instruction contains the high order byte of the address and the second byte after the instruction contains the low order byte.

Here is ADDA written in the extended address mode:

Label	Opcode	Operand	Comment
	ADDA	$0AFC;	add contents of location 0AFC to the A Accumulator

Relative Addressing

In **relative addressing**, the address of the operand must be calculated by the 6800. The relative addressing mode uses a **displacement byte** following the instruction. This byte is added to the program counter to point to the location of the operand.

The displacement byte appears in the 2's complement form, which means that displacement numbers from -128 to $+127$ can be represented. In practice, the program counter always increments after the fetch, so the actual range possible for relative addresses is -126 to $+129$. Relative addressing is used for *branch*-type instructions.

An example of relative addressing is:

Label	Opcode	Operand	Comment
	BRA	$0A;	BRanch Always to location indicated by adding +10 to whatever address is in the PC

Indexed Addressing

The indexed mode of addressing also uses a calculation method to find the address of the operand. An indexed-mode instruction uses the byte following the instruction, called the **offset byte**, to add to the address contained in the index register. The result of adding the offset to the index register address is called the **effective address**. It is important to note that this calculation does not change the value in the index register. An example of how the indexed mode of addressing is accomplished follows.

For this example, assume the index register contains a value of 4000H (the base address).

Label	Opcode	Operand	Comment
	ADDA	$0B;	add the byte pointed to by the offset plus the index register to the A Accumulator

The 6800 calculates the location of the operand by adding

$$
\begin{array}{ll}
4000 & \text{index register} \\
+\ 0B & \text{offset} \\
\hline
400B & \text{location of the operand}
\end{array}
$$

 **SELF-CHECK FOR SECTION 14-5**

17. What is the implied mode of addressing?
18. Give and example of an implied-mode instruction.
19. How many bytes of memory does an implied-mode instruction require?
20. Explain immediate-mode addressing.
21. What is the purpose of the direct mode of addressing?
22. Explain extended-mode addressing.
23. Explain relative addressing.
24. The byte in the index register plus the offset byte equals the _____ _____.

14-6   THE MC6800 INSTRUCTION SET

The instruction set for the MC6800 consists of 72 different opcodes. There are 72 different mnemonics and their 8-bit binary equivalents. Each of the 72 mnemonics, when assembled, translates into a 1, 2, or 3-byte instruction. The opcode is always the first byte and the second or third byte will depend on the addressing mode.

The MC6800 does *not* have a unique mnemonic for each possible opcode. The same mnemonic is used for several different address modes. For example:

Mnemonic	Opcode	Addressing Mode
ADDA	8B	Immediate
ADDA	9B	Direct
ADDA	AB	Indexed
ADDA	BB	Extended

This is why the assembler language for the 6800 must have an indicator of some sort to tell it what addressing mode is intended. Given all the different addressing modes, 197 possible instructions for the 6800 exist.

For clarity, Motorola has divided the instruction set into groups. They are:

1. Accumulator and Memory Operations
2. Index and Stack-Pointer Instructions
3. Jump and Branch Instructions
4. Condition Code Register Instructions

Accumulator and Memory Operations

This group of instructions is by far the largest group. The list of accumulator and memory operations is found in Table 14-1. The MC6800 is generally referred to as a **memory-oriented** microprocessor. This is because the largest group of instructions is based on transfers to and from memory. Not only that, the MC6800 treats I/O devices as though they were a memory location. In an MC6800 system, a portion of memory is blocked out and assigned to peripheral devices. When the processor wishes to transfer data to or from a peripheral, it uses its assigned memory address. This method is called a **memory-mapped** system.

Table 14-1 lists the mnemonic and five different addressing modes. In the address mode columns, we find the header:

$$\text{OP} \quad \sim \quad \#$$

The OP refers to the opcode and lists the hex equivalent of the 8-bit machine code.

The listing under the ~ (tilde) symbol gives the number of MPU (microprocessor unit) cycles required to complete the instruction. There are no instructions that can complete in less than two cycles. The first cycle of the clock is required for the fetch operation. During the next cycle, the decode and execute phase take place. (Fig. 14-10).

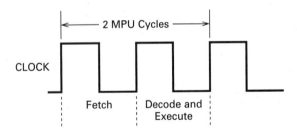

FIGURE 14-10 Illustration of Instruction That Completes in Two MPU Cycles

The # symbol gives the number of bytes required by the instruction.

Table 14-1 uses a shorthand to describe the action of an instruction. For example, the ADDA instruction is accompanied by the symbols:

$$\text{A} + \text{M} \longrightarrow \text{A}$$

This means that the contents of the A accumulator is added to the contents of the memory location and the result appears in the A accumulator.

MC6800

ACCUMULATOR AND MEMORY OPERATIONS

OPERATIONS	MNEMONIC	IMMED OP ~ #	DIRECT OP ~ #	INDEX OP ~ #	EXTND OP ~ #	IMPLIED OP ~ #	BOOLEAN/ARITHMETIC OPERATION (All register labels refer to contents)	H I N Z V C
Add	ADDA	8B 2 2	9B 3 2	AB 5 2	BB 4 3		A + M · A	↕ • ↕ ↕ ↕ ↕
	ADDB	CB 2 2	DB 3 2	EB 5 2	FB 4 3		B + M · B	↕ • ↕ ↕ ↕ ↕
Add Acmltrs	ABA					1B 2 1	A + B · A	↕ • ↕ ↕ ↕ ↕
Add with Carry	ADCA	89 2 2	99 3 2	A9 5 2	B9 4 3		A + M + C · A	↕ • ↕ ↕ ↕ ↕
	ADCB	C9 2 2	D9 3 2	E9 5 2	F9 4 3		B + M + C · B	↕ • ↕ ↕ ↕ ↕
And	ANDA	84 2 2	94 3 2	A4 5 2	B4 4 3		A · M · A	• • ↕ ↕ R •
	ANDB	C4 2 2	D4 3 2	E4 5 2	F4 4 3		B · M · B	• • ↕ ↕ R •
Bit Test	BITA	85 2 2	95 3 2	A5 5 2	B5 4 3		A · M	• • ↕ ↕ R •
	BITB	C5 2 2	D5 3 2	E5 5 2	F5 4 3		B · M	• • ↕ ↕ R •
Clear	CLR			6F 7 2	7F 6 3		00 · M	• • R S R R
	CLRA					4F 2 1	00 · A	• • R S R R
	CLRB					5F 2 1	00 · B	• • R S R R
Compare	CMPA	81 2 2	91 3 2	A1 5 2	B1 4 3		A − M	• • ↕ ↕ ↕ ↕
	CMPB	C1 2 2	D1 3 2	E1 5 2	F1 4 3		B − M	• • ↕ ↕ ↕ ↕
Compare Acmltrs	CBA					11 2 1	A − B	• • ↕ ↕ ↕ ↕
Complement, 1's	COM			63 7 2	73 6 3		M̄ · M	• • ↕ ↕ R S
	COMA					43 2 1	Ā · A	• • ↕ ↕ R S
	COMB					53 2 1	B̄ · B	• • ↕ ↕ R S
Complement, 2's	NEG			60 7 2	70 6 3		00 − M · M	• • ↕ ↕ ① ②
(Negate)	NEGA					40 2 1	00 − A · A	• • ↕ ↕ ① ②
	NEGB					50 2 1	00 − B · B	• • ↕ ↕ ① ②
Decimal Adjust, A	DAA					19 2 1	Converts Binary Add. of BCD Characters into BCD Format	• • ↕ ↕ ↕ ③
Decrement	DEC			6A 7 2	7A 6 3		M − 1 · M	• • ↕ ↕ ④ •
	DECA					4A 2 1	A − 1 · A	• • ↕ ↕ ④ •
	DECB					5A 2 1	B − 1 · B	• • ↕ ↕ ④ •
Exclusive OR	EORA	88 2 2	98 3 2	A8 5 2	B8 4 3		A⊕M · A	• • ↕ ↕ R •
	EORB	C8 2 2	D8 3 2	E8 5 2	F8 4 3		B⊕M · B	• • ↕ ↕ R •
Increment	INC			6C 7 2	7C 6 3		M + 1 · M	• • ↕ ↕ ⑤ •
	INCA					4C 2 1	A + 1 · A	• • ↕ ↕ ⑤ •
	INCB					5C 2 1	B + 1 · B	• • ↕ ↕ ⑤ •
Load Acmltr	LDAA	86 2 2	96 3 2	A6 5 2	B6 4 3		M · A	• • ↕ ↕ R •
	LDAB	C6 2 2	D6 3 2	E6 5 2	F6 4 3		M · B	• • ↕ ↕ R •
Or, Inclusive	ORAA	8A 2 2	9A 3 2	AA 5 2	BA 4 3		A + M · A	• • ↕ ↕ R •
	ORAB	CA 2 2	DA 3 2	EA 5 2	FA 4 3		B + M · B	• • ↕ ↕ R •
Push Data	PSHA					36 4 1	A · Msp, SP − 1 · SP	• • • • • •
	PSHB					37 4 1	B · Msp, SP − 1 · SP	• • • • • •
Pull Data	PULA					32 4 1	SP + 1 · SP, Msp · A	• • • • • •
	PULB					33 4 1	SP + 1 · SP, Msp · B	• • • • • •
Rotate Left	ROL			69 7 2	79 6 3		M	• • ↕ ↕ ⑥ ↕
	ROLA					49 2 1	A	• • ↕ ↕ ⑥ ↕
	ROLB					59 2 1	B	• • ↕ ↕ ⑥ ↕
Rotate Right	ROR			66 7 2	76 6 3		M	• • ↕ ↕ ⑥ ↕
	RORA					46 2 1	A	• • ↕ ↕ ⑥ ↕
	RORB					56 2 1	B	• • ↕ ↕ ⑥ ↕
Shift Left, Arithmetic	ASL			68 7 2	78 6 3		M	• • ↕ ↕ ⑥ ↕
	ASLA					48 2 1	A	• • ↕ ↕ ⑥ ↕
	ASLB					58 2 1	B	• • ↕ ↕ ⑥ ↕
Shift Right, Arithmetic	ASR			67 7 2	77 6 3		M	• • ↕ ↕ ⑥ ↕
	ASRA					47 2 1	A	• • ↕ ↕ ⑥ ↕
	ASRB					57 2 1	B	• • ↕ ↕ ⑥ ↕
Shift Right, Logic	LSR			64 7 2	74 6 3		M	• • R ↕ ⑥ ↕
	LSRA					44 2 1	A	• • R ↕ ⑥ ↕
	LSRB					54 2 1	B	• • R ↕ ⑥ ↕
Store Acmltr.	STAA		97 4 2	A7 6 2	B7 5 3		A · M	• • ↕ ↕ R •
	STAB		D7 4 2	E7 6 2	F7 5 3		B · M	• • ↕ ↕ R •
Subtract	SUBA	80 2 2	90 3 2	A0 5 2	B0 4 3		A − M · A	• • ↕ ↕ ↕ ↕
	SUBB	C0 2 2	D0 3 2	E0 5 2	F0 4 3		B − M → B	• • ↕ ↕ ↕ ↕
Subtract Acmltrs.	SBA					10 2 1	A − B · A	• • ↕ ↕ ↕ ↕
Subtr. with Carry	SBCA	82 2 2	92 3 2	A2 5 2	B2 4 3		A − M − C · A	• • ↕ ↕ ↕ ↕
	SBCB	C2 2 2	D2 3 2	E2 5 2	F2 4 3		B − M − C · B	• • ↕ ↕ ↕ ↕
Transfer Acmltrs	TAB					16 2 1	A · B	• • ↕ ↕ R •
	TBA					17 2 1	B · A	• • ↕ ↕ R •
Test, Zero or Minus	TST			6D 7 2	7D 6 3		M − 00	• • ↕ ↕ R R
	TSTA					4D 2 1	A − 00	• • ↕ ↕ R R
	TSTB					5D 2 1	B − 00	• • ↕ ↕ R R
								H I N Z V C

LEGEND:

OP Operation Code (Hexadecimal);
~ Number of MPU Cycles;
# Number of Program Bytes;
+ Arithmetic Plus;
− Arithmetic Minus;
· Boolean AND;
Msp Contents of memory location pointed to be Stack Pointer;
+ Boolean Inclusive OR;
⊙ Boolean Exclusive OR;
M̄ Complement of M;
→ Transfer Into;
0 Bit = Zero;
00 Byte = Zero;

CONDITION CODE SYMBOLS:

H Half-carry from bit 3;
I Interrupt mask
N Negative (sign bit)
Z Zero (byte)
V Overflow, 2's complement
C Carry from bit 7
R Reset Always
S Set Always
↕ Test and set if true, cleared otherwise
• Not Affected

CONDITION CODE REGISTER NOTES:
(Bit set if test is true and cleared otherwise)

1 (Bit V) Test: Result = 10000000?
2 (Bit C) Test: Result = 00000000?
3 (Bit C) Test: Decimal value of most significant BCD Character greater than nine? (Not cleared if previously set.)
4 (Bit V) Test: Operand = 10000000 prior to execution?
5 (Bit V) Test: Operand = 01111111 prior to execution?
6 (Bit V) Test: Set equal to result of N⊕C after shift has occurred.

Note – Accumulator addressing mode instructions are included in the column for IMPLIED addressing

TABLE 14-1 Accumulator and Memory Operations

The condition code column in Table 14-1 lists the change, if any, in the various bit positions in the condition code register that occur as a result of the operation.

Here are some examples of accumulator and register instructions:

Instruction

Mnemonic	Hex	
CLRA	4F	(Implied)

Example

Opcode	Operand
CLRA	

Description

The CLRA instruction is a one-byte instruction to clear accumulator A. After this instruction is executed the A accumulator will contain all zero's.

Instruction

Mnemonic	Hex	
INCA	4C	(Implied)

Example

Opcode	Operand
INCA	

Description

The increment-A instruction is a one-byte instruction that adds +1 to the A accumulator.

Instruction

Mnemonic	Hex	
DECA	4A	(Implied)

Example

Opcode	Operand
DECA	

Description

The decrement-A instruction is a one-byte instruction that adds −1 to the A accumulator.

Instruction

Mnemonic	Hex	
LDAA	86	(Immediate)

Example

Opcode	Operand
LDAA	$FA

Description

The load-A accumulator instruction, written in the immediate form, requires two program bytes; one for the instruction and one for the *immediate byte*. This instruction will load the immediate byte, FAH, into the A accumulator.

Instruction

Mnemonic	Hex	
STAA	97	(Direct)

Example

Opcode	Operand
STAA	$0A

Description

The store-A instruction, written in the direct mode, requires two program bytes; one for the instruction and one for the direct-address byte. This example will store the byte existing in the A accumulator to the memory location 0AH.

Instruction

Mnemonic	Hex
ORAA	8A

Example

Opcode	Operand	
ORAA	$02	(Immediate)

Description

The "OR" A instruction in the immediate mode requires two program bytes, one for the instruction and one for the byte to be ORed. This instruction performs the logical OR-function. In this example, it will OR the byte existing in the A accumulator with 00000010_{10}.

Instruction

Mnemonic	Hex	
CMPA	81	(Immediate)

Example

Opcode	Operand
CMPA	$01

Description

The compare instruction is less obvious than other instructions. It compares the value in the A accumulator with the byte following the instruction itself. The result of the comparison must be looked for in the condition code register. The compare instruction causes the processor to subtract the operand from the value existing in the A accumulator. The resulting ALU operation will cause the appropriate bit in the condition code register to be either set or clear.

If for example, the A accumulator contains 01H and the above instruction is performed, the result, $1 - 1 = 0$, will cause the Z-bit to be set. The actual results of such subtractions are discarded and do not appear anywhere. The only result will be the effect on the condition code register. There are of course, instructions which test the various bits in the CC register.

Instruction

Mnemonic	Hex	
ASLA	48	(Implied)

Example

Opcode	Operand
ASLA	

Description

The Arithmetic Shift Left for the A accumulator is a one byte implied mode instruction. It shifts every bit position in the A accumulator one bit position to the left. Note the diagram in the column headed Boolean/Arithmetic Operation opposite the ASLA instruction in Table 14-1. The diagram shows a 0 is shifted into the LSB position while the MSB is shifted into the C-bit position of the condition code register. Shift instructions such as this, are found in nearly all microprocessors. There is also a shift right instruction, ASRA. Note its action in the diagram across from ASRA in Table 14-1. When shifting right, the MSB is retained. This is because changing it might change the sign of the value.

Instruction

Mnemonic	Hex	
ROLA	46	(Implied)

Example

Opcode	Operand
ROLA	

Description

The rotate left for the A accumulator is also diagramed in Table 14-1 opposite the instruction ROLA. The rotate left shifts all bit positions to the left except for the MSB, which is shifted into the C bit position of the CC register. The LSB accepts the bit that was in the C bit position before the rotate instruction. The rotate right, RORA, is essentially the same except the direction of rotation is right.

Index-Register and Stack-Pointer Instructions

Table 14-2 lists the Index and Stack Pointer Instructions. All of these instructions center on the stack pointer register or the index register. The possible operations include incrementing, decrementing, loading, storing, transferring, and comparing.

TABLE 14-2 Index Register and Stack Pointer Instructions

POINTER OPERATIONS	MNEMONIC	IMMED OP	~	#	DIRECT OP	~	#	INDEX OP	~	#	EXTND OP	~	#	IMPLIED OP	~	#	BOOLEAN/ARITHMETIC OPERATION	H	I	N	Z	V	C
Compare Index Reg	CPX	8C	3	3	9C	4	2	AC	6	2	BC	5	3				$X_H - M, X_L - (M+1)$	•	•	①	↕	②	•
Decrement Index Reg	DEX													09	4	1	$X - 1 \rightarrow X$	•	•	•	↕	•	•
Decrement Stack Pntr	DES													34	4	1	$SP - 1 \rightarrow SP$	•	•	•	•	•	•
Increment Index Reg	INX													08	4	1	$X + 1 \rightarrow X$	•	•	•	↕	•	•
Increment Stack Pntr	INS													31	4	1	$SP + 1 \rightarrow SP$	•	•	•	•	•	•
Load Index Reg	LDX	CE	3	3	DE	4	2	EE	6	2	FE	5	3				$M \rightarrow X_H, (M+1) \rightarrow X_L$	•	•	③	↕	R	•
Load Stack Pntr	LDS	8E	3	3	9E	4	2	AE	6	2	BE	5	3				$M \rightarrow SP_H, (M+1) \rightarrow SP_L$	•	•	③	↕	R	•
Store Index Reg	STX				DF	5	2	EF	7	2	FF	6	3				$X_H \rightarrow M, X_L \rightarrow (M+1)$	•	•	③	↕	R	•
Store Stack Pntr	STS				9F	5	2	AF	7	2	BF	6	3				$SP_H \rightarrow M, SP_L \rightarrow (M+1)$	•	•	③	↕	R	•
Indx Reg → Stack Pntr	TXS													35	4	1	$X - 1 \rightarrow SP$	•	•	•	•	•	•
Stack Pntr → Indx Reg	TSX													30	4	1	$SP + 1 \rightarrow X$	•	•	•	•	•	•

COND. CODE REG. columns: 5 4 3 2 1 0

① (Bit N) Test: Sign bit of most significant (MS) byte of result = 1?
② (Bit V) Test: 2's complement overflow from subtraction of ms bytes?
③ (Bit N) Test: Result less than zero? (Bit 15 = 1)

Some examples follow:

Instruction

	Mnemonic	Hex	
	LDX	C3	(Immediate)

Example

	Opcode	Operand
	LDX	$F0A6

Description

The load-index register in the immediate mode requires three program bytes, one for the instruction and the next two for the 16-bit value to be placed in the index register. In this example, the two bytes are A6H and F0H, representing the low order and high order byte respectively. The instruction and the operand would appear in sequential memory locations like this:

Binary	Hex
11000011	C3
11110000	F0
10100110	A6

It is important to note that the high order byte is loaded first, right after the instruction, and low order byte second.

Instruction

	Mnemonic	Hex	
	STS	9F	(Direct)

Example

	Opcode	Operand
	STS	$FA

Description

The store stack (STS) pointer register instruction, in the direct mode, requires only two bytes; one for the instruction and one for the direct address. The instruction will take the 16-bit value existing in the stack pointer register and load it into two sequential memory locations, FAH and FBH. The microprogram in the MC6800 is aware that this instruction will need two bytes of memory, so that it will always load the high order byte in the stack pointer first. It then increments and loads the low order byte next. This action can be seen in the description column opposite the instruction in Table 14-2.

$SP_H \longrightarrow M$, means the high order byte is loaded in memory location M

$SP_L \longrightarrow M + 1$, means the low order byte is loaded in memory location M plus 1 (the next higher location)

Jump and Branch Instructions

Table 14-3 lists the jump and branch instructions. These instructions transfer the control and execution of the program from one area of memory to another. Note that branch instructions are only written in the relative addressing mode.

OPERATIONS	MNEMONIC	RELATIVE OP	~	#	INDEX OP	~	#	EXTND OP	~	#	IMPLIED OP	~	#	BRANCH TEST	COND. CODE REG. 5 H	4 I	3 N	2 Z	1 V	0 C
Branch Always	BRA	20	4	2										None	•	•	•	•	•	•
Branch If Carry Clear	BCC	24	4	2										C = 0	•	•	•	•	•	•
Branch If Carry Set	BCS	25	4	2										C = 1	•	•	•	•	•	•
Branch If = Zero	BEQ	27	4	2										Z = 1	•	•	•	•	•	•
Branch If ≥ Zero	BGE	2C	4	2										N ⊕ V = 0	•	•	•	•	•	•
Branch If > Zero	BGT	2E	4	2										Z + (N ⊕ V) = 0	•	•	•	•	•	•
Branch If Higher	BHI	22	4	2										C + Z = 0	•	•	•	•	•	•
Branch If ≤ Zero	BLE	2F	4	2										Z + (N ⊕ V) = 1	•	•	•	•	•	•
Branch If Lower Or Same	BLS	23	4	2										C + Z = 1	•	•	•	•	•	•
Branch If < Zero	BLT	2D	4	2										N ⊕ V = 1	•	•	•	•	•	•
Branch If Minus	BMI	2B	4	2										N = 1	•	•	•	•	•	•
Branch If Not Equal Zero	BNE	26	4	2										Z = 0	•	•	•	•	•	•
Branch If Overflow Clear	BVC	28	4	2										V = 0	•	•	•	•	•	•
Branch If Overflow Set	BVS	29	4	2										V = 1	•	•	•	•	•	•
Branch If Plus	BPL	2A	4	2										N = 0	•	•	•	•	•	•
Branch To Subroutine	BSR	8D	8	2											•	•	•	•	•	•
Jump	JMP				6E	4	2	7E	3	3				See Special Operations	•	•	•	•	•	•
Jump To Subroutine	JSR				AD	8	2	BD	9	3					•	•	•	•	•	•
No Operation	NOP										01	2	1	Advances Prog. Cntr. Only	•	•	•	•	•	•
Return From Interrupt	RTI										3B	10	1		①					
Return From Subroutine	RTS										39	5	1	See Special Operations	•	•	•	•	•	•
Software Interrupt	SWI										3F	12	1		•	•	•	•	•	•
Wait for Interrupt*	WAI										3E	9	1		•	②	•	•	•	•

*WAI puts Address Bus, R/W, and Data Bus in the three-state mode while VMA is held low.

① (All) Load Condition Code Register from Stack. (See Special Operations)
② (Bit 1) Set when interrupt occurs. If previously set, a Non-Maskable Interrupt is required to exit the wait state.

TABLE 14-3 Jump and Branch Instructions

Instruction

	Mnemonic	Hex	
	JMP	7E	(Extended)

Example

	Opcode	Operand
	JMP	$4567

Description

The jump instruction will cause the program to jump to a new specified location in memory and begin execution there. In the extended mode, the instruction requires three program bytes. The two following the instruction specify the new memory location.

In this example, the program counter will be loaded with the address 4567H. In memory, the instruction will look like this:

Binary	Hex
11000011	C3
01111110	7E
01000101	45
01100111	67

Note again that the high order of the address to jump to will be in memory first, then the low order byte.

Instruction

Mnemonic	Hex	
BBC	24	(Relative)

Example

Opcode	Operand
BBC	$08

Description

Branch instructions are used in decision–making. They are among the most powerful and useful instructions for the microprocessor. A branch is sometimes called a *conditional branch*, because a program branch will only occur under a given condition. If the condition is not true, the program will not branch to a new location but will simply continue its sequential execution.

The Branch if Carry Clear (BCC) instruction shown here, will test the C-bit in the condition code register. If the C-bit is clear, the branch will be performed. It will be a relative branch, that is, a + 8 will be added to the value in the program counter to determine the new location to branch to.

If the carry bit is set, the branch will not take place. It will be ignored and the next sequential instruction will be executed.

Condition Code Register Operations

Table 14-4 lists the condition code register instructions. These instructions use only the implied mode of addressing and manipulate some of the individual bits within the condition code register.

Instruction

Mnemonic	Hex	
CLI	OE	(Implied)

Example

Opcode	Operand
CLI	

Description

The clear "I" bit instruction is a one-byte, implied-mode-only instruction. It simply clears the "I" bit position in the condition-code register.

Instruction

Mnemonic	Hex	
TAP	06	(Implied)

Example

Opcode	Operand
TAP	

Description

The TAP instruction is used to change all six bits in the condition code register to a predetermined value. The CC register is loaded from the byte in the A accumulator and sets or clears each bit position according to the value in the A accumulator. It can be thought of as a *load CC register* instruction.

$$b_5 \quad b_4 \quad b_3 \quad b_2 \quad b_1 \quad b_0$$

H	I	N	Z	V	C

H = Half-carry; set whenever a carry from b_3 to b_4 of the result is generated by ADD, ABA, ADC; cleared if no b_3 to b_4 carry; not affected by other instructions.

I = Interrupt Mask; set by hardware or software interrupt or SEI instruction; cleared by CLI instruction. (Normally not used in arithmetic operations.) Restored to a zero as a result of an RT1 instruction if I_m stored on the stacked is low.

N = Negative; set if high order bit (b_7) of result is set; cleared otherwise.

Z = Zero; set if result = 0; cleared otherwise.

V = Overlow; set if there was arithmetic overflow as a result of the operation; cleared otherwise.

C = Carry; set if there was a carry from the most significant bit (b_7) of the result; cleared otherwise.

— CONDITION CODE REGISTER INSTRUCTIONS

OPERATIONS	MNEMONIC	IMPLIED			BOOLEAN OPERATION	COND. CODE REG.					
		OP	~	=		5 H	4 I	3 N	2 Z	1 V	0 C
Clear Carry	CLC	0C	2	1	0 → C	●	●	●	●	●	R
Clear Interrupt Mask	CLI	0E	2	1	0 → I	●	R	●	●	●	●
Clear Overflow	CLV	0A	2	1	0 → V	●	●	●	●	R	●
Set Carry	SEC	0D	2	1	1 → C	●	●	●	●	●	S
Set Interrupt Mask	SEI	0F	2	1	1 → I	●	S	●	●	●	●
Set Overflow	SEV	0B	2	1	1 → V	●	●	●	●	S	●
Acmltr A → CCR	TAP	06	2	1	A → CCR	①					
CCR → Acmltr A	TPA	07	2	1	CCR → A	●	●	●	●	●	●

R = Reset

S = Set

● = Not affected

① (ALL) Set according to the contents of Accumulator A.

TABLE 14-4 Condition Code Register Instructions

14-7   EVOLUTION OF THE MC6800

Motorola has continually brought out enhancements and upgrades to the original 6800 microprocessor. Some of the releases are significant changes in the architecture and capability of the microprocessor.

What follows is not intended to be a comprehensive study of all the variations and changes in the 6800 series. Rather, we will look briefly at the major milestones on the way to the more current versions.

The MC6802

The first improvement to the MC6800 was the MC6802. The 6802 has all the registers and accumulators that the 6800 had but adds an internal clock oscillator and driver. It also has 128 bytes of *on board RAM*. The first 32 bytes of this RAM can be retained in a low power Vcc mode. This on board RAM can be used as a **scratch pad** (usually temporary registers used to hold data during an operation). The main complaint about the 6800 was the lack of registers. The addition of on board RAM serves effectively as extra registers.

The MC6801/6803

The MC6801 is an enhanced version of the MC6800. The execution time has been improved and some new instructions have been added. There is an on-board, 128 byte RAM, and 2048 bytes of mask-programmable ROM. The chip also has a built-in serial communication interface and a three-function programmable timer.

The MC6809

All chips previous to the MC6809 were true 8-bit microprocessors. The MC6809 is also an 8-bit microprocessor, but it has the ability to process some instructions in a 16-bit mode. This is done by combining the A and B accumulator, for some instructions, into one 16-bit accumulator called the "D" accumulator.

The main feature of the 6809, however, is the addition of several new addressing modes.

The *direct page* mode allows direct addressing within a 256-byte page, located anywhere in memory, by using an internal, direct-page register to hold the high byte of the memory address. The low order byte is a one-byte address following the instruction.

There are several new types of **indirect-addressing** modes. For example, the **extended-indirect** mode makes use of the two bytes following the instruction to point to an address where the actual address of the instruction is located. This is sort of an *address of the address*.

The 68000

The 68000 first appeared in the late 70's and is really the progenitor of the current versions. It is considered to be a 16-bit microprocessor because it uses a 16-bit data bus. Internally, however, it has the ability to process many instructions in a 32-bit mode. The register array includes two banks of eight 32-bit registers. There are eight interrupt levels available. The 68000 can directly address 16 Mbytes of memory using a 24-bit address bus. The speed of operation was significantly enhanced and there are 8, 10 and 12.5 MHz versions available.

The 68010

The 68010 is an enhanced version of the 68000 and has **virtual memory** capability. A virtual memory allows the programmer to write programs as if there were no limit on the size of the memory. The memory beyond the size of the RAM is actually stored on disk. The programmer can refer to disk storage as if it were part of the main memory. The 68010 also has multiple-vector tables and fourteen addressing modes.

The 68020

The 68020, evolved from the 68010, is a full, 32-bit microprocessor with a 32-bit address and data bus. Introduced in 1984, it contains sixteen, 32-bit general-purpose and address registers, and will operate at 16.67, 20, 25, and 33 MHz. Another interesting feature is a 256-byte **cache memory** used for instruction **pipelining**. Pipelining is a procedure whereby the processor *prefetches* instructions and places them in the cache memory. These prefetched instructions can be executed much faster, because the access time required for the on-board, cache memory is considerably faster than memory access.

The 68030

In 1986, Motorola announced the 68030 as the successor to the 68020. It is now available in versions that will operate to 50 MHz. The 68030 is fully compatible with the 68020 and the main improvements lie in its ability to manage memory more efficiently than previous models. Some speed has been gained in the way data-cache and instruction-cache memory is handled.

The 68040

The third generation of the 68000 compatible series, the 68040, is also on the market. It has some new features and enhancements over the 68030 architecture. For instance, cache memory is expanded to four Kbytes. Internally, it makes use of multiple, independent-execution pipelines.

There is no reason to believe the improvements and advances in microprocessor design are anywhere near an end. Using and understanding advanced processors still begins with learning the original MC6800.

 SELF-CHECK FOR SECTIONS 14-6, 14-7

25. Does the 6800 have a unique mnemonic for each op code?
26. Why is the 6800 referred to as being memory oriented?
27. What is the minimum number of clock cycles required to complete an instruction?
28. What would the byte in the accumulator be after a CLRA instruction is performed?
29. What is the advantage of prefetching?

SUMMARY OF IDEAS

- The MC6800 is an 8-bit microprocessor and the first in a long series of processors developed by Motorola.
- A basic MC6800 system consists of the 6800 with a 2-phase clock input, ROM, RAM, and a 6821 PIA chip.
- The RESET signal vector addresses are FFFEH and FFFFH.
- The IRQ (Interrupt Request) vector addresses are FFF8H and FFF9H.
- The NMI (Nonmaskable Interrupt) vector addresses are FFFCH and FFFDH.
- The SWI (Software Interrupt) vector addresses are FFFAH and FFFBH.
- The address and data buses in the MC6800 are three-state buses. Both internally generated signals and external signals are capable of placing the buses in a high-impedance state.
- The MC6800 has three internal 16-bit registers, the program counter, the stack pointer, and the index register.
- The MC6800 has three internal 8-bit registers, the A and B accumulator, and the condition code register.
- There are seven possible address modes for the MC6800— accumulator, inherent, immediate, direct, extended, relative, and indexed.
- The MC 6800 instruction set can be divided into four distinct groups: accumulator and register instructions; index and stack instructions; jump and branch instructions; and condition code register instructions.
- The evolution of the MC6800 began with the 8-bit, 1 MHz version introduced in the mid-70's and has lead to the advanced 32-bit, 50 Mhz MC68040 microprocessor currently available.

CHAPTER QUESTIONS & PROBLEMS

True or False

1. The MC6800 has an *on board*, 2-phase clock system.
2. Both the IRQ and the NMI interrupt must first test the "I" bit (interrupt mask) in the condition code register before allowing an interrupt.
3. The TSC input signal can cause the address bus to go into a high-impedance state.
4. The DBE signal causes the address bus to go into the high-impedance state.
5. The BA (bus available) is strictly an output signal from the MC6800.

Fill in the Blanks

6. A microprocessor that treats I/O devices as though they were memory locations is said to be _____ _____.
7. When the MC6800 operates in the direct-addresses mode, it also is operating on the _____ _____.
8. An instruction written the extended mode of addressing will require _____ byte(s) of memory.
9. An indexed-mode instruction uses an 8-bit byte following the instruction called the _____ byte.
10. The top or last locations in memory on an MC6800 system are reserved for _____ interrupts.

Multiple Choice

11. Which of the following is not a 16-bit register?
    a. Program Counter Register
    b. The B accumulator
    c. The Stack Pointer Register
    d. The Index Register

12. The largest group of MC6800 instructions are centered around the
    a. stack pointer operations.
    b. jump and branch operations.
    c. condition code register.
    d. accumulator and registers.

13. The *reset* routine is vectored to addresses
    a. FFF8H and FFF9H.
    b. FFFCH and FFFDH.
    c. FFFEH and FFFFH.
    d. FFFAH and FFFBH.

14. Which address mode is *not* one of the MC6800 modes?
    a. Extended
    b. Direct
    c. Indirect
    d. Relative

15. If the "I" flag in the condition code register is set, which of the following signals will *not* cause the normal processing to be discontinued?
    a. NMI
    b. IRQ
    c. HALT
    d. RESET

16. In base-page or direct addressing, the MC6800 addresses are
    a. limited to the first 256 Kbytes.
    b. limited to 64 Kbytes.
    c. limited to the first 256 bytes.
    d. not limited.

17. Which sentence best describes jump and branch instructions?
    a. They are used with vectored interrupts.
    b. They cannot be used beyond the first 256 bytes of memory.
    c. They use the relative addressing mode.
    d. They transfer control of the program to accumulator instructions.

18. In the indexed mode of addressing, the index register contains FD00H and the offset byte 4H. What is the effective address?
    a. FD00H
    b. FDFFH
    c. 4H
    d. FD04H

19. The MC6800 can operate at 1 MHz which means the time for 1 cycle is 1 microsecond. How many microseconds are needed for the MC6800 to complete its fastest instructions?
    a. 1
    b. 4
    c. 2
    d. 10

20. An on-board memory area in a microprocessor for storing instructions about to be executed best describes a
    a. scratch pad memory.
    b. virtual memory.
    c. ROM.
    d. cache memory.

CHAPTER 15

THE INTEL 8080/8085

OUTLINE

NEW TERMS TO WATCH FOR

System Controller
Functional Block
Destination Register
DMA
Loop
Instruction Queue

Status Word
Source Register
Hold
Rotate
Two-Phase Clock
T-State

Restart
Interrupt Enable
Load And Store
Wait State
Conditional Machine Cycle

After completing this chapter, you should be able to:

1. List the additional chips needed for a basic 8080A system and an 8085A system.
2. Work with the various input and output signals from the 8080A and the 8085A.
3. Illustrate the timing signals and understand the various machine states.
4. Explain the 8080A interrupt signal and the resulting microprocessor action.
5. Discuss the register structure and the use of the individual registers in the 8080A and the 8085A.
6. Name and explain the five addressing modes available to the 8080A/85.
7. Identify various instructions in the instruction set and detail their actions.
8. Explain the interrupts available on the 8085A chip and describe their actions.
9. Recognize the newer versions of the Intel microprocessor line and appreciate their enhancements.

15-1   INTRODUCTION

The Intel 8080A made its first appearance in 1974 and, for several years, it was the best selling microprocessor. The 8080A has largely been replaced with newer, more advanced versions, but it is still found in a vast amount of existing electronic equipment. Understanding the 8080 is the first step in learning the newer and more advanced versions now available from Intel.

15-2   THE BASIC SYSTEM

The 8080A microprocessor chip needs three power supplies: +5, −5, and +12 volts. In addition, a crystal-controlled, **two phase clock** generator/driver (8224) and a **system controller**/bus driver (8228) are needed. Figure 15-1 shows the chips required for a basic 8080 system.

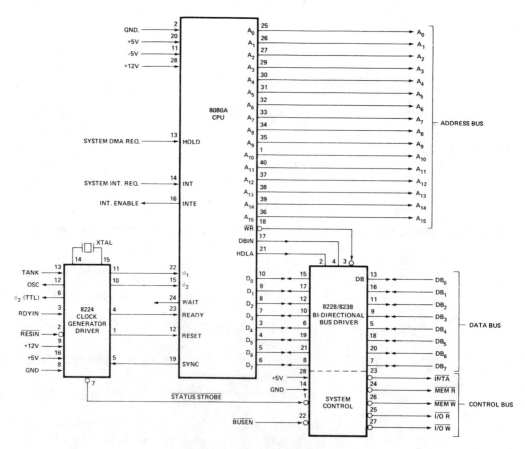

FIGURE 15-1 Basic 8080 System

The address bus is 16-bits wide, making the 8080A capable of directly addressing up to 64K bytes of memory. It is a three-state bus.

The data bus is 8-bits wide, bidirectional and, like the address bus, is a three-state bus. The control signals are under the direction of the 8228 chip. This chip also serves as a bus driver and interface for ROM, RAM, and all I/O devices. The pin out configuration of the 8080A itself is seen in Figure 15-2.

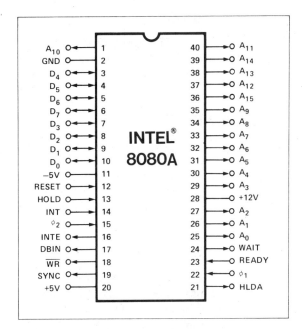

FIGURE 15-2 Pin Configuration for 8080A

15-3   THE 8080 SIGNAL DESCRIPTIONS

The **functional block** diagram for the 8080A is shown in Figure 15-3. The signal input and output pins can be seen going to and from the timing and control block at the bottom of the diagram.

WR

The WR or write/read output is for controlling the memory write and read functions. The WR output is normally high (read) and is brought low for a memory write operation.

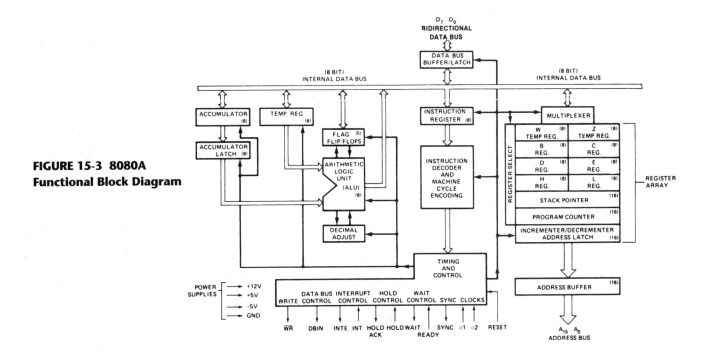

FIGURE 15-3 8080A Functional Block Diagram

DBIN

The Data Bus IN, DBIN, is an output signal. It is used by external devices like memory to determine if the data bus is ready to be used to input data. When DBIN is high, data can be gated onto the data bus.

INTE

The **INTerrupt Enable** line is an output. This output indicates the status of an internal interrupt flip-flop. The flip-flop is set and reset by the interrupt enable and interrupt disable (EI, DI) instructions. When set, the 8080A accepts interrupts. When it is reset, the 8080A will not accept interrupts. It is reset by an instruction or when an interrupt is being serviced.

INT

The INT input is the interrupt request line for use by devices generating hardware interrupts. The 8080A will accept an interrupt on the INT line whenever INTE is set. If INTE is reset or if the processor is in a **HOLD** state, the interrupt will be rejected.

HOLD

The HOLD input signal allows an external device to place the microprocessor in a HOLD state. Bringing the HOLD input high places the processor in HOLD and allows an external device to use the bus system. The microprocessor will go into the HOLD state only after the current instruction is finished. HOLD suspends microprocessor operation and places the address bus, data bus, and control bus, in a high-impedance state.

The HOLD state is used mainly for **DMA** or direct memory access. Peripheral devices that can handle DMA, like disk drives, take over the bus system and transfer large blocks of data to or from memory or other I/O devices. This is inherently more efficient than going through the microprocessor.

HLDA

The HLDA, Hold Acknowledge signal, works in conjunction with the HOLD signal. It indicates that the address, data, and control buses are in the high-impedance state.

WAIT

The WAIT output simply acknowledges that the microprocessor is in the **WAIT state**. The WAIT state will be discussed under the timing signals section.

READY

A high on the READY input signals the 8080A that valid data is available on the data bus. This input synchronizes the processor with slower devices. If the 8080A outputs an address but does not immediately receive a return READY signal, it will enter the WAIT state and will remain in WAIT until it receives a high on the READY input.

SYNC

The SYNC pin provides an output that indicates the beginning of each **machine cycle**. Machine cycles are discussed under timing signals.

RESET

The RESET signal clears the program counter register and resets both the INTE and HLDA flip-flops. It does not, however, clear any of the other internal registers.

✔ SELF-CHECK FOR SECTIONS 15-1, 15-2, 15-3

1. What other chips are needed for a basic 8080 system?
2. What is the purpose of the 8228 chip?
3. Is DBIN an input or an output signal?
4. What is the purpose of DBIN?
5. What is the INTE pin on the 8080 used for?
6. What is the INT input?
7. What is the function of the HOLD pin?
8. Describe the purpose of READY pin.

15-4   TIMING SIGNALS

Clock Signals

The 8080A requires a 2-phase clock input. The signals and their relation to each other are illustrated in Figure 15-4.

The instruction cycle for the 8080A consists of the fetch, decode, and execute phases, just as in any other microprocessor. But the instruction cycle is further divided into *machine cycles*. The machine cycles are labeled M1, M2, M3, M4, and M5. Fetch, decode, and execute can require up to five machine cycles, depending on the nature of the instruction.

The machine cycles are divided into **T-states** and each machine cycle is made up of three to six T-states— T1, T2, T3, T4, T5, and T_w (wait state). The T-state is defined by the phase-1 clock and is equal to the time from the leading edge of one clock cycle to the leading edge of the next.

Figure 15-4 shows an instruction that requires ten T-states or ten phase-1 clock cycles. An example of an instruction needing ten cycles is the IN instruction. This instruction can be used to place a data byte from a port location into a register. The states T1, T2, and T3 of M1 are used to fetch the instruction. T4 is needed to decode it. The M2 cycle deals with the register, while M3 is for addressing the port and finishing execution. Note that M1 requires four clock cycles and M2 and M3 require three each.

The minimum clock period for the 8080A is .32 microseconds and the maximum is 2 microseconds. If the 8080A was operating at .32 microseconds per clock period it would be able to complete the IN instruction in 3.2 microseconds. In general, however, the 8080A is rated as a 2 microsecond or .5 MHz processor.

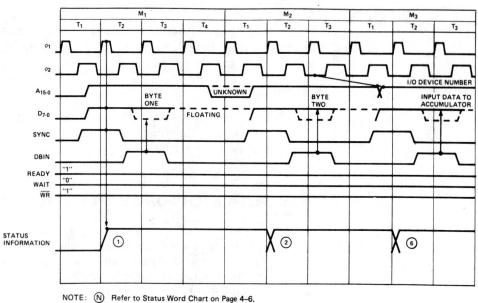

NOTE: (N) Refer to Status Word Chart on Page 4–6.

Input Instruction Cycle

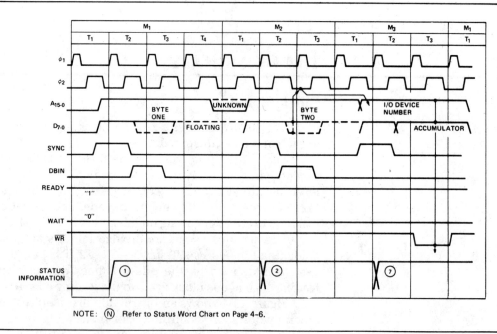

NOTE: (N) Refer to Status Word Chart on Page 4–6.

Output Instruction Cycle

FIGURE 15-4 Timing Signals

WAIT

Now that we have an idea of how the timing on the 8080A works, we can examine the WAIT state. The 8080A sends out an address and expects a *high* to be returned on the Ready line from the I/O or memory that was addressed. If it does not receive this high after T2 of M2, it will enter the wait state at the end of T2.

It will continue in this suspended state until a high is received on the READY input. It will extend the wait state T_w, for as many cycles or T-states as necessary. As soon as the Ready goes high, it resumes at T3 of machine cycle two (M2). The WAIT output on the 8080A will be high while the processor is in the WAIT state. It goes low when a high on the READY line is received.

The WAIT state is essentially to accommodate I/O devices or memory which are always slower than the microprocessor.

Address Bus

The address bus is 16-bits wide and labeled A0 through A15 (Fig. 15-2). It is a three-state, buffered output bus. It can directly address up to 64K bytes of memory. The address bus serves a dual purpose in that it can address either I/O devices or memory.

The first 256 bytes can be designated and addressed as Input/Output ports. For I/O addressing, the addresses, consisting of eight bits, are on the lower eight lines of the address bus and duplicated on the upper eight lines. The system control chip, 8228, then determines whether the address is meant for an I/O device or for memory. This I/O addressing scheme works in conjunction with the IN and OUT instructions discussed later.

Data Bus

The data bus is a three-state, 8-bit, buffered, bidirectional bus. It is labeled D0 through D7 (Fig. 15-2). The data bus outputs a **status word** during the first clock cycle of each machine cycle. The status word describes the action of the current machine cycle. There are ten possible operations for a machine cycle:

1. Instruction fetch
2. Memory read
3. Memory write
4. Stack read
5. Stack write
6. Input read
7. Output write
8. Interrupt acknowledge
9. Halt acknowledge
10. Interrupt acknowledge while Halt

Of course, the main purpose of the data bus is to transfer data and instructions between the processor, memory, and I/O.

✔ SELF-CHECK FOR SECTION 15-4

9. Machine cycles are divided into _____.
10. The WAIT output on the 8080A will be _____ (high or low) while the processor is in the WAIT state.
11. The 8080 can directly address up to _____ bytes of memory.
12. The data bus outputs a _____ _____ during the first clock cycle of each machine cycle.

15-5   THE 8080A INTERRUPT

The INT input is the hardware interrupt line for the 8080A. In order to enable this input, the software instruction EI must be executed. The EI instruction is a one-byte instruction that allows the 8080A to accept an interrupt.

When an interrupt signal arrives, the microprocessor will finish the instruction it is on and then output a status word on the data bus called *interrupt acknowledge*. The INTE line is then reset, inhibiting any further interrupts. The microprocessor now waits for an instruction on the data bus to begin the interrupt routine. This instruction must come from external hardware.

The interrupt instruction is called RST or **ReSTart**. There are eight RST instructions, RST-0 through RST-7. The RST instruction is an 8-bit instruction that uses only bits D3, D4, and D5. The other bit positions are 1's. With three bits, 2^3 or 8 instructions are possible.

The RST instruction byte looks like this:

$$1\ 1\ N\ N\ N\ 1\ 1\ 1$$

When it appears on the data bus, the microprocessor loads this byte into the program counter register so that it will contain:

$$0\ 0\ 0\ 0\ 0\ 0\ 0\ 0\ 0\ 0\ N\ N\ N\ 0\ 0\ 0$$

What this boils down to is that the eight starting addresses for interrupt routines are:

Hex		Lower Address Byte
00H	=	00000000
08H	=	00001000
10H	=	00010000
18H	=	00011000
20H	=	00100000
28H	=	00101000
30H	=	00110000
38H	=	00111000

The programmer inserts the interrupt routines at these starting addresses. The RST instruction also automatically stores the program counter return address on the stack.

15-6   8080A REGISTERS

Accumulator

The accumulator register is an 8-bit register connected to the data bus and the ALU. It performs exactly as described in Chapter 8, namely, it holds one of the ALU operands and, after execution, receives the result of the ALU operation.

Register Array

The register array can be seen on the right side of Figure 15-3. The top two registers, temporary registers W and Z, are not accessible to the user. The next six, 8-bit registers are for the programmer. They can be used as individual 8-bit registers— B, C, D, E, H, and L—or they can be addressed in pairs. When designated as BC, DE, and HL, they act as 16-bit registers.

Stack-Pointer Register

The stack-pointer register is a 16-bit register used to hold the address of the stack. The registers are *pushed* onto the stack in pairs. In other words, the push operation "PUSH B" actually puts the contents of B *and* C in the stack. We'll examine this in more detail during the discussion of the instruction set.

Program-Counter Register

The program-counter register is a 16-bit register that holds the address of the current instruction. It is automatically incremented after a decode operation so that it always points to the next instruction to be executed.

Flag Register

The flag register or flag flip-flops are connected to the ALU as they must monitor ALU operations. Note that the flag register is also connected to the data bus. The 8080A flag register is organized like this:

Bits 7 6 5 4 3 2 1 0

S Z X AC X P X CY

Bits 1, 3, and 5 are not used.

The operation of these flags was covered in detail in the chapter on microprocessor status.

The S-flag is the *Sign* flag; it is used to indicate the sign of the resulting ALU operation.

The Z-flag is the *Zero* flag which is set if an ALU operation results in zero.

The AC is *Auxiliary Carry*, used to indicate that a carry occurred from bit-3 to bit-4 during an ALU operation. This is most often used in BCD operations.

The P-flag is the *Parity flag*. If the accumulator holds an even number of bits, the P-flag will be set. If odd parity exists in the accumulator, the P-flag will be clear.

The *carry-flag*, CY, is set when an arithmetic operation results in a carry from bit 7.

Decimal Adjust

In Figure 15-2, note the block attached to the ALU called "Decimal Adjust." The is not a register, but a function. This area of the microprocessor is activated by the DAA instruction (Decimal Adjust Accumulator). It is used after a BCD-operation to test for and correct any illegal BCD numbers that may have resulted. Recall that BCD code does not use all possible 4-bit binary combinations.

✔ SELF-CHECK FOR SECTIONS 15-5, 15-6

13. The interrupt instruction for the 8080 is called _____.
14. How many RST instructions are there?
15. What is the size of registers B, C, D, E, H and L?
16. What size are registers BC, DE and HL?
17. What is the size of the flag register?
18. Explain the purpose of the AC position in the flag register.
19. What is the DAA instruction used for?

15-7   ADDRESSING MODES

The 8080A makes use of five addressing modes:

1. Implied Addressing
2. Immediate Addressing
3. Register Addressing
4. Direct Addressing
5. Register-Indirect Addressing

Many of the 8080A instructions use *implied* or inherent addressing. The operand is implied in the instruction. An example is the CMA instruction which complements the byte in the accumulator. All implied-mode instructions are one byte.

The *immediate-mode* instructions use the byte immediately following the instruction as the data byte. An example is the LXI B instruction.

Label	Opcode	Operand	Comment
	LXI	B,F018H;	Loads BC pair with Hex F018

The LXI B is a 3-byte, immediate-mode instruction. It loads the B and C register pair with the two bytes immediately following the instruction. The first byte after the instruction is moved into the low order register (C) while byte-3 is moved into the high order register (B).

Several of the instructions for the 8080A use *register addressing*. The operand names the register source for an operation. All registers involved in register addressing will be internal to the microprocessor and are thus faster and more efficient than memory operations. An example of register addressing is the ADD B instruction.

Label	Opcode	Operand	Comment
	ADD	B;	Contents of B added to A

The register-addressing instructions are not only fast, they require only one byte of memory. In this example, the content of the B register is added to the contents of the accumulator. The result will appear in the accumulator.

When *direct addressing* is used in the 8080A, three program bytes are needed. The first byte is the instruction and the next two bytes specify the 16-bit address location of the operand. The LDA instruction is an example of direct addressing.

Label	Opcode	Operand	Comment
	LDA	01FAH;	Load Accumulator with byte located at FA01 Hex

The second byte after the instruction is the low order byte of the address and the third byte is the high order byte of the address.

The *register-indirect* instructions use a register pair to point to the memory address location of the operand. An example of the register indirect mode is the instruction LDAX B.

Label	Opcode	Operand	Comment
	LDAX	B;	Contents of memory location pointed to by BC loaded into A

For this instruction, only the BC and DE register pairs may be used.

✔ SELF-CHECK FOR SECTION 15-7

20. How many addressing modes does the 8080 have?
21. Explain the difference between register addressing and memory addressing.
22. How many bytes are needed for direct addressing in the 8080?

15-8   THE 8080A INSTRUCTION SET

The instruction set for the 8080A consists of 111 basic instruction formats (Table 15-1). With these basic formats over 200 instructions are possible. For example, the instruction format INR r means increment the register r. The registers that can be incremented are the Accumulator, B, C, D, E, H, and L registers. The INR r format then includes seven instructions.

The 8080A uses 1, 2, and 3-byte instructions. In fact, the instruction itself is never more than one byte, but may include two more bytes, as in the direct addressing mode. This is called *generalized opcode* because the opcode in this sense includes the address bytes needed in some instructions. Appendix A has a complete listing of the Intel instructions for the 8080/85.

The Intel Corporation groups the instructions into five operative work functions:
1. Data Transfer Group
2. Arithmetic Group
3. Logic Group
4. Branch and Control Group
5. I/O, Stack and Machine Control Group

Data Transfer Group

The data transfer group is largest group of instructions. These instructions are for moving data between registers or between registers and memory.

Many of these instructions employ the mnemonic MOV for *move.*

Instruction	MOV A,L	
	Mnemonic	Hex
	MOV A,L	7D
Example		
	Opcode	Operand
	MOV	A,L
Description		

The MOV A,L instruction moves the contents of register L into register A. These instructions are always written with the **destination register** before the comma and the **source register** after the comma.

8080 INSTRUCTION SET

Summary of Processor Instructions

Mnemonic	Description	D7	D6	D5	D4	D3	D2	D1	D0	Clock Cycles
MOVE, LOAD, AND STORE										
MOVr1,r2	Move register to register	0	1	D	D	D	S	S	S	5
MOV M,r	Move register to memory	0	1	1	1	0	S	S	S	7
MOV r,M	Move memory to register	0	1	D	D	D	1	1	0	7
MVI r	Move immediate register	0	0	D	D	D	1	1	0	7
MVI M	Move immediate memory	0	0	1	1	0	1	1	0	10
LXI B	Load immediate register Pair B & C	0	0	0	0	0	0	0	1	10
LXI D	Load immediate register Pair D & E	0	0	0	1	0	0	0	1	10
LXI H	Load immediate register Pair H & L	0	0	1	0	0	0	0	1	10
STAX B	Store A indirect	0	0	0	0	0	0	1	0	7
STAX D	Store A indirect	0	0	0	1	0	0	1	0	7
LDAX B	Load A indirect	0	0	0	0	1	0	1	0	7
LDAX D	Load A indirect	0	0	0	1	1	0	1	0	7
STA	Store A direct	0	0	1	1	0	0	1	0	13
LDA	Load A direct	0	0	1	1	1	0	1	0	13
SHLD	Store H & L direct	0	0	1	0	0	0	1	0	16
LHLD	Load H & L direct	0	0	1	0	1	0	1	0	16
XCHG	Exchange D & E, H & L Registers	1	1	1	0	1	0	1	1	4
STACK OPS										
PUSH B	Push register Pair B & C on stack	1	1	0	0	0	1	0	1	11
PUSH D	Push register Pair D & E on stack	1	1	0	1	0	1	0	1	11
PUSH H	Push register Pair H & L on stack	1	1	1	0	0	1	0	1	11
PUSH PSW	Push A and Flags on stack	1	1	1	1	0	1	0	1	11
POP B	Pop register Pair B & C off stack	1	1	0	0	0	0	0	1	10
POP D	Pop register Pair D & E off stack	1	1	0	1	0	0	0	1	10
POP H	Pop register Pair H & L off stack	1	1	1	0	0	0	0	1	10
POP PSW	Pop A and Flags off stack	1	1	1	1	0	0	0	1	10
XTHL	Exchange top of stack, H & L	1	1	1	0	0	0	1	1	18
SPHL	H & L to stack pointer	1	1	1	1	1	0	0	1	5
LXI SP	Load immediate stack pointer	0	0	1	1	0	0	0	1	10
INX SP	Increment stack pointer	0	0	1	1	0	0	1	1	5
DCX SP	Decrement stack pointer	0	0	1	1	1	0	1	1	5
JUMP										
JMP	Jump unconditional	1	1	0	0	0	0	1	1	10
JC	Jump on carry	1	1	0	1	1	0	1	0	10
JNC	Jump on no carry	1	1	0	1	0	0	1	0	10
JZ	Jump on zero	1	1	0	0	1	0	1	0	10
JNZ	Jump on no zero	1	1	0	0	0	0	1	0	10
JP	Jump on positive	1	1	1	1	0	0	1	0	10
JM	Jump on minus	1	1	1	1	1	0	1	0	10
JPE	Jump on parity even	1	1	1	0	1	0	1	0	10
JPO	Jump on parity odd	1	1	1	0	0	0	1	0	10
PCHL	H & L to program counter	1	1	1	0	1	0	0	1	5
CALL										
CALL	Call unconditional	1	1	0	0	1	1	0	1	17
CC	Call on carry	1	1	0	1	1	1	0	0	11/17
CNC	Call on no carry	1	1	0	1	0	1	0	0	11/17
CZ	Call on zero	1	1	0	0	1	1	0	0	11/17
CNZ	Call on no zero	1	1	0	0	0	1	0	0	11/17
CP	Call on positive	1	1	1	1	0	1	0	0	11/17
CM	Call on minus	1	1	1	1	1	1	0	0	11/17
CPE	Call on parity even	1	1	1	0	1	1	0	0	11/17
CPO	Call on parity odd	1	1	1	0	0	1	0	0	11/17
RETURN										
RET	Return	1	1	0	0	1	0	0	1	10
RC	Return on carry	1	1	0	1	1	0	0	0	5/11
RNC	Return on no carry	1	1	0	1	0	0	0	0	5/11
RZ	Return on zero	1	1	0	0	1	0	0	0	5/11
RNZ	Return on no zero	1	1	0	0	0	0	0	0	5/11
RP	Return on positive	1	1	1	1	0	0	0	0	5/11
RM	Return on minus	1	1	1	1	1	0	0	0	5/11
RPE	Return on parity even	1	1	1	0	1	0	0	0	5/11
RPO	Return on parity odd	1	1	1	0	0	0	0	0	5/11
RESTART										
RST	Restart	1	1	A	A	A	1	1	1	11
INCREMENT AND DECREMENT										
INR r	Increment register	0	0	D	D	D	1	0	0	5
DCR r	Decrement register	0	0	D	D	D	1	0	1	5
INR M	Increment memory	0	0	1	1	0	1	0	0	10
DCR M	Decrement memory	0	0	1	1	0	1	0	1	10
INX B	Increment B & C registers	0	0	0	0	0	0	1	1	5
INX D	Increment D & E registers	0	0	0	1	0	0	1	1	5
INX H	Increment H & L registers	0	0	1	0	0	0	1	1	5
DCX B	Decrement B & C	0	0	0	0	1	0	1	1	5
DCX D	Decrement D & E	0	0	0	1	1	0	1	1	5
DCX H	Decrement H & L	0	0	1	0	1	0	1	1	5
ADD										
ADD r	Add register to A	1	0	0	0	0	S	S	S	4
ADC r	Add register to A with carry	1	0	0	0	1	S	S	S	4
ADD M	Add memory to A	1	0	0	0	0	1	1	0	7
ADC M	Add memory to A with carry	1	0	0	0	1	1	1	0	7
ADI	Add immediate to A	1	1	0	0	0	1	1	0	7
ACI	Add immediate to A with carry	1	1	0	0	1	1	1	0	7
DAD B	Add B & C to H & L	0	0	0	0	1	0	0	1	10
DAD D	Add D & E to H & L	0	0	0	1	1	0	0	1	10
DAD H	Add H & L to H & L	0	0	1	0	1	0	0	1	10
DAD SP	Add stack pointer to H & L	0	0	1	1	1	0	0	1	10

NOTES: 1. DDD or SSS: B 000, C 001, D 010, E 011, H 100, L 101, Memory 110, A 111.
2. Two possible cycle times. (6/12) indicate instruction cycles dependent on condition flags.

TABLE 15-1 8080A Instruction Set

Summary of Processor Instructions

Mnemonic	Description	D7	D6	D5	D4	D3	D2	D1	D0	Clock[2] Cycles
SUBTRACT										
SUB r	Subtract register from A	1	0	0	1	0	S	S	S	4
SBB r	Subtract register from A with borrow	1	0	0	1	1	S	S	S	4
SUB M	Subtract memory from A	1	0	0	1	0	1	1	0	7
SBB M	Subtract memory from A with borrow	1	0	0	1	1	1	1	0	7
SUI	Subtract immediate from A	1	1	0	1	0	1	1	0	7
SBI	Subtract immediate from A with borrow	1	1	0	1	1	1	1	0	7
LOGICAL										
ANA r	And register with A	1	0	1	0	0	S	S	S	4
XRA r	Exclusive Or register with A	1	0	1	0	1	S	S	S	4
ORA r	Or register with A	1	0	1	1	0	S	S	S	4
CMP r	Compare register with A	1	0	1	1	1	S	S	S	4
ANA M	And memory with A	1	0	1	0	0	1	1	0	7
XRA M	Exclusive Or memory with A	1	0	1	0	1	1	1	0	7
ORA M	Or memory with A	1	0	1	1	0	1	1	0	7
CMP M	Compare memory with A	1	0	1	1	1	1	1	0	7
ANI	And immediate with A	1	1	1	0	0	1	1	0	7
XRI	Exclusive Or immediate with A	1	1	1	0	1	1	1	0	7
ORI	Or immediate with A	1	1	1	1	0	1	1	0	7
CPI	Compare immediate with A	1	1	1	1	1	1	1	0	7
ROTATE										
RLC	Rotate A left	0	0	0	0	0	1	1	1	4
RRC	Rotate A right	0	0	0	0	1	1	1	1	4
RAL	Rotate A left through carry	0	0	0	1	0	1	1	1	4
RAR	Rotate A right through carry	0	0	0	1	1	1	1	1	4
SPECIALS										
CMA	Complement A	0	0	1	0	1	1	1	1	4
STC	Set carry	0	0	1	1	0	1	1	1	4
CMC	Complement carry	0	0	1	1	1	1	1	1	4
DAA	Decimal adjust A	0	0	1	0	0	1	1	1	4
INPUT/OUTPUT										
IN	Input	1	1	0	1	1	0	1	1	10
OUT	Output	1	1	0	1	0	0	1	1	10
CONTROL										
EI	Enable Interrupts	1	1	1	1	1	0	1	1	4
DI	Disable Interrupt	1	1	1	1	0	0	1	1	4
NOP	No-operation	0	0	0	0	0	0	0	0	4
HLT	Halt	0	1	1	1	0	1	1	0	7

TABLE 15-1 8080A Instruction Set (continued)

Technically the contents of L are *copied* into A because the contents of the L register are not disturbed. This is characteristic of all data transfer instructions.

Instruction MOV C,M

Mnemonic	Hex
MOV C,M	4E

Example

Opcode	Operand
MOV	C,M

Description

This instruction moves a byte of data into register C. The byte will be located at the memory address (M) pointed to by the HL register. Obviously the HL register must first be loaded with the required address before the MOV C,M instruction will work.

Another smaller subgroup of instructions in the data transfer group are called **Load and Store** instructions. An example of this type instruction is LDAX D.

Instruction   LDAX D

	Mnemonic	Hex
	LDAX D	1A

Example

	Opcode	Operand
	LDAX	D

Description

This instruction will load the accumulator with the byte pointed to by the DE register pair. Only the BC and DE register can be referred to by this instruction.

Note that "B" refers to the BC pair while "D" would refer to the DE pair.

Instruction   STAX B

	Mnemonic	Hex
	STAX B	2

Example

	Opcode	Operand
	STAX	B

Description

The STAX B instruction is an example of a *store* operation. The contents of the accumulator will be stored in a memory location contained in the BC register pair. Only the BC and DE pair may be used in this instruction.

Arithmetic Group

This group of instructions includes all addition and subtraction functions. It also includes the increment and decrement functions.

Instruction   INX H

	Mnemonic	Hex
	INX H	23

Example

	Opcode	Operand
	INX	H

Description

The increment-H instruction will increment the 16-bit HL register pair.

Instruction   ADC D

	Mnemonic	Hex
	ADC D	8A

Example

	Opcode	Operand
	ADC	D

Description

The add-with-carry instruction adds the carry bit, if any, and the contents of the D register to the accumulator. The result appears in the accumulator.

The Logic Group

The logical group performs boolean logic operations on both registers and memory locations. It also includes the compare and **rotate** instructions.

Instruction	ANA D	
	Mnemonic	Hex
	ANA D	A2
Example		
	Opcode	Operand
	ANA	D
Description		

The ANA D performs the logical-AND function with the D register and the byte in the accumulator. The result will be in the accumulator.

Instruction	CMP B	
	Mnemonic	Hex
	CMP B	B8
Example		
	Opcode	Operand
	CMP	B
Description		

The compare instruction is normally used as a decision making instruction. It tests for a given condition and then, based on the condition, a branch-type instruction can be executed next. The compare instruction in this example will subtract the value in the B register from the accumulator. The actual result of the subtraction is discarded and the registers are unchanged. The flag-register bits will be set or cleared based on the result of the subtraction.

Instruction	RLC	
	Mnemonic	Hex
	RLC	07
Example		
	Opcode	Operand
	RLC	H
Description		

The RLC is a *rotate* instruction. This instruction shifts each bit in the accumulator one bit position to the left. The high-order bit is transferred to the low-order bit and the CY bit in the flag register is set according to the value of the high-order bit.

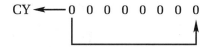

Branch and Control Group

The branch and control group is responsible for **conditional** or unconditional jumps, calls, returns or restarts. They essentially transfer control from one part of the program to another.

Instruction	JMP	
	Mnemonic	Hex
	JMP adr	C3
Example		
	Opcode	Operand
	JMP	18F0H
Description		

The jump instruction is a 3-byte instruction. It will cause the program counter to be loaded with the address specified in the operand. The first byte after the instruction will be the low-order address byte and the second byte after the instruction will be the high-order address byte. In this example, the program will begin execution at location F018H.

The JMP instruction is an unconditional jump and the program will always jump to the location specified. It is sometimes used to **loop** a program. If the JMP is the last instruction and the jump address specified is the beginning address of the program, the program will loop or run continuously.

Instruction	JNZ	
	Mnemonic	Hex
	JNZ adr	C2
Example		
	Opcode	Operand
	JNZ	18F0H

Description

The JNZ instruction is a conditional jump. In this case, the program counter will be loaded with the new address only if the Z-bit in the flag register is not clear. If Z is set (Z=1), then a jump will be executed. If Z is clear (Z=0), the program will continue on sequentially.

Instruction	CALL	
	Mnemonic	Hex
	CALL adr	CS
Example		
	Opcode	Operand
	CALL	12FAH

Description

The CALL instruction is used to *call* a subroutine. The subroutine is located in another part of memory and out of the normal program sequence. The *call* instruction differs from the jump instruction. This is because the call instruction is designed so that the program can return to the normal sequence of execution. A *return* (RET) instruction is placed at the end of a subroutine and causes the subroutine to return to the instruction in the main program that would have normally executed had the *call* not be encountered.

The subroutine return (RET) works because the CALL instruction causes the address of the next instruction after the call to be loaded onto the stack. The RET instruction, then, causes the return address to be loaded from the stack into the program counter so the main program can resume.

I/O, Stack, and Machine-Control Group

The I/O instructions input data *from* a port, or output data *to* a port. Stack instructions are used to build a stack, or use the stack to restore the processor registers. The machine-control group includes interrupt enable, interrupt disable, no operation (NOP), HALT, and exchange instructions.

Instruction	PUSH B	
	Mnemonic	Hex
	PUSH C5r	C2
Example		
	Opcode	Operand
	PUSH	B

Description

The PUSH instruction is a stack-operation instruction and it is designed so that the register to be pushed onto the stack can be named as the operand.

This example pushes the contents of the BC register onto the stack. Note that the registers are *pushed* in pairs only. The PUSH instruction is for the BC, DE, and HL pairs. The only other push operation will place the accumulator and the flags onto the stack (PUSH PSW). The register named in the operand is assumed to be a 16-bit register and the high-order byte will be stored before the low-order byte.

Instruction	POP B	
	Mnemonic	Hex
	POP B	C1
Example		
	Opcode	Operand
	POP	B

Description

The POP instruction is the reverse of the PUSH instruction. It removes the data stored on the stack and restores it to the designated register pair. It works in reverse (LIFO) so that the low-order byte will be restored before the high-order byte.

Instruction	OUT	
	Mnemonic	Hex
	OUT byte	D3
Example		
	Opcode	Operand
	OUT	61H

Description

The OUT instruction is a 2-byte instruction that sends the data byte in the accumulator to the port address specified. Since only one address byte is allowed, all port addresses are restricted to the first 256 address bytes.

The address of the port appears on both the upper and lower address lines. The status word that results from an out instruction indicates to the 8228 chip that the port addressed is to be written to, (output write).

Instruction	IN	
	Mnemonic	Hex
	IN byte	DB
Example		
	Opcode	Operand
	IN	61H

Description

The IN instruction reads the port designated by the byte in the operand. IN instructions, like OUT instructions, are restricted to the first 256 address bytes.

The address of the port appears on both the upper and lower address lines. The status word indicates to the 8228 chip that the port addressed is to be read, (input read).

Instruction	EL	
	Mnemonic	Hex
	EL	FB
Example		
	Opcode	Operand
	EL	18F0H

Description

The EI or Enable Interrupt is a 1-byte instruction that enables the interrupt input, INT. The instruction resets the interrupt flip-flop and the INTE output indicates that the processor will accept interrupts.

✔ **SELF-CHECK FOR SECTION 15-8**

23. For the MOV instruction, what is a source and destination register?
24. Explain a conditional branch.
25. What is meant by "loop?"
26. What is the CALL instruction for?

15-9 THE BASIC 8085A SYSTEM

The 8085A is an enhancement of the original 8080A microprocessor and the instruction set is 100% compatible with the 8080A. The 8085A has two additional instructions to be discussed later.

The 8085A, however, needs only a single +5 volt supply instead of the three needed by the 8080A. In addition, in keeping with the trend toward integration, the 8085A has an on-board clock circuit. The controller chip necessary for 8080A has also been done away with. The minimum configuration of an 8085A system is shown in Figure 15-5.

The other major enhancement to the 8085A is the interrupt circuitry. Recall the 8080A had only one interrupt input.

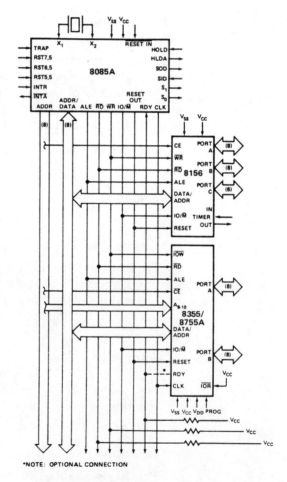

*NOTE: OPTIONAL CONNECTION

FIGURE 15-5 Minimum Configuration

15-10   THE 8085A SIGNAL DESCRIPTIONS

Figure 15-6 shows the functional block diagram of the 8085A. While the architecture is quite similar to the 8080A, there are some differences to be discussed. The actual pin outs can be seen in Figure 15-7.

For the following descriptions, it is helpful to refer to the functional block diagram in Figure 15-6.

X1 and X2

Since the 8085A has a built-in clock, it is necessary to connect a crystal to these two pins. The crystal frequency must be at least twice the desired clock frequency. Normally a 6 MHz crystal is employed for the maximum 3 MHz operating speed.

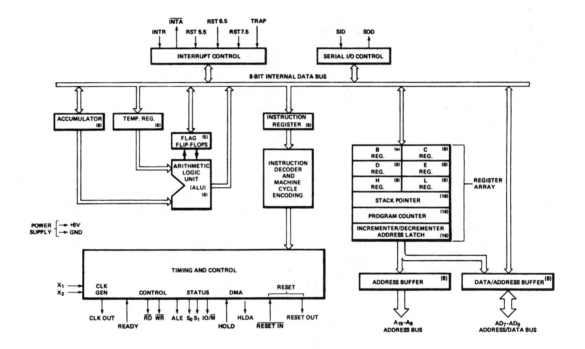

FIGURE 15-6 Functional Block Diagram of the 8085A System

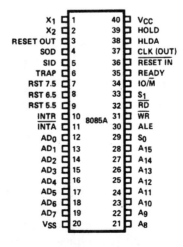

FIGURE 15-7 8085A Pin Configuration

Clock Out

The clock circuitry is integrated onto the 8085A chip. The clock output enables external devices to "synchronize" with the 8085A.

Ready

The *Ready* pin is an input from memory or peripherals. If it is high, the processor will complete the read or write cycle. If it is low, the processor inserts wait states until it is brought high. This is essentially the same as the 8080A.

RD

The ReaD control (RD) is a three-state output. When it is low, data is available on the data bus for transfer. It is three-stated during halt, hold, and reset modes.

WR

The write control output is also a three-state output. When it is brought low, data is available on the data bus for the write operation. It is three-stated during halt, hold, and reset modes.

Address Latch Enable

The need for this output arises because of the 40-pin limitation on the chip package. There simply were not enough pins to have all the new signals and to have separate data and address bus pins, so the data bus is actually multiplexed on the lower 8-bits of the address bus.

The ALE output is a status output indicating whether these pins are being used as the lower 8-bits of the address or as the 8-bit data bus.

S_0 S_1 IO/M

The three outputs indicate the status of the microprocessor at the beginning of each machine cycle. This system takes the place of the status words used on the 8080A. The possible output combinations are:

S_0	S_1	IO/M	
1	0	0	Memory Write
0	1	0	Memory Read
1	0	1	I/O Write
0	1	1	I/O Read
1	1	0	Op Code Fetch
0	0	*	Halt
X	X	*	Hold
X	X	*	Reset

* = Three-state, Hi-Z
X = unspecified

Hold

The Hold input is for peripheral devices with the capability of using the bus system. When a Hold input is received, the microprocessor finishes its current instruction and places the address and data buses, the WR, the RD, and the IO/M lines, in the third state (high-impedance). Operation is suspended.

HLDA

The HLDA, Hold Acknowledge, is an output to indicate that a hold request has been received and the bus will be relinquished.

RESET IN

The RESET IN is an input that zeros the program counter and resets the HLDA and Interrupt Enable flip-flops.

RESET OUT

This output signals that the microprocessor has received a reset. The output can be used to reset the rest of the system in synchronization with the processor.

15-11   8085A INTERRUPTS

The 8080A had only one interrupt input, the INT. The 8085A has the INT interrupt, called INTR, and four other levels of interrupts.

INTR

The INTR is a general-purpose interrupt that is tested or checked by the microprocessor during the next to last clock cycle of a given instruction. If the interrupt control has been enabled by the software (EI instruction) the processor accepts the interrupt and the program counter will not increment. At the same time, the INTA, interrupt acknowledge, signal is issued.

The processor now expects a restart (RST 0 – RST 7) instruction to direct it to the interrupt routine. This is actually the same procedure used by the 8080A.

INTA

The INTA output is the interrupt acknowledge. The 8080A depended on the 8228 controller chip to generate the acknowledge. In the 8085A, the INTA is an output from the processor itself and is designed for peripheral devices or chips that are tracking the interrupt.

RST 5.5, RST 6.5, RST 7.5

These additional hardware interrupts have the same timing as the INTR, but instead of expecting an external Restart input, they have an internal automatic Restart. This essentially makes them vectored interrupts.

When the RST 5.5 input is activated, the program counter is saved to stack and the program jumps to memory location 002CH. The RST 6.5 interrupt saves the program counter and jumps to location 0034H, and RST 7.5 jumps to 003CH. These interrupts have a higher priority than the INTR, but they do not all have the same priority. The priority comes into play if two interrupt signals arrive at the same time. Table 15-2 shows the priority of each of the five hardware interrupts.

TRAP

The TRAP interrupt is the highest priority interrupt on the 8085A. It is a nonmaskable interrupt recognized at the same time as the other interrupts. It cannot be disabled by the Disable Interrupt and it is not dependent on the EI instruction. The TRAP interrupt also saves the program counter to stack. It then jumps to memory location 0024H for the interrupt routine.

INTERRUPT PRIORITY, RESTART ADDRESS, AND SENSITIVITY

TABLE 15-2 Interrupt Priority

Name	Priority	Address Branched To (1) When Interrupt Occurs	Type Trigger
TRAP	1	24H	Rising edge AND high level until sampled.
RST 7.5	2	3CH	Rising edge (latched).
RST 6.5	3	34H	High level until sampled.
RST 5.5	4	2CH	High level until sampled.
INTR	5	See Note (2).	High level until sampled.

NOTES:

(1) The processor pushes the PC on the stack before branching to the indicated address.
(2) The address branched to depends on the instruction provided to the cpu when the interrupt is acknowledged.

Serial I/O Control

The serial I/O control block (Fig. 15-6) has an SID, Serial Input Data line, and an SOD, Serial Output Data line. The SID input is a primitive serial input port. The RIM instruction, one of the two new instructions, transfers the bit on the SID input to bit-7 in the accumulator (Fig. 15-8). Once in the accumulator, it is subject to all of the instructions possible with the accumulator.

In the same way, the SIM instruction will transfer a bit from the bit-7 position of the accumulator to the SOD output, forming a serial output port. These two new instructions, RIM and SIM also have other uses.

FIGURE 15-8 Serial Data Input to Bit 7 of Accumulator

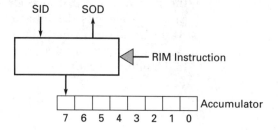

Interrupt Control

There are two general instructions in the 8080A and the 8085A that control the interrupts. The EI, interrupt enable, sets the interrupt-enable flip-flop permitting all five interrupts (one in the 8080A) to work. The DI, disable interrupt, resets the interrupt flip-flop to 0 and disables all interrupts except the TRAP. These instructions deal with the interrupts as a group.

SIM

The RST 5.5, RST 6.5, and RST 7.5 interrupts are maskable and can be individually controlled. This is accomplished via an interrupt status register in the interrupt-control section. The SIM, Set Interrupt Mask, instruction will place the contents of the accumulator into the interrupt status register. The bits in this status register then control the interrupt by enabling or disabling the appropriate bit. Figure 15-9 shows the bit assignments in the interrupt status register.

Bits 0, 1, and 2 control the RST interrupts as shown in Figure 15-9. Bit position-3 (MSE) must be set in order to change bits 0, 1, and 2. If bit-3 is clear, bits 1, 2, and 3 are unaffected. Bit-4 controls the RST 7.5 individually and bit-5 is not used. Bit-6 is the serial output enable and bit-7 is the serial output data.

Briefly, the SIM instruction works through the accumulator. First the accumulator is loaded with the appropriate mask; then the SIM instruction is executed.

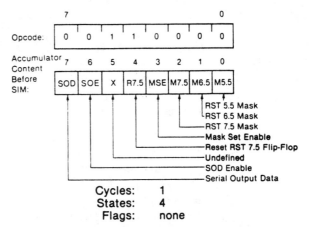

FIGURE 15-9 Bit Assignment Interrupt

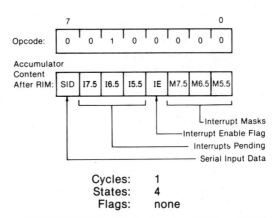

FIGURE 15-10 Bit Assignment After RIM

RIM

The RIM, Read Interrupt Mask, instruction reads the contents of the internal latches and puts the information into the accumulator. Figure 15-10 illustrates the assignment of each of the bits in the accumulator after the RIM instruction is executed.

15-12   EVOLUTION OF THE 8080A

Intel has a research and development program that is producing faster microprocessors with innovative features. Every introduction, however, is not a major innovation or landmark development.

What follows is an overview of the series of processors that Intel has developed over the years. The models with important changes structural and performance changes are covered. This section is not intended to offer a comprehensive discussion of the entire Intel microprocessor line.

The 8086

The 8085A was the first enhancement of the 8080A, but it remained an 8-bit microprocessor. The 8086 is Intel's first 16-bit microprocessor. Some of the 8080 architecture remains, but the 8080 and the 8086 are not directly compatible.

The 8086 has a 20-bit address bus, which means 1M byte of memory is accessible. Although it has a 20-pin address bus, internally all address registers are 16-bits wide. In addition, because of the 40-pin limitation on the package, the data bus is multiplexed on the lower 16 bits of the address bus.

To speed execution, the 8086 has an **instruction queue**. Up to six instructions can be *prefetched* and placed in the instruction queue registers. This is called *pipelining*. The 8086 is offered in 5, 8, and 10MHz versions.

The 8088

The 8088 was introduced shortly after the 8086, and, from a programmers point of view, it is the same as the 8086. A substantial amount of equipment and peripheral devices are designed around a standard 8-bit data bus. These devices cannot easily be adapted to the 16-bit data bus on the 8086. For this reason, the 8088 has all the features of the 8086, but it uses only the lower eight bits of the address bus to form a standard, 8-bit data bus.

The 80286

The 80286 is well-known because of its use in the IBM PS-line and the Compaq 286. The 80286 is manufactured in a 68-pin package, which makes room for separate data and address buses. The address bus is increased to 24 pins, allowing 16M bytes of memory to be addressed.

It can also be operated in a virtual mode which maps up to 1 giga byte (1 billion bytes) of virtual memory. The data bus is 16 bits wide. The advances and features in the 80286 make it useful in multi-user and multi-tasking environments. The 80286 is offered in a range of 8,10, and 12.5 MHz versions.

The 80386

The 80386 is an advanced, 32-bit microprocessor manufactured in a 132-pin, grid-array package. There are 32 address lines for accessing 4-giga bytes of physical memory. The internal registers and the data bus are 32-bits wide. The virtual memory mode expands to 64 trillion bytes. It is offered with clock speeds of 20, 25, and 33 MHz.

The 80386 and 80486

The improved 80486 from Intel is widely available and is rapidly becoming the microprocessor of choice for users of IBM and IBM-compatible machines. Part of the 80486's popularity comes from its 100 percent binary compatibility with the 80386. With a 168-pin grid-array package and complete 32-bit architecture the 80486 is faster and more powerful than other microprocessors. The 1 million-transistor on-board cache memory and available 25 and 33 MHz clock frequencies allow the 80486 to challenge some mainframe computers.

✔ SELF-CHECK FOR SECTIONS 15-9, 15-10, 15-11, 15-12

27. What are two major differences between the 8080 and the 8085A?
28. What is the maximum operating frequency for the 8085A?
29. Explain the purpose of the ALE output.
30. Explain the function of the RESET IN and RESET OUT pins for the 8085A.

31. What is the 8085A interrupt with the highest priority?
32. The ___ instruction will place the contents of the accumulator into the interrupt status register.
33. The ___ instruction reads the contents of the internal latches and puts the information into the accumulator.
34. How large is the address bus on the 8086?

SUMMARY OF IDEAS

- The basic 8080A system requires a two-phase clock generator and an 8228 system controller chip.
- Control of the 8080A chip is achieved though six input and six output lines. Much of the control of peripherals is delegated to the system controller chip.
- The instruction cycle is divided into machine cycles M1 through M5.
- Each machine cycle is further divided into T-states. A T-state lasts from the rising edge of one clock cycle to the rising edge of the next.
- The 8080A hardware interrupt is called the INT input. After an interrupt, the 8080A waits for an external device to place the RST instruction on the data bus.
- There are eight RST instructions, each with its own vectored address for the interrupt routine.
- The 8080A has six user registers: the accumulator, the BC, the DE, the HL, the stack pointer, and the program counter.
- The BC, DE, and HL registers are 16-bit registers that can be addressed and treated as two individual 8-bit registers.
- The 8080A has five addressing modes: implied, immediate, register, direct, and register indirect.
- The 8080A instruction set consists of 111 basic 8-bit instruction formats from which over 200 combinations are possible.
- The 8085A enhancement of the 8080A has an on board clock and integrated system control functions.
- Through its control signals, the 8085A has more ability to manage RAM, ROM, and I/O devices.
- The 8085A has four added interrupts, bringing the total to five, including the nonmaskable TRAP interrupt.
- The 8080A began as an 8-bit processor with operating speeds around .5 MHz and has led to the current advanced version, the 80386, a 32-bit processor with operating speeds up to 33 MHz.

CHAPTER QUESTIONS & PROBLEMS

True or False
1. The 8080A generates a two-phase clock signal.
2. The data bus outputs a status word during the first clock cycle of each machine cycle.
3. Every instruction cycle will make reference to a memory location.
4. The INTE input is the hardware interrupt input line.
5. The HOLD input signal allows an external device to place the microprocessor in a HOLD state.

Fill in the Blanks
6. The flag that monitors the state of the bit-3-to-bit-4 carry during a math operation is called the _____ _____ flag.

7. A T-state has the same duration as a _____ _____.
8. The I/O ports in an 8080A system are reached by the _____ and _____ instructions.
9. To service an interrupt, the 8080A needs an _____ instruction from an external device.
10. The _____ _____ instructions use a register pair to point to the memory address location of the operand.

Multiple Choice

11. Which of the following correctly lists the flags in the 8080/85 flag register?
   a. CY I N S C
   b. AC P C Z N
   c. S Z AC P CY
   d. S Z AC V CY

12. All 8080/85 instructions consist of
   a. one byte.
   b. one or two bytes.
   c. one, two, or three bytes.
   d. as many bytes as necessary.

13. How many address bytes are required for direct-addressing in the 8080A and 8085A?
   a. One byte.
   b. Two bytes.
   c. Three bytes.
   d. Either one or two.

14. Which two instructions will not work on the 8080A?
   a. IN, OUT
   b. RST 6, RST 7
   c. RIM, SIM
   d. EI, DI

15. Which of the following 8085A interrupts cannot be masked by the SIM instruction?
   a. RST 5.5
   b. INTA
   c. RST 7.5
   d. TRAP

16. The RST interrupts will cause the microprocessor to save to stack the
   a. program counter, stack pointer.
   b. accumulator, program counter, stack pointer.
   c. program counter.
   d. all internal registers.

17. Which of the following instructions would not work?
   a. MOV B,C
   b. MOV D,C
   c. MOV BC,DE
   d. MOV B,DE

18. Which of the following best describes the instruction, INX H?
   a. The H register is incremented.
   b. The index register is loaded from H.
   c. The HL register is incremented.
   d. The content of the X register is loaded with the contents of the H register.

19. Which of the following best describes SID and SOD?
   a. The instructions to mask or read the interrupt control register.
   b. Serial input data and serial output data connections for the 8080A.
   c. Instructions to control the input or output of serial data.
   d. Serial data input and output pins on the 8085A.

20. The instruction JNZ checks the Z-bit in the flag register and is called a
   a. load and store instruction.
   b. unconditional branch instruction.
   c. data transfer instruction.
   d. conditional branch instruction.

CHAPTER 16

MICROPROCESSOR INTERFACING AND BUS STRUCTURE

OUTLINE

NEW TERMS TO WATCH FOR

Interface	Octal Three-State Buffer	Port
Polling	DMA Controller	Initialize
DMA Request	PPI	USART
S-100	IEEE-696	PC Bus
Multibus	GPIB	HPIB
IEEE-488	Listener	Talker
VME	IEEE-583	Crate
Card Rack	Controller	

After completing this chapter, you should be able to:

1. Correctly interface ROM or RAM memory with a microprocessor.
2. Describe polling and explain how a microprocessor uses this technique.
3. Show how interrupt signals are related to microprocessor interfacing.
4. Explain the direct memory access process.
5. Discuss programmable peripheral interface IC's.
6. Work with keyboard interfaces.
7. Identify CRT interface techniques and recognize CRT interface chips.
8. Define the USART device and describe its characteristics.
9. Recognize and define the S-100 bus interface.
10. Distinguish the character of the popular bus interfaces in use today.
11. Determine the types of microprocessors commonly used with the various buses.

16-1   INTRODUCTION

The microprocessor, in spite of all of its capabilities, is not of much use by itself. Peripheral devices are necessary to make the microprocessor a useful device. Without peripheral devices to provide input and take output from the microprocessor it would be a non-functioning bit of silicon.

In general, a microprocessor system will consist of both ROM and RAM memory, and I/O devices, such as keyboards, disk drives, displays, screens, and printers.

A world of peripheral devices must be interfaced with the microprocessor itself. The interconnections will be wire, printed circuits, and IC-chips. These interconnections are called **interfaces**.

There are few peripheral devices that will connect directly to the microprocessor without an interface. This can be attributed to the specialized nature of the microprocessor and the diversity of peripheral products. There are many more peripheral devices than there are types of microprocessors and this variety seems to preclude a standard connection.

When the essential elements of interconnection are accounted for, some standards are possible. Interfacing includes three major considerations: signal levels, synchronization, and compatible physical layout. This chapter will cover the common techniques and devices used to connect the microprocessor to the outside world.

16-2   ROM AND RAM INTERFACING

In some cases, the address and data outputs of the microprocessor can be directly connected to memory devices with a minimum of interfacing. It is a necessary precaution to choose memory chips specifically designed for the connections.

TYPICAL 16K EPROM SYSTEM

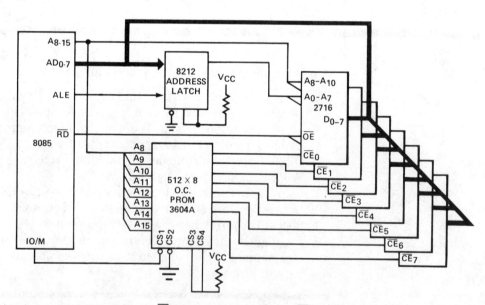

**FIGURE 16-1
Typical
Connection
to EPROM**

- This scheme accomplished by using $\overline{CE}$ (PD) as the primary decode. $\overline{OE}$ (CS) is now controlled by previously unused signal. RD now controls data on and off the bus by way of $\overline{OE}$.

- A selected 2716 is available for systems which require $\overline{CE}$ access of less than 450 ns for decode network operation.

- The use of a PROM as a decoder allows for:

  a) Compatibility with upward (and downward) memory expansion.

  b) Easy assignment of ROM memory modules, compatible with PL/M modular software concepts.

ROM

Figure 16-1 shows a typical 8085A connection to a 16K EPROM memory system. The 2716 is a 2K × 8 memory chip and, therefore, eight chips constitute a 16K × 8 memory.

Address lines A0 to A10 are connected to the 2716 array. The address lines are sufficient to select any of 2,048 8-bit words on a given chip. The chip select is used to enable one of the eight chips in the array.

Chip select is accomplished with a 512 × 8 PROM decoder. The upper address byte, A8 through A15, carries the chip select information. This is overkill for a 16K array, when only three chip select address lines are needed. This system, however, can be easily expanded.

The RD enable output from the 8085A controls the OE input on the 2716. The OE pin enables the output of the memory chips. The RD signal from the 8085A will not call for the output of a memory chip, until the

MOTOROLA

| MC54F/74F240 |
| MC54F/74F241 |
| MC54F/74F244 |

OCTAL BUFFER/LINE DRIVER WITH 3-STATE OUTPUTS

DESCRIPTION — The F240, F241 and F244 are octal buffers and line drivers designed to be employed as memory address drivers, clock drivers and bus oriented transmitters/receivers which provide improved PC board density.

- 3-STATE OUTPUTS DRIVE BUS LINES OR BUFFER MEMORY ADDRESS REGISTERS
- OUTPUTS SINK 64 mA
- 15 mA SOURCE CURRENT
- INPUT CLAMP DIODES LIMIT HIGH-SPEED TERMINATION EFFECTS

OCTAL BUFFER/LINE DRIVER with 3-STATE OUTPUTS

FAST™ SCHOTTKY TTL

FIGURE 16-2 MC54/74F240 Buffer and Line Driver

CONNECTION DIAGRAMS

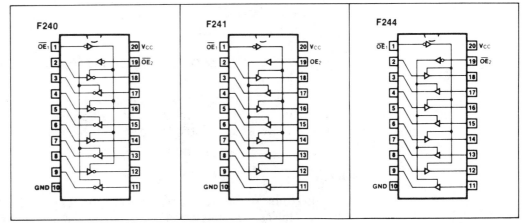

J Suffix — Case 732-03 (Ceramic)
N Suffix — Case 738-03 (Plastic)
DW Suffix — Case 751D-03 (SOIC)

TRUTH TABLES

F240

INPUTS		OUTPUT
$\overline{OE}_1$, $\overline{OE}_2$	D	
L	L	H
L	H	L
H	X	Z

F241

INPUTS			OUTPUT
$\overline{OE}_1$	OE₂	D	
L	H	L	L
L	H	H	H
H	L	X	Z

F244

INPUTS		OUTPUT
$\overline{OE}_1$, $\overline{OE}_2$	D	
L	L	L
L	H	H
H	X	Z

H = HIGH Voltage Level   L = LOW Voltage Level   X = Immaterial   Z = High Impendance

GUARANTEED OPERATING RANGES

SYMBOL	PARAMETER		MIN	TYP	MAX	UNIT
V_{CC}	Supply Voltage	54, 74	4.50	5.0	5.50	V
T_A	Operating Ambient Temperature Range	54	−55	25	125	°C
		74	0	25	70	
I_{OH}	Output Current — High	54			−12	mA
		74			−15	
I_{OL}	Output Current — Low	54			48	mA
		74			64	

DC CHARACTERISTICS OVER OPERATING TEMPERATURE RANGE (unless otherwise specified)

SYMBOL	PARAMETER		LIMITS			UNITS	TEST CONDITIONS	
			MIN	TYP	MAX			
V_{IH}	Input HIGH Voltage		2.0			V	Guaranteed Input HIGH Voltage	
V_{IL}	Input LOW Voltage				0.8	V	Guaranteed Input LOW Voltage	
V_{IK}	Input Clamp Diode Voltage				−1.2	V	$I_{IN} = -18$ mA	V_{CC} = MIN
V_{OH}	Output HIGH Voltage	54, 74	2.4	3.4		V	$I_{OH} = -3.0$ mA	$V_{CC} = 4.50$ V
		74	2.7	3.4		V	$I_{OH} = -3.0$ mA	$V_{CC} = 4.75$ V
		54	2.0			V	$I_{OH} = -12$ mA	$V_{CC} = 4.50$ V
		74	2.0			V	$I_{OH} = -15$ mA	$V_{CC} = 4.5$ V
V_{OL}	Output LOW Voltage	54			0.55	V	$I_{OL} = 48$ mA	V_{CC} = MIN
		74			0.55	V	$I_{OL} = 64$ mA	
I_{OZH}	Output Off Current HIGH				50	µA	$V_{OUT} = 2.7$ V	V_{CC} = MAX
I_{OZL}	Output Off Current LOW				−50	µA	$V_{OUT} = 0.5$ V	V_{CC} = MAX
I_{IH}	Input HIGH Current				20	µA	$V_{IN} = 2.7$ V	V_{CC} = MAX
					100		$V_{IN} = 7.0$ V	
I_{IL}	Input LOW Current	Data Inputs F241, F244			−1.6	mA	$V_{IN} = 0.5$ V	V_{CC} = MAX
		Other			−1.0			
I_{OS}	Output Drive Current Note 2	54	−100		−275	mA	V_{OUT} = GND	V_{CC} = MAX
		74	−100		−275			
I_{CCH}	Power Supply Current HIGH	F240			35			
		F241, F244			60			
I_{CCL}	Power Supply Current LOW	F240			75	mA	V_{CC} = MAX	
		F241, F244			90			
I_{CCZ}	Power Supply Current OFF	F240			75			
		F241, F244			90			

NOTES:
1. For conditions shown as MIN or MAX, use the appropriate value specified under recommended operating conditions for the applicable device type.
2. Not more than one output should be shorted at a time, nor for more than 1 second.

FIGURE 16-2 MC54/74F240 Buffer and Line Driver (continued)

address has stabilized. This is necessary, as you will recall, because the 8085A multiplexes the lower 8 bits of the address bus with the data bus. This is also why the address latch is present for the lower eight address bits.

RAM

It is not always desirable or even possible to directly connect address and data buses to memory circuits. In many cases, connections are made with bus-driver chips. The microprocessor does not have the output power required to drive a large bus system. Nearly all memory circuits, especially dynamic RAMS, would overload the bus output of the microprocessor.

A common solution is to use a chip such as the MC74F240 (Figure 16-2). This chip is an **octal three-state buffer** and line driver. The 74F240 provides the microprocessor with the power needed to drive a memory circuit. These chips also supply the power needed to drive other I/O devices that may be connected to the bus.

 **MOTOROLA**

DESCRIPTION — The SN54LS/74LS245 is an Octal Bus Transmitter/ Receiver designed for 8-line asynchronous 2-way data communication between data buses. Direction Input (DR) controls transmission of Data from bus A to bus B or bus B to bus A depending upon its logic level. The Enable input (E̅) can be used to isolate the buses.

- HYSTERESIS INPUTS TO IMPROVE NOISE IMMUNITY
- 2-WAY ASYNCHRONOUS DATA BUS COMMUNICATION
- INPUT DIODES LIMIT HIGH-SPEED TERMINATION EFFECTS

SN54/74LS245

OCTAL BUS TRANSCEIVER

LOW POWER SCHOTTKY

TRUTH TABLE

INPUTS		OUTPUT
E̅	DIR	
L	L	Bus B Data to Bus A
L	H	Bus A Data to Bus B
H	X	Isolation

H = HIGH Voltage Level
L = LOW Voltage Level
X = Immaterial

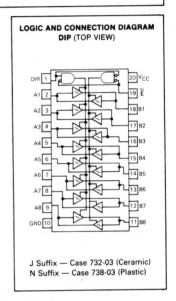

LOGIC AND CONNECTION DIAGRAM
DIP (TOP VIEW)

J Suffix — Case 732-03 (Ceramic)
N Suffix — Case 738-03 (Plastic)

FIGURE 16-3 SN54/74LS245 Bus Interface

The data bus may use a chip such as the MC74F245. (Figure 16-3). This chip is essentially the same as the MC74F240, except that it is bidirectional. This is a necessary requirement for a data bus interface.

Usually the control bus is interfaced to provide buffering and adequate signal levels. A typical control-bus-interface IC is the Intel 8288 chip. This chip (Figure 16-4) not only provides the driving power necessary, it also enhances the ability of the microprocessor to control peripheral devices.

Figure 16-5 shows how a typical 8086 microprocessor might be interfaced with a memory. The block is somewhat simplified. In truth, the 8086 must have the memory divided into two banks, odd addressed banks and even addressed banks. Both banks receive the address, but the A0 line and a control line are used to select the proper bank.

GUARANTEED OPERATING RANGES

SYMBOL	PARAMETER			MIN	TYP	MAX	UNIT
V_{CC}	Supply Voltage		54	4.5	5.0	5.5	V
			74	4.75	5.0	5.25	
T_A	Operating Ambient Temperature Range		54	−55	25	125	°C
			74	0	25	70	
I_{OH}	Output Current — High		54,74			−3.0	mA
			54			−12	mA
			74			−15	
I_{OL}	Output Current — Low		54			12	mA
			74			24	

DC CHARACTERISTICS OVER OPERATING TEMPERATURE RANGE (unless otherwise specified)

SYMBOL	PARAMETER		LIMITS			UNITS	TEST CONDITIONS	
			MIN	TYP	MAX			
V_{IH}	Input HIGH Voltage		2.0			V	Guaranteed Input HIGH Voltage for All Inputs	
V_{IL}	Input LOW Voltage	54			0.7	V	Guaranteed Input LOW Voltage for All Inputs	
		74			0.8			
$V_{T+}-V_{T-}$	Hysteresis		0.2	0.4		V	V_{CC} = MIN	
V_{IK}	Input Clamp Diode Voltage			−0.65	−1.5	V	V_{CC} = MIN, I_{IN} = −18 mA	
V_{OH}	Output HIGH Voltage	54,74	2.4	3.4		V	V_{CC} = MIN, I_{OH} = −3.0 mA	
		54,74	2.0			V	V_{CC} = MIN, I_{OH} = MAX	
V_{OL}	Output LOW Voltage	54,74		0.25	0.4	V	I_{OL} = 12 mA	V_{CC} = V_{CC} MIN, V_{IN} = V_{IL} or V_{IH} per Truth Table
		74		0.35	0.5	V	I_{OL} = 24 mA	
I_{OZH}	Output Off Current HIGH				20	μA	V_{CC} = MAX, V_{OUT} = 2.7 V	
I_{OZL}	Output Off Current LOW				−200	μA	V_{CC} = MAX, V_{OUT} = 0.4 V	
I_{IH}	Input HIGH Current	A or B, DR or $\overline{E}$			20	μA	V_{CC} = MAX, V_{IN} = 2.7 V	
		DR or $\overline{E}$			0.1	mA	V_{CC} = MAX, V_{IN} = 7.0 V	
		A or B			0.1	mA	V_{CC} = MAX, V_{IN} = 5.5 V	
I_{IL}	Input LOW Current				−0.2	mA	V_{CC} = MAX, V_{IN} = 0.4 V	
I_{OS}	Output Short Circuit Current		−40		−225	mA	V_{CC} = MAX	
I_{CC}	Power Supply Current Total, Output HIGH				70	mA	V_{CC} = MAX	
	Total, Output LOW				90			
	Total at HIGH Z				95			

AC CHARACTERISTICS: T_A = 25°C, V_{CC} = 5.0 V

SYMBOL	PARAMETER	LIMITS			UNITS	TEST CONDITIONS
		MIN	TYP	MAX		
t_{PLH} t_{PHL}	Propagation Delay, Data to Output		8.0 8.0	12 12	ns	C_L = 45 pF R_L = 667 Ω
t_{PZH}	Output Enable Time to HIGH Level		25	40	ns	
t_{PZL}	Output Enable Time to LOW Level		27	40	ns	
t_{PLZ}	Output Disable Time from LOW Level		15	25	ns	C_L = 5.0 pF R_L = 667 Ω
t_{PHZ}	Output Disable Time from HIGH Level		15	25	ns	

FIGURE 16-3 SN54/74LS245 Bus Interface (continued)

8288
BUS CONTROLLER FOR THE 8086 CPU

- **Bipolar Drive Capability**
- **Provides Advanced Commands**
- **Provides Wide Flexibility in System Configurations**

- **3-State Command Output Drivers**
- **Configurable for Use with an I/O Bus**
- **Facilitates Interface to One or Two Multi-Master Busses**

The Intel® 8288 Bus Controller is a 20-pin bipolar component for use with medium-to-large 8086 processing systems. The bus controller provides command and control timing generation as well as bipolar bus drive capability while optimizing system performance.

A strapping option on the bus controller configures it for use with a multi-master system bus and separate I/O bus.

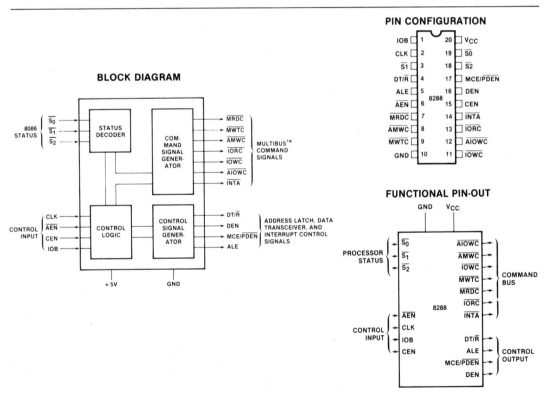

FIGURE 16-4 Intel 8288 Bus Controller

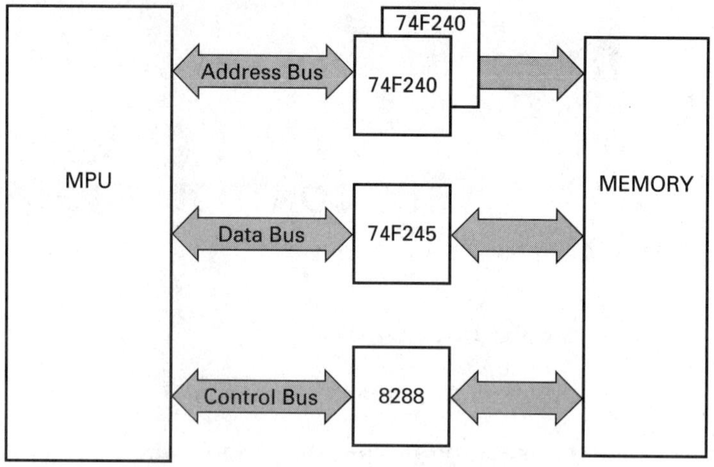

FIGURE 16-5 Memory Interfacing

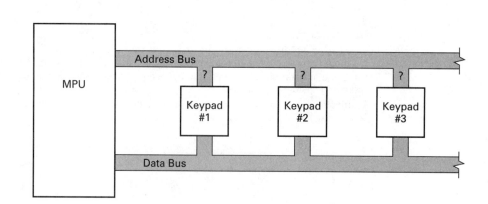

FIGURE 16-6 Alarm System

FIGURE 16-7 Service Routine

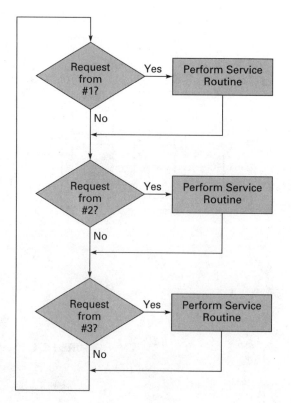

✔ SELF-CHECK FOR SECTIONS 16-1, 16-2

1. Microprocessor _____ includes three major considerations, signal levels, synchronization and compatible physical layout.
2. Name at least two other devices commonly found in microprocessor systems.
3. Explain the need for bus driver chips.
4. Describe an octal three-state buffer.
5. What is the size of a 2716 chip?

16-3   THE BASICS OF I/O INTERFACING

I/O transfers occupy a large part of the microprocessor's business life. Data must flow to and from peripheral devices on a regular basis and the center of this activity is the microprocessor. The interface connection for an I/O or peripheral device is called an input or output **port**.

There are three basic ways that a microprocessor controls I/O ports. The methods are **polling**, interrupt, or Direct Memory Access.

Polling

Polling is not a difficult or complex process to understand. Here is an analogy. Some electronic phone systems depend on the in-house line voltage to operate. With a power failure, the phones cannot ring. During a power failure, if you picked up the phone every few minutes to see if someone was calling, you would be *polling.*

Polling is the least-complicated way of handling I/O and it requires minimal hardware.

Polling can be initiated through a program. The polling program directs the microprocessor to check each I/O device to see if service is required. For example, a microprocessor might control a security system equipped with remote keypads. The polling program would interrogate the keypads to see if there was input to indicate a request to enter the building. Figure 16-6 shows a simplified block diagram of such a system.

Figure 16-7 shows how the polling sequence in the program might be flowcharted. The actual polling technique would consist of the microprocessor testing the byte in the status register of each keypad. Usually one bit is assigned (say bit 0) to the polling request. When a key is pressed, the bit is set to indicate that the keypad needs service.

The polling scheme operates synchronously with the program. The programmer always knows when a device will be checked and how long it will take to service it. On the other hand, polling has a lot of useless overhead, all devices are checked continuously. Service requirements, however, may be infrequent. Finally, the number of units that can be polled, without causing a device to wait excessively long for service, has limits.

Interrupts

Interrupt strategy relies on the I/O devices to initiate the request for service. All microprocessors have the capability to be interrupted. An interrupt is analogous to the phone ringing. Just as we interrupt what we are doing to answer the phone, the microprocessor interrupts its normal program execution to service the interrupting device.

Interrupts can occur at any point in the program, so provisions are made to suspend program execution to perform the interrupt routine. After servicing the interrupt, an arrangement exists to return the microprocessor to the previous activity. Both hardware and software are required to do the job.

Interrupt processing was covered in Chapter 12 and in the chapters on the Motorola and Intel microprocessors. The number of interrupt connections allowed on a microprocessor chip is limited, due to its physical size. Special IC circuits are available that will prioritize a number of I/O devices and manage the interrupt facility. The final drawback to an interrupt is the speed with which the microprocessor can execute an interrupt routine.

For example, transferring large blocks of data from disk to memory is not the most efficient operation a microprocessor can perform. It becomes a third wheel so to speak. The transfer is more efficient if data travels directly between the disk and memory without microprocessor involvement. This is called DMA.

Direct Memory Access

To understand the need for DMA, it is helpful to remember that the microprocessor carries out instructions based on the instruction words that reside in memory. It cannot execute an instruction cycle faster than the basic timing frequency under which it operates. Many memories and disk drives, however, can transfer bytes of data much faster than the instruction cycle of the processor will allow.

DMA allows the buses to be taken over and used by the I/O devices exchanging data. This is not to say that there is no microprocessor control over the bus at all. In fact, a DMA operation is under the direction of a **DMA controller**. Oddly enough, many DMA controllers are also microprocessor-equipped. When used as a controller, the microprocessor is narrowly specialized and serves only to supervise the transfer of data at hardware speed.

The Intel 8257 is a four-channel, DMA controller chip (Figure 16-8). The chip monitors the peripherals that have DMA and accepts their requests. Upon receiving a request, the controller chip places the microprocessor chip in a wait state. The controller then acknowledges the request for service. The microprocessor then places the buses in a high impedance state while the 8257 DMA controller chip makes the transfer.

The actual interface connections and chips for the 8257 controller are shown in Figure 16-9. Before a channel is ready, it must be **initialized**. Each DMA channel has a 16-bit register that is first loaded with the starting memory address. Another 16-bit register is loaded with the number of DMA cycles to be executed.

A priority can be established by rotating between the four channels. If the rotation priority is not used, the DRQ 0 channel has the highest priority while DRQ 3 has the lowest.

DMA is not restricted to disk drives. For example, the newer color graphics terminals also make good use of DMA. The large amount of data needed to map the multicolored displays must be moved at high rates of speed.

16-4   INTERFACE CHIPS

The microprocessor is usually surrounded by special IC chips that have been specifically designed to facilitate the interface with peripheral devices and users. Many of these interface chips are also programmable, that is, their assignments and functions can be controlled with 8-bit, binary words. Loading the programming statement or "word" takes place before the device is activated and is called *initializing*.

8257/8257-5
PROGRAMMABLE DMA CONTROLLER

- ■ **MCS-85™ Compatible 8257-5**
- ■ **4-Channel DMA Controller**
- ■ **Priority DMA Request Logic**
- ■ **Channel Inhibit Logic**

- ■ **Terminal Count and Modulo 128 Outputs**
- ■ **Single TTL Clock**
- ■ **Single +5V Supply**
- ■ **Auto Load Mode**

The Intel® 8257 is a 4-channel direct memory access (DMA) controller. It is specifically designed to simplify the transfer of data at high speeds for the Intel® microcomputer systems. Its primary function is to generate, upon a peripheral request, a sequential memory address which will allow the peripheral to read or write data directly to or from memory. Acquisition of the system bus in accomplished via the CPU's hold function. The 8257 has priority logic that resolves the peripherals requests and issues a composite hold request to the CPU. It maintains the DMA cycle count for each channel and outputs a control signal to notify the peripheral that the programmed number of DMA cycles is complete. Other output control signals simplify sectored data transfers. The 8257 represents a significant savings in component count for DMA-based microcomputer systems and greatly simplifies the transfer of data at high speed between peripherals and memories.

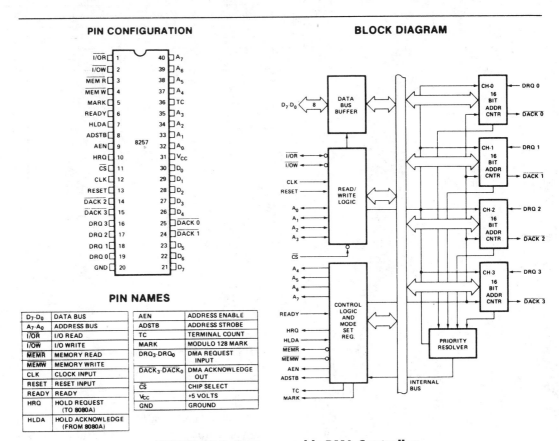

PIN CONFIGURATION

BLOCK DIAGRAM

PIN NAMES

D_7-D_0	DATA BUS	AEN	ADDRESS ENABLE
A_7-A_0	ADDRESS BUS	ADSTB	ADDRESS STROBE
I/OR	I/O READ	TC	TERMINAL COUNT
I/OW	I/O WRITE	MARK	MODULO 128 MARK
MEMR	MEMORY READ	DRQ_3-DRQ_0	DMA REQUEST INPUT
MEMW	MEMORY WRITE	$DACK_3$-$DACK_0$	DMA ACKNOWLEDGE OUT
CLK	CLOCK INPUT	CS	CHIP SELECT
RESET	RESET INPUT	Vcc	+5 VOLTS
READY	READY	GND	GROUND
HRQ	HOLD REQUEST (TO 8080A)		
HLDA	HOLD ACKNOWLEDGE (FROM 8080A)		

FIGURE 16-8 Programmable DMA Controller

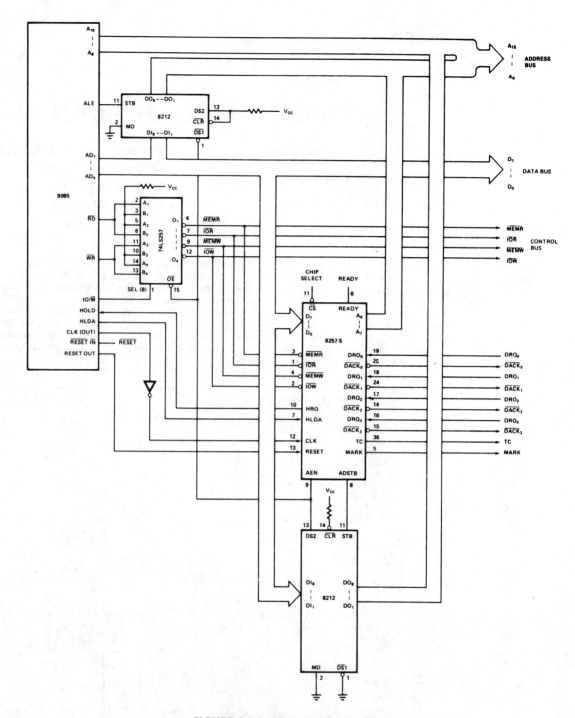

FIGURE 16-9 8257 Configuration

Memory with I/O Ports

Figure 16-10 shows a basic 8085A configuration. Note that the 8156 chip has three general-purpose I/O ports and that the 8355/8755 has two. The 8156 actually is a 2K RAM and the 8355 is a 16K EPROM. The additional general-purpose I/O ports make the chips dual-purpose chips. The ports will serve to interface with simple peripheral devices. However, for complex peripherals like keyboards, printers, and networked terminals, more control over a port is desirable.

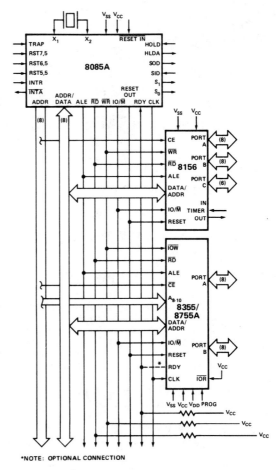

*NOTE: OPTIONAL CONNECTION

FIGURE 16-10 8085 Basic Configuration

Programmable Peripheral Interface

The 8255 (Fig. 16-11) is an example of a programmable peripheral interface chip, **(PPI)**. The chip is programmable through the system software and has three basic functional modes.

The three basic functional modes control the port configurations (Fig. 16-12). The mode is established with a control word input on the data lines, D0 - D7. Each of the three modes have several configuration definitions controlled by inputting the proper control word. As a result, the 8255 can be adapted to a wide variety of peripheral devices, each of which may demand different numbers of data and control lines.

In a sense, this chip becomes an extension of an interrupt service routine. Figure 16-13 is an application of the 8255 used to interface with a paper tape reader used to control a machine tool. Note the interrupt request line output to the microprocessor.

A Keyboard Interface

The 8279 (Fig. 16-14) is an even more specialized interface chip. The 8279 is specifically for keyboard interfacing. The left side of the logic symbol diagram (Fig. 16-14) shows the direct connections to the CPU. On the right side of this diagram are the SL_{0-3} scan line outputs to the keyboard matrix. The RL_{0-7} lines are return inputs from the keyboard matrix.

8255A/8255A-5
PROGRAMMABLE PERIPHERAL INTERFACE

- **MCS-85™ Compatible 8255A-5**
- **24 Programmable I/O Pins**
- **Completely TTL Compatible**
- **Fully Compatible with Intel® Microprocessor Families**
- **Improved Timing Characteristics**

- **Direct Bit Set/Reset Capability Easing Control Application Interface**
- **40-Pin Dual In-Line Package**
- **Reduces System Package Count**
- **Improved DC Driving Capability**

The Intel® 8255A is a general purpose programmable I/O device designed for use with Intel® microprocessors. It has 24 I/O pins which may be individually programmed in 2 groups of 12 and used in 3 major modes of operation. In the first mode (MODE 0), each group of 12 I/O pins may be programmed in sets of 4 to be input or output. In MODE 1, the second mode, each group may be programmed to have 8 lines of input or output. Of the remaining 4 pins, 3 are used for handshaking and interrupt control signals. The third mode of operation (MODE 2) is a bidirectional bus mode which uses 8 lines for a bidirectional bus, and 5 lines, borrowing one from the other group, for handshaking.

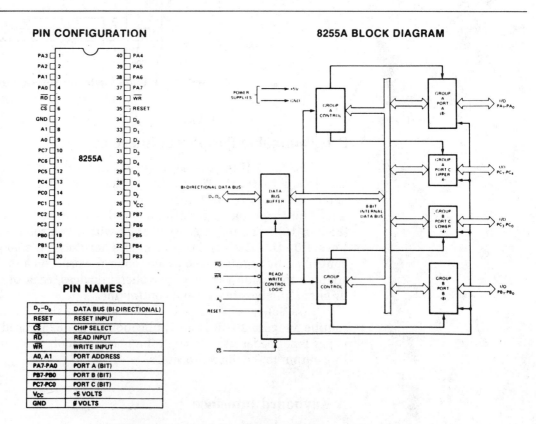

FIGURE 16-11 Programmable Peripheral Interface

An application of this interface chip is seen in the SDK-85 development board (Fig. 16-15). The scan line outputs are connected to the matrix through a 74LS156, a 1-of-4 decoder. The output switch closures of the keys are connected directly to the RL inputs of the interface chip. In this way, the keys generate an 8-bit, encoded input that is routed to an internal 8 × 8 RAM. The contents of the RAM are output to the data bus and the output is then accessible to the microprocessor chip. Whenever data exists in the internal 8 × 8 RAM, the IRQ interrupt output is high, requesting service from the microprocessor.

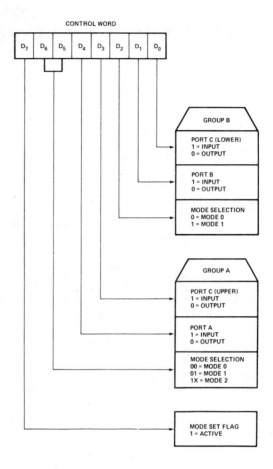

FIGURE 16-12 Mode Control

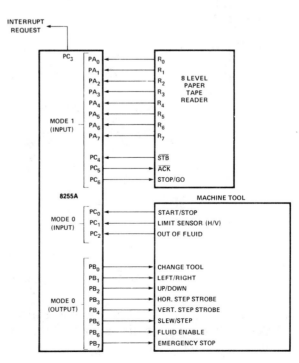

FIGURE 16-13 8255 Application

8279/8279-5
PROGRAMMABLE KEYBOARD/DISPLAY INTERFACE

- **MCS-85™ Compatible 8279-5**
- **Simultaneous Keyboard Display Operations**
- **Scanned Keyboard Mode**
- **Scanned Sensor Mode**
- **Strobed Input Entry Mode**
- **8-Character Keyboard FIFO**
- **2-Key Lockout or N-Key Rollover with Contact Debounce**

- **Dual 8- or 16-Numerical Display**
- **Single 16-Character Display**
- **Right or Left Entry 16-Byte Display RAM**
- **Mode Programmable from CPU**
- **Programmable Scan Timing**
- **Interrupt Output on Key Entry**

The Intel® 8279 is a general purpose programmable keyboard and display I/O interface device designed for use with Intel® microprocessors. The keyboard portion can provide a scanned interface to a 64-contact key matrix. The keyboard portion will also interface to an array of sensors or a strobed interface keyboard, such as the hall effect and ferrite variety. Key depressions can be 2-key lockout or N-key rollover. Keyboard entries are debounced and strobed in an 8-character FIFO. If more than 8 characters are entered, overrun status is set. Key entries set the interrupt output line to the CPU.

The display portion provides a scanned display interface for LED, incandescent, and other popular display technologies. Both numeric and alphanumeric segment displays may be used as well as simple indicators. The 8279 has 16X8 display RAM which can be organized into dual 16X4. The RAM can be loaded or interrogated by the CPU. Both right entry, calculator and left entry typewriter display formats are possible. Both read and write of the display RAM can be done with auto-increment of the display RAM address.

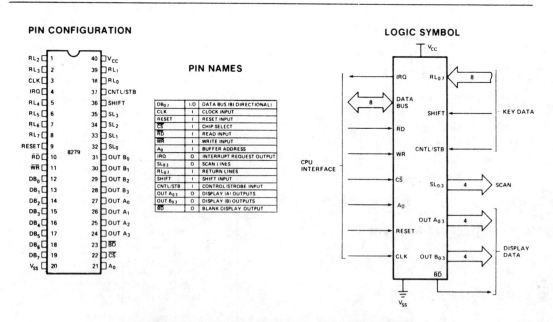

FIGURE 16-14 Programmable Keyboard Interface

The chip also has a display mode. The mode of operation, keyboard input, or display output, can be controlled with the system software via the data bus.

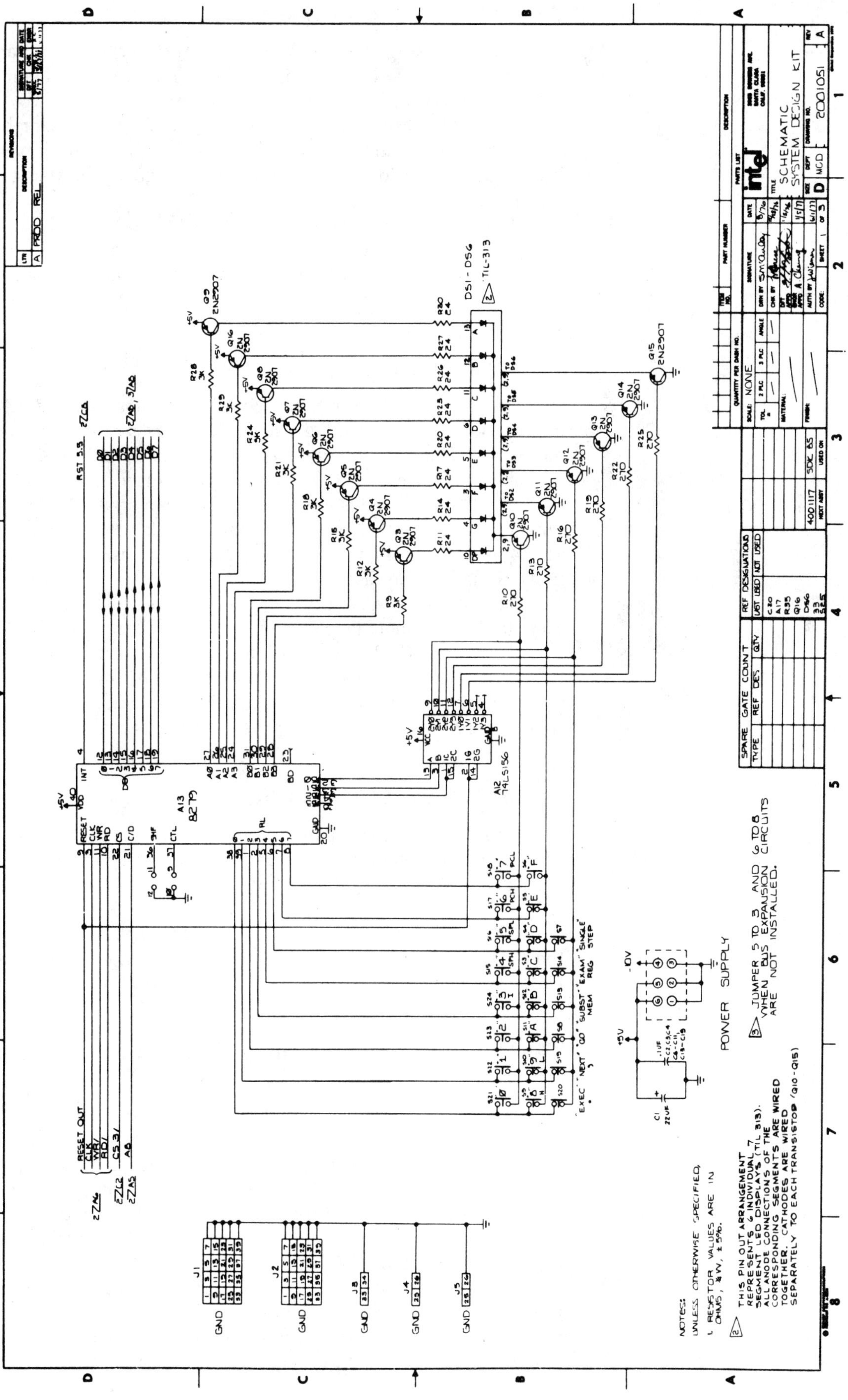

FIGURE 16-15 SDK-85 Development Board

Dot Matrix Printer Interface

The 8295 (Fig. 16-16) is designed to interface dot matrix printers to a microprocessor. This specialized chip contains a character generator for 64 ASCII characters encoded for a 7×7 dot matrix print head.

The 8295 eases the workload of the microprocessor by generating the necessary printer characters and the various control signals, such as paper feed signals. The job of the processor is basically limited to inputting the 8-bit data words.

The job can be further simplified through a DMA arrangement. The DRQ/CST output is meant for the 8257 DMA controller. With this additional interfacing, the microprocessor allows the printer a DMA channel for high speed data transfer.

The CRT Interface

An example of a relatively simple interface is one between a CRT and a microprocessor. Interfacing usually requires a combination of software and hardware. The hardware needed to interface a CRT and a microprocessor is probably much simpler than the software routines that had to be developed.

Figure 16-17 shows an interface between an 8085A and a CRT. The SOD output on the 8085A is only capable of driving a single TTL load. The MC1488 essentially changes the TTL level into an RS-232 level used to transmit data to the CRT.

The MC1489 takes the serial RS-232 levels from the CRT and reduces them to the TTL logic levels needed by the SID input of the 8085A.

There are three parts to the software routines that drive the CRT interface. One part identifies the baud rate of the received characters based upon the timing of a bits in the ASCII characters. The other two parts deal with transmitting and receiving the characters themselves.

The 8275 CRT Interface Chip

True control over a modern CRT requires complicated arrangements. The 8275 is designed to accommodate not only CRT control signals such as vertical and horizontal timing, but, in addition, it can handle a light pen input (Fig. 16-18).

The chip is also equipped to take advantage of a DMA controller through the **DMA request** output, DRQ. Because the interface chores are largely handled by the 8275, the microprocessor is not necessarily needed to display characters.

The Universal Synchronous-Asynchronous Receiver/Transmitter

The 8251A (Fig. 16-19) is an industry standard communications interface chip known as a **USART**, Universal Synchronous-Asynchronous Receiver Transmitter.

This chip does essentially what its name says it does, that is, it receives and transmits. It accepts the parallel format of data from the microprocessor and transmits it in a serial bit stream. The bit stream can be in a synchronous or asynchronous mode. It also accepts the serial input stream and outputs 8-bit parallel data to the microprocessor via the data bus.

The chip is controlled by the system software and must be initialized by the microprocessor for the desired communications interface. An 8-bit word from the microprocessor on the data bus will set the baud rate, character length, number of stop bits, synchronous or asynchronous mode, and parity.

8295
DOT MATRIX PRINTER CONTROLLER

- ■ **Interfaces Dot Matrix Printers to MCS-48™, MCS-80™, MCS-85™ Systems**

- ■ **40 Character Buffer On Chip**

- ■ **Serial or Parallel Communication with Host**

- ■ **DMA Transfer Capability**

- ■ **Programmable Character Density (10 or 12 Chararcters/Inch)**

- ■ **Programmable Print Intensity**

- ■ **Single or Double Width Printing**

- ■ **Programmable Multiple Line Feeds**

- ■ **3 Tabulations**

- ■ **2 General Purpose Outputs**

The Intel® 8295 Dot Matrix Printer Controller provides an interface for microprocessors to the LRC 7040 Series dot matrix impact printers. It may also be used as an interface to other similar printers.

The chip may be used in a serial or parallel communication mode with the host processor. Furthermore, it provides internal buffering of up to 40 characters and contains a 7 × 7 matrix character generator accommodating 64 ASCII characters.

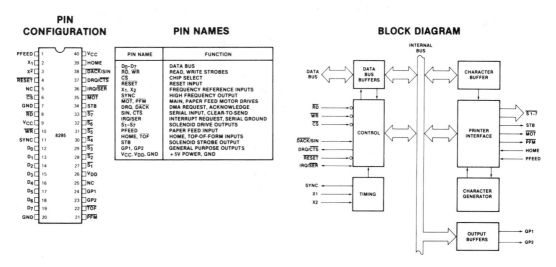

FIGURE 16-16 8295 Dot Matrix Printer Controller

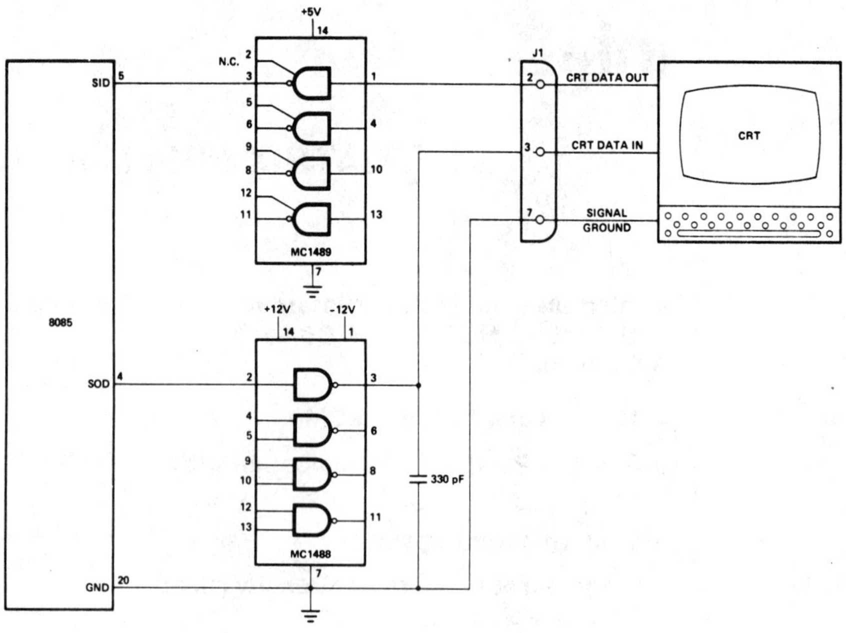

FIGURE 16-17 CRT Interface

✔ SELF-CHECK FOR SECTIONS 16-3, 16-4

6. The interface connection for I/O or a peripheral device is called an input or output _____.
7. What are the three basic ways that a microprocessor controls I/O ports?
8. What is the least complicated way of handling I/O?
9. A _____ strategy relies on the I/O devices to initiate the request for service.
10. The _____ process allows the buses to be taken over and used by the I/O devices exchanging data.
11. DMA operation is under the direction of a _____ _____.
12. What is a PPI?
13. What is the purpose of the MC1488 in the CRT interface?
14. What is the purpose of the MC1489 in the CRT interface?
15. Explain the purpose of a USART.

8275
PROGRAMMABLE CRT CONTROLLER

■ **Programmable Screen and Character Format**

■ **6 Independent Visual Field Attributes**

■ **11 Visual Character Attributes (Graphic Capability)**

■ **Cursor Control (4 Types)**

■ **Light Pen Detection and Registers**

■ **Fully MCS-80™ and MCS-85™ Compatible**

■ **Dual Row Buffers**

■ **Programmable DMA Burst Mode**

■ **Single +5V Supply**

■ **40-Pin Package**

The Intel® 8275 Programmable CRT Controller is a single chip device to interface CRT raster scan displays with Intel® microcomputer systems. Its primary function is to refresh the display by buffering the information from main memory and keeping track of the display position of the screen. The flexibility designed into the 8275 will allow simple interface to almost any raster scan CRT display with a minimum of external hardware and software overhead.

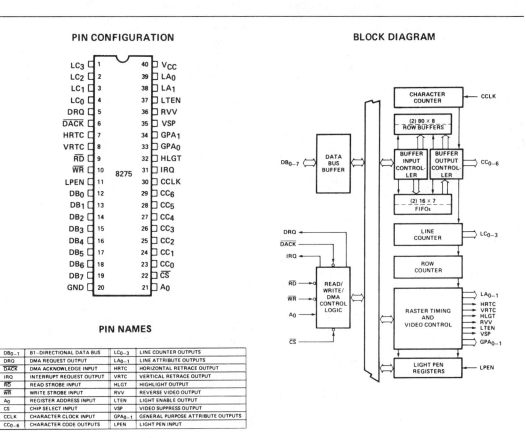

FIGURE 16-18 8275 Programmable CRT Controller

intel®

8251A
PROGRAMMABLE COMMUNICATION INTERFACE

- ■ **Synchronous and Asynchronous Operation**

- ■ **Synchronous 5-8 Bit Characters; Internal or External Character Synchronization; Automatic Sync Insertion**

- ■ **Asynchronous 5-8 Bit Characters; Clock Rate—1, 16 or 64 Times Baud Rate; Break Character Generation; 1, 1½, or 2 Stop Bits; False Start Bit Detection; Automatic Break Detect and Handling.**

- ■ **Synchronous Baud Rate — DC to 64K Baud**

- ■ **Asynchronous Baud Rate — DC to 19.2K Baud**

- ■ **Full Duplex, Double Buffered, Transmitter and Receiver**

- ■ **Error Detection — Parity, Overrun and Framing**

- ■ **Fully Compatible with 8080/8085 CPU**

- ■ **28-Pin DIP Package**

- ■ **All Inputs and Outputs are TTL Compatible**

- ■ **Single +5V Supply**

- ■ **Single TTL Clock**

The Intel® 8251A is the enhanced version of the industry standard, Intel® 8251 Universal Synchronous/Asynchronous Receiver/Transmitter (USART), designed for data communications with Intel's new high performance family of microprocessors such as the 8085. The 8251A is used as a peripheral device and is programmed by the CPU to operate using virtually any serial data transmission technique presently in use (including IBM "bi-sync"). The USART accepts data characters from the CPU in parallel format and then converts them into a continuous serial data stream for transmission. Simultaneously, it can receive serial data streams and convert them into parallel data characters for the CPU. The USART will signal the CPU whenever it can accept a new character for transmission or whenever it has received a character for the CPU. The CPU can read the complete status of the USART at any time. These include data transmission errors and control signals such as SYNDET, TxEMPTY. The chip is constructed using N-channel silicon gate technology.

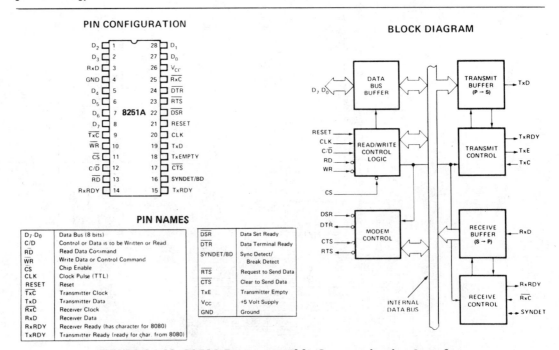

FIGURE 16-19 8251A Programmable Communication Interface

16-5   INTERFACING AND BUS STANDARDS

The real obstacle in interfacing to the microprocessor is the huge variety of devices that must interconnect with the microprocessor. It would be unrealistic to expect that all peripheral devices could be made to directly interface with the microprocessor. However, devices can be made to conform to an interface standard. The interface standards are in the form of *buses.*

Over the years, several bus standards have developed out of necessity. Some bus standards have been adopted by or developed for the Institute for Electrical and Electronic Engineers (IEEE). Other bus standards are the property of the manufacturer. If a manufacturer wishes to develop a peripheral, he is well-advised to build according to the bus standard used with the microprocessor.

The S-100 Bus

One of the first bus standards was developed by MITS, Inc., an early computer manufacturer. MITS built the Altair computer which used the 8080A. Their **S-100**, introduced in 1976, has since become the IEEE standard, **IEEE-696**.

The S-100 is a 100-pin, parallel circuit card with three power supplies, +8v, +18v, and −18v. The peripheral boards plug into the 100-pin connectors. Provisions are available for up to 16 DMA functions as well as 8- or 16-bit data bus connections. There are eight pins for interrupt lines, (4 through 11), making the board useful for a variety of microprocessors. In fact, the S-100 bus interface has been used with the 8085, 8086/88 as well as the MC6800 and MC68000 to name just a few applications.

There have been complaints of crosstalk, (mutual interference) between the clock and control lines and criticism that it is too easy to accidentally short the +8v and −18v lines (pins 51 and 52).

Today the S-100 bus is largely used in industrial and controller environments.

The PC Bus

The **PC bus** standard was actually developed for the first IBM PC. There are 20 address lines, allowing for 1 Megabyte of memory, and 8 data lines. Provisions are made for six interrupt levels as well as four DMA channels. The power supply voltages are +5V, −5V, +12V, and −12V.

The basic bus has from six to eight *expansion slots* into which circuit cards containing the peripherals can be plugged. Circuit card functions are, for example, CRT controllers, memory, disk drive controllers, and modems.

The PC bus is used on the PC XT, which uses the 8088, but has to be expanded for 16-bit microprocessors like the 8086 and 80286. The expanded PC bus is called the PC AT bus and has 16 data lines with eleven interrupt levels. The address bus is expanded to 28 bits.

The GPIB or IEEE-488

The General Purpose Interface Bus or **GPIB** was developed largely by the Hewlett Packard Co., where it is called the **HPIB**. Hewlett Packard makes a large variety of electronic instruments as well as computers. The bus was adopted in 1975 by the IEEE and is called the **IEEE-488** standard.

The IEEE-488 as a bus standard is somewhat different from the standards previously discussed. Not surprisingly, the bus can be used to connect a large number of instruments together and place them under microprocessor control.

TABLE 16–1 S-100 IEEE 696 Bus

**TABLE 16-1 S-100
IEEE 696 Bus**

PIN	SYMBOL	DESCRIPTION
1	+8V	8 volts, unregulated
2	+16V	16 volts, unregulated
3	XRDY	External ready input
4	V10	Vectored interrupt 0
5	V11	Vectored interrupt 1
6	V12	Vectored interrupt 2
7	V13	Vectored interrupt 3
8	V14	Vectored interrupt 4
9	V15	Vectored interrupt 5
10	V16	Vectored interrupt 6
11	V17	Vectored interrupt 7
12	NMI	Non-maskable interrupt
13	PWRFAIL	Power failure signal
14	DMA3	Master priority bit 3
15	A18	Extended address bit-18
16	A16	Extended address bit-16
17	A17	Extended address bit-17
18	SDSB	Status disable
19	CDSB	Control disable
20	GND	System ground
21	NDEF	Not to be defined
22	ADSB	Address disable
23	DOBSB	Data out disable
24		Master timing signal
25	pSTVAL	Status valid strobe
26	pHLDA	Hold acknowledge
27	RFU	Reserved for future use
28	RFU	Reserved for future use
29	A5	Address bit-5
30	A4	Address bit-4
31	A3	Address bit-3
32	A15	Address bit-15
33	A12	Address bit-12
34	A9	Address bit-9
35	DO1/DATA1	Data out bit-1
36	DO0/DATA0	Data out bit-0
37	A10	Address bit 10
38	DO4/DATA4	Data out bit-4, bidirectional data bit-4
39	DO5/DATA5	Data out bit-5, bidirectional data bit-5
40	DO6/DATA6	Data out bit-6, bidirectional data bit-6
41	DI2/DATA10	Data in bit-2, bidirectional data bit-10
42	DI3/DATA11	Data in bit-3, bidirectional data bit-11
43	DI7/DATA17	Data in bit-7, bidirectional data bit-17
44	sML	Status signal for current cycle
45	sOUT	Status signal for transferring data to an output device
46	sINP	Status signal for transferring data from an input device
47	sMEMR	Memory read
48	sHLTA	Status signal acknowledging HLT
49	CLOCK	2 MHz clock
50	GND	System ground
51	+8V	Unregulated 8 volts (common to pin 1)
52	−16V	16 volts negative, unregulated
53	GND	System ground
54	SLAVE CLR	Signal to reset but slaves
55	DMA0	Master priority bit-0
56	DMA1	Master priority bit-1
57	DMA2	Master priority bit-2

The standard specifies three types of devices to be connected to the bus, a **listener**, a **talker** and a **controller**. A *listener* is a device like a printer, CRT display, or a signal generator. These devices are receiving devices. The *talker* is a transmitter type such as a digital multi-meter, tape reader, or a frequency analyzer. Some peripherals can act as either type. The *controller* is the device that controls the listener and the talker. While all this sounds reasonably simple, the listeners and talkers must themselves have a degree of intelligence.

The controller communicates over the specified control lines by means of status words, instructions and/or address signals. The listeners and talkers must be able to understand and act on these signals.

The complicated data stream traveling on the GPIB has given rise to specialized interface chips. These chips interface devices with the GPIB bus. An example is the Motorola MC68488 (Fig. 16-20).

On the left in Figure 16-20 is the GPIB and on the right are the usual three microprocessor buses. The MC68488 can be thought of as a translator, allowing the microprocessor to interface with the standard IEEE 488 bus.

Intel Multibus

Intel developed the first **Multibus**, called Multibus I, for its own 8088 microprocessor. Later, the standard was expanded to accommodate the 8086 16-bit microprocessor.

But with the introduction of 32-bit microprocessors, simply making the data bus wider was not adequate. The 32-bit microprocessors have enormous capabilities, so the 32-bit buses include features like advanced interrupt facilities and bus arbitration schemes.

The Intel 32-bit bus is called the Multibus II and is actually a network of five different, but interconnected, buses. There is a main bus called the system bus, which carries both data and addresses. There is a bus for serial messaging, one for local bus extension used for local memory expansion, a multichannel DMA bus, and an I/O expansion bus.

Motorola VME Bus

The Motorola standard, the **VME**, will accommodate either 16- or 32-bit architectures. It is not as advanced as the Multibus II, but it has enjoyed wide popularity because of the ability to handle 32-bit data.

The VME bus consists of four individual buses as opposed to the five in Multibus II. The buses are: the data transfer bus, the arbitration bus, the interrupt bus, and the utility bus.

The VME bus uses asynchronous protocol for transfers which do not depend on the status of the clock. The Multibus II, on the other hand, is a synchronous bus that transfers data only on the leading edge of the clock.

The synchronous bus proponents claim that asynchronous buses are noisy and not as reliable, while the asynchronous group claims that the synchronous delays, while waiting for the proper clock cycle, are intolerable. In fact, however, both buses are widely and successfully used.

SEMICONDUCTORS

3501 ED BLUESTEIN BLVD., AUSTIN, TEXAS 78721

MC68488
(1.0 MHz)
MC68A488
(1.5 MHz)
MC68B488
(2.0 MHz)

MOS

(N-CHANNEL, SILICON-GATE
DEPLETION LOAD)

**GENERAL PURPOSE
INTERFACE ADAPTER**

GENERAL PURPOSE INTERFACE ADAPTER

The MC68488 GPIA provides the means to interface between the IEEE-488 standard instrument bus and the M6800 MPU Family. The GPIB instrument bus provides a means of controlling and moving data between instruments connected to it.

The MC68488 will automatically handle all handshake protocol needed on the instrument bus.

- Single- or Dual-Primary Address Recognition
- Secondary Address Capability (Talker or Listener)
- Complete Source and Acceptor Handshakes
- Programmable Interrupts
- RFD Holdoff to Prevent Data Overrun
- Operates with DMA Controller
- Serial- and Parallel-Polling Capability
- Talk-Only or Listen-Only Capability
- Selectable Automatic Features to Minimize Software
- Synchronization Trigger Output
- M6800 Bus Compatible

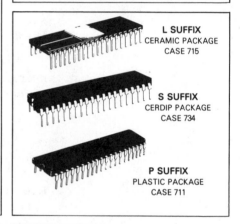

L SUFFIX
CERAMIC PACKAGE
CASE 715

S SUFFIX
CERDIP PACKAGE
CASE 734

P SUFFIX
PLASTIC PACKAGE
CASE 711

MAXIMUM RATINGS

Rating	Symbol	Value	Unit
Supply Voltage	V_{CC}	−0.3 to +7.0	V
Input Voltage	V_{in}	−0.3 to +7.0	V
Operating Temperature Range	T_A	0 to +70	°C
Storage Temperature Range	T_{stg}	−55 to +150	°C

THERMAL CHARACTERISTICS

Characteristics	Symbol	Value	Rating
Thermal Resistance Ceramic Cerdip Plastic	θ_{JA}	50 60 100	°C/W

This device contains circuitry to protect the inputs against damage due to high static voltages or electric fields; however, it is advised that normal precautions be taken to avoid application of any voltage higher than maximum rated voltages to this high-impedance circuit. Reliability of operation is enhanced if unused inputs are tied to an appropriate logic voltage (e.g., either V_{SS} or V_{CC}).

FIGURE 1 — PIN ASIGNMENT

V_{SS}	1	40	$\overline{IRQ}$
DMA Grant	2	39	RS2
$\overline{CS}$	3	38	RS1
$\overline{ASE}$	4	37	RS0
R/$\overline{W}$	5	36	$\overline{IB0}$
E	6	35	$\overline{IB1}$
DB0	7	34	$\overline{IB2}$
DB1	8	33	$\overline{IB3}$
DB2	9	32	$\overline{IB4}$
DB3	10	31	$\overline{IB5}$
DB4	11	30	$\overline{IB6}$
DB5	12	29	$\overline{IB7}$
DB6	13	28	T/$\overline{R}1$
DB7	14	27	T/$\overline{R}2$
DMA Request	15	26	$\overline{ATN}$
$\overline{DAV}$	16	25	$\overline{EOI}$
DAC	17	24	TRIG
RFD	18	23	$\overline{SRQ}$
$\overline{RESET}$	19	22	$\overline{REN}$
V_{CC}	20	21	$\overline{IFC}$

FIGURE 16-20 MC68488 General Purpose Interface Adapter

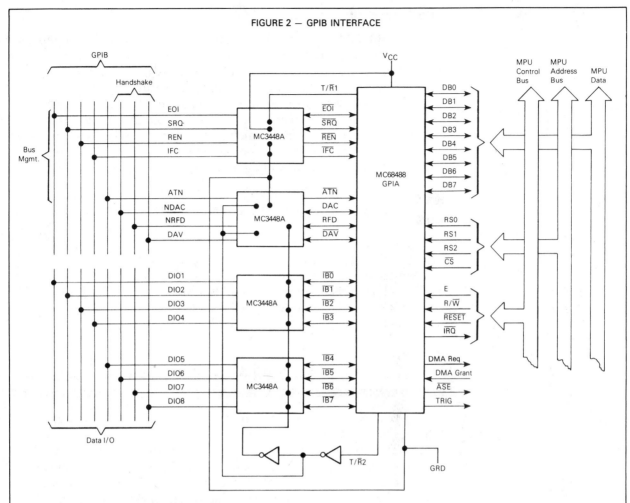

FIGURE 2 — GPIB INTERFACE

Note: The four MC3448A quad bus transceivers can be replaced by two MC3447 octal bus transceivers.

DC ELECTRICAL CHARACTERISTICS ($V_{CC} = 5.0$ Vdc $\pm 5\%$, $V_{SS} = 0$, $T_A = 0$ to 70°C unless otherwise noted)

Characteristic		Symbol	Min	Typ	Max	Unit
Input High Voltage		V_{IH}	$V_{SS} + 2.0$	—	V_{CC}	V
Input Low Voltage		V_{IL}	$V_{SS} - 0.3$	—	$V_{SS} + 0.8$	V
Input Leakage Current ($V_{in} = 0$ to 5.25 V)		I_{in}	—	1.0	2.5	μA
Three State (Off State) Input Current ($V_{in} = 0.4$ to 2.4 V)	D0-D7	I_{TSI}	—	2.0	10	μA
DC Output High Voltage ($I_{load} = -205\,\mu A$)	D0-D7	V_{OH}	$V_{SS} + 2.4$	—	—	V
DC Output Low Voltage ($I_{Load} = 1.6$ mA) ($I_{Load} = 3.2$ mA)	D0-D7 $\overline{SRQ}, \overline{IRQ}$	V_{OL}	— —	— —	$V_{SS} + 0.4$ $V_{SS} + 0.4$	V
Output Leakage Current (Off State) ($V_{OH} = 2.4$ V)	$\overline{SRQ}, \overline{IRQ}$	I_{LOH}	—	1.0	10	μA
Internal Power Dissipation		P_{INT}	—	600	750	mW
Input Capacitance ($V_{in} = 0$, $T_A = 25$°C, f = 1.0 MHz)	D0-D7 All Others	C_{in}	— —	— —	12.5 7.5	pF

 MOTOROLA *Semiconductor Products Inc.*

FIGURE 16-20 MC68488 General Purpose Interface Adapter (continued)

The IEEE-583

The **IEEE-583** standard is an example of a **card rack** or **crate** standard. The card rack has room for up to 25 modules. The modules plug into 86-pin connectors. Each crate has a controller module that is microprocessor-based. The IEEE-583 standard is widely used in industry and in nuclear power control.

The bus systems discussed in this chapter are representative of the bus systems in use today. This list does not pretend to cover them all. For example, there are other buses such as the Q-Bus, Nubus, and Futurebus, but nearly all buses are a variation on the types covered and you should be well equipped to understand any of the types you meet.

✔ SELF-CHECK FOR SECTION 16-5

16. The S-100 is a _____ _____.
17. What is the purpose of an expansion slot in a PC?
18. Which bus standard has a "listener" and a "talker?"
19. Which manufacturer developed Multibus?
20. Which manufacturer developed the VME bus?
21. Which bus standard is for card racks?

SUMMARY OF IDEAS

- Interfacing includes three major considerations; signal levels, synchronization, and compatible physical layout.
- The microprocessor can be directly connected to memory devices, if the memory chips are specifically designed for such connections.
- Some memory chips also have primitive I/O ports as well as storage.
- There are three basic ways that a microprocessor controls I/O ports: polling, interrupt, or Direct Memory Access.
- In polling, the microprocessor checks with each I/O device in turn, to see if service is required.
- Interrupt I/O relies on the I/O devices to initiate the request for service.
- The DMA process allows the buses to be taken over and used by I/O devices exchanging data.
- The programmable peripheral interface chip, (PPI). is programmable through the system software. The software controls the port configurations.
- The 8279 is an interface chip specifically for keyboard interfacing.
- The 8295 is designed to interface dot matrix printers to a microprocessor.
- The 8275 will interface a CRT to the microprocessor and handle details such as vertical and horizontal timing. It will also handle a light pen input.
- The 8251A, is an industry-standard, communications interface chip, a Universal Synchronous-Asynchronous Receiver Transmitter (USART).
- One of the first bus standards was the S-100, introduced in 1976, now the IEEE standard 696. The S-100 is a 100 pin parallel circuit card with three power supplies, +8v, +18v, and −18v.
- The PC bus standard was developed for the first IBM PC. There are 20 address lines, 8 data lines, 6 interrupt levels and 4 DMA channels. The power supply voltages are +5V, −5V, +12V, and −12V.

- The General Purpose Interface Bus or GPIB was developed largely by the Hewlett Packard Co. The bus was adopted in 1975 by the IEEE and is called the IEEE-488 standard.
- The IEEE-488 bus can be used to connect a large number of instruments together and place them under microprocessor control.
- Intel developed Multibus for its own microprocessors. Multibus I handles 8 and 16-bit processors while Multibus II is for the 32-bit line.
- The Motorola standard, the VME, will accommodate either 16 or 32-bit architectures.
- The IEEE-583 standard is an example of a card rack or *crate* standard.

CHAPTER QUESTIONS & PROBLEMS

True or False
1. There is no way to directly interface memory chips with microprocessor buses.
2. During polling, the microprocessor waits for an interrupt to start the polling sequence.
3. There are no standard microprocessors, but there are interface standards for microprocessors.
4. The GPIB, General Purpose Interface Bus, is so simple that the microprocessor usually plugs directly into it.
5. The USART is a general purpose communications interface chip.

Fill in the Blanks
6. The interface connection for an I/O or a peripheral device is called an input or output _____.
7. When the microprocessor continuously checks with each I/O device to see if service is required, the activity is called _____.
8. When the microprocessor allows the buses to be taken over and used by the I/O devices, this process is usually supervised with a _____ controller.
9. Programmable interface chips have configurable ports and can be controlled by loading 8-bit words. Loading the word is called _____.
10. The GPIB, General Purpose Interface Bus is also the IEEE standard _____.

Multiple Choice
11. Which of the following devices could be connected directly to the microprocessor data bus?
    a. Disk drives   c. ROM
    b. Printers   d. Keyboards

12. Select the most convincing reason why a microprocessor cannot be connected directly to a CRT.
    a. The microprocessor does not have enough control lines.
    b. The microprocessor operates at too great a speed.
    c. The microprocessor does not have enough driving power.
    d. The output of the processor is usually RS-232 while the CRT signals are at TTL level.

13. Which of the following is not true of polling?
   a. The length of the polling time is directly proportional to the number of devices polled.
   b. The processor always checks the I/O devices in a specific order.
   c. The requesting device has to wait until it is polled before it is serviced.
   d. The programmer can never be sure exactly when a device is polled.

14. Which of the following is not true of interrupts?
   a. They can occur at any point in the program.
   b. Interrupts can be implemented either as hardware or software.
   c. The programmer can never be sure exactly when a device will interrupt.
   d. Provisions cannot be made to suspend the program while performing the interrupt routine.

15. Which statement is not true of DMA?
   a. A priority can be established between DMA channels.
   b. DMA is not restricted to disk drives.
   c. Many DMA controllers are actually microprocessor chips.
   d. The DMA speed is controlled by the microprocessor.

16. Which of the following peripherals would not use a DMA channel?
   a. Printers
   b. Keyboards
   c. Disk Drives
   d. CRTs

17. Which statement does not apply to a USART?
   a. It can operate as a SIPO device (Serial-In, Parallel-Out).
   b. It will transmit synchronous protocol data.
   c. The number of stop bits cannot be controlled.
   d. It receives asynchronous protocol data.

18. Interfacing with this bus requires a 100 pin connector and peripherals adapted to +8V +18V, and −18V, best describes
   a. GPIB.
   b. IEEE-488.
   c. S-100.
   d. VME.

19. Interfacing with this bus requires that peripherals be designated as talkers and listeners, best describes
   a. IEEE-488.
   b. VME.
   c. Multibus.
   d. GPIB.

20. Which of the following buses was specifically designed for 32-bit microprocessors?
   a. Multibus II.
   b. VME.
   c. IEEE-488.
   d. PC Bus.

BIBLIOGRAPHY

Babbage, Henry Prevost. *Babbage's Calculating Engine.* Tomash Publishers, Los Angeles, CA., 1982.

Harold, Fred G. *Introduction to Computers.* West Publishing, 1984.

Hill, H., Arnold, R., Nichols, A. *Modern Data Processing.* John Wiley and Sons, 1978.

McGlinn, Daniel R. *Microprocessors.* John Wiley and Sons, 1976.

Esquire Magazine, "Tinkerings of Robert Noyce," Dec. 1983, p. 345, Wolfe, Thomas.

Malone, Michael S. *The Big Score.* Doubleday and Co., 1985.

Flamm, Kenneth. *Creating the Computer.* The Brookings Institute, 1988.

Soma, John T. *The Computer Industry.* Lexington Books, 1985.

Braun, E., MacDonald, S. *Revolution in Miniature.* Cambridge University Press, 1978.

Alessi, Stephen M., Trollip, Stanley R. *Computer Based Instruction.* Prentice-Hall, Inc., 1985.

Long, Larry, Long, Nancy. *Computers.* Prentice-Hall, Inc., 1986.

APPENDIX

MCM6256B

AC OPERATING CONDITIONS AND CHARACTERISTICS
($V_{CC} = 5.0$ V $\pm 10\%$, $T_A = 0$ to 70°C, Unless Otherwise Noted)

READ, WRITE, AND READ-MODIFY-WRITE CYCLES (See Notes 1, 2, 3, and 5)

Parameter	Symbol		MCM6256B-10		MCM6256B-12		MCM6256B-15		Unit	Notes
	Standard	Alternate	Min	Max	Min	Max	Min	Max		
Random Read or Write Cycle Time	t_{RELREL}	t_{RC}	190	—	220	—	260	—	ns	4, 5
Read-Write Cycle Time	t_{RELREL}	t_{RWC}	200	—	240	—	265	—	ns	4, 5
Read-Modify-Write Cycle Time	t_{RELREL}	t_{RMW}	220	—	260	—	310	—	ns	4, 5
Access Time from $\overline{RAS}$	t_{RELQV}	t_{RAC}	—	100	—	120	—	150	ns	6, 7
Access Time from $\overline{CAS}$	t_{CELQV}	t_{CAC}	—	50	—	60	—	75	ns	7, 8
Output Buffer and Turn-Off Delay	t_{CEHQZ}	t_{OFF}	5	25	5	30	5	35	ns	9
$\overline{RAS}$ Precharge Time	t_{REHREL}	t_{RP}	80	—	90	—	100	—	ns	—
$\overline{RAS}$ Pulse Width	t_{RELREH}	t_{RAS}	100	10,000	120	10,000	150	10,000	ns	—
$\overline{CAS}$ Pulse Width	t_{CELCEH}	t_{CAS}	50	10,000	60	10,000	75	10,000	ns	—
$\overline{RAS}$ to $\overline{CAS}$ Delay Time	t_{RELCEL}	t_{RCD}	25	50	25	60	25	75	ns	10
Row Address Setup Time	t_{AVREL}	t_{ASR}	0	—	0	—	0	—	ns	—
Row Address Hold Time	t_{RELAX}	t_{RAH}	15	—	15	—	15	—	ns	—
Column Address Setup Time	t_{AVCEL}	t_{ASC}	0	—	0	—	0	—	ns	—
Column Address Hold Time	t_{CELAX}	t_{CAH}	20	—	25	—	30	—	ns	—
Column Address Hold Time Referenced to $\overline{RAS}$	t_{RELAX}	t_{AR}	70	—	85	—	105	—	ns	—
Transition Time (Rise and Fall)	t_T	t_T	3	50	3	50	3	50	ns	—
Read Command Setup Time	t_{WHCEL}	t_{RCS}	0	—	0	—	0	—	ns	—
Read Command Hold Time Referenced to $\overline{CAS}$	t_{CEHWX}	t_{RCH}	0	—	0	—	0	—	ns	11
Read Command Hold Time Referenced to $\overline{RAS}$	t_{REHWX}	t_{RRH}	10	—	15	—	20	—	ns	11
Write Command Hold Time	t_{CELWH}	t_{WCH}	20	—	25	—	30	—	ns	—
Write Command Hold Time Referenced to $\overline{RAS}$	t_{RELWH}	t_{WCR}	70	—	85	—	105	—	ns	—
Write Command Pulse Width	t_{WLWH}	t_{WP}	20	—	25	—	30	—	ns	—
Write Command to $\overline{RAS}$ Lead Time	t_{WLREH}	t_{RWL}	25	—	35	—	45	—	ns	—
Write Command to $\overline{CAS}$ Lead Time	t_{WLCEH}	t_{CWL}	25	—	35	—	45	—	ns	—
Data in Setup Time	t_{DVCEL}	t_{DS}	0	—	0	—	0	—	ns	12
Data in Hold Time	t_{CELDX}	t_{DH}	20	—	25	—	30	—	ns	12
Data in Hold Time Referenced to $\overline{RAS}$	t_{RELDX}	t_{DHR}	70	—	85	—	105	—	ns	—
$\overline{CAS}$ to $\overline{RAS}$ Precharge Time	t_{CEHREL}	t_{CRP}	10	—	10	—	10	—	ns	—
$\overline{RAS}$ Hold Time	t_{CELREH}	t_{RSH}	50	—	60	—	75	—	ns	—
Refresh Period	t_{RVRV}	t_{RFSH}	—	4	—	4	—	4	ms	—

NOTES:
1. V_{IH} min and V_{IL} max are reference levels for measuring timing of input signals. Transition times are measured between V_{IH} and V_{IL}.
2. An initial pause of 200 μs is required after power-up followed by 8 $\overline{RAS}$ cycles before proper device operation is guaranteed.
3. The transition time specification applies for all input signals. In addition to meeting the transition rate specification, all input signals must transmit between V_{IH} and V_{IL} (or between V_{IL} and V_{IH}) in a monotonic manner.
4. The specifications for t_{RC} (min) and t_{RMW} (min) are used only to indicate cycle time at which proper operation over the full temperature range ($0°C \leq T_A \leq 70°C$) is assured.
5. AC measurements $t_T = 5.0$ ns.
6. Assumes that $t_{RCD} \leq t_{RCD}$ (max).
7. Measured with a current load equivalent to 2 TTL (-200 μA, $+4$ mA) loads and 100 pF with the data output trip points set at $V_{OH} = 2.0$ V and $V_{OL} = 0.8$ V.
8. Assumes that $t_{RCD} \geq t_{RCD}$ (max).
9. t_{OFF} (max) defines the time at which the output achieves the open circuit condition and is not referenced to output voltage levels.
10. Operation within the t_{RCD} (max) limit ensures that t_{RAC} (max) can be met. t_{RCD} (max) is specified as a reference point only; if t_{RCD} is greater than the specified t_{RCD} (max) limit, then access time is controlled exclusively by t_{CAC}.
11. Either t_{RRH} or t_{RCH} must be satisfied for a read cycle.
12. These parameters are referenced to $\overline{CAS}$ leading edge in random write cycles and to $\overline{WRITE}$ leading edge in delayed write or read-modify-write cycles.

THE INSTRUCTION SET

A.1 What The Instruction Set Is

A computer, no matter how sophisticated, can do only what it is instructed to do. A program is a sequence of instructions, each of which is recognized by the computer and causes it to perform an operation. Once a program is placed in memory space that is accessible to your CPU, you may run that same sequence of instructions as often as you wish to solve the same problem or to do the same function. The set of instructions to which the 8085A CPU will respond is permanently fixed in the design of the chip.

Each computer instruction allows you to initiate the performance of a specific operation. The 8085A implements a group of instructions that move data between registers, between a register and memory, and between a register and an I/O port. It also has arithmetic and logic instructions, conditional and unconditional branch instructions, and machine control instructions. The CPU recognizes these instructions only when they are coded in binary form.

A.2 Symbols and Abbreviations:

The following symbols and abbreviations are used in the subsequent description of the 8085A instructions:

Symbols	Meaning
accumulator	Register A
addr	16-bit address quantity
data	8-bit quantity
data 16	16-bit data quantity
byte 2	The second byte of the instruction
byte 3	The third byte of the instruction
port	8-bit address of an I/O device
r, r1, r2	One of the registers A, B, C, D, E, H, L
DDS, SSS	The bit pattern designating one of the registers A, B, C, D, E, H, L (DDD = destination, SSS = source):

DDD or SSS	Register Name
111	A
000	B
001	C
010	D
011	E
100	H
101	L

rp	One of the register pairs:

B represents the B, C pair with B as the high-order register and C as the low-order register;

D represents the D, E pair with D as the high-order register and E as the low-order register;

H represents the H, L pair with H as the high-order register and L as the low-order register;

SP represents the 16-bit stack pointer register.

RP	The bit pattern designating one of the register pairs B, D, H, SP:

RP	Register Pair
00	B-C
01	D-E
10	H-L
11	SP

rh	The first (high-order) register of a designated register pair.
rl	The second (low-order) register of a designated register pair.
PC	16-bit program counter register (PCH and PCL are used to refer to the high-order and low-order 8 bits respectively).
SP	16-bit program counter register (SPH and SPL are used to refer to the high-order and low-order 8 bits respectively).
r$_m$	Bit m of the register r (bits are number 7 through 0 from left to right).
LABEL	16-bit address of subroutine. The condition flags:
Z	Zero
S	Sign
P	Parity
CY	Carry
AC	Auxiliary Carry
( )	The contents of the memory location or registers enclosed in the parentheses.
←	"Is transferred to"
∧	Logical AND
∀	Exclusive OR
∧	Inclusive OR

THE INSTRUCTION SET

+	Addition
−	Two's complement subtraction
*	Multiplication
↔	"Is exchanged with"
⎯	The one's complement (e.g., $(\overline{A})$)
n	The restart number 0 through 7
NNN	The binary representation 000 through 111 for restart number 0 through 7 respectively.

The instruction set encyclopedia is a detailed description of the 8085A instruction set. Each instruction is described in the following manner:

1. The 8085 Family macro assembler format, consisting of the instruction mnemonic and operand fields, is printed in **BOLDFACE** on the first line.

2. The name of the instruction is enclosed in parentheses following the mnemonic.

3. The next lines contain a symbolic description of what the instruction does.

4. This is followed by a narrative description of the operation of the instruction.

5. The boxes describe the binary codes that comprise the machine language.

6. The last four lines contain information about the execution of the instruction. The number of machine cycles and states required to execute the instruction are listed first. If the instruction has two possible execution times, as in a conditional jump, both times are listed, separated by a slash. Next, data addressing modes are listed if applicable. The last line lists any of the five flags that are affected by the execution of the instruction.

A.3 Instruction and Data Formats

Memory used in the 8085 system is organized in 8-bit bytes. Each byte has a unique location in physical memory. That location is described by one of a sequence of 16-bit binary addresses. The 8085A can address up to 64K (K = 1024, or 2^{10}; hence, 64K represents the decimal number 65,536) bytes of memory, which may consist of both random-access, read-write memory (RAM), and read-only memory (ROM), which is also random-access.

Data in the 8085A is stored in the form of 8-bit binary integers:

```
              DATA WORD
        ┌──┬──┬──┬──┬──┬──┬──┬──┐
        │D₇│D₆│D₅│D₄│D₃│D₂│D₁│D₀│
        └──┴──┴──┴──┴──┴──┴──┴──┘
        MSB                  LSB
```

When a register or data word contains a binary number, it is necessary to establish the order in which the bits of the number are written. In the Intel 8085A, BIT 0 is referred to as the **Least Significant Bit (LSB)**, and BIT 7 (of an 8-bit number) is referred to as the **Most Significant Bit (MSB)**.

An 8085A program instruction may be one, two, or three bytes in length. Multiple-byte instructions must be stored in successive memory locations; the address of the first byte is always used as the address of the instruction. The exact instruction format will depend on the particular operation to be executed.

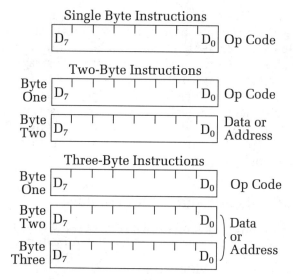

A.4 Addressing Modes:

Often the data that is to be operated on is stored in memory. When multi-byte numeric data is used, the data, like instructions, is stored in successive memory locations, with the least significant byte first, followed by increasingly significant bytes. The 8085A has four different modes for addressing data stored in memory or in registers:

- Direct — Bytes 2 and 3 of the instruction contain the exact memory address of the data item (the low-order bits of the address are in byte 2, the high-order bits in byte 3).

- Register — The instruction specifies the register or register pair in which the data is located.

- Register Indirect — The instruction specifies a register pair which contains the memory address where the data is located (the high-order bits of the address are in the first register of the pair, the low-order bits in the second).

THE INSTRUCTION SET

• Immediate — The instruction contains the data itself. This is either an 8-bit quantity or a 16-bit quantity (least significant byte first, most significant byte second).

Unless directed by an interrupt or branch institution, the execution of instructions proceeds through consecutively increasing memory locations. A branch instruction can specify the address of the next instruction to be executed in one of two ways:

• Direct — The branch instruction contains the address of the next instruction to be executed. (Except for the 'RST' instruction, byte 2 contains the low-order address and byte 3 the high-order address.)

• Register Indirect — The branch instruction indicates a register-pair which contains the address of the next instruction to be executed. (The high-order bits of the address are in the first register of the pair, the low-order bits in the second.)

The RST instruction is a special one-byte call instruction (usually used during interrupt sequences). RST includes a three-bit field; program control is transferred to the instruction whose address is eight times the contents of this three-bit field.

A.5 Condition Flags:

There are five condition flags associated with the execution of instructions on the 8085A. They are Zero, Sign, Parity, Carry, and Auxiliary Carry. Each is represented by a 1-bit register (or flip-flop) in the CPU. A flag is set by forcing the bit to 1; it is reset by forcing the bit to 0.

Unless indicated otherwise, when an instruction affects a flag, it affects it in the following manner:

Zero: If the result of an instruction has the value of 0, this flag is set; otherwise it is reset.

Sign: If the most significant bit of the result of the operation has the value 1, this flag is set; otherwise it is reset.

Parity: If the modulo 2 sum of the bits of the result of the operation is 0, (i.e., if the result has even parity), this flag is set; otherwise it is reset (i.e., if the result has odd parity).

Carry: If the instruction resulted in a carry (from addition), or a borrow (from subtraction or a comparison) out of the high-order bit, this flag is set; otherwise it is reset.

Auxiliary Carry: If the instruction caused a carry out of bit 3 and into bit 4 of the resulting value, the auxiliary carry is set; otherwise it is reset. This flag is affected by single-precision additions, subtractions, increments, decrements, comparisons, and logical operations, but is principally used with additions and increments preceding a DAA (Decimal Adjust Accumulator) instruction.

A.6 Instruction Set Encyclopedia

In the ensuing dozen pages, the complete 8085A instruction set is described, grouped in order under five different functional headings, as follows:

1. **Data Transfer Group** — Moves data between registers or between memory locations and registers. Includes moves, loads, stores, and exchanges. (See below.)

2. **Arithmetic Group** — Adds, subtracts, increments, or decrements data in registers or memory. (See page 5-13.)

3. **Logic Group** — ANDs, ORs, XORs, compares, rotates, or complements data in registers or between memory and a register. (See page 5-16.)

4. **Branch Group** — Initiates conditional or unconditional jumps, calls, returns, and restarts. (See page 5-20.)

5. **Stack, I/O, and Machine Control Group** — Includes instructions for maintaining the stack, reading from input ports, writing to output ports, setting and reading interrupt masks, and setting and clearing flags. (See page 5-22.)

The formats described in the encyclopedia reflect the assembly language processed by Intel-supplied assembler, used with the Intellac® development systems.

A.6.1 Data Transfer Group

This group of instructions transfers data to and from registers and memory. **Condition flags are not affected by any instruction in this group.**

---

* All mnemonics copyrighted © Intel Corporation 1976.

THE INSTRUCTION SET

MOV r1, r2   (Move Register)
(r1) ← (r2)
The content of register r2 is moved to register r1.

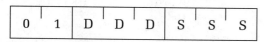

0	1	D	D	D	S	S	S

Cycles: 1
States: 4 (8085), 5 (8080)
Addressing: register
Flags: none

MOV r, M   (Move from memory)
(r) ← ((H) (L))
The content of the memory location, whose address is in registers H and L, is moved to register r.

0	1	D	D	D	1	1	0

Cycles: 2
States: 7
Addressing: reg. indirect
Flags: none

MOV M, r   (Move to memory)
((H) (L)) ← (r)
The content of register r is moved to the memory location whose address is in registers H and L.

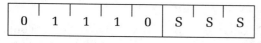

0	1	1	1	0	S	S	S

Cycles: 2
States: 7
Addressing: reg. indirect
Flags: none

MVI r, data   (Move immediate)
(r) ← (byte 2)
The content of byte 2 of the instruction is moved to register r.

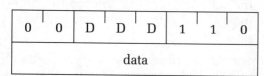

0	0	D	D	D	1	1	0
data							

Cycles: 2
States: 7
Addressing: immediate
Flags: none

MVI M, data   (Move to memory immediate)
((H) (L)) ← (byte 2)
The content of byte 2 of the instruction is moved to the memory location whose address is in registers H and L.

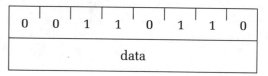

0	0	1	1	0	1	1	0
data							

Cycles: 3
States: 10
Addressing: immed./reg. indirect
Flags: none

LXI rp, data 16   (Load register pair immediate)
(rh) ← (byte 3),
(rl) ← (byte 2)
Byte 3 of the instruction is moved into the high-order register (rh) of the register pair rp. Byte 2 of the instruction is moved into the low-order register (rl) of the register pair rp.

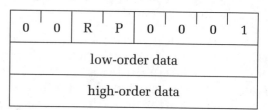

0	0	R	P	0	0	0	1
low-order data							
high-order data							

Cycles: 3
States: 10
Addressing: immediate
Flags: none

LDA addr   (Load Accumulator direct)
(A) ← ((byte 3)(byte 2))
The content of the memory location, whose address is specified in byte 2 and byte 3 of the instruction, is moved to register A.

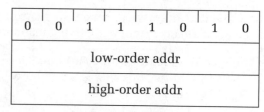

0	0	1	1	1	0	1	0
low-order addr							
high-order addr							

Cycles: 4
States: 13
Addressing: direct
Flags: none

THE INSTRUCTION SET

STA addr   (Store accumulator direct)

((byte 3)(byte 2)) ← (A)

The content of the accumulator is moved to the memory location whose address is specified in byte 2 and byte 3 of the instruction.

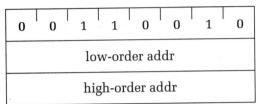

0	0	1	1	0	0	1	0
low-order addr							
high-order addr							

Cycles: 4
States: 13
Addressing: direct
Flags: none

LHLD addr   (Load H and L direct)

(L) ← ((byte 3)(byte 2))

(H) ← (byte 3)(byte 2) + 1)

The content of the memory location, whose address is specified in byte 2 and byte 3 of the instruction, is moved to register L. The content of the memory location at the succeeding address is moved to register H.

0	0	1	0	1	0	1	0
low-order addr							
high-order addr							

Cycles: 5
States: 16
Addressing: direct
Flags: none

SHLD addr   (Store H and L direct)

((byte 3)(byte 2)) ← (L)

(byte 3)(byte 2)+1) ← (H)

The content of register L is moved to the memory location whose address is specified in byte 2 and byte 3. The content of register H is moved to the succeeding memory location.

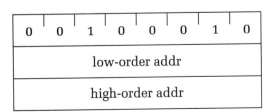

0	0	1	0	0	0	1	0
low-order addr							
high-order addr							

Cycles: 5
States: 16
Addressing: direct
Flags: none

LDAX rp   (Load accumulator indirect)

(A) ← ((rp))

The content of the memory location, whose address is in the register pair rp, is moved to register A. Note: only register pairs rp=B (registers B and C) or rp = D (registers D and E) may be specified.

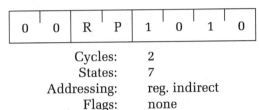

0	0	R	P	1	0	1	0

Cycles: 2
States: 7
Addressing: reg. indirect
Flags: none

STAX rp   (Store accumulator indirect)

((rp)) ← (A)

The content of register A is moved to the memory location whose address is in the register pair rp. Note: only register pairs rp=B (registers B and C) or rp = D (registers D and E) may be specified.

0	0	R	P	0	0	1	0

Cycles: 2
States: 7
Addressing: reg. indirect
Flags: none

XCHG   (Exchange H and L with D and E)

(H) ↔ (D)

(L) ↔ (E)

The contents of registers H and L are exchanged with the contents of registers D and E.

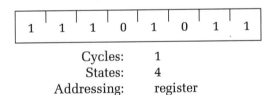

1	1	1	0	1	0	1	1

Cycles: 1
States: 4
Addressing: register
Flags: none

THE INSTRUCTION SET

A.6.2 Arithmetic Group

This group of instructions performs arithmetic operations on data in registers and memory.

Unless indicated otherwise, all instructions in this group affect the Zero, Sign, Parity, Carry, and Auxiliary Carry flags according to the standard rules.

All subtraction operations are performed via two's complement arithmetic and set the carry flag to one to indicate a borrow and clear it to indicate no borrow.

ADD r   (Add register)

(A) ← (A) + (r)

The content of register r is added to the content of the accumulator. The result is placed in the accumulator.

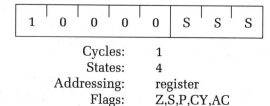

1	0	0	0	0	S	S	S

    Cycles: 1
    States: 4
    Addressing: register
    Flags: Z,S,P,CY,AC

ADD M   (Add memory)

(A) ← (A) + ((H) (L))

The content of the memory location whose address is contained in the H and L registers is added to the content of the accumulator. The result is placed in the accumulator.

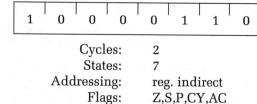

1	0	0	0	0	1	1	0

    Cycles: 2
    States: 7
    Addressing: reg. indirect
    Flags: Z,S,P,CY,AC

ADI data   (Add immediate)

(A) ← (A) + (byte 2)

The content of the second byte of the instruction is added to the content of the accumulator. The result is placed in the accumulator.

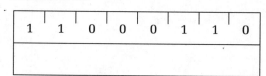

1	1	0	0	0	1	1	0

    Cycles: 2
    States: 7
    Addressing: immediate
    Flags: Z,S,P,CY,AC

ADC r   (Add register with carry)

(A) ← (A) + (r) + (CY)

The content of register r and the content of the carry bit are added to the content of the accumulator. The result is placed in the accumulator.

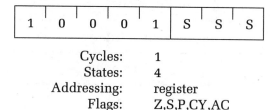

1	0	0	0	1	S	S	S

    Cycles: 1
    States: 4
    Addressing: register
    Flags: Z,S,P,CY,AC

ADC M   (Add memory with carry)

(A) ← (A) + ((H) (L)) + (CY)

The content of the memory location whose address is contained in the H and L registers and the content of the CY flag are added to the accumulator. The result is placed in the accumulator.

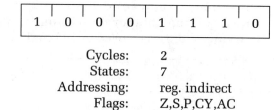

1	0	0	0	1	1	1	0

    Cycles: 2
    States: 7
    Addressing: reg. indirect
    Flags: Z,S,P,CY,AC

ACI data   (Add immediate with carry)

(A) ← (A) + (byte 2) + (CY)

The content of the second byte of the instruction and the content of the CY flag are added to the contents of the accumulator. The result is placed in the accumulator.

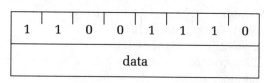

1	1	0	0	1	1	1	0
data							

    Cycles: 2
    States: 7
    Addressing: immediate
    Flags: Z,S,P,CY,AC

THE INSTRUCTION SET

SUB r   (Subtract Register)

(A) ← (A) − (r)

The content of register r is subtracted from the content of the accumulator. The result is placed in the accumulator.

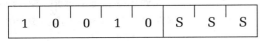

1	0	0	1	0	S	S	S

Cycles: 1
States: 4
Addressing: register
Flags: Z,S,P,CY,AC

SUB M   (Subtract memory)

(A) ← (A) − ((H) (L))

The content of the memory location whose address in contained in the H and L registers is subtracted from the content of the accumulator. The result is placed in the accumulator.

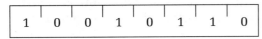

1	0	0	1	0	1	1	0

Cycles: 2
States: 7
Addressing: reg. indirect
Flags: Z,S,P,CY,AC

SUI data   (Subtract immediate)

(A) ← (A) − (byte 2)

The content of the second byte of the instruction is subtracted from the content of the accumulator. The result is placed in the accumulator.

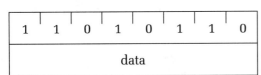

1	1	0	1	0	1	1	0
data							

Cycles: 2
States: 7
Addressing: immediate
Flags: Z,S,P,CY,AC

SBB r   (Subtract register with borrow)

(A) ← (A) − (r) − (CY)

The content of register r and the content of the CY flag are both subtracted from the accumulator. The result is placed in the accumulator.

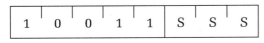

1	0	0	1	1	S	S	S

Cycles: 1
States: 4
Addressing: register
Flags: Z,S,P,CY,AC

SBB M   (Subtract memory with borrow)

(A) ← (A) − ((H) (L)) − (CY)

The content of the memory location whose address is contained in the H and L registers and the content of the CY flag are both subtracted from the accumulator. The result is placed in the accumulator.

1	0	0	1	1	1	1	0

Cycles: 2
States: 7
Addressing: reg. indirect
Flags: Z,S,P,CY,AC

SBI data   (Subtract immediate with borrow)

(A) ← (A) − (byte 2) − (CY)

The content of the second byte of the instruction and the contents of the CY flag are both subtracted from the accumulator. The result is placed in the accumulator.

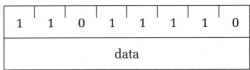

1	1	0	1	1	1	1	0
data							

Cycles: 2
States: 7
Addressing: immediate
Flags: Z,S,P,CY,AC

INR r   (Increment register)

(r) ← (r) + 1

The content of register r is incremented by one. Note: All condition flags **except CY** are affected.

0	0	D	D	D	1	0	0

Cycles: 1
States: 4(8085), 5(8080)
Addressing: register
Flags: Z,S,P,AC

INR M   (Increment memory)

((H) (L)) ← ((H) (L)) + 1

The content of the memory location whose address is contained in the H and L registers is incremented by one. Note: All condition flags **except CY** are affected.

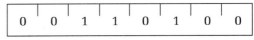

0	0	1	1	0	1	0	0

Cycles: 3
States: 10
Addressing: reg. indirect
Flags: Z,S,P,AC

THE INSTRUCTION SET

DCR r   (Decrement register)

(r) ← (r) − 1

The content of register r is decremented by one.
Note: All condition flags **except CY** are affected.

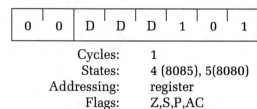

0	0	D	D	D	1	0	1

Cycles: 1
States: 4 (8085), 5(8080)
Addressing: register
Flags: Z,S,P,AC

DCR M   (Decrement memory)

((H) (L)) ← ((H) (L)) − 1

The content of the memory location whose
address is contained in the H and L registers is
decremented by one. Note: All condition flags
except CY are affected.

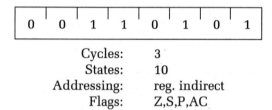

0	0	1	1	0	1	0	1

Cycles: 3
States: 10
Addressing: reg. indirect
Flags: Z,S,P,AC

INX rp   (Increment register pair)

(rh)(rl) ← (rh)(rl) + 1

The content of the register pair rp is
incremented by one. Note: **No condition flags
are affected.**

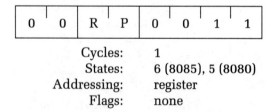

0	0	R	P	0	0	1	1

Cycles: 1
States: 6 (8085), 5 (8080)
Addressing: register
Flags: none

DCX rp   (Decrement register pair)

(rh)(rl) ← (rh)(rl) − 1

The content of the register pair rp is
decremented by one. Note: **No condition flags
are affected.**

0	0	R	P	1	0	1	1

Cycles: 1
States: 6 (8085), 5 (8080)
Addressing: register
Flags: none

DAD rp   (Add register pair to H and L)

((H) (L)) ← ((H) (L)) + (rh)(rl)

The content of the register pair rp is added to
the content of the register pair H and L. The
result is placed in the register pair H and L.
Note: **Only the CY flag is affected.** It is set if
there is a carry out of the double precision
add; otherwise it is reset.

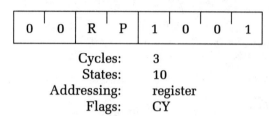

0	0	R	P	1	0	0	1

Cycles: 3
States: 10
Addressing: register
Flags: CY

DAA   (Decimal Adjust Accumulator)

The 8-bit number in the accumulator is
adjusted to form two, 4-bit Binary-Coded-
Decimal digits by the following process:

1. If the value of the least significant 4 bits of
   the accumulator is greater than 9 **or** if the
   AC flag is set, 6 is added to the accumulator.

2. If the value of the most significant 4 bits of
   the accumulator is now greater than 9, **or**
   the CY flag is set, 6 is added to the most
   significant 4 bits of the accumulator.

NOTE: All flags are affected.

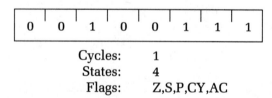

0	0	1	0	0	1	1	1

Cycles: 1
States: 4
Flags: Z,S,P,CY,AC

A.6.3 Logical Group

This group of instructions performs logical
(Boolean) operations on data in registers and
memory and on condition flags.

Unless indicated otherwise, all instructions in this
group affect the Zero, Sign, Parity, Auxiliary Carry,
and Carry flags according to the standard rules.

THE INSTRUCTION SET

ANA r   (AND register)

(A) ← (A) ∧ (r)

The content of register r is logically ANDed with the content of the accumulator. The result is placed in the accumulator. **The CY flag is cleared and AC is set (8085). The CY flag is cleared and AC is set to the OR'ing of bits 3 of the operands (8080).**

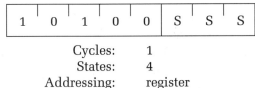

Cycles:	1
States:	4
Addressing:	register
Flags:	Z,S,P,CY,AC

ANA M   (AND memory)

(A) ← (A) ∧ ((H) (L))

The content of the memory location whose address is contained in the H and L registers is logically ANDed with the content of the accumulator. The result is placed in the accumulator. **The CY flag is cleared and the AC is set (8085). The CY flag is cleared and AC is set to the OR'ing of bits 3 of the operands (8080).**

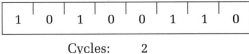

Cycles:	2
States:	7
Addressing:	reg. indirect
Flags:	Z,S,P,CY,AC

ANI data   (AND immediate)

(A) ← (A) ∧ (byte 2)

The content of the second byte of the instruction is logically ANDed with the contents of the accumulator. The result is placed in the accumulator. **The CY flag is cleared and AC is set (8085). The CY flag is cleared and AC is set to the OR'ing of bits 3 of the operands (8080).**

Cycles:	2
States:	7
Addressing:	immediate
Flags:	Z,S,P,CY,AC

XRA r   (Exclusive OR register)

(A) ← (A) ∀ (r)

The content of the register r is exclusive-OR'd with the content of the accumulator. The result is placed in the accumulator. **The CY and AC flags are cleared.**

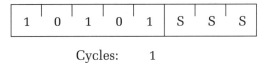

Cycles:	1
States:	4
Addressing:	register
Flags:	Z,S,P,CY,AC

XRA M   (Exclusive OR memory)

(A) ← (A) ∀ ((H) (L))

The content of the memory location whose address is contained in the H and L registers is exclusive-OR'd with the content of the accumulator. The result is placed in the accumulator. **The CY and AC flags are cleared.**

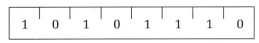

Cycles:	2
States:	7
Addressing:	reg. indirect
Flags:	Z,S,P,CY,AC

XRI data   (Exclusive OR immediate)

(A) ← (A) ∀ (byte 2)

The content of the second byte of the instruction is exclusive-OR'd with the content of the accumulator. The result is placed in the accumulator. **The CY and AC flags are cleared.**

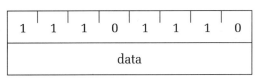

Cycles:	2
States:	7
Addressing:	immediate
Flags:	Z,S,P,CY,AC

THE INSTRUCTION SET

ORA r   (OR register)

(A) ← (A) ∨ (r)

The content of register r is inclusive-OR'd with the content of the accumulator. The result is placed in the accumulator. **The CY and AC flags are cleared.**

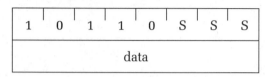

1	0	1	1	0	S	S	S
data

Cycles:	1
States:	4
Addressing:	register
Flags:	Z,S,P,CY,AC

ORA M   (OR memory)

(A) ← (A) ∨ ((H) (L))

The content of the memory location whose address is contained in the H and L registers is inclusive-OR'd with the content of the accumulator. The result is placed in the accumulator. **The CY and AC flags are cleared.**

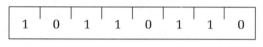

1	0	1	1	0	1	1	0

Cycles:	2
States:	7
Addressing:	reg. indirect
Flags:	Z,S,P,CY,AC

ORI data   (OR immediate)

(A) ← (A) ∨ (byte 2)

The content of the second byte of the instruction is inclusive-OR'd with the content of the accumulator. The result is placed in the accumulator. **The CY and AC flags are cleared.**

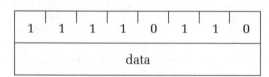

1	1	1	1	0	1	1	0
data

Cycles:	2
States:	7
Addressing:	immediate
Flags:	Z,S,P,CY,AC

CMP r   (Compare register)

(A) − (r)

The content of register r is subtracted from the accumulator. The accumulator remains unchanged. The condition flags are set as a result of the subtraction. **The Z flag is set to 1 if (A) = (r). The CY flag is set to 1 if (A) < (r).**

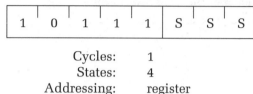

1	0	1	1	1	S	S	S

Cycles:	1
States:	4
Addressing:	register
Flags:	Z,S,P,CY,AC

CMP M   (Compare memory)

(A) − ((H) (L))

The content of the memory location whose address is contained in the H and L registers is subtracted from the accumulator. The accumulator remains unchanged. The condition flags are set as a result of the subtraction. **The Z flag is set to 1 if (A) = ((H) (L)). The CY flag is set to 1 if (A) < ((H) (L)).**

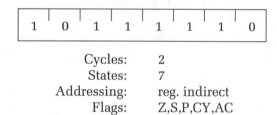

1	0	1	1	1	1	1	0

Cycles:	2
States:	7
Addressing:	reg. indirect
Flags:	Z,S,P,CY,AC

CPI data   (Compare immediate)

(A) − (byte 2)

The content of the second byte of the instruction is subtracted from the accumulator. The condition flags are set as a result of the subtraction. **The Z flag is set to 1 if (A) = (byte 2). The CY flag is set to 1 if (A) < (byte 2).**

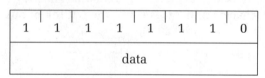

1	1	1	1	1	1	1	0
data

Cycles:	2
States:	7
Addressing:	immediate
Flags:	Z,S,P,CY,AC

THE INSTRUCTION SET

RLC   (Rotate left)

$(A_n+1) \leftarrow (A_n); (A_0) \leftarrow (A_7)$

The content of the accumulator is rotated left one position. The low-order bit and the CY flag are both set to the value shifted out of the high-order bit position. **Only the CY flag is affected.**

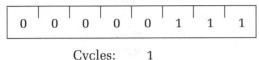

0	0	0	0	0	1	1	1

Cycles: 1
States: 4
Flags: CY

RRC   (Rotate right)

$(A_n) \leftarrow (A_n+1); (A_7) \leftarrow (A_0)$
$(CY) \leftarrow (A_0)$

The content of the accumulator is rotated right one position. The high-order bit and the CY flag are both set to the value shifted out of the low-order bit position. **Only the CY flag is affected.**

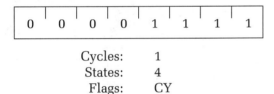

0	0	0	0	1	1	1	1

Cycles: 1
States: 4
Flags: CY

RAL   (Rotate left through carry)

$(A_n+1) \leftarrow (A_n); (CY) \leftarrow (A_7)$
$(A_0) \leftarrow (CY)$

The content of the accumulator is rotated left one position through the CY flag. The low order bit is set equal to the CY flag and the CY flag is set to the value shifted out of the high order bit. **Only the CY flag is affected.**

0	0	0	1	0	1	1	1

Cycles: 1
States: 4
Flags: CY

RAR   (Rotate right through carry)

$(A_n) \leftarrow (A_n+1); (CY) \leftarrow (A_0)$
$(A_7) \leftarrow (CY)$

The content of the accumulator is rotated right one position through the CY flag. The high-order bit is set equal to the CY flag and the CY flag is set to the value shifted out of the low-order bit. **Only the CY flag is affected.**

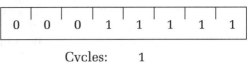

0	0	0	1	1	1	1	1

Cycles: 1
States: 4
Flags: CY

CMA   (Complement accumulator)

$(A) \leftarrow (\overline{A})$

The contents of the accumulator are complemented (zero bits become 1, one bits become 0). **No flags are affected.**

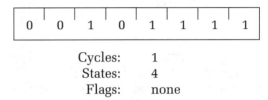

0	0	1	0	1	1	1	1

Cycles: 1
States: 4
Flags: none

CMC   (Complement carry)

$(CY) \leftarrow (\overline{CY})$

The CY flag is complemented. **No flags are affected.**

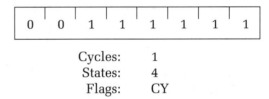

0	0	1	1	1	1	1	1

Cycles: 1
States: 4
Flags: CY

STC   (Set carry)

$(CY) \leftarrow 1$

The CY flag is set to 1. **No other flags are affected.**

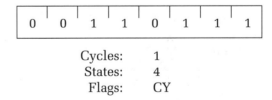

0	0	1	1	0	1	1	1

Cycles: 1
States: 4
Flags: CY

A.6.4 Branch Group

This group of instructions alter normal sequential program flow.

Condition flags are not affected by any instruction in this group.

The two types of branch instructions are unconditional and conditional. Unconditional transfers simply perform the specified operation on

THE INSTRUCTION SET

register PC (the program counter). Conditional transfers examine the status of one of the four processor flags to determine if the specified branch is to be executed. The conditions that may be specified are as follows:

Condition		CCC
NZ —	not zero (Z=0)	000
Z —	zero (Z=1)	001
NC —	no carry (CY=0)	010
C —	carry (CY=1)	011
PO —	parity odd (P=0)	100
PE —	parity even (P=1)	101
P —	plus (S=0)	110
M —	minus (S=1)	111

JMP addr   (Jump)

(PC) ← (byte 3) (byte 2)

Control is transferred to the instruction whose address is specified in byte 3 and byte 2 of the current instruction.

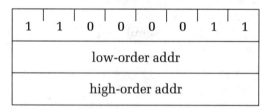

1	1	0	0	0	0	1	1

low-order addr

high-order addr

Cycles:	3
States:	10
Addressing	immediate
Flags:	none

Jcondition addr   (conditional jump)

If (CCC),

(PC) ← (byte 3) (byte 2)

If the specified condition is true, control is transferred to the instruction whose address is specified in byte 3 and byte 2 of the current instruction; otherwise, control continues sequentially.

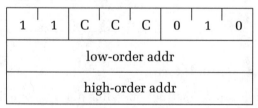

1	1	C	C	C	0	1	0

low-order addr

high-order addr

Cycles:	2/3 (8085), 3 (8080)
States:	7/10 (8085), 10 (8080)
Addressing:	immediate
Flags:	none

CALL addr   (Call)

((SP) − 1) ← (PCH)

((SP) − 2) ← (PCL)

(SP) ← (SP) − 2

(PC) ← (byte 3) (byte 2)

The high-order eight bits of the next instruction address are moved to the memory location whose address is one less than the content of register SP. The low-order eight bits of the next instruction address are moved to the memory location whose address is two less than the content of register SP. The content of register SP is decremented by 2. Control is transferred to the instruction whose address is specified in byte 3 and byte 2 of the current instruction.

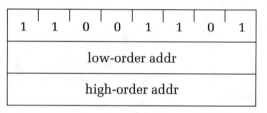

1	1	0	0	1	1	0	1

low-order addr

high-order addr

Cycles:	5
States:	18 (8085), 17 (8080)
Addressing:	immediate/ reg. indirect
Flags:	none

Ccondition addr   (Condition call)

If (CCC),

((SP) − 1) ← (PCH)

((SP) − 2) ← (PCL)

(SP) ← (SP) − 2

(PC) ← (byte 3) (byte 2)

If the specified condition is true, the actions specified in the CALL instruction (see above) are performed; otherwise, control continues sequentially.

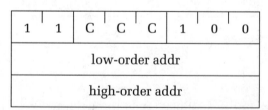

1	1	C	C	C	1	0	0

low-order addr

high-order addr

Cycles:	2/5 (8085), 3/5 (8080)
States:	9/18 (8085), 11/17 (8080)
Addressing:	immediate/ reg. indirect
Flags:	none

THE INSTRUCTION SET

RET   (Return)

(PCH) ← ((SP));

(PCH) ← ((SP) + 1);

(SP) ← (SP) + 2;

The content of the memory location whose address is specified in register SP is moved to the low-order eight bits of register PC. The content of the memory location whose address is one more than the content of register SP is moved to the high-order eight bits of register PC. The content of register SP is incremented by 2.

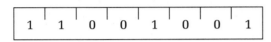

1	1	0	0	1	0	0	1

Cycles:	3
States:	10
Addressing:	reg. indirect
Flags:	none

Rcondition   (Conditional return)

If (CCC),

(PCH) ← ((SP))

(PCH) ← ((SP) + 1)

(SP) ← (SP) + 2

If the specified condition is true, the actions specified in the RET instruction (see above) are performed; otherwise, control continues sequentially.

1	1	C	C	C	0	0	0

Cycles:	1/3
States:	6/12 (8085), 5/11 (8080)
Addressing:	reg. indirect
Flags:	none

RST n   (Restart)

((SP) − 1) ← (PCH)

((SP) − 2) ← (PCL)

(SP) ← (SP) − 2

(PC) ← 8 * (NNN)

The high-order eight bits of the next instruction address are moved to the memory location whose address is one less than the content of register SP. The low-order eight bits of the next instruction address are moved to the memory location whose address is two less than the content of register SP. The content of register SP is decremented by two. Control is transferred to the instruction whose address is eight times the content of NNN.

1	1	N	N	N	1	1	1

Cycles:	3
States:	12 (8085), 11 (8080)
Addressing:	reg. indirect
Flags:	none

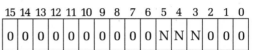

15	14	13	12	11	10	9	8	7	6	5	4	3	2	1	0
0	0	0	0	0	0	0	0	0	0	N	N	N	0	0	0

Program Counter After Restart

PCHL   (Jump H and L indirect — move H and L to PC)

(PCH) ← (H)

(PCL) ← (L)

The content of register H is moved to the high-order eight bits of register PC. The content of register L is moved to the low-order eight bits of register PC.

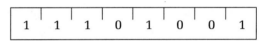

1	1	1	0	1	0	0	1

Cycles:	1
States:	6 (8085), 5 (8080)
Addressing:	register
Flags:	none

A.6.5 Stack, I/O, and Machine Control Group

This group of instructions performs I/O, manipulates the Stack, and alters internal control flags.

Unless otherwise specified, **condition flags are not affected by any instructions in this group.**

PUSH rp   (Push)

((SP) − 1) ← (rh)

((SP) − 2) ← (rl)

(SP) ← (SP) − 2

The content of the high-order register of register pair rp is moved to the memory location whose address is one less than the content of register SP. The content of the low-order register of register pair rp is moved to the memory location whose address is two less than the content of register SP. Then content of register SP is decremented by 2. **Note: Register pair rp = SP may not be specified.**

* All mnemonics copyrighted © Intel Corporation 1976.

THE INSTRUCTION SET

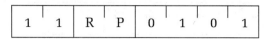

1	1	R	P	0	1	0	1

Cycles: 3
States: 12 (8085), 11 (8080)
Addressing: reg. indirect
Flags: none

PUSH PSW   (Push processor status word)

$((SP) - 1) \leftarrow (A)$
$((SP) - 2)_0 \leftarrow (CY), ((SP) - 2)_1 \leftarrow X$
$((SP) - 2)_2 \leftarrow (P), , ((SP) - 2)_3 \leftarrow X$
$((SP) - 2)_4 \leftarrow (AC), ((SP) - 2)_5 \leftarrow X$
$((SP) - 2)_6 \leftarrow (Z), ((SP) - 2)_7 \leftarrow (S)$
$(SP) \leftarrow (SP) - 2$ X: Undefined.

The content of register A is moved to the memory location whose address is one less than register SP. The contents of the condition flags are assembled into a processor status word and the word is moved to the memory location whose address is two less than the content of register SP. The content of register SP is decremented by two.

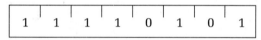

1	1	1	1	0	1	0	1

Cycles: 3
States: 12 (8085), 11 (8080)
Addressing: reg. indirect
Flags: none

FLAG WORD

D_7	D_6	D_5	D_4	D_3	D_2	D_1	D_0
S	Z	X	AC	X	P	X	CY

X: undefined

POP rp   (Pop)

$(rl) \leftarrow ((SP))$
$(rh) \leftarrow ((SP) + 1)$
$(SP) \leftarrow (SP) + 2$

The content of the memory location, whose address is specified by the content of register SP, is moved to the low-order register of register pair rp. The content of the memory location, whose address is one more than the content of register SP, is moved to the high-order register of register rp. The content of register SP is incremented by 2. **Note: Register pair rp = SP may not be specified.**

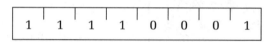

1	1	R	P	0	0	0	1

Cycles: 3
States: 10
Addressing: reg. indirect
Flags: none

POP PSW   (Pop processor status word)

$(CY) \leftarrow ((SP))_0$
$(P) \leftarrow ((SP))_2$
$(AC) \leftarrow ((SP))_4$
$(Z) \leftarrow ((SP))_6$
$(S) \leftarrow ((SP))_7$
$(A) \leftarrow ((SP) + 1)$
$(SP) \leftarrow (SP) + 2)$

The content of the memory location whose address is specified by the content of register SP is used to restore the condition flags. The content of the memory location whose address is one more than the content of register SP is moved to register A. The content of register SP is incremented by 2.

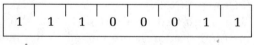

1	1	1	1	0	0	0	1

Cycles: 3
States: 10
Addressing: reg. indirect
Flags: Z, S, P, CY, AC

XTHL   (Exchange stack top with H and L)

$(L) \leftrightarrow ((SP))$
$(H) \leftrightarrow ((SP) + 1)$

The content of the L register is exchanged with the content of the memory location whose address is specified by the content of register SP. The content of the H register is exchanged with the content of the memory location whose address is one more than the content of register SP.

1	1	1	0	0	0	1	1

Cycles: 5
States: 16 (8085), 18 (8080)
Addressing: reg. indirect
Flags: none

THE INSTRUCTION SET

SPHL (Move HL to SP)
(SP) ← (H) (L)
The contents of registers H and L (16 bits) are moved to register SP.

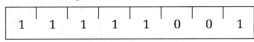

Cycles:	1
States:	6 (8085), 5 (8080)
Addressing:	register
Flags:	none

IN port (Input)
(A) ← (data)
The data placed on the 8-bit bidirectional data bus by the specified port is moved to register A.

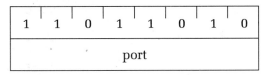

Cycles:	3
States:	10
Addressing:	direct
Flags:	none

OUT port (Output)
(data) ← (A)
The content of register A is placed on the 8-bit bidirectional data bus for transmission to the specified port.

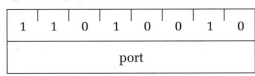

Cycles:	3
States:	10
Addressing:	direct
Flags:	none

EI (Enable interrupts)
The interrupt system is enabled **following the execution of the next instruction. Interrupts are not recognized during the EI instruction.**

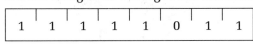

Cycles:	1
States:	4
Flags:	none

NOTE: Placing an EI instruction on the bus in response to INTA during an INA cycle is prohibited. (8085)

DI (Disable interrupts)
The interrupt system is disabled **immediately following the execution of the DI instruction. Interrupts are not recognized during the DI instruction.**

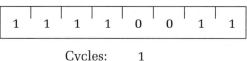

Cycles:	1
States:	4
Flags:	none

NOTE: Placing a DI instruction on the bus in response to INTA during an INA cycle is prohibited. (8085)

HLT (Halt)
The processor is stopped. The registers and flags are unaffected. (8080) A second ALE is generated during the execution of HLT to strobe out the Halt cycle status information. (8085)

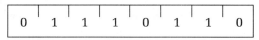

Cycles:	1 + (8085), 1 (8080)
States:	5 (8085), 7 (8080)
Flags:	none

NOP (No op)
No operation is performed. The registers and flags are unaffected.

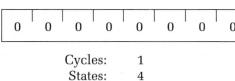

Cycles:	1
States:	4
Flags:	none

RIM (Read Interrupt Masks) (8085 only)
The RIM instruction loads data into the accumulator relating to interrupts and the serial input. This data contains the following information:

- Current interrupt mask status for the RST 5.5, 6.5, and 7.5 hardware interrupts (1 = mask disabled)

- Current interrupt enable flag status (1 = interrupts enabled) except immediately following a TRAP interrupt. (See below.)

THE INSTRUCTION SET

- Hardware interrupts pending (i.e., signal received but not yet serviced), on the RST 5.5, 6.5, and 7.5 lines.

- Serial input data.

Immediately following a TRAP interrupt, the RIM instruction must be executed as a part of the service routine if you need to retrieve current interrupt status later. Bit 3 of the accumulator is (in this special case only) loaded with the interrupt enable (IE) flag status that existed prior to the TRAP interrupt. Following an RST 5.5, 6.5, 7.5, or INTR interrupt, the interrupt flag flip-flop reflects the current interrupt enable status. Bit 6 of the accumulator (I7.5) is loaded with the status of the RST 7.5 flip-flop, which is always set (edge-triggered) by an input on the RST 7.5 input line, even when that interrupt has been previously masked. (See SIM instruction.)

SIM   (Set Interrupt Masks) (8085 only)
The execution of the SIM instruction uses the contents of the accumulator (which must be previously loaded) to perform the following functions:

- Program the interrupt mask for the RST 5.5, 6.5, and 7.5 hardware interrupts.

- Reset the edge-triggered RST 7.5 input latch.

- Load the SOD output latch.

To program the interrupt masks, first set accumulator bit 3 to 1 and set to 1 any bits 0, 1, and 2, which disable interrupts RST 5.5, 6,5, and 7.5, respectively. Then do a SIM instruction. If accumulator bit 3 is 0 when the SIM instruction is executed, the interrupt mask register will not change. If accumulator bit 4 is 1 when the SIM instruction is executed, the RST 7.5 latch is then reset. RST 7.5 is distinguished by the fact that its latch is always set by a rising edge on the RST 7.5 input pin, even if the jump to service routine is inhibited by masking. This latch remains high until cleared by a RESET IN, by a SIM instruction with accumulator bit 4 high, or by an internal processor acknowledge to an RST 7.5 interrupt subsequent to the removal of the mask (by a SIM instruction). The RESET IN signal always sets all three RST mask bits.

If accumulator bit 6 is at the 1 level when the SIM instruction is executed, the state of accumulator bit 7 is loaded into the SOD latch and thus becomes available for interface to an external device. The SOD latch is unaffected by the SIM instruction if bit 6 is 0. SOD is always reset by the RESET IN signal.

INDEX